D1252401

'SIR, THEY'RE TAKING THE KIDS INDOORS'

THE BRITISH ARMY IN NORTHERN IRELAND 1973-4

An Oral and Historical Analysis of the Troubles During the Bloody 1970s

Ken M. Wharton

Helion & Company Ltd

Helion & Company Limited
26 Willow Road
Solihull
West Midlands
B91 1UE
England
Tel. 0121 705 3393
Fax 0121 711 4075
Email: info@helion.co.uk
Website: www.helion.co.uk

Published by Helion & Company 2012
Designed and typeset by Farr Out Publications, Wokingham, Berkshire
Cover designed by Euan Carter, Leicester
Printed by Gutenberg Press Limited, Tarxien, Malta

The opinions expressed in this book are those of the individuals quoted and do not necessarily accord with views held by the author or publisher.

ISBN 978 1 907677 67 0

British Library Cataloguing-in-Publication Data.
A catalogue record for this book is available from the British Library.

For details of other military history titles published by Helion & Company Limited please contact the above address, or visit our website www.helion.co.uk.

We always welcome receiving book proposals from prospective authors.

Dedications

To every soldier, no matter which Regiment, no matter which arm of the British Army you served in Northern Ireland. You learned to walk backwards with such style

To the Royal Green Jackets and my many friends in
that superb Regiment: *Celer et Audux*

To Mick Hill, Andy Thomas and Steve Norman and the Royal Anglians

To Tommy Clarke, Kev Wright, Dead Horse and the Royal Corps of Transport.

To Paddy Lenaghan, George Prosser, 'Cav' and the King's Regiment

To Slapper and the Tankies

To Slops and the Catering Corps lads who kept us going

To Andrew MacDonald and the King's Own Royal Border Regiment

To Mike Sangster, the Swaine Brothers, Mick Potter and the
rest of the 'Seven Mile Snipers' of the Royal Artillery

To Ken, Stevie, Ronnie Mark and the other magnificent lads of the Ulster Defence Regiment, and sad that it is still too dangerous to use their surnames.

To Haydn and Roy Davies, Arfon Williams, Andy Bull and Ken Donavan
and the Royal Regiment of Wales: *Gwell Angau na Chywilydd*

To my many Australian and New Zealand friends, especially
the ever patient Rebecca Kolsteeg and Rachel Barnard

To my cousin John Leighton; a Territorial Long Range Sniper

To the memory of my late parents, Mark and Irene Wharton

My partner, Helen MacDonald who comforts me and whose love keeps me going

As always to my children: Anne-Marie, Anna, Jonathan,
Jenny, Robbie, Alex and Nathan and grandchildren:
Sheriden and Kelsey Wharton, William and
Sammy Thomas and Layla-Mae Addy-Wharton

To my lovely Aussie friend, Sophie Sheldon

To the memory of the late Pete Whittall of the Cheshire Regiment who passed away in 2010; the IRA couldn't beat you, sadly Cancer did. 18/11/2010.

To the late Eddie French, King's Regiment who also
lost his fight with Cancer, August 2011

To everyone who served with me and to all who followed
*And if you come, when all the flowers are dying
And I am dead, as dead I well may be
You'll come and find the place where I am lying
And kneel and say an "Ave" there for me.*
(From 'Danny Boy', traditional Irish ballad)

*An' for each an' ev'ry underdog soldier in the night, we
gazed upon the chimes of freedom flashing.*
(From 'Chimes of Freedom' Bob Dylan)

*There was a checkpoint Charlie; he didn't crack a smile. But it's no
laughing **party when you've been on the murder mile.***
(From 'Oliver's Army' Elvis Costello & the Attractions)

*Some say troubles abound; someday soon they're gonna pull the old town
down; one day we'll return here, when the Belfast child sings again.*
(From 'Belfast Child' by Simple Minds)

*In my mind, I can still smell the acrid smoke of Brompton Park burning from end
to end, see the petrol bombs and nail bombs coming over the 'peace wall' opposite
Holy Cross; the fireman lying on the road, shot through the chest; the RUC inspector
hit by a petrol bomb on Butler Street, and the sniper's shots that missed us embedded
in the wall at the Woodvale Junction. I still have vivid pictures of the young
Marine, holding his guts in with one hand as he carried his rifle with the other
after getting hit by a nail bomb, and the Ferret Scout Car in a sea of flames.*

*Over forty years have passed since I saw, heard and smelled all this, witnessed the
grief, and shed the tears over fallen comrades, yet here we are again, same place, same
circumstances and same the hatred. My heart is heavy at our wasted sacrifice*
Dave Von Slaps, Royal Tank Regiment

*On a small residential road beside the chapel, about 30 metres up was a small girl;
probably about five years old, she was playing with her dog and was wearing a white
dress. She looked very pretty, against the drab backdrop of terraced housing. Upon
spotting me kneeling down, she pointed to her dog and gestured in my direction, sending
her dog to attack us. I think the dog got a kick in the head and went scampering back.
Nothing unusual, but another generation of hatred was being produced by her parents.*
Jamie Tyrell, RAF Regiment

In 1972 and 1973, the IRA really tried so hard to make their boast of killing a British soldier a day, come true. I was based at North Howard Street Mill and the minute we burst onto the streets, you could sense the hatred; the loathing that the people had for us was so thick that you could have cut it with a knife.
Rifleman 'W', Royal Green Jackets

'How many rounds did you fire?' Answer: 'Two.' 'What did you fire at; was it an identifiable target? Answer: 'I saw a target behind the shops in the Broadway. I saw dust kicking up at the same time as the gunfire.' 'Did you hit anyone?' Answer: 'Don't know, but the shooting stopped!' End of interview.
Steve Norman, Royal Anglian Regiment

'I only saw Belfast from behind me, as I was always the one man in the patrol walking backwards.'
Dave Sherlock, Cheshire Regiment

'Rewriting history is what failed terrorists always do.'
Kevin Myers, Author

'The troubles were just the latest episode in an on-going saga which had raged in Ireland for 500 years.'
Ken Wharton, Former Soldier

℘

The Best Mate I Ever Had

I would like to dedicate this book to the memory of my best mate, Chris Johnson, who was killed in a motorcycle crash in May, 1968 aged only 18 years. From the age of 11 we were inseparable; we did everything together, went everywhere together, shared the same girls and got into many scrapes…but always together.

Before I joined the Army in January 1967, we had a weekly ritual called 'York Roading' which involved drinking – illegally of course, as we were both under 18 – a pint of Bitter in all ten pubs which littered one of the longest roads in Leeds. One of those drinking holes was the Irish Centre – complete with Irish Tricolour – and it was merely one of our ports of call and in we would innocently and perhaps naively traipse, having had some friendly Paddy sign us in. We stayed long enough to imbibe the ritualistic pint, joined in with a chorus or two of 'Merry Ploughboy' or 'The Fields of Athenry' and sing away merrily before moving on to the White Horse.

We would sing out the words "And we're all off to Dublin in the green, in the green; where the helmets glisten in the sun, where the bayonets flash and the rifles crash to the rattle of a Thompson gun." As I sang along with gusto – courtesy of the typewritten sheets passed around – I had no inkling that one day soon I would be fighting elements of the IRA. Only, unlike the romanticism and the tributes to the 'heroes' of the song, the real thing was something a little different, motivated by a psychopathic evil and dedicated to the destruction of decency.

It is so easy to sing "… and we're off to join the IRA and we're off tomorrow morn'…" and "… there's one I leave behind me …" as though it was some romantic adventure about 'rob the rich to give to the poor' freedom fighters. The reality was starker, more sinister; it was an 'army' which became increasingly professional and professionally equipped with arms by naïve Americans and hateful Libyans and Soviets. They became very good at what they did best: killing people.

Still love you, mate: RIP my friend.

Contents

List of Maps and Illustrations

Foreword

In October 1973, I left a comrade, my sight, my right hand, much of my hearing and my career in Northern Ireland. Ken's fifth book on the Troubles is a tribute to those like my comrade, 2nd Lieutenant Lindsay Dobbie. He was killed in the same explosion in which I was injured. Many other members of HM Forces and civilians made the ultimate sacrifice. Ken revives that headline which is printed today, forgotten tomorrow, but lasts a lifetime for those involved. One has to feel great sympathy for those who had to live amongst the daily acts of bestiality and cruelty perpetuated by the lunatic few. But great admiration must go to all members of HM Forces who faced tour after tour with patience and a very remarkable degree of restraint. To maintain impartiality at a time when bottles, rocks, petrol and pipe bombs and bullets are flying towards you demands well-disciplined and well trained troops – who better than Tommy Atkins? I believe the situation would have worsened very much earlier had our troops descended to the level of the terrorists in those early years

Ken's approach to the history of this period through unbiased account, meticulous research and the actual words of those who served in Northern Ireland at the time makes this dark period very readable. It will bring back memories, sad, tragic, happy and amusing to those who were there. To find oneself in a 'civil war' situation, patrolling suburban British streets with loaded rifle; Christmas shopping in familiar UK stores with a pistol on one's belt created an almost surreal atmosphere to one who had never fired a shot in anger. The experience has taught me one positive lesson. The world of disability and handicap is full of people who devote their lives to helping others. Many are paid to carry out this work, but there are many who volunteer. The good people far outweigh the terrorists and have certainly restored my faith in human nature; thank goodness! I have been back to Ulster several times since 1973. I have always found the local people cheerful, witty and with a good sense of humour. If only they could bury the congenital bigotry, which has nothing to do with religion, and let peace and prosperity thrive!

Raymond Hazan, OBE
President St Dunstan's for Blind and Partially Sighted ex-Servicemen and Women

Preface by Darren Ware

In 1988 at the age of 18 I deployed to Lisnaskea, Co Fermanagh, Northern Ireland on my first operational tour which lasted four months. In 1991 I was posted back to Northern Ireland to Omagh, Co Tyrone for my second tour that lasted just over two years.

Like the hundreds of soldiers before and after me, we just got on and done the task. To assist the RUC in the defeat of terrorism – to kill or capture the terrorist! We slogged our guts out night and day, week in and week out. We moaned, cursed everything, and got fed up, cold, tired and hungry. We missed home, we missed our loved ones, we couldn't go out and we could not drink for the time we were there. We watched each other's backs on every patrol, on every street and through every highway and hedgerow until we concluded our patrol.

Our rest and recuperation was short and before long our tour was over. We left the Province and returned home and just mingled back in to life on the mainland. There was no huge welcome home! There was no fanfare either! And it was not unusual for people not to know what went on *over the water*; a mere 45 minute plane flight.

Well, that's where this book comes into it. Ken Wharton's books: *A Long Long War*; *Bullets Bombs and Cups of Tea*; *Bloody Belfast* and *The Bloodiest Year: Northern Ireland, 1972* gives the opportunity for every serviceman, service woman, civilian and loved ones' story to be told, and for each of those, there is a unique account. My brother, LCpl Simon Ware was serving with the 2nd Battalion Coldstream Guards when he was killed in South Armagh in 1991. The circumstances of his death are told in detail in my book *A Rendezvous with the Enemy: My brother's life and death with the Coldstream Guards in Northern Ireland.*

I first met Ken Wharton in the summer of 2007 when I answered a request on an army website for soldiers to contribute to a book that he was writing about soldiers' stories of Northern Ireland. At the time, I was writing my book about my brother's death and felt it was an ideal opportunity to tell my story. Ken has continued to triumph with continuing to tell 'the soldiers' story' of what life in Northern Ireland was like. This book continues that strength to keep 'the Troubles' in the public eye. It details all deaths in a concise way with just the right amount of information to interestingly read each set of circumstances. It is not biased, so will tell the stories from all sides. There is an 'impact' comment in this book describing the level of atrocities as "… a conveyor belt of slaughter" and this is not far from the truth! It is written from the eye of those who have dealt with what was sent to confront them. And we must remember that for every soldier or civilian killed then there are many more who are left behind to pick up the physical, emotional and physiological scars. It is all of these that we should remember.

Darren Ware
Author of *A Rendezvous With The Enemy: My brother's life and death with the Coldstream Guards in Northern Ireland*
May 2011, Lancashire, UK

Author's Note

"Sir, they're taking the kids indoors" was a cry heard by most, if not all, of the British soldiers who served on either the four month emergency or the two year resident battalion tours of Northern Ireland. It refers to the IRA (Irish Republican Army) tactic of warning the civilian population in Republican areas of the impending arrival of one of their gunmen. Clearly, as witnessed by the number of civilian deaths among the Catholic population directly or indirectly at the hands of their 'protectors' in the IRA, they were not averse to killing or causing the deaths of Catholics. Once the 'jungle drums' had warned mothers of the approaching death at the hands of the 'widow maker' they would bring their offspring indoors and thus give the IRA the 'moral high ground' of not shooting their own supporters.

Once a soldier had called out these words to comrades, the patrol would know that the angel of death was in the area, although it was never far away at the best of times. It would alert them to the fact that they had to be ready for something more lethal than the aimed bricks, Molotov cocktails, dead animals, dog excrement and used sanitary towels which the women of the Republican areas so charmingly saved for the optimum moment. It would herald the approach of a gunman or gunmen and the locals, especially those who revelled in the prospect of 'shooting a Brit' or adherents to the Provisionals' line of killing a soldier a day. They would have their sadistic hatred sated for at least a day at the sight of British blood staining the streets.

One only needs to consult the roll of honour in any of my books to know that there were many streets in Belfast and Londonderry where the Republican mobs had danced in the blood of a young man from England, Scotland, Wales or even their own Northern Ireland. Spamount Street, New Lodge; Flax Street, Ardoyne; Glenalina Gardens, Ballymurphy; Ardmonagh Gardens, Turf Lodge and Shaw's Road, Andersonstown; Lecky Road and Iniscarn Road, Londonderry. All saw British blood stain the tarmac; in some cases on more than occasion.

In this, my fifth oral history of the Northern Ireland troubles, I will examine and discuss the events of the period 1973/4. Although this was a period which never paralleled the bloodiest year of 1972, in terms of loss of life, it was nonetheless a time of constant death and mayhem. Moreover, the two years under review saw the peak deployment of British troops in the Province. During 1973 a total of 25,343 soldiers – the highest in a single year – served in Northern Ireland. The following year, the tally was 24,015; never again would the numbers of British soldiers deployed throughout the Province scale these heights.

The blinkered Irish-Americans so willingly, and sometimes not as willingly as there were generally IRA supporters on hand to 'encourage' contributions, gave their hard-earned dollars to support these people. The money was collected on the pretext that it was for the 'families of the men behind the wire' or alms for the people 'back home.' Huge sums were raised which, far from providing alms actually provided arms for the perpetration and perpetuation of the misery for over 1.5 million people living in

Northern Ireland. But it wasn't just the Irish-Americans – it was the Irish-Australians, Colonel Gaddafi of Libya and the provocateurs of the USSR also.

Abbreviations

2IC	Second in Command
3LI	Third Battalion Light Infantry
AAC	Army Air Corps
ADU	Army Dog Handling Unit
APC	Armoured Personnel Carrier
APNI	Alliance Party of Northern Ireland
ASU	Active Service Unit
ATO	Ammunition Technical Officer
AWOL	Absent Without Leave
BFBS	British Forces Broadcasting Service
Bn HQ	Battalion Headquarters
BOI	Board of Inquiry
CESA	Catholic Ex-serviceman's Association
CO	Commanding Officer
CS	Tear Gas
CVO	Casualty Visiting Officers
DC	Detective Constable
DERR	Duke of Edinburgh's Royal Regiment
DOE	Department of the Environment
DoW	Died of Wounds
DOWR	Duke of Wellington's Regiment
DUP	Democratic Unionist Party
DWR	Duke of Wellington's Regiment
EOD	Explosive Ordnance Disposal
ETA	*Euskadi Ta Askatasuna* (Basque Separatist Terrorist group)
FOI	Freedom of Information
FRG	Federal Riot Guns
GAA	Gaelic Athletic Association (Irish: *Cumann Lúthchleas Gael*)
GC	George Cross
GHQ	General Head Quarters
GPMG	General Purpose Machine Gun
GPO	General Post Office
HET	Historical Enquiries Team
HQNI	Head Quarters Northern Ireland
IJLB	Infantry Junior Leaders Battalion
INLA	Irish National Liberation Army
INT	Intelligence
IRA	Irish Republican Army
IRSP	Irish Republican Socialist Party
KIA	Killed in Action
KOSB	King's Own Scottish Borderers

LSL	Landing Ship Logistics
MO	Medical Officer
MoD	Ministry of Defence
NAAFI	Navy, Army and Air Force Institute
NCND	neither confirm nor deny
NCO	Non-Commissioned Officer
NG	Negligent Discharge
NI	Northern Ireland
NIVA	Northern Ireland Veteran's Association
NMA	National Memorial Arboretum
NORAID	Northern Aid Committee
NTH	Newtownhamilton
ODC	Ordinary decent Catholics
OP	Observation Post
OTR	On the Run
PIG	Armoured Vehicle (named as such due to its pig-like appearance)
PIRA	Provisional Irish Republican Army
PLA	People's Liberation Army
POA	Prison Officers' Association
POW	Prisoner of War
PRO	Public Relations Officer
PSNI	Police Service Northern Ireland
QLR	Queen's Lancashire Regiment
QOH	Queen's Own Highlander's
QRF	Quick Reaction Force
RAF	Royal Air Force
RSF	Republican Sinn Féin
RCT	Royal Corps of Transport
RE	Royal Engineers
REHQ	Royal Engineers Headquarters
REME	Royal Electrical and Mechanical Engineers
RGJ	Royal Green Jackets
RIRA	Real Irish Republican Army
RMP	Royal Military Police
RAOC	Royal Army Ordnance Corps
ROE	Rules of Engagement
RPG-7	Rocket Propelled Grenade
RRF	Royal Regiment of Fusiliers
RRW	Royal Regiment of Wales
RSM	Regimental Sergeant Major
RTA	Road Traffic Accident
RUC	Royal Ulster Constabulary
RUCR	Royal Ulster Constabulary Reserve
RVH	Royal Victoria Hospital
SB	Special Branch
SDLP	Social Democratic and Labour Party

SF	Security Forces
SIB	Special Investigation Branch
SLR	Self Loading Rifle
SOP	Standard Operating Procedure
SUIT	Sight Unit Infantry Trilux
TA	Territorial Army
TD	*Teachta Dála* (Member of the Irish Parliament)
TAOR	Tactical Area of Responsibility
UDA	Ulster Defence Association
UDR	Ulster Defence Regiment
UFF	Ulster Freedom Fighters
USC	Ulster Special Constabulary
UTV	Ulster Television
UUP	Ulster Unionist Party
UVBT	Under vehicle booby trap
UWC	Ulster Worker's Council
VCP	Vehicle Check Point
WOII	Warrant Officer Second Class
WRAC	Women's Royal Army Corps

A Letter Home

DEAR MUM, THE SKY IS ON FIRE
Dave Parkinson, Royal Armoured Corps

It's three in the afternoon, and I'm really hungry. It's been many hours since the cooks dropped the hay box of soup and the sack of loaves off to us, and I have an appetite like all other youngsters, that somehow the many cigarettes I'm smoking won't quench. I'm aching and sore, my shoulder stiff from where the piece of broken gravestone from Milltown Cemetery hit me, thrown by God knows whom. It will be dark soon, yet even in this ghostly daylight, the pungent smell of burning mixed with the faint whiff of CS stings my eyes. To my right, just twenty yards away, the smouldering remains of a once loved and treasured Ford Anglia lie in the road, its paint-less wheels starting to rust over, even now, in the fine mist of rain that's falling. To my left, the gaunt remains of a whole row of burnt out terraced houses stretches away into the disappearing distance, once lived in, and full of the laughter of a million children, but now just the bare bones of what once was. In the distance, I see the shadow of Divis Tower, a place filled with hate and death, the fortress of the enemy; it rises like some sort of medieval castle but from a base of fire and hate, not from a swan lake.

For this is Belfast, a town, a city even, where hate breeds. I'm tired. We are all so very tired. Not just a sleep tired, but a body and mind exhaustion. The tears are running down my face. I'm not crying; it's just sheer fatigue. The tears are forming running black lines through the filth of last night's fires, a goo so thick and encrusted I can feel it. My combat trousers are stuck to my legs, and my jersey heavy wool stinks of mothballs and burnt rubber. The flak jacket I'm wearing came from another war, many miles from here, and the paint I once thought stained the back of it, is from another soldier, from another country. Did he ever get home, either on his legs or in a body bag? I'm really past caring. The black remains of some lorry tyres are still burning down the road, their flames in constant combat with the rain, casting a lurid glow into the grey mist. It's quite just now, the boyos have gone for a rest, maybe for their teas, but they will be back, fortified by sleep, a luxury we can't, no daren't, take. This morning, in a lull from the stone throwers, we got ten minutes in a smashed bus shelter, the hard Yorkshire stone is better than any duck-down mattress. The sheer joy of being able to lie down, and take the weight off our burning, feet, fall instantly asleep, to be awakened by the distant boom of another large bomb, somewhere near the City Centre. Just how much more of this can we take? I'm sick of fire, the rain and the bits of people we all see lying in the road. The stench of death fills the air here, and I don't want to die.

Soon it will begin all over again, another night of terror, the stones, then the petrol and nail bombs, and then, when our backs are illuminated by fresh fires, the snipers will crawl out of their graves, slither into the gaunt, wrecked houses, with their deadly Garand rifles, loaded with armour piercing bullets and orders to kill anything wearing a uniform, be it the green of the RUC, or the green of the British Army. Their women will goad us with their shouted insults, and blow their whistles, crash their dustbin lids and spit in our faces. Their barefoot and ragged children will fire their catapults at us, using the ball bearings taken from the wheels of burnt out cars. Slowly, over the hours, they will wear us down even more, until we can't think, can't reason, and even the autopilot that controls us starts to disengage.

Oh mum, I want to come home. I want to see you again, and see your house, sit in your garden, and go for a pint with dad. I want to see the sun, see flowers again, smell a clean woman again, sleep; oh I so need to sleep. What happened to the clean air I love to breathe? Am I never going to breathe clean air again? I don't want to die here, to rot in this stinking place, with its stinking people.

I just want to come home.

Maps

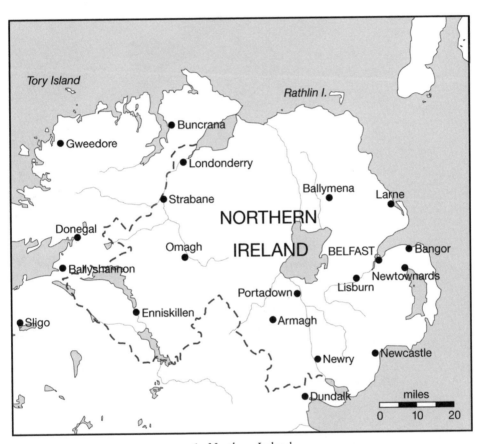

1. Northern Ireland

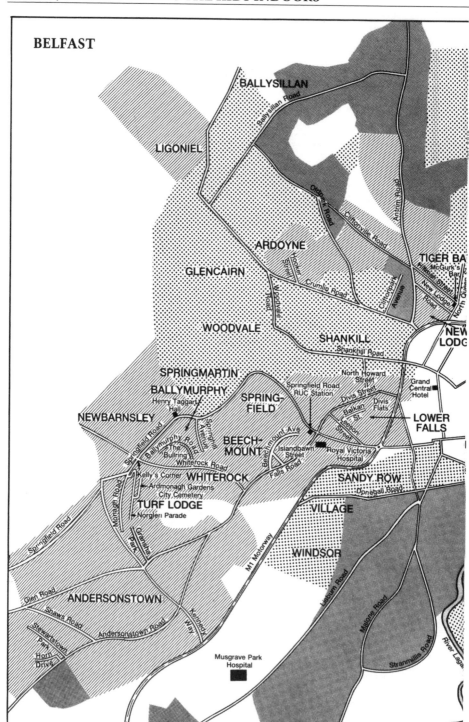

2. Belfast

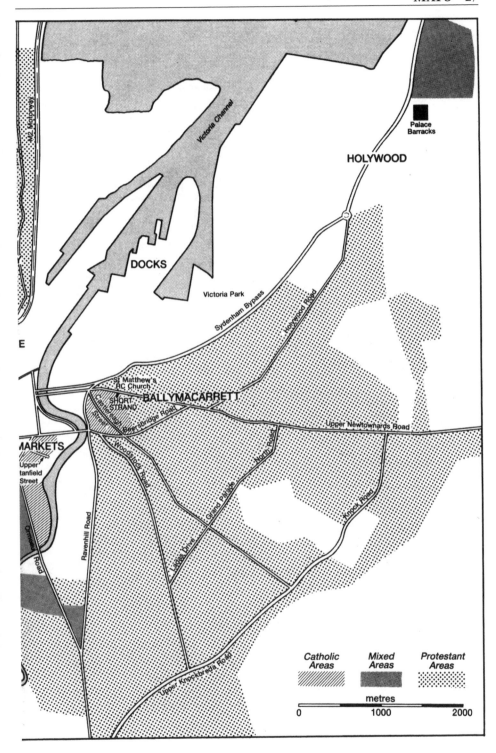

HOLYWOOD

Palace
Barracks

Victoria Channel

DOCKS

Victoria Park

Sydenham Bypass

Holywood Road

M2 Motorway

E

St Matthew's
RC Church

SHORT
STRAND

BALLYMACARRETT

Castlereagh Road

Beersbridge Road

Upper Newtownards Road

North Road

Knock Road

MARKETS

Upper
Stanfield
Street

Woodstock Road

Grand Parade

Ladas Drive

Ravenhill Road

Ormeau Road

Upper Knockbreda Road

Catholic
Areas

Mixed
Areas

Protestant
Areas

metres

0   1000   2000

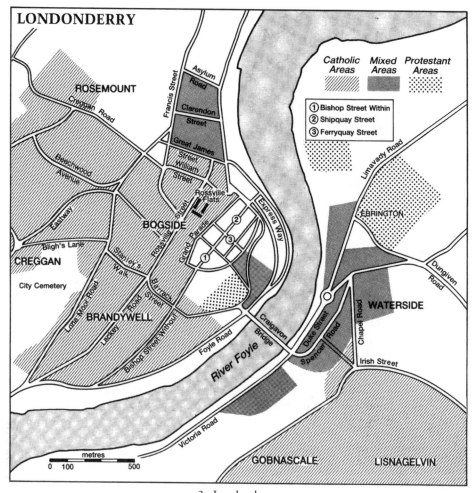

3. Londonderry

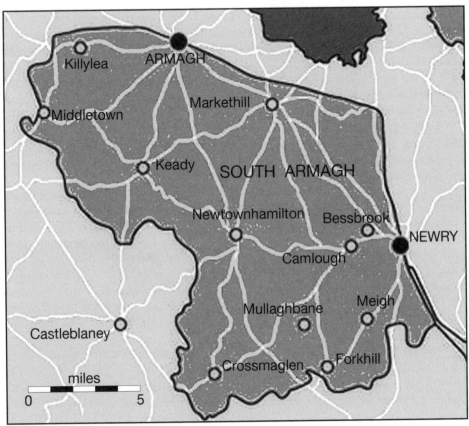

4. South Armagh ('bandit country')

Introduction

As I start this, my fifth book on the Northern Ireland troubles – again from the perspective of the British soldier – it is a hot and humid day on the Gold Coast of Australia where I currently reside. It is 12,000 miles away, and approaching 42 years since the Labour Government of Harold Wilson sent troops onto the streets of Belfast and Londonderry in order to restore order and save lives and property in the law and order vacuum created by the forced withdrawal of the beleaguered RUC. It might as well be a million miles away and a million years ago. Harold Wilson died on 24 May, 1995. By the time this oft-criticised Huddersfield born Prime Minister died, approaching 1,300 British soldiers had been killed in order to achieve his original objectives; that of restoring law and order in the lawless Province.

Every soldier who trod the streets of Belfast, Londonderry, Newry, Crossmaglen, and Lurgan and a dozen other towns and villages or tramped the beautiful yet lethal countryside of Counties Londonderry, Antrim, Down, Armagh, Tyrone and Fermanagh, will remember their days during this troubled time.

Between 1969 and 1998 a total of 1,294 – identified to date – British military personnel were killed or died in a variety of circumstances in or as a direct consequence of the somewhat euphemistically named 'troubles.' To the mandarins of Whitehall in the giant Ministry of Defence, the total is given, variously, as c. 730 as they include only those killed as a consequence of terrorist activity. That figure does not include Trooper Eddie Maggs of the Blues and Royals or his comrade John Tucker killed at Woodbourne RUC station on February 25, 1979. It does not include Tommy Stoker of the Light Infantry who died of wounds, sustained earlier, on September 19, 1972. Nor does it include Owen Pavey of the King's Own Royal Border Regiment who was killed on March 11, 1980.

Trooper Eddie Maggs, it is alleged, had been drinking heavily and was on duty at the RUC station in Woodbourne in south-west Belfast. He shot and killed Corporal of Horse John Tucker before he himself was also shot and killed by RUC officers. Tommy Stoker, a Private in the Light Infantry who attended the same school as the author was only 18 and had only been in Northern Ireland for a few days. On the evening of Thursday July 27, 1972 whilst manning an Army OP in Berwick Road in the Republican Ardoyne he was accidentally shot by a comrade in an adjoining room; he lingered bravely for seven weeks before succumbing to the wound. Private Owen Pavey was preparing to leave for a foot patrol in the Crossmaglen area and in a moment of horseplay, so common amongst young soldiers even in times of war, another comrade shot and killed him with his General Purpose Machine Gun (GPMG). Young Pavey was estranged from his family and his Father never attended his own son's funeral.

That these four young soldiers were killed, and killed in different parts of Northern Ireland is not disputed by the MoD and nor is an acknowledgement, however tacit or forced, of the grief of the Maggs, Tucker, Stoker or Pavey families. That their young lives were prematurely, violently and tragically cut short is not disputed but as they were not 'direct victims of terrorism' their deaths are cast aside in an almost callous manner and only the National Memorial Arboretum (NMA), Palace Barracks Garden of Remembrance and the NIVA recall their names with honour, pride and dignity. Their names and several hundred others may not appear on the 'official' rolls of honour, but they are remembered daily by their comrades and they are of course remembered in the hearts of their families. One contributor to this book writes of the tears he sheds each time he reads the names of his fallen comrades from his Regiment. One maintains that each and every soldier who served in Northern Ireland during Op Banners feels precisely the same way; this author certainly does.

One does not wish to either insult or denigrate what the MoD thinks or states publically but the toll in or as a consequence of Northern Ireland is simply much less prosaic and needs to put into some kind of perspective alongside the already tragically high death toll of the current conflict in Afghanistan where British troops continue to die in their struggle against the evils of militant and archaic Moslem terrorism.

From the death of Trooper Hugh McCabe of the Queen's Royal Irish Hussars, home on leave from Germany, killed by 'friendly fire' in the Divis Street area of Belfast on Friday August 15, 1969 to the first 'official' death, that of Gunner Robert 'Geordie' Curtis on Saturday February 6, 1971, no less than 21 Regimental Officers were dispatched to families on the mainland.

My contention is that the 21 soldiers killed between the early days of deployment and the murder of Gunner Curtis in the New Lodge area of Belfast 18 months later, deserve official recognition from the Government and the MoD just as we, their comrades, recognise their sacrifice and their loss and the emptiness in the hearts of their families.

Again, what is not disputed is that between the deaths of Trooper McCabe and the death of Corporal Gary Fenton on June 22, 1998, over that intervening 29 years, British military fatalities grew exponentially and tragically.

Following on from my last book, *The Bloodiest Year: Northern Ireland, 1972*, this volume will look at the bloody years which followed and will attempt to cover every tragedy faced by the men and women in uniform and will also look at the murder and mayhem caused by the Provisional IRA and their murderous counterparts on the opposite side of the sectarian divide.

Given the continuing antipathy between Protestants and Catholics since partition in 1921, and the centuries old pattern of sectarian murder, it was perhaps inevitable that the Troubles were a bloodbath just waiting to happen. But this one was different; it wasn't just bloody or short-lived like other IRA 'campaigns' of the 20th Century, this one ran for almost 30 years – is still continuing in many ways – and has claimed nearly 5,000 lives in all. It wasn't just British soldiers, sailors and airmen, it was British civilians, Spanish, American and, in a case of 'mistaken identity,' Australian tourists also. Two Pakistanis also died as well, one riddled with 17 bullets and his body dumped near Crossmaglen; his crime? His Dad was an Army camp barber and another young Pakistani was murdered for selling tea to soldiers!

Could it have been stopped? The will or noticeable absence of it from the British Government certainly prolonged matters; making the soldiers fight with one hand tied behind their backs and then blindfolded didn't help. Nor did the succour, sympathy and arms supply to the IRA by misguided Irish-Americans. In particular, there are many former soldiers who hold an especial hatred for Senator Edward Kennedy, who they believe was one of the most significant apologists for the IRA in the United States.

Colonel Gaddafi, the fanatical leader of Libya helped train and equip the IRA and not only exacerbated the security situation in Ulster, but prolonged the murder campaign for far longer than was necessary or desired. As I write this, his life is also over; one trusts that the two will reflect upon their crimes in a fiery place.

During the course of this book, we will examine the American role in the prolonging of this 'forgotten war' in Northern Ireland and the support that they, as a nation, albeit heavily influenced by the powerful Irish-American lobby, gave to the Provisional IRA. Several Hollywood movies have portrayed the British as oppressors in Northern Ireland and whether or not this is influenced by the anti-Brit lobby or simply by blind prejudice, one will almost certainly never know. One must remember that the Americans have this 'jolly old England' view which they like to portray to the world but beneath the surface and sometimes more manifestly, were they attempting to justify their hatred for the days of England's[1] Empire by descriptively romanticising the IRA as 'freedom fighters'? How else would one explain NORAID (Northern Aid Committee) and their fund-raising activities; how else would one explain the pressure that the late and, by some, unlamented Senator Edward Kennedy allegedly placed on the US State Department to allow convicted IRA men to enter the US; how else would one explain the filibustering and blocking tactics of the US Supreme Court in ensuring that on the run Republican terrorists could remain at large in the USA whilst dodging British justice; and how else would one explain the appalling sight of President Clinton shaking the blood-stained hands of Gerry Adams and Martin McGuinness on the steps of the White House?

This book will look at those two years which followed the 'bloodiest year of the Troubles and examine the role of the squaddie on the street, described by that excellent author Kevin Myers thus: "… unfortunate soldiers fruitlessly walking the deserted streets in the rain, their hands cold and wet on their rifle stocks." Using anecdotal evidence and verbal testimony it will give the reader an insight into the daily tensions, violence and bloody death that each young lad from every part of the United Kingdom who had accepted the 'Queen's shilling' faced on an almost daily basis. In short, it will pay tribute to all those who learned to walk backwards, up and down the bloody streets and fields of Ulster with such grace and professionalism.

Ken Wharton, Gold Coast, Australia. December 18, 2010

---

1   Some Americans, Australians and the Irish don't appear to recognise 'British'.

Part One: 1973

Preamble

The previous year, 1972, had been the bloodiest year of the conflict and had witnessed the deaths of 172 British military personnel. The figures of that terrible year were, thankfully, never repeated. Although the Provisionals and the Loyalist murder gangs attempted to emulate, or even surpass, their bloody work. In terms of the military toll, the year had ended on Christmas Eve when Lance Corporal Colin Harker (23) of REME, who had been shot and wounded by the IRA in Londonderry on September 14, died of those wounds.

The year of 1973 resulted in the deaths of 106 British military and ex-military personnel, as a consequence, directly or indirectly, of the Troubles. It was a massive reduction on the toll of the previous year, but it was still a high 'butcher's bill' as the carnage continued into a fifth year. Even so, optimists at the year-end would claim a slight decline in violence and point to a new hope and a new future. But 1973 was to be yet another false dawn in Ulster's troubles.

I will always maintain that the Army, of which I was a member, was professional, impartial (in the main) and behaved (again in the main) with restraint and tolerance. Undoubtedly, there were times when the Army overstepped the mark and behaved in a less than professional and restrained manner and allowed an overzealous attitude to colour its judgement and actions. The vast bulk of these instances came under extreme provocation in the face of IRA attacks which caused death and severe injury and the attitude of the inhabitants of the Republican areas. To witness a comrade's lifeblood spill into the filthy streets of the Lower Falls, of the Beechmounts, of the Clonards and the Ardoyne causes a profound metamorphosis of even the most restrained soldier. To witness – as I did – the white, pained face of a mate clutching his mouth after being hit by a brick or to stare at the bloody mess which was once a leg or a foot, would test the tolerance and professionalism of Saint Patrick himself.

Houses and bars were turned over and wrecked during searches and civilians were roughed up or violently shoved aside but generally under the most extreme circumstances of sorrow or bile-filled provocation. There were certain regiments and units who had a reputation for this sort of out-of-control behaviour and it was these soldiers and their leaders who did the Army a grave disservice. In the main, discipline and professionalism were maintained, although there are countries whose armies would never have been so tolerant or as well behaved.

Chapter 1

January

As Old Father Time representing 1972 faded away, an elderly and heartbroken man as a consequence of the past year, so a nappy-clad younger version heralded the dawn of 1973. His first encounter would be to witness the murders of Oliver Boyce (25) and his fiancé Briege Porter (21) both of whom had been stabbed and shot by Loyalist murderers in Donegal. The young couple had been returning home from a New Year's dance when they were slaughtered; their crime had been to be Catholics in the wrong place at the wrong time. It was to be a pattern of sectarian murder which would be repeated again and again over the course of the next 26 long and depressing years.

The January of 1973 had started in a depressingly familiar vein to how 1972 and December had ended. Only hours after the two lovers had been murdered in cold blood, gunmen from the Ulster Freedom Fighters (UFF) – hidden in bushes – opened fire with automatic weapons on a packed car which was arriving at a car factory in Dundonald. One man, a married father-of-two, Jack Mooney (31) was killed in the carefully planned ambush. It is thought that the men – all Catholics – were earmarked for assassination purely because they "had the audacity to be Catholics in a Protestant workforce."

Three days later, the first member of the Security Forces (SF) to die that year would be Captain James Hood (48), an officer in the Ulster Defence Regiment (UDR) who was murdered by the IRA in his home in the hamlet of Straidarran. This was close to the scene of the Claudy slaughter, which had taken place some five months earlier. As the Captain returned home from work IRA gunmen, skulking in bushes close to his front door, shot him in the head before making good their escape; the officer died instantly. Several known Republicans were arrested shortly afterwards and this prompted a number of local Catholic schools to close in protest and teachers in those schools to strike in support of the release of the suspects.

Daily Mirror, Thursday 7th December, 1972

35

Rooftop brickies shot by mistake

By IAN SMITH

A BRICKLAYER was shot dead and his mate badly wounded yesterday by an Army marksman who mistook them for snipers.

But the men were on a life-saving operation—bricking up empty homes overlooking an Army post in Belfast to prevent them being used by terrorist gunmen.

Last night the Army expressed its 'deepest regret at the incident'. A top-level inquiry has been ordered.

Six shots had been fired at the Army observation post at the junction of Alliance Avenue and Berwick Road, Ardoyne, when the two men were spotted.

Bricklayer William Bell, 30, was on the roof of the terraced house in Berwick Road stripping lead, while his 25-year-old assistant worked in an upstairs bedroom.

Two shots rang out and father-of-two Mr Bell was dead. Last night the other man was seriously ill in the Royal Victoria Hospital.

Soldiers from the 3rd Light Infantry f o u n d both men lying in the house—still clutching the piping and spanners that had been mistaken for guns.

The bricklayers were employed by the Northern Ireland Housing Executive and had been working in the area for two weeks with orders to block up the deserted houses.

The executive said last night: 'We are deeply shocked. The men were doing a twofold job—making the homes safe, and also stopping them being used by snipers.

Mr Bell, a Protestant, lived in Forster Road, Woodvale, Belfast. His mate, a Catholic, came from Carrickfergus.

DAILY MAIL IRISH EDITION WEDNESDAY DECEMBER 6TH 1972.

Daily Mail Irish Edition, Wednesday 6th December 1972

The following day, the IRA shot and killed Trevor Rankin (18) as he attended to his car at a petrol station in Shore Road, in the northern part of Belfast. The fleeing gunmen were observed running into the nearby Republican Bawnmore Estate after what was a clearly sectarian murder by the IRA. Rankin, a Protestant had no links with any organisation and was killed carrying out a routinely simple task, that of putting air into his tyres. But then, was there ever anything routine during the Troubles?

Nigel Ely in his excellent book, *Fighting for Queen and Country,* speaks of the Northern Irish Republicans and Loyalists alike and their obsession with the past and how they are able to justify every single atrocity:

At times there seemed to be no end to the problems of Northern Ireland especially when most of the population lived 300 years in the past. How can you deal with people who constantly refer to wrongdoings vested upon their ancestors all those years ago. This may seem a simplistic view of the differences between Protestants and Catholics, but that was my view and it hasn't changed. The daily bombings,

DECEMBER 6TH 1972

New IRA weapon kills Army expert

By MICHAEL KELLY

A BOMB disposal expert was killed last night while dismantling what the Army described as a 'home-made mortar' at Lurgan in County Armagh.

Two bombs were fired at the Kitchen Hill Army post from a yard alongside a convent.

One exploded prematurely, injuring an IRA man, and the other hit wire mesh in front of the post and rebounded into the yard before exploding.

The Army expert was working on the mortar, which had a bomb in the barrel, when it exploded.

The IRA's new weapon was also used in attacks on Army posts at Kilrea, County Londonderry, and Bligh's Lane, Londonderry.

No casualties were caused by a total of six bomb blasts.

The attacks came on a night when UDR Pte. William Bogle, 26, of Gortnacross, was gunned down and killed in Killeter as he went to a post office with his wife and children.

In Armagh, a woman was critically ill with a bullet wound in the head after a rocket and gunfire attack on an Army post at a factory.

Daily Mail, 7th September 1972

Dave Sherlock (Cheshires) policing an evacuation in Belfast city centre after an IRA bomb scare (Dave Sherlock)

killings, knee-cappings by both sides kept happening no matter how many patrols we carried out or how many arrests we made.[1]

Another civilian, Elizabeth McGregor (76), lost her life when she was tragically caught in the crossfire between British soldiers and the IRA in the Ardoyne. Late on the morning of 12 January, soldiers manning an OP saw an armed gunman take up a firing position as a patrol approached in his (the gunman's) direction. Alerted by the OP, members of the patrol opened fire and Mrs McGregor was hit and sadly died a few hours later in the Royal Victoria Hospital (RVH). There was, however, some discrepancy and confusion about the incident as the fatal shots may have also been fired by the soldiers in the OP. Whatever the reason, the terrorists had again, albeit indirectly, caused the death of an innocent civilian due to their choosing a suburban street to be part of their battlefield.

A reserve policeman was then killed as his vehicle passed over an IRA landmine near Cappagh, a solid Republican area in Co Tyrone. RUCR Constable Henry Sandford (34) was killed instantly in the massive explosion which also seriously injured a Royal Ulster Constabulary (RUC) colleague. That day – the 14th – continued in the same tragic way for the Northern Ireland police when two more of their officers were killed, after an IRA UVBT (under vehicle booby trap) exploded beneath their car after they stopped briefly in Harbour Square, in Londonderry city centre. Constables Samuel Wilson (23) and David Dorsett (37) who was a father of three were both killed by the IRA bomb.

---

1   Ely, Nigel, *Fighting for Queen and Country: one man's true story of blood and violence inside the Paras and the SAS*, (London: John Lake Publishing, 2007) p. 62.

Dave Sherlock (centre) with two comrades from the Cheshire
Regiment arrive in Belfast (Dave Sherlock)

The SF toll continued and the following day, UDR soldier Corporal David Bingham (22) was abducted en-route to the RVH for an appointment. He was held for 48 hours and tortured before being shot in the head and dumped in a stolen car near Divis Street, Belfast. It was thought that the IRA merely intended to steal his car for use in a bomb attack, but discovered that he was a member of the UDR and in their twisted logic, got 'two for the price of one!' Corporal Bingham's car was used as a getaway vehicle after an explosion on the day of the abduction.

WHAT WAS IT LIKE?
Rifleman 'C' Royal Green Jackets
I was a soldier in the Royal Green Jackets and I did one of my tours during the period you are writing about; you won't remember me, but I remember you, Yorkie. Fondly, of course. I was back in Belfast for this latest tour and by this time, the Army had been trying to keep the peace for almost five years. I think that most of what was happening over the water wasn't being reported back home on the mainland. Perhaps it was because it wasn't considered as 'newsworthy' or maybe we were just an embarrassment to the Government which was sending us over to Ireland. When I got a spot of leave, I'd go see my folks in London and they'd be dead pleased to see me, but I couldn't talk to them about what I had experienced, because I knew how much it would upset them.

So off I'd go to see my civvie mates down the local pub. I think that I noticed it after my second tour; just how little they wanted to talk about what I was doing. Maybe they were bored of the whole thing, but I just wanted to talk about what was happening, what I was seeing and how bad it was over there. I'd start talking about what was happening and one would pipe up: "Fucking Ireland; that's all we hear from you!" Another variation was: "Boring, mate! Talk about something else for fuck's sake!" Eventually, I used to come home and spend my time in my bedroom until it was time to go back over the water. I remember how in the last day or two before my leave was up, that I'd feel sick and I used to look around my room and try to imagine that I'd never see it again. I was seeing this girl called April, but she'd gone off with a toe-rag called Martin. I was a soldier and very proud of it; I used to look real smart in my number twos[2] and he was a driver's mate! For Christ's sake; what could he offer her? I suppose he was at home and I was off fighting in one of my country's wars!

Now, some 30 years on, people suddenly have an interest, especially after the Saville Report into 'Bloody Sunday'. People are more likely to ask me what it was like being a soldier, fighting on British soil. Let me say that I have absolutely nothing against the Irish; especially the people who didn't like to live in what the author calls 'an urban battlefield'. But I do hate the IRA and I hate the Protestant thugs as well. Between them, they came near to destroying their own country. I read a word in one of the author's books; opprobrium it was. I didn't know what it meant at the time so I looked it up and I see that the word is correct and it was used correctly in describing the feelings in Northern Ireland.

What was it like? Imagine you've just worked for 16 hours solid and you've just gone home and your boss comes around to your house, kicks you out of bed and drags you back to work and the people where you work shout abuse and try and kill you. Try and imagine, because that is exactly what it was like to be a British soldier on the streets of Belfast or Derry or Newry or any of a dozen other places in the Province.

We used to do patrols on the streets and we'd go out in batches of four men – which we called a 'brick' – several minutes between these batches so that back up was never far away. Once we were outside our base, away from our mates, we would feel the hatred; hatred so thick that you could feel it, could taste it. We would turn into a street; the back man always walking backwards to watch for trouble from behind and those residents on the streets would call for others to come out. Women would appear from their filthy hovels, dustbin lids in hand and begin pounding on the pavement and soon all the 'natives' would be there. The chanting would soon begin: 'English fuck-pigs' 'Brit bastards' 'Fuckin' English gob-shite' and this from the children; the adults were much worse! I walked past a house in the Balkans and I felt a whack on the back of my calves and I turned around to see a kid of five with a piece of timber in his hands! That kid will be 50 now; wonder if he still feels the same hatred?

Sure enough, the brick commander would inform us that kids were gathering in Leeson Street or down in the Falls Road and we would link up with other bricks

---

2   Ceremonial Dress Uniform.

and make our way down there. We would see more than 50 kids, faces masked, all wearing those jeans with tartan turn-ups and long hair and we would see some of our lads in riot gear. Steel lids[3], riot shields, pick-axe staves, Federal Riot Guns, rubber bullets at the ready. There would be smoke from the hurled petrol bombs – the Falls Road always smelled to me like a garage forecourt – and rocks all over the road. Behind the front line, you would see lads being dragged away by his mates, white-faced, blood pouring from head wounds caused by bricks and metal filings fired from catapults. Then all of a sudden, a big gap would appear in the front ranks of the rioters and a gunman or several gunmen would open fire on the lads with rifles or Tommy guns. Before we could fire back, the rioters would close ranks again and we were unable to shoot the bastards.

If we had been Nazis or American soldiers, we would have fired straight into the rioters and fuck any 'collateral damage!' Eventually, the rioters would tire, or our snatch squads would grab some of their ring-leaders, give them a good kicking and then hand them over to the RUC. The scumbags would return home to lick their wounds or brag about a soldier who had gone down injured, under a hail of rocks or paving stones. We would evacuate the area and return to our base for a few hours' kip on the floor. Our beds were blankets on the floor, small pack as a pillow and a blanket over us and we would try and sleep. Minutes after drifting off, stinking of petrol and shit, we would be kicked awake and 'crashed out' to a new riot on Springfield Road or somewhere else. That was what it was like. I was only a Rifleman, later a Lance Corporal, but that was my war. Next leave, I would keep my mouth shut, keep schtumm and say nothing!

For Mickey Pearce, Johnny Keeney, Mike Boswell, Bob Bankier, 'Geordie' Walker, 'Joe' Hill, John Taylor, Davie Card, Jim Meredith, Dave Griffiths and Ian George ; never forgotten lads; I still cry when I see your names. *Celer et Audux.*

On 18 January, the IRA carried out a fundraising bank robbery at a branch of the Northern Bank located inside the RVH. Arthur Liggett (25), a member of the IRA, and two others held up the clerks and grabbed a bag of money. However, a passing soldier forced his way into the bank and shot Liggett whose other two companions escaped through the complex lay out of the hospital. On the same day, the Ulster Volunteer Force (UVF) shot and killed Joseph Weir (48) in West Street, Portadown. Weir, who was drunk at the time, was thought to have been killed in either an internal UVF feud or as a simple falling out between paramilitaries. An equally bizarre death occurred three days later at a drinking session in the same town of Portadown when Margaret Rowland (18) was shot dead by an alleged Ulster Defence Association (UDA) member; again drink played its part.

On the Saturday of that week, taking a leaf out of the IRA's bloody book of urban terrorism, the UVF left a device inside a car in the centre of Dublin as they 'took the war to the Republic.' Thomas Douglas (21), in Dublin for his wedding, was walking past the car in Sackville Place when it detonated, wounding him fatally and hideously wounding another passer-by. Douglas died shortly afterwards in a Dublin hospital.

---

3   Helmets.

On 22 January, a 23-year-old RUC officer was accidentally shot whilst off duty, when an officer dropped his police revolver, discharging a round. Constable Samuel Culbert Hyndman was a victim of the Troubles, as surely as if the fatal shot was fired by an IRA gunman.

On the 25th, William Staunton, a 48-year-old Magistrate, died of his wounds after an IRA assassination attempt on his life the previous October. Magistrates were known targets of the IRA and, as Staunton was a Catholic and considered a 'traitor' by the Republicans, he was a marked man and had been fatally wounded as he had dropped his two daughters off at St Dominic's High School on the Catholic Falls Road area of Belfast.

The Falls Road (from the Irish: *tuath-na-bhFál* meaning district of the falls or hedges) is the main road through west Belfast; from Divis Street in Belfast City Centre to Andersonstown in the suburbs. The Falls Road was originally a country lane leading from the city centre but the population of the area expanded rapidly in the nineteenth century with the construction of several large linen mills. All of these have now closed. The housing in the area developed in the nineteenth century and was organised in narrow streets of small terraced back-to-back housing. Many of these streets were named after characters and events in the Crimean War (1853-1856) which was being fought at that time. These included Raglan Street – named after Lord Raglan, commander of British forces in the Crimean War, Alma Street – named after the Battle of Alma, Balaklava

UDR foot patrol, Belfast (Mark Campbell)

Street – named after the Battle of Balaklava, Inkerman Street – named after the Battle of Inkerman, and Sevastopol Street – named after the Siege of Sevastopol.

As the month drew to an end, sectarianism, surely the most evil crime of this most malicious period, reared its ugly head with a UFF murder gang was cruising around the Falls Road. As they drove along, intent on cold-blooded murder, they spotted an easy target in Peter Watterson, who was only 15, as he stood outside his widowed mother's shop, talking to his equally juvenile friends. Young Peter had that very day, dashed inside a burning building and rescued an elderly woman from the fire. As he no doubt, and quite justifiably basked in the adulation of his friends, gunmen opened fire, killing him and severely wounding a boy of 14. The estimable *Lost Lives* claims that one of the UFF gunmen was Francis 'Hatchet' Smith who himself, as we shall see, was killed by the IRA in the very early hours of the following morning.

That day – the 29th – was not yet over and a UFF murder gang – in all probability the same one led by Smith – struck at a petrol station at Kennedy Way, killing James Trainor (23) as he unwittingly went to serve the men who would prove to be his killers. Young Peter Watterson was killed at the junction of the Falls and Donegall Roads, and Kennedy Way is only a little over 1.5 miles away.

THE SKIRMISH
Corporal Hiram Dunn, 'A' Company, 1 King's Own Scottish Borderers
Just after midnight on the 30 January 1973, the anniversary of 'Bloody Sunday', a patrol from 1 KOSB was fired on in the Turf Lodge area. This led to a running gun-battle which went on for a number of hours between several patrols from 'C' Coy and 'A' companies and a group of IRA gunmen, believed at the time to be CESA (Catholic Ex Servicemen Association). Well over a 1,000 rounds were fired by the Borderers and three hits were claimed; two were confirmed.

The previous day, a section from King's Own Scottish Borderers was the QRF Section in Andersonstown RUC and Bus Station. As the section commander, I was in the OP's Room in the RUC Station, while my section was in the portakabin across the road in the Bus Depot. Not just any road, by the way; this was the junction of the Falls and Glen Road, where a numbers of soldiers had been shot dead crossing in the past. It was always a risk crossing this piece of road, not just from enemy fire but the crazy drivers in Northern Ireland who either did not have a drivers' licence or were just drunk.

Just after midnight the battalion radio came to life informing us that one of our patrols had come under fire in the Turf Lodge area a few streets to our north. One of our patrols, led by Corporal Ian 'Skip' Little had left our base, tasked to take the daily Sit Rep up to Bn HQ in Fort Monagh; he too was under fire and pinned down in the area of Upton Cottages and Arizona Street. The Op's officer Colour Sergeant Peter Seggie tasked me to take my section and come in from the east of Skip's location and give him covering fire to extract his patrol. I did not have to run the gauntlet as Lance Corporal Rab Baptie, my 2IC, had the section in the RUC station yard ready to go. I gave a quick sit rep on the situation and on our approach route. As I came out of the gate, I met the Company Commander Capt. Clive Fairweather, running across the road towards us. I can still see him today, wearing chukka boots, laces undone, blue and white striped Army issue pyjamas, 58 pat belt with a 9mm Pistol round his waist, open flak jacket, TOS (hat) and the cheroot in the mouth! As we bolted out the gate like rats from a trap, he told us to take care and keep your heads down; it was good advice which we were to put into practice.

After the initial burst out of the gate and into cover, we paused for a few seconds to collect our thoughts and our senses before moving off. As we moved up the Glen Road, Rab with two men on the left, myself and two men on the right, we used the leap frog method, keeping one foot on the ground while the other moved. My group took up fire positions at the junction of Glen Road and Norfolk Drive, whilst Rab's group crossed the gap and moved up to secure the next junction of Glen Road and Norfolk Parade. Fire fights continued to go on to our north in the Turf as we moved, and we headed in that direction. Once Rab's group were firm, my group moved up and turned into Norfolk Parade, and we all moved off in the same formation. As we approached the junction with Norbury Street, we came under machine gun fire from the Park at the top of the Road, some 400 metres in front.

I shouted: "Take cover!" and looked around before diving over the hedge to my right. I needn't have bothered; the Jocks were gone, obviously quicker than me. I sent a contact report to the Op's Room giving my location and where the fire was coming from and asking them to confirm that there were no friendly

The UDR on alert in Belfast city centre after an IRA bomb threat (Mark Campbell)

troops in that area. We did not return fire as there was no clear target; the burst of fire was high and could have come from well within the Falls Park which was like looking into a black hole. Ops confirmed that there were no friendly troops in that area and we should advance with caution; as if we needed telling. About ten minutes had passed with no movement seen or shots fired at us. We now started to advance up Norfolk Grove keeping to the gardens rather than on the road. The streetlights were out which was to our advantage as we moved, keeping in the shadows. After about five minutes we reached some open ground to our left, this was waste ground, undulating, with a small burn running down the middle. The ground rises up at the far end with semi-detached house in a semi-circle, some 150 metres away and all in darkness, and we had to cross this to reach the other section.

Rab and myself crawled from under the hedge, on to a bank of earth, to have a good look at the area so as to see how best to cross it. We called the rest of the section forward and spread them out either side of us and were about to brief them when this voice to our front shouted out: "I want to surrender!" We all looked at each other in disbelief, and as I could not see anyone, I was unsure where it came from. I told Rab that I didn't trust this and told the guys to keep their eyes peeled in case it was a come on. I spoke to Ops and was told to proceed with extreme caution and shout: "Come in".

I crawled forward in line again and shouted out: "Come in" but received no reply, then without warning, Rab got on his knees and belted out: "Come in!" which was followed by a burst of fire hitting the hedge row behind us. The Jocks were on the ball and a volley of shots was returned towards the area of the houses. The gunman had no intention of surrendering; he had obviously lost sight of us and was trying to find our location; you had to admire his balls because he could have just as easily given away his position. I did not want to hang about here any longer so I gave the order: "Prepare to skirmish in your pairs!" The adrenalin was running; up we got up together and darted forward, taking two zig-zag paces and down, as in training, except you don't take more than two paces or look for some where nice to get down again. I looked back and saw the next two move; Wee Jimmy (Jimmy Ingram) and Willy 'G,' (William Gordon) and they were followed by Rab, Robert Baptie and Rab (Robert McDowell).

We covered the ground in no time doing about five or six skirmishes each and reached the relative safety of Upton Cottages, out of breath and exhilarated. We never took any fire as we moved across the open ground, and to me, the gunman must have felt that his position was threatened by our aggression and legged it. I radioed Skip and gave him our location; he was at the opposite end of Upton Cottages. We moved off and came under fire again but this time, it was single rife fire from the area of Norfolk Gardens. The shots were a bit closer this time, hitting the stone wall and gate post, we didn't return fire, as again a clear target could not be identified. It would be a further four hours before we returned to relative safety of the Bus Depot. Skip never did deliver the Company Sit-Rep as he left that morning to go on a course. The heart-warming thing for me was the courage shown by the Jocks when asked to risk their lives in this notorious area of West Belfast; they met the challenge head on with steadfast determination.

It rarely gives this author pleasure to report any death during the long and tortuous course of the Troubles, but one is prepared to make an exception in the case of the aforementioned 'Hatchet' Smith. Just hours after the double killings of the two Catholics, Smith had been involved in a brief armed struggle with an IRA unit, during which several shots were fired, hitting him in the head. It is likely that one or two further shots were fired into his head as he lay prostrate, his body was found in Rodney Street not far from the murder scene of Peter Watterson. A suitably fitting end for a mad dog!

The remainder of the day passed without further deaths, although there was much rioting in Catholic areas in several parts of Ulster as the first anniversary of the 'Bloody Sunday' killings was 'celebrated'. However, the rabid dogs of the UFF didn't wait long before extracting reprisals for the killing by the IRA of 'Hatchet' Smith. The next day, a Wednesday, UFF killers abducted Phillip Rafferty (14) from Tullymore Gardens, Andersonstown and took him to Giant's Ring on the southern outskirts of Belfast where his bound, hooded and beaten body was found having been shot in the head. It is both easy and quite natural in these appalling circumstances to wax lyrical and eulogise these young victims. However, young Phillip was a frail and asthmatic boy who had barely passed his 14th birthday. This author is not afraid to accuse the IRA of wanton and cowardly murders but is equally condemnatory of the sub-humans who populated the Loyalist murder gangs. That very same day Gabriel Savage (17) was abducted, also in the Andersonstown area and his body, having been beaten and tortured, was dumped in the Protestant Village area of Belfast. Two young Catholic teenagers had been abducted, beaten, tortured and their dead bodies dumped like some old rubbish all in the name of the Loyalist cause.

Rossington soldier Private Edward Blazaitis (19) serving with the 3rd Battalion the Light Infantry in Belfast, had a lucky escape when a gunman's bullet struck the muzzle of his rifle.

Edward (pictured with the smashed rifle) was in an observation post looking down the Berwick Road, in the Ardoyne area of Belfast, during a gun battle against the Provisional IRA.

During the evening about 230 shots were fired in the area of Edward's post. He said of the incident, "My rifle vibrated and I looked at the muzzle and it was smashed. I shouted to my section commander for another rifle and then carried on with my duties."

Edward's parents, Mr. and Mrs. I. V. Blazaitis, live at Chestnut Avenue, Rossington.

Doncaster Evening Post, early 1973

LONDONDERRY ANTI-CLIMAX
Alan McMillan, Royal Artillery

I suppose the final memorable event on the tour was the anniversary of 'Bloody Sunday.' The anniversary turned out to be one of the most boring days of the whole tour for Reserve Troop. In the early hours of the morning, we were deployed to 73 Battery's TAOR (Tactical Area of Responsibility) in the City centre; we were briefed in the Victoria car park base as to our duties for the day. Basically, a memorial stone for those killed on 'Bloody Sunday' was to be unveiled at that day's parade. The Security Forces would have eyes in the crowd and depending on the wording – anything inflammatory such as 'Murdered by British Army' or something along those lines – we would be moving in to remove it.

Now I would never claim to be a tactical expert but there were going to be more than 10,000 people at this march, while at a push the army could have maybe supplied 1,000 for whole of Derry's west bank. To my way of thinking it would have made more sense to let them unveil the stone, see what was on it and if it had to be removed, wait till 3am the next morning and run a bulldozer over it. Quite simple and removes the obvious threat to personnel; as it turned out it was a complete waste of time. We sat from 10am until 6pm in the back of the PIGs with the engines running, with cups of tea being ferried out or having comfort breaks. After all that time we were de-briefed and sent home.

The thing is from that day, if I pass a bus or HGV vehicle at a standstill with its engine running, the smell from its exhaust always brings the memories of that day flooding back. That is one smell I have never forgotten, even more so than the smell after bomb explosions. Weird or what! Looking back over the intervening years I suppose the memories are a mixture of togetherness, fear, laughter, adrenalin rushes and boredom; and of course the drabness on a rainy day, and there was plenty of them.

Things had been fairly quiet for some time, or as quiet as Londonderry could be at that time, so the powers that be decided that we could go on shopping trips to Coleraine which was about 40 miles from Derry. Now this was an area I knew very well and had quite a few friends in. We were taken in for a briefing about areas to avoid and bars that were out of bounds for one reason or another. Now I don't know who provided the intelligence for these briefings but I couldn't believe my ears at what was being said. With the exception of the RBL, every bar they classified as safe would have been the most unwelcoming establishment for any soldier to enter. Indeed, one in particular was so well known for its Republican sympathies, that even the ODC's (ordinary decent Catholics) wouldn't use it. Fortunately on the way to Coleraine, I was able to set the lads straight about safe bars for a drink. Happily a good day out was had by all, but through bad intelligence it could have turned out disastrously. Some weeks later a soldier from another unit entered this particular Republican bar and was severely beaten up; it is widely believed if it hadn't been for the intervention of a UDR patrol, his attackers intended throwing him into the river.

Unnoticed in the turmoil of this month was the death of UDR soldier Private Johnstone Bradley, who was killed in unknown circumstances on the 23 January.

It was certainly a lighter month than its 1972 counterpart, but of the 22 who lost their lives, three were soldiers, four were policemen; the IRA lost one; the Loyalists lost three members and a total of 11 innocent civilians were killed. The Provisional IRA was responsible for eight of the deaths, and the Protestant murder gangs also killed the same number.

Chapter 2

February

February 1 fell on a Thursday and, as the working day began, a bus carrying workers to the site of a new school in Gilnahirk; East Belfast was attacked by a Loyalist gang as it approached the building site. The driver had slowed to let an apparently disabled youth cross in front of it, although this was an elaborate ruse by the gang and the 'disabled' youth was faking. A bomb was tossed on board the bus and it detonated almost immediately, killing Patrick Heenan (50) a labourer from Andersonstown and father of five children. In addition, almost all the other 13 passengers received injuries ranging from minor to very severe. Edward 'Ned' McCreery, the local UDA man who was accused of the murder, was killed in an internal Loyalist feud in April, 1992.

Just moments later, this time in Strabane, an IRA unit phoned in a hoax call stating that they had planted a bomb in a building on Main Street close to the town centre. A mobile patrol of the King's Own Scottish Borderers (KOSB) stopped to investigate, not immediately realising that this was a hoax and that it was designed to lure soldiers or Police into an IRA killing zone. Colour Sergeant William Boardley (30) was standing close to their Saracen armoured vehicle when two or three shots rang out; the Barrow-in-Furness man was hit in the neck and chest and collapsed to the ground. He was rushed to the nearest hospital but was already dead. The married soldier was the father of two and was killed by an IRA gunman who, at the time of the killing was only 16 years old.

On 4 February, Constable Robert James McIntyre (41) collapsed and died on duty and, as such, is commemorated on the RUC, GC roll of honour, alongside the names of his other fallen comrades, who fell in the fight against terrorism.

As children, we played a game called tit-for-tat; we raced around trying to 'tig' a friend. During the Troubles both Republican and Loyalists also played a version – albeit a much bloodier version – of this innocent childhood game. This one involved a revenge sectarian killing for a sectarian murder by the other side. The IRA would kill a Protestant and the UFF or UVF would kill a Catholic, and then the IRA would kill a Protestant and the UFF or UVF would kill a Catholic in retaliation, and then the whole deadly game would continue. Sometimes one group would kill someone 'out of turn' but in the end, any pretence of 'revenge' was lost in the senseless slaughter.

Apparently in retaliation for the attack on the work bus at Gilnahirk, the IRA shot and killed James Greer (21) at a glazier's shop on Springfield Road, Belfast. At that stage of the conflict, Springfield Road, although in the main a Catholic area, still contained Protestant families. Greer, a Protestant who was due to move to Scotland, was singled out because of his religion and shot several times in the head, dying more or less immediately at the scene.

As my late father was fond of saying 'as sure as eggs are eggs' the UFF struck next and abducted Patrick Brady (28) from outside a pub on Linden Street. Linden Street is close to the Catholic Falls Road and at the time of the abduction, it was already dark and it would not have been difficult in the gloom to have taken him. His body was found, badly beaten, his hands tied and hooded, shot through the head and dumped just off Springfield Road. That Friday was not finished and the IRA then engaged in their game of bloody tit-for-tat that same evening. Six Protestant boys – none of whom had any known paramilitary leanings – were engaged in conversation on a street corner standing outside a chemist shop near the sectarian interface of the Oldpark Road in North Belfast. As they discussed women or football or any other variety of 'weighty' topics, a car drove up and a burst of automatic fire came from it, hitting five of the boys and killing Robert Burns (18). The car, a yellow Mini, was traced by the Army and as a small foot patrol attempted to make an arrest, they were forced back by a massive crowd of Catholics and also came under fire, according to later forensic evidence, from the same gun used to kill Burns.

NEAR MISS IN DUNGIVEN
Malcolm Phillips, 2nd Battalion, Royal Green Jackets

The reluctance of the RUC to come out to incidents where shots had been fired was well known, and I can only remember one time when they were there before us. We were doing our stint in Dungiven. Not a very nice area and the locals did not appreciate what we were trying to do for them. One night we had reports of shots being fired at a house where a police inspector lived. The immediate section, myself included, rushed round there to see what was happening. With gunmen supposedly on the ground, I had one up the spout. . I took up a position by a hedge while the Boss went to the house. A minute or two after that, a bloke walked out of the trees a few yards in front of me, holding an M1 Carbine. I had taken first pressure on my trigger before I noticed his policeman's hat. Never known police to be anywhere before we were, but I suppose they look after their own. Damn fool nearly got himself killed.

The weekend arrived, but there was to be no let up from the senseless sectarian slaughter, as no less than nine people lost their lives during the course of those 48 hours. In any British mainland city, such an appalling number of murders would have every available police officer and that of neighbouring forces working flat out on door-to-door enquiries, fingertip searches, and lifting the 'usual suspects.' Indeed, during the long course of the 'Yorkshire Ripper' murders, forces from Leeds, Bradford and Huddersfield might have found themselves working alongside each other to stop and catch Peter Sutcliffe. For all the herculean tasks which faced them, they could at least enter all areas without the need for armed soldiers to protect them and know, in the main, that the local communities were united in helping find the notorious and cowardly killer of women. But this was Northern Ireland and it was the Troubles, and the factors which worked in favour of the English police, worked to the detriment of the Northern Ireland police, the RUC.

ANDERSONSTOWN, FEBRUARY 1973
George Clarke, MM, Green Howards

The company was stationed in Andersonstown for our tour; it was the usual for Belfast, nothing but a collection of buildings surrounded by a wriggly tin fence. The IRA was in full swing at this period in history as everyone knows. We carried out the usual rota for the time; patrols, guards, standby, rest or training. We were continually being shot at from a row of garages overlooking the camp, and the Company Commander decided that something had to be done about this. As the area in question was part of my platoon's responsibility, it became our job to do something. 'Big Moo' got myself and the section commanders all together, and asked for any ideas on how to do this. We knew the area quite well and there was no doubt in our minds that this wasn't going to be an easy task. After deliberation, it was decided that one of us was going to have to wait in the garage alone for the gunman to turn up; as it was my idea, I volunteered. It was decided that we would patrol the area, and see how easy it was to get into the garage without being see, and also we had the added problem that it could be booby trapped. As it was, it turned out fairly easy and it was decided that I would go in the garage for a few minutes, to see what happened and in I went. I can't say that I wasn't scared but once inside, I waited for the platoon to come and get me. It was decided that the signal that it was my men coming to get me, was three taps followed by two taps. After 15 minutes, which felt a lot longer, there was a tapping on the door and I was extracted easily. We did this for a couple of nights and on the third night we decided that I would go in and stay.

The night came more quickly than I thought it would. I made sure that my rifle was working at its peak performance and was clean and well oiled; I was only going to get one chance. I was tense on the briefing and a little apprehensive, but the adrenalin was flowing. We set out on patrol with me in the centre. As we approached the garages, my training kicked in and I was ready for action; I slid a round into the breach and I was ready. I followed the patrol into the garage area and as they went into position to cover me, I slipped into the garage. As my eyes adjusted to the darkness, all my senses came alert and I could smell stale urine, it smelled as though someone had just been in and relieved himself. I could just make out an old mattress in the corner and wondered what it could have been used for. I settled down to wait; it was eerily quiet. I could see the light coming from a hole in the corner wall of the garage, where the gunman would stand when he was shooting at us. I kept looking at my watch and the time seemed to stand still.

All the time I was thinking: can I do this? Can I be brave enough to shoot before he shoots me? He would have the advantage over me, because I had a yellow card that I must obey; I must give him a chance to give himself up. I sat there and waited and waited. After what seemed like hours there was a rustling outside the garage door, and I thought: 'This is it'. It seemed like an eternity then the door started lifting; I got myself ready then the door stopped moving and I heard the signal: three taps followed by two taps, and realised that my hand had tightened around the pistol grip. I had taken off my safety and my finger was on the trigger; I seemed to have frozen to the spot. I finally let myself relax, as I saw the outline of Big Moo; he was indicating that it was time to come out.

We returned to camp and after debriefing, I went to bed; my mind was in turmoil all night, knowing that for a split second I could have killed one of my own men. I went in a couple more times, until it was decided not to continue with the operation; amazingly enough we stopped getting shot at from the garages after that.

York Road, to the north west of the Catholic New Lodge, today sits alongside the modern and very busy M2 Motorway, with all the 21st century noise of the hustle and bustle of transport. In February, 1973, it was quieter and less well-developed. The small café there attracted many lorry drivers, cab drivers or any of the local people from Seaview Street, Parkmount Street, North Derby Street or Mountcollyer Road or any of scores of other Protestant enclaves. It was run by James Fusco (58) a local man of Italian extraction and, shamefully, a Catholic; shamefully that is, in the eyes of the Protestant extremists. Masked gunmen from the UDA and UFF burst into the café and shot and killed Fusco and indirectly caused the death of Samuel Reynolds (70) who was so shocked by the shooting that he collapsed and died from a heart attack.

On 28th February 2011, as the result of a PSNI (Police Service Northern Ireland) Historical Enquiries Team investigation, Loyalist terrorist Robert James Clarke (58) was found guilty of Alfredo Fusco's murder. In 2009, when the Historical Enquiries Team (HET) reviewed the case, Clarke was never a suspect. His fingerprints were not even on file until he murdered Margaret O'Neill (58) two years after killing Mr Fusco. When HET reopened the Fusco murder case in February 2009 they gathered all the files. By then automatic computerised checks could be run on the prints. Almost immediately a match was thrown up and that match was of Clarke.

In August 2009 fresh fingerprints were taken from Clarke in the custody suite at Antrim police station. Fingerprint experts then compared these fresh prints with those lifted in 1973. The similarity of the characteristics led the expert to conclude that in "… no doubt these imprints were made by the defendant. And they were the only fingerprints on the door." That was the evidence officers needed to feel confident enough to charge him with Mr Fusco's murder. The evidence was also significant in convincing Mr Justice McLaughlin of his guilt at a non-jury trial. The Historical Enquiries Team has completed 1,100 cases relating to some 1,400 deaths. In February 1976, Clarke was one of four men convicted and given life sentences for the random sectarian killing of Margaret O'Neill, shot dead on 14 June 1975 as she walked home along the New Lodge Road after a night out with her husband and their youngest son. Under the terms of the Good Friday Agreement, Clarke is expected to serve a maximum of two years for the 1973 offence, the same rules and sentence that would apply to Colour Sergeant Boardley's killer were he, or she, ever identified.

During the research for this book, I spoke with a Belfast Catholic and, whilst he requested not to be identified, was willing to tell me the following:

I knew Alfie Fusco; he owned a chip shop on York Road at the junction with Mountcollyer Road where I lived as a kid and was famous for his Italian ice cream. My Grandad used to buy a big tub every Friday night and we all shared it; it was heaven! Alfie was a lovely inoffensive wee man, he had owned and served in the shop for years and was popular and well respected in the community. Before and during the Troubles, he always gave the local kids free ice cream for their 11th of July bonfire parties. His killers went into the shop one Saturday night looking for his son who was rumoured to be in the IRA. However, I don't know if that's true or just a malicious rumour, but he wasn't there so they shot Alfie instead, simply because he was a Catholic. I'm glad they finally caught up with his killer; I hope he has a long time to think about it.

Shortly after the murder of Mr Fusco, a group of men, including two IRA members were standing outside Lynch's Bar on the New Lodge Road when a car containing gunmen from the UFF opened fire indiscriminately. IRA man James Sloan (19) was shot and died at the scene and fellow terrorist James McCann (18) was fatally wounded, dying in hospital in the early hours of Sunday morning. It does appear, with the undoubted benefit of hindsight, that the Loyalist murder gang was simply trying to kill Catholics and couldn't believe their good fortune in killing two of their hated enemies.

Soldiers immediately flooded the New Lodge area on the Sunday, to follow up the killings amidst the inevitable accusations from Republicans of collusion with the Loyalists. There have been constant claims over the years, that RUC/Army INT had advised soldiers to leave an area clear when they were informed that Loyalists planned a hit on the IRA or that random sectarian killings were scheduled. Several gun battles broke out between soldiers and the IRA and with a variety of weapons being used, at least eight IRA gunmen were involved, using several US-made and no doubt US-smuggled Armalites. Over 500 rounds were expounded and the Army claimed to have hit at least six gunmen. During the firefights, Tony Campbell (19) of the IRA and three other Catholics: John Loughran (35), Brendan Maguire (32) and Ambrose Hardy (26) were all shot and killed by the Army. There is no evidence to suggest that the latter three were IRA members and they may have been killed in the crossfire. The Provisional IRA's Belfast propaganda sheet 'Battleground' had a field day with the six killings on what many soldiers referred to as the 'long streets.' Their 'reporter' wrote:

> … the people of the New Lodge area, hardened as they are to explosions and shots[1] were startled by the sound of heavy gunfire coming from the immediate area. After the furore died down we were left with six men dead and many more wounded. The British Army had opened up indiscriminately with their SLRs and murdered six young men in cold blood.

The Provisionals had, as always, put their 'spin' on matters and it was true that the Army had killed one of their gunmen, but it was a legitimate shooting under ROE and the 'yellow card.' Two of their members were killed by a UFF murder gang and although there is evidence that the three innocent Catholics were shot by the Army, they could have been killed by either side in the murderous crossfire on the 3rd. The Provisional IRA chose to turn the New Lodge into a battleground and the 'Battleground' writer conveniently chose to ignore that fact.

The night before, a UDA/UFF gang had abducted John Boyd (33), a fellow Protestant in the Ann Street area, east of the Catholic Short Strand. He was beaten, tortured and then murdered by fellow Protestants in what may have been either an internal feud or a mistaken identity sectarian killing. No less than nine people – all of them civilians

---

1   Author: Most of them by the IRA.

– had been killed during that fateful weekend in Belfast and it was amongst the worst weekends of the Troubles.

The killings resumed in the early hours of Monday morning, when gunmen from the UVF – one of whom was just 14 years old – drove into a petrol station in Ballysillan Road in North Belfast and shot dead Seamus Gilmore (18) as he worked on a car. Gilmore, described as 'car mad' with no paramilitary leanings, was cut down, his life barely started, by masked cowards from the Loyalist side of the sectarian divide.

The following day, the IRA fired a rocket at an Army mobile patrol in the Falls Road area and the explosion killed Private Michael Murtagh (23) of the Queen's Lancashire Regiment. The firing point was a car, hijacked earlier by terrorists and positioned on derelict ground near Cullingtree Road. The soldier from Lancashire was fatally wounded and despite the superb medical treatment received at the nearby Royal Victoria hospital, died within an hour. The armoured vehicle had been on a routine mobile patrol and had just reached Servia Street when the attack took place.

Despite their oft uttered cries of support for 'Queen and country' and a professed desire to remain 'British' the Loyalists were not averse to attacking soldiers, rioting or injuring and killing members of the SF. On 7 February – a bloody day on which five people lost their lives – during major riots in the Newtownards Road, Belfast, the Army came under fire. The Loyalists had staged a one day 'general strike' to protest against the continued killings by Republicans ('kettle calling the pot black' syndrome?) and no doubt to complain about the alleged hand over of some power to the Catholics.

UDR soldiers seen at Unity flats, Belfast (Mark Campbell)

During the course of the heavy rioting, two local Protestant women were accidentally knocked over by armoured cars and both were slightly injured. The news of this soon spread and soldiers came under fire, although this was subsequently denied by the Godfathers of the UDA. The Army shot and killed Ulster Freedom Fighters (UFF) member Andrew Petherbridge (18) near to Newtownards Road. Soldiers from the Green Howards came under increasing fire and in a shoot-out close to where Petherbridge was killed, they shot Robert Bennett (31) who was a member of another Loyalist terror group, the UVF; Bennett died at the scene. He had been firing into the street below, when a Green Howard shot him from a higher vantage point.

SHOOTING A TERRORIST
George Clarke, MM, Green Howards

We were into our third month of a four month tour and the problems for the Government had swung in a different direction. The Protestants had started to flex their muscles. It seemed that the Loyalists were protesting the internment of Protestants; no doubt convinced that only Catholics should be interned. The Ulster Workers' Council was placing considerable demands on both Stormont and Westminster governments and a day of protest was planned. The military had to make contingency plans in case of violence, not in the Catholic areas but in the Protestant areas of East Belfast. As the Belfast reserve was on leave, other units had to make up a reserve force and the Mortar Platoon, strengthened by the Drums Platoon, and the Anti-Tank Platoon from Support Company was to be part of this force; together with a with a platoon from 'B' Company. This happened to be seven platoon.

By noon there were reports of large crowds gathering in East Belfast; word came from Brigade headquarters that we were required there. Whilst the Company Commander disappeared to find out what was going on, we left under the command of WOII Terry Moore to go out to the east of the city. We arrived at the Short Strand Bus Depot just after 2pm to be met by the Company Commander, and we were ordered to go Albertbridge Road because we had reports of large and angry crowds massing.

As we arrived, we were confronted by a large crowd of Loyalists; our vehicles were spaced out one behind the other. We dismounted and started moving up the street, behind our vehicle, to disperse them, when we came under fire from the rooftops. The Company Commander said: "Don't worry; they are not shooting at us," when at that moment a bullet went into one of the vehicle's tyres. I shouted out to him that we needed to get to higher ground, so that we have better control of the situation. He ordered me to go into the TA centre, which we happened to be passing at the time, and get as high as I could. I dashed into the building and flew up the stairs; at the top there were floor to ceiling windows which went out to a balcony. I went out and found that I commanded a good view of the area. As I went out, I heard shooting and looked across the street onto a roof a little lower than me; there I saw three men, one of whom had a rifle and was shooting down into the street at my platoon.

All of this seemed to be happening in slow motion; the noise was horrendous from the crowd and they were egging the gunmen on. I cocked my rifle, loading a round into the breach, took careful aim at the gunman and fired. Immediately, I realised I hadn't allowed for the fall from my height to a lower height and my round struck the wall in front of the gunman. The impact splattered him with debris and he fell out of sight, dropping the weapon which was picked up by another man. Now that I had been seen, the one who had picked up the rifle started firing at me; I could hear rounds passing close by. I knew that as long as I could hear the rounds passing by, I was ok. I fired two or three quick rounds and one struck the gunman and he fell backwards; the other man suddenly disappeared.

I was not in communication at all with my platoon, so I stayed on the roof for what seemed like hours, but was probably less than 30 minutes, and covered my men as they moved forward and cleared the street. Two of my platoon came up, and we stayed securing the high ground until, at last, the streets had been cleared and we went down and out of the building. I emerged into the street and looked around; the place was covered in debris and my platoon seemed to be walking around in a daze. It was at this stage that we learned that 'Tapper' Hall who had been with 7 platoon, had been severely wounded. My platoon had fortunately not suffered any casualties. What we didn't know at the time was that 'Tapper' had been fatally wounded and died some time afterwards.

I had been to Northern Ireland several times before this, but this was my first real taste of a gun battle; I could still smell the cordite and feel the heat of my weapon. I thought that these smells and this feeling would never go away, but I also knew that, as a soldier, this probably wouldn't be my last gun battle. I was later awarded the Military Medal for this action and Lieutenant Richard Dannatt, now Lord Dannatt, who had commanded 7 Platoon, was awarded the Military Cross. I gladly accepted the award on behalf of all my men; one man does not win a conflict; it needs every person in the team to bring an operation to a successful conclusion.[2]

The Loyalist strike – and the violence – continued and paramilitaries deliberately set fire to a clothing shop in the Sandy Row area, some two miles or so across Belfast. The Belfast fire brigade raced to the scene and as firemen fought the blaze, they came under fire from UFF gunmen. In the chaos of the gunfire and the blazing building, Brian Douglas (23) was shot and killed, ironically by fellow Protestants in what was later described as a 'show of strength' by the UDA. The funeral was attended by over a thousand of his fellow firemen from all over the UK.

That bloody day continued when a member of the UFF, Glen Clarke (18) was foolish enough to walk through the Unity Street flats area, a notorious and violent breeding ground for the IRA. He was abducted and later his beaten and bound body was dumped behind a pub on the nearby Antrim Road. The bloodletting for February 7 finally ended close to midnight, with the death of Hugh Connolly (38) when an Army foot patrol came under fire on Springfield Road, Belfast from gunmen in Clonard Gardens. Clonard Gardens is situated in the heart of Republican country and the soldiers returned fire and shot Mr Connolly who was badly wounded and crawled to a nearby house. He was not a member of the IRA and nor was he a known Republican. Regrettably he appears to have

---

2   See Chapter 3, March 1972, for more information on Private Raymond 'Tapper' Hall.

Firemen tackle a blaze after an IRA bomb, Wellington Street Belfast (Mark Campbell)

been accidentally killed by the Army. Again, it was the IRA who had chosen to make a suburban street their battlefield and much of the blame must rest with their irresponsible use of built up areas and the consequent killing of civilians caught in the crossfire.

As the reader will see, with February only a week old, already 21 people had been killed in or as a direct consequence of the euphemistically named troubles. By now two CVOs (Casualty Visiting Officers) had made their way to households in Cumbria and Lancashire and in order to impart their sad news to an Army wife or parent and the RUC, no doubt under heavy military protection would have done the same in a number of households in Belfast and elsewhere. To the reader who has never experienced sectarianism or sectarian murder, the very concept of killing another human being on the simple basis of which church he or she worshipped at or even in which district he lived must seem not only utterly repulsive but also quite bizarre. The author as a young boy was brought up in a Jehovah's Witness background and did suffer the 'slings and arrows' of a form of mild sectarianism from former school friends who belonged to the Church of England. This, though irritating and at times frightening, was a mere discomfort compared with the abhorrent and illogical blood-letting which had plagued Ireland for centuries, and now manifested itself in a modern pattern of deliberate, but totally indiscriminate, murder. The reader will witness how many people had their lives prematurely – and violently – ended by simple virtue of the fact that they were in the wrong place at the wrong time! Or were asked that most obscene of all questions: "Are yez, Protestant or Catholic?"

On the mainland, worried Army parents and families alike and, no doubt, even the uninvolved pub drinkers asked themselves the same question: can it get any worse? As posterity shows, it could and did!

BLACK MAFIA DON'T LIKE COWS!
Malcolm Phillips, 2nd Battalion, Royal Green Jackets

At the time, I was in 'C' section of the Assault Pioneer Platoon of 'I' Company, 2RGJ. During one particular night, we had been patrolling the countryside and doing snap VCPs all over the place, in a couple of land rovers. Someone took offence to that, and at one spot they took a few pot shots at us. We de-bussed and did a follow up, with part of the section in a field full of cows, and part of the section going up to the high ground where the shots had come from. From our position we could see them; clearly silhouetted against the night sky.

Suddenly the 'tail end Charlie' of our group began to run; he passed the radio operator and then the NCO in charge. Then the radio operator began to run also, and passed the NCO! The next thing, all three were running up the hill and there, chasing them, was a cow! Despite the situation, we were in fits of laughter. Needless to say we did not find any gunmen. Getting back into our wagons, we had another incident. I had just climbed into the back, when a car going at speed came over the humpback rise behind us, literally leaving the ground for a few feet before landing again and slamming into the back of the land rover I had just got into. It bent the bumper of the land rover and bounced off. Turning over as it did so. Just a second or two earlier and I would have been squashed; as it was I was not hurt at all. We pulled the driver from his car, an old Cortina, which was a write-off. He wasn't badly hurt but we then had the usual wait for the Police and Ambulance services; never quick going to anywhere where shots had been fired.

The next morning I got home to my married quarters in Ballykelly; I left my combats in a heap in the bath, all covered in cow dung and mud and showered before crashing out, leaving my poor missus to clean them. She was not amused.

Earlier we touched on the obstacles placed in the path of the RUC in the execution of their duty, and how it differed greatly from the rest of the British police forces. No more was that more borne out that on the very next day of the month after a road traffic accident in Dungannon. The question on every one's lips though was it in some bizarre way planned by the IRA or was one of their so-called active service units (ASU) encountering a target of opportunity or reacting with lightning speed to the situation. In Dungannon, in the immediate aftermath of the accident, RUC Constable Charles Morrison (26) arrived on the scene and raced to assist an injured woman. As he knelt down by the wreckage, he was shot in the back several times by an IRA gunman and died shortly afterwards en-route for the hospital.

The IRA lost two of their members 48 hours later in a classic 'own goal' when a device being planted in a wood close to Strangford Lough prematurely detonated. A teacher, Lee O'Hanlon (23) and a student Vivienne Fitzsimmons (17) were killed instantly in the blast and their mutilated bodies lay undisturbed until a Catholic priest notified the Army.

The Queen's Lancashire Regiment (motto: 'Loyally I Serve') were to suffer two tragedies in the space of 23 days in February/ March. The first occurred, on 14 February, when a QLR foot patrol was attacked in Cyprus Street, in the Lower Falls area and two soldiers were hit. One of the men was only slightly wounded, but Private Edwin Weston (21) was mortally wounded and despite being rushed to nearby RVH, died not long after he was admitted. His comrades returned fire but were unable to confirm any hits on the one, possibly two terrorists, who participated in the attack. The young soldier who was single came from the Lancashire town of Preston.

IN THE FALLS
Soldier 'A' Queen's Lancashire Regiment

I wasn't on the patrol when Weston was killed but I spoke to other lads and I also had my own time being shot at, spat at, insulted and bricked along with the rest. When we first got there, although we knew what was happening, we all felt – well I did, anyway, that we could make a difference and things would be better. You know what I mean? Like giving sweets to the kids in the area, and stuff like that. The toddlers would take them and we were always having them run up to us and shout: 'Got any sweets, mistah?' but sometimes their mothers or older brothers and sisters would pull them away. Sometimes they would tell us to 'Fuck orf' and that was girls as well as boys and as young as four or five.

We walked, or sometimes drove, around the Lower Falls and I remember the streets were all like 'Coronation Street' on the telly but the difference was that the Ena Sharples and the Len Fairclough there wanted to kill you, not buy you a pint in the 'Rover's Return.' Some of the places like Albert Street, where Gary Barlow was murdered,[3] and Servia Street and others you could feel the hatred and it was hard to imagine that you were in a part of the UK. After a while, you became cynical and you thought, if they treat us like animals, we'll act like animals. One day, somewhere around Raglan Street, we were just patrolling and some guy swore at us. The Lance Jack (Lance Corporal) said to me: 'We'll have a word with that fella!' and we walked over to him. I pointed my SLR at him and screamed: 'Name, you Paddy bastard!' and he told me to go fuck myself. I stood back and a couple of lads pushed him back against a wall and started searching him and I said very quietly: 'Give me a reason you Irish twat and I'll fucking shoot you without blinking!' You know what? I hated him so much, I would have done it!

I was home on leave once and I went to see City play at Maine Road, and I'd had a few before the game and I was bursting for a piss, so I went in the bogs where there was the usual half-time queue.[4] I was stood behind these two lads, both with City scarves on, discussing the match in Paddy accents. I nearly pissed myself there and then and it unnerved me. I did a Google search for Raglan Street and Cyprus Street where Weston was shot and they weren't there anymore! They'll always be there inside my head, though.

---

3   On the 5th March.

4   Manchester City Football Club.

On February 15, the UVF targeted the 'Bunch of Grapes' bar, in Garmoyle Street, close to Belfast Docks. Several people were injured, including George Keatings. Ironically, he was killed in a carbon-copy attack almost exactly 13 months later.

Three days later, the sectarian killing commenced after a short pause for breath and the UFF abducted Francis Taggart (23) apparently as a spontaneous reaction to a failed IRA gun attack on a Protestant in Roden Street, some 300 or so yards from the RVH. Taggart's mortally wounded body was found in an abandoned car close to Ravenhill Road, Belfast, near the Catholic Short Strand area. He died shortly after admittance to the RVH, killed because he was a Catholic who had the 'temerity' to work for a Protestant company.

The following day, the bloody killings continued, and this time, the UVF targeted two off-duty postmen as they were returning home after their day's work and were walking, chatting to each other along Divis Street, Belfast. The two General Post Office (GPO) employees, Michael Coleman (30) from the Falls Road and Joseph McAleese (38) from the Ballymurphy Estate were shot when a car containing the Loyalist murder gang stopped and the men inside opened fire with sub-machine guns. Both men were hit repeatedly with some of the shots being fired into their prostrate bodies and they both died at the scene.

The UVF struck again the following day, when they cold-bloodedly 'executed' William Cooke (29) whom they had accused of being an informant, or 'tout' in the vernacular of Northern Ireland during the Troubles.

Less than 24 hours later, the IRA turned their attention again to the British Army and made two major attacks in the Belfast area. At approximately 9am on 20, February, a foot patrol from the Royal Marines was in the New Lodge Road when a device exploded. In the incident Royal Marine Tom Rivenberg was blown off his feet and terribly injured. His dedicated wife Frances did me the great honour of writing a piece in conjunction with her husband, Tom.

Frances Dodworth Rivenberg:

Tom has no problem at all with you including him in your book but doesn't want to name any people that were with him that night. As you probably know he was threatened by the IRA when he was in the Royal Victoria Hospital and they did try to gain access to him whilst he was in the intensive care unit. This is dictated by Tom to me because he doesn't know how to type.

NEW LODGE ROAD, BELFAST

We were on patrol in a side street off New Lodge Road on 20 February, 1973. It was about 8:45am and the weather was a cold, sleety drizzle. We were on the opposite side of the road to a Working Men's Club, passing a disused Fish 'n' Chip shop. A device had been left in the doorway of the shop and as we passed by, it detonated. I was in direct line of fire, so to speak, and was thrown into the air and then landed, rather unceremoniously, a bit further down the road minus a leg and with the other one badly mangled. My rifle didn't come off any better than me; it was bent into a horseshoe shape! The rest is common knowledge. I lost both legs and have spent most of the rest of my days in a wheelchair. There has been the odd threat by IRA since then but we are well looked after.

On the same day, and less than a mile away, the IRA turned their attention again to the British Army and attacked a mobile patrol of the Coldstream Guards close to the Falls Road. Using their new favourite weapon, the American Armalite plus a World War II Garrand and a Thompson sub-machine gun, they fired a fusillade of shots and followed this up with a blast bomb. The bomb severely injured one of the Guardsmen, but Guardsman Robert Pearson (20) a Leeds boy and Guardsman Malcolm Shaw (23) who were travelling in separate vehicles were both hit and died shortly afterwards. Three of the alleged killers were said to be teenagers with the oldest being only 15 years old. The 'Coldcreamers', as they are known to rival regiments, were to suffer another tragedy the following day just up the road from this attack, this time close to the Whiterock Road.

As thousands of Northern Ireland veterans will know, the Whiterock Road is a long, initially straight but becoming winding, road which leads off the upper section of the Falls Road and neatly bisects the Ballymurphy Estate and its equally notorious Republican sister, the Turf Lodge. Almost as a reminder of their own mortality, as the soldiers headed north, is Belfast City Cemetery with its row after row of different coloured gravestones and a wall behind which, stone throwers and gunmen alike could crouch, hidden, until the last minute. With the regiment still reeling from the double loss of the day before and with another comrade seriously ill, the Coldstream Guards were tasked with guarding a party of Sappers who were laying telephone cables outside a fortified Army base in the Whiterock area. Londoner Michael Doyle (20) was shot by an IRA gunman concealed nearby but within easy reach of a bolthole in the upper part of the Ballymurphy Estate. Doyle fell, fatally wounded and a Catholic Nun had the courage and presence of mind to bravely dash to where he lay dying. She desperately fought to save the life of a young stranger from England and when she failed was seen walking away, crying her heart out and covered in the soldier's blood. At this stage, further comment from the author would be entirely superfluous other than to add his admiration for the unknown Sister.

The previous October, during a riot on Newtownards Road, Corporal of Horse, Leonard Godber (26) was involved in quelling Loyalist rioters. He had been hit in the face by a brick and had received further injuries when the vehicle he was driving smashed into a wall. On the same day that the Nun had tried to save Michael Doyle's life, he passed away in the Royal Herbert Hospital in London after a long fight for life. A Stoke-on-Trent boy, he left a widow and two young children. As a further sad epitaph, he became the first soldier – officially at least – to be killed by Loyalists.

February 1973 was a truly horrible month both in terms of casualties, but also in respect of the sheer scale of lawlessness and the continued use of sectarianism in order to justify murder. No doubt both the IRA and the Protestant murder gangs were able to smugly justify this type of killing in that they were 'protecting' their respective communities by 'taking the war to their enemy.' If the Loyalists hoped that by killing innocent Catholics, by abducting them in the dead of night as they walked home in a drunken stupor or machine-gunning them from a passing car in broad daylight, they would sicken the IRA's supporters into putting pressure on them into withdrawing from their terror campaign, they were clearly wrong. For just as every Protestant death at the hands of the IRA stiffened the resolve of the Protestants, so too did the Loyalist's atrocities have the same effect on the Catholics. It was bloody tit-for-tat and both sides soon realised that their respective campaigns of sectarian murder were not having the desired effect. It did not, however, bring about a cessation of these nefarious and bloody activities, despite the evidence being clear that their policies were just not working. The perpetrators of these killings were too heady with the pleasure of bloodletting – they were too addicted to quit now. Martin Dillon's superb book, *The Shankill Butchers,* clearly illustrates just how much sadistic pleasure, for example, that the mad dog, Lenny Murphy, obtained from his cowardly campaign of indiscriminate murder.

All wars, and especially terrorist wars, claim the lives of children and despite the pious words of Adams, McGuinness et al, the war involving the Provisional IRA was no different. On the morning of Sunday, 25 February, little William Gallagher, who was only nine, was playing outside his home in Leenan Gardens on the Creggan Estate. Local Provisionals had planted a bomb with trip wire activation in the Gallagher's garden and telephoned a warning through to the Army in the hope of killing or maiming a soldier. Tragically, the little boy triggered the device and received hideous leg wounds. Mortally wounded, he crawled over to a passing man and begged him: "Help me, mister, I'm hurt!" He was rushed at once to Altnagelvin Hospital where surgeons amputated his shattered legs in an effort to save his life but he died shortly afterwards.

The IRA quickly wheeled out their spokesman from their 'Department of Pious and Meaningless Apologies' who claimed that it was an attempt to kill soldiers and that it was a 'tragic accident' that young Gallagher had been killed. The IRA's callous indifference to the loss of innocent civilians, especially from the very community which they professed to 'defend' is simply staggering and small wonder that Sinn Féin's respected political leader who now sits in the Northern Ireland Executive was once known as the 'Londonderry butcher.'

Two days after the tragedy of Leenan Gardens, the IRA were in action again, this time Aghagallon, close to the town of Lurgan. A routine RUC patrol stopped when they thought that they had spotted an abandoned car on a remote country road close to Caranagh Bridge. Hidden inside the car were at least two IRA gunmen who opened fire and hit both the two RUC officers who were walking towards the vehicle. Constable Raymond Wylie (26) was hit, fired back but was hit a second time and died almost immediately. The other policeman, Constable Ronald Macauley (43) was badly wounded but still continued to engage the terrorists for several minutes both of whom escaped and left the policeman for dead. He died of his wounds on 25 March, his passing will be dealt with in a later chapter.

As the month entered its final day, the IRA struck again, this time in Belfast's Ardoyne district. A routine patrol of the Third Battalion, Light Infantry (3LI) was supervising children as they left school for the day and Lance Corporal Alan Kennington (20) from Somerset had just walked into the street from a shop and was handing out sweets to his comrades. An IRA gunman, hiding in nearby Butler Street opened fire and hit the 3LI soldier in the head and fatally wounded him. He died shortly after reaching hospital. The excellent *Lost Lives* quotes the poignant words of the shopkeeper who had just served him. "He was a nice boy. He was very friendly and in a jolly mood. I sold him the sweets and minutes after he left the shop, I heard the shots which killed him."[5] The fact that there were many schoolchildren in the immediate vicinity appears not to have deterred the IRA killer and again demonstrates the callous indifference of this organisation. The fact that children were around, ensured that the soldiers would not fire back; something which the IRA generally relied upon.

That same day, it was the turn of another innocent child to suffer, as soldiers shot and killed Kevin Heatley (12) on the Republican Derrybeg Estate in Newry. A foot patrol came under attack from a mob in the notorious run down estate when a soldier of the Royal Hampshire Regiment claimed that he had witnessed someone with a gun. He fired one shot from his SLR and the boy was hit and died at the scene. The soldier was later arrested and charged with unlawful killing and was sentenced to three years after some unacceptable behaviour in court from both sides. He was later released on appeal, but the death of young Heatley merely served to deepen the already deep hatred the residents of the Derrybeg held for the soldiers. The author does not seek, nor will he justify in any way, the tragic death of this youngster.

So February ended, but lost in all this bloody mayhem were the mysterious, or at best, unexplained deaths of three soldiers: Sergeant (23217746) James William Robinson (34) of the Royal Pioneer Corps, whom the author understands died on duty on 7 February. Corporal (24122242) Alan John Holman (21) of the Royal Military Police who died on 11 February and Private (24150244) James Francis Leadbeater, a Bradford boy of the Prince Of Wales' Own Regiment of Yorkshire who died on the same day.

The month witnessed a staggering 41 deaths. Of the dead, 11 were soldiers including three who had died in unknown circumstances and three were Policemen; 18 innocent civilians were killed and the IRA lost five and the Loyalists lost four. The Protestant murder gangs were responsible for 14 killings and the IRA for 12. Of the 18 civilians killed, 13 were sectarian slayings. The death of Fireman Douglas is included in the toll of innocent civilians.

---

5   McKitterick, David et al, *Lost Lives: The stories of the men, women and children who died as a result of the Northern Ireland Troubles*, (Edinburgh: Mainstream, 2000) pp. 334-335.

Chapter 3

March

The carnage in Northern Ireland was to continue throughout March. Thirty-nine people were to lose their lives, the majority of whom were soldiers making up 21 of the dead. At this stage in 1973 the Troubles were over three and a half years old and to the decreasing and cynical audience back home in England, Scotland and Wales, the capacity to be shocked had almost been lost. In March, two incidents were to change all that as they involved the death of a young Lancashire soldier in a street close to the Falls Road, and three Sergeants lured to their deaths by the IRA at a flat on the Antrim Road.

The month was only a few hours old when Stephen Kernan (56) was found shot and dying in a car which had been abandoned in the Protestant Shankill area. His attackers had shot him in the chest, and, shortly after being rushed to hospital, he died of his wounds. The car in which he was found was a borrowed vehicle as an IRA gang had hijacked his taxi in the Ardoyne to use in a shooting some weeks previously. He had been threatened by the IRA and they were first considered to have carried out the murder. He had been lured into the Loyalist heartland by the UVF and cynically shot and left for dead. *Lost Lives* reports that the murder weapon was one stolen from the RUC and later found in a house in a staunchly Loyalist area.[1]

Shortly before midnight on the same day Daniel Bowen (38) was shot and killed in Linenhall Street, just south of Donegall Square and close to Belfast City Centre. He was a Catholic living in the Falls Road area, and, as there were soldiers and RUC around, he probably thought that he was safe. Although his killers were never found, it is thought that they were part of a Loyalist murder gang who were aiming at a Catholic-owned black cab, which was driving along Linenhall Street. Sources suggest that is the case, as the shot hit the cab first and ricocheted into Mr Bowen.

The Loyalists struck again, killing a third Catholic in a little over 24 hours when they shot bus driver Patrick Crossan (30) in Woodvale Road. He had stopped his bus to pick up passengers when a gunman or gunmen from the UVF opened fire with automatic weapons and he died on the spot. Ever much as cynical as their counterparts on the Republican side, the gunmen took no notice of the fact that the bus contained several passengers, including children, and also wounded one of Mr Crossan's colleagues. By the time the RUC arrived, most of the passengers – all of them potential witnesses – had melted away. A later strike by bus drivers, protesting about the killing of their colleague absolutely paralysed public transport in the Province.

Revenge was in the air and the IRA struck later that same day and killed a Protestant outside an Orange Lodge meeting place in Glenbank Drive, Belfast. It is believed that they were targeting an off-duty UDR soldier who was actually not there at the time. George Walmsley (52) was standing next to the man, believed to be UDR when IRA gunmen opened fire. He was hit nine times but although he survived, the shots fatally

1   McKitterick, David, et al, *op cit.* pp. 335-336.

wounded the other equally innocent Protestant. He died later in the day at the RVH from the dreadful wounds that he had received.

Earlier that day, English born David Deacon (39), a father of four and a soldier in the UDR, was abducted by the IRA. Off-duty at the time, the Sergeant was attacked and bundled into his own car close to Londonderry city. He was taken to an unknown destination where he was beaten, tortured and finally shot in the head at close range in classic IRA 'execution' style. The following day, his body was dumped near a border crossing at Molenan in the Irish Republic.

PRIVATE DAVE SHERLOCK, CHESHIRE REGIMENT
Not A Great Start in The Lenadoon

Our training was now far behind us and the goodbyes were all completed by the families at Weeton Camp near Kirkham, Lancashire. Soon the Battalion was bussed down in coaches to the Liverpool docks. The ship taking us over to Belfast was one of the LSL troop carrying vessels, belonging to some unknown part of the Army or Navy. Coming from Birkenhead it was a whole new world to me; my first cruise in fact. Weapons were stowed away and preparations were made for the 12-hour voyage to the Emerald isle, well the North part anyway.

The ship sailed out from Liverpool and we saluted the Liverbird statues as we headed out into a grey, foreboding Irish Sea. The night soon approached and with it the sea became as choppy as a night out around the Cape Horn. Shit, it was rough, lucky for us soon we were issued with sea sickness cans filled with lager, although the prescription costs were in the form of pound notes. There seemed to be no limit to these wonderful alcoholic sea-sickness tablets. The night went fast and with the beer and the sea combined, it was the best cruise I've experienced.

Dawn came and with it a wash of orange and black clouds centred on the backdrop of the Black Mountain. It was eerie and as the ship sailed close into the docks we all looked over the sides forming an unbroken line of boys and men, each wondering how the next four months of our lives would unfold. No words were spoken and a sombre mood hung in the air. I remember thinking: 'Hey I can't hear any bombs or shooting!' I cannot recall how we got to the base but I do remember feeling very vulnerable having no bullets for my SLR.

We arrived at our new home, the Woodbourne Hotel. It was a recently bombed hotel which now had a collection of caravans and some prefabricated buildings complementing what was left from the original hotel. Two companies were based here; 'B' company and my own Company 'C'. Although we shared the same base we had a totally different role to play. 'B' Company were to patrol in the mainly Protestant area near the base and we had the infamous, Republican Lenadoon.

Our area was small, but was infamous for the open hostility shown by the residents of the estate and was a very prominent IRA area. The next few hours were taken up getting the kit off the outgoing unit, issuing ammo and gaining as much local knowledge as you could absorb in the limited time that the few remaining outgoing troops could offer.

These handover periods were vital and it is worth noting a couple of incidents where the outgoing unit either created mischief or where the incoming unit failed to heed advice. The Parachute Regiment was touring Newry in the 1980s and, knowing that their hated rivals, the Royal Marines were taking over their TAOR, deliberately stirred up the Republicans on the notorious Derrybeg Estate. On another occasion, an outgoing Gloucester unit warned the incoming Light Infantry to be careful of any come-ons which might lead them into the abandoned Match factory in the Markets area of Belfast. This advice was not heeded and it cost the lives of two of their soldiers.

One platoon was on camp duties; one patrolling and one platoon was to live in three separate locations right in the middle of the local Catholic community. These were changed over after five to ten days, to offset any obvious routine. That first night was the most apprehensive of my life. The dread, the unknowing, the silence; my imagination was running wild.

I was staring from the sangar window, wondering if I would ever see the Liverbirds again, when, within minutes the sound of automatic fire rang out like metallic thunder piercing the darkness that had descended. Headlights were shone into the back of a nearby Saracen vehicle which had its back doors open. This neutralised the Night scopes, and allowed an IRA gunman to empty a magazine from his Armalite into the rear of the vehicle. Bullets zipped into the interior and ricocheted around the inside the Saracen, missing all but the Browning gunner who received a gunshot wound to the arm. Needless to say, this open door routine soon changed. The guy shot in the PIG was Lance Corporal Glyn Jones, our Browning gunner.

We were four hours into a four month tour and one down already. I did a quick calculation and came to the conclusion that if we lost one every four hours then the chances of me even getting a chance of my R&R, which was only a weekend off in the whole tour in those days, was not very good odds. Shit! I trained up to be a Browning gunner, why could I not be a cook, I thought!

The Lenadoon Estate was, in the period before the Troubles, a mixed area, but given its location – north of the Stewartstown and Andersonstown Road and to the immediate south-west of the Republican Andersonstown – it was an uneasy 'alliance'. Eventually the remaining Protestants were forced out and while it lacked the firebrand Republicanism of the 'big three' of Andytown, Turf Lodge and the Ballymurphy, it was, nevertheless, not a safe place for the Security Forces.

The author knows the Troubles intimately from a British soldier's perspective and admits to being shocked by the murder of the three unarmed Jocks at Ligoniel in March, 1971. Additionally this author is familiar with the lynching of the Signals' Corporals at Penny Lane, Andersonstown in April, 1988, after the funerals of those murdered at Milltown by Michael Stone.[2] The death of Gary Barlow, of the Queen's Lancashire Regiment (QLR) left one feeling shocked and horrified; incredibly bewildered as to just how, so called 'civilised women' involved in this murder, could behave in such a manner as they did on that day.

---

2   See all previous books by Ken Wharton for further details.

On Monday, March 5, a routine foot patrol by the QLR was passing through an area of the Lower Falls and reached Albert Street and McDonnell Street. The area is to the east of the Falls Road and close to Leeson Street where 3RGJ (3rd battalion, Royal Green Jackets) had their first major shoot-out with the IRA later that year. Mysteriously, and for a reason which only Private Gary Barlow (19) knew and took to his premature grave, he lost contact with his comrades and found himself separated from them. His absence was only noted once the remainder of the patrol had returned to their base at either North Howard Street mill or to Springfield Road police station, after being collected by an armoured vehicle.

A soldier on the rooftop op at the nearby Divis Tower was observing the area with binoculars and he noticed that a crowd was gathering at the junction of the two aforementioned streets. Gary Barlow may have laid low for a time or nervously searched for his comrades and en-route to safety encountered some of the Falls hags. These hags were clearly direct descendants of the toothless crones who cheered the separation of each aristocrat's head by Madame Guillotine during the French Revolution. He was immediately surrounded by a gaggle of angry, spitting Catholics who, emboldened by his solitude, scratched his face and seized his SLR. However, some decent women from the area tried to shepherd him to safety and one has to speculate here that he didn't trust them and unwittingly allowed himself to be pushed into a lock up garage out of view of the Divis flats OP. Some witnesses state that poor Gary was crying for his mother in his hour of darkness. The women attracted some teenagers from the area and an IRA gunman was sent for. Trapped inside of the garage, the young soldier was helpless. A gunman, said to be younger than himself shot young Barlow twice in the head at close range and he died almost immediately. No doubt the Falls' hags went away and congratulated themselves on the death of a soldier whilst others contemplated the sheer horror and mental torture the soldier suffered before his cold-blooded murder.

There is now a suggestion that the soldier suffered from deafness; possibly in one ear. If this is so, he may not have heard the pre-arranged signal of a whistle which would have alerted him of an RV with the armoured vehicle at the pickup point. If this was the case, why was this lad not confined to base, in an administrative role or on sangar duty? Why was his life endangered – to the point of his horrible, tortured death – by his officers if indeed he suffered this slight disability? The author's own training included the safety-first 'count them out – count them back.' Why was this allowed to happen?

In June, 2011, there was a further postscript to the murder of Barlow, when Labour MP for Warrington North, Helen Jones, made a call in the British Parliament for him to be posthumously awarded a medal; it was not successful. The MP said:

> The lieutenant in charge ordered his men to withdraw. They all got back into the Saracen except Gary. No roll-call was taken at the time. It appears from the witness statements that the Lieutenant asked the two corporals to account for all their men. Gary's corporal asked if they were all back and someone said yes. It was only when they got back to their base that Gary's room-mate realised he was missing.' Ms Jones added: 'I think this young man was a fine British soldier, a very brave young man indeed, and it is time we recognised that. His mother is proud of him, we should be proud of him too.

Speaking in the Commons, Defence Minister Andrew Robathan said Private Barlow's mother, Rona, was presented with the Elizabeth Cross last year, as a recognition of her sacrifice and loss. The soldier's mother said: "He's not going to get a medal, which I thought he should have had, but he got recognition. At least he has been recognised for what he did."

This author is aware of at least three other incidents in which a soldier was accidentally separated from his patrol comrades; the Gary Barlow tragedy was not an isolated occurrence. Fortunately there were no deaths as a consequence of the other incidents. It was reported to the author that a young paratrooper, newly arrived in the Province was abandoned by his comrades as a 'laugh' but was collected shortly afterwards. This type of behaviour will never be condoned by either myself or any other rationally thinking individuals.

As a consequence of being contacted by the Historical Enquiries Team (HET), I was privileged enough to be put in touch with Gary Barlow's family. It is an honour to include their poignant comments below, and this author and those who served in Northern Ireland now hope that the Barlow family can find comfort in the knowledge that their lad will never be forgotten.

Tina Naylor, sister of Gary, wrote to me and told me: "Our family has read your piece and it is an accurate account."

RONA AND JACK BARLOW

When Gary died, especially the way he died, all our family; myself, Tina, Keith and Jack, our world changed. He was a very strong gentle lad and for him to be taken from us was awful. There is not a day that goes by without us thinking about him. The fellow who did this to Gary is walking the streets and we have a life sentence. I will never get over the death of Gary. Jack and I will be having our diamond wedding in two weeks' time and we will both be wearing the Elizabeth Cross we received from the Queen. I feel that a bit of him will be there with us. It is very gratifying to think that, 39 years on, he is still remembered by people who are not family. One of his mates in the Army managed to get our address and came to see us after it was in the paper about Helen Jones going to Parliament about Gary. Thank you all for remembering him.

TINA NAYLOR AND KEITH BARLOW, SISTER AND BROTHER OF GARY BARLOW

As a family we know that Gary was brave and courageous to take the decision he took. Maybe if we had been given all the facts at the time of Gary's death, he would have been entitled to a posthumous award, but due to the length of time which had elapsed, this is no longer possible

We are not sure whether this piece is appropriate for your book but what else can we say? He is sadly missed.

GARY BARLOW AND OTHER SIMILAR INSTANCES
Stephen Corbett, Royal Artillery

A friend of mine is interested in this story, as he was left behind one night after a cordon and search back in the 70s. He was told to go in a ditch at Shaw's Road, Andersonstown, while the search was carried out. The PIGs withdrew and left him there. It was only after the patrol got back to base that they realised he was missing. Immediately, a PIG was sent back for him, and my friend recalls how he saw them arrive – but was scared stiff of just stepping out in case they thought he was a gunman. He crouched there, going 'Psst, psst' in an effort to attract their attention. Dave 'Lindo' – the Sergeant in charge of the PIG spent the rest of the day taking the piss out of him – going 'Psst, psst' every time he saw him. The incident was investigated, but nothing was done.

Another friend of mine – 'Addi' Adamson was left behind after a search in Rosnareen Avenue. He was left under a privet hedge, but the PIG only got to the end of the road before he was missed. I really feel for Gary Barlow's parents; I think the poor bastard was just too scared to attempt to get away, and ended up doing what many would have done in the same situation; he stayed put. It always amazes me though how cornered soldiers have never used their weapons to save their own life. Take for instance the two poor bastards back in the 80's in the 'Q' car on Stockman's estate, they chose to fire their pistols into the air in an effort to scare off the rioters. Can you imagine American troops doing that?[3]

Stephen Corbett:
That is just my opinion over Gary. I think he just stayed where he was out of fear of doing anything else. I'm quite sure he was shit-scared; as anyone would be! What exactly do you want to use? The story of Richard 'R' being left behind is in my book. I have only really given you the basics of it which wouldn't do any harm to use. I am in regular touch with Richard, and that story over him being left behind has caused me more trouble than anything. The basics are that he was dropped off and told to stay where he was and the PIG would pick him up at the end of the search. He followed this order to the letter and stayed at his post – even when he heard the order 'everybody mount up.'

I never recorded this incident in my diaries, but at the back of my mind I always vaguely remembered someone being left behind under a privet hedge after a search. It was while I was ill that I got in touch with Richard and I told him of my intention to do the book. He then told me of the incident when he was left behind. I just assumed that this must have been the one I vaguely remembered, but not so! Last year the friend of mine who was left behind under a privet hedge came over to see me; the first time in 38 years. He recounted how he had been left behind under some privets, and that I had gone back to rescue him. For the life of me I cannot remember that!

A serving officer made a statement at the end of the tour that said our Battery (9 Plassey Battery) had come under the longest period of sustained attack that

---

3   The incident which the contributor refers to involves the lynching and cowardly murders of two soldiers from the Royal Signals; on May 19, 1988, the world witnessed the horrifying abduction, beating and eventual murder of Corporal Derek Wood (24) who had been in the country for some time and Corporal David Howes (23) who had only been in the Province for a week. The murder was not only a seminal moment in the history of the Troubles but probably the most sickening sight ever shown on British television. It was akin, to "watching a hunting pack of Lions tear some poor Antelope to pieces on some natural history programme" The two men were abducted outside Milltown Cemetery, savagely beaten, then shot and their bodies dumped at Penny Lane in the Turf Lodge area.

any unit in the British army had endured since the end of the Second World War. I know it sounds far-fetched, but that is indeed what was said.

In July, 2011, a former UDR soldier and a friend of the author reported back to me on his efforts to see if there was a Board of Inquiry (BOI) into the circumstances surrounding this soldier's death.

Stevie, Ulster Defence Regiment

Today I received a reply from the Land Forces Secretariat to my Freedom of Information (FOI) request for information on Private Barlow's death. I quote below their reply.

Q: Please would it be possible to obtain a copy of minutes of any BOI and /or any similar report compiled by RMP or RUC operational log, regimental or other source, regarding the death of the following soldier:

24211767 Pte Gary Albert BARLOW, 1 QLR, killed in the Lower Falls Road area of Belfast, March 5th 1973.

A: 'The only document that we have been able to locate that may fall into the scope of your request is a copy of the HET report that was prepared in 2010 on behalf of the family of Private Barlow. We are unable to disclose this report as it falls within the scope of Section 41 of the FOI Act – that is Information provided in confidence. This is because we were given permission by the family to have a copy of the report for a **specific purpose** (my emphasis) with the reasonable expectation that it would be treated in confidence for that purpose only. As this is an absolute exemption, an assessment of the public interest for and against disclosure is not required under the terms of the Act.

If you are not satisfied with this response or you wish to complain about any aspect of the handling of your request, then you should contact me in the first instance. If informal resolution is not possible and you are still dissatisfied then you may apply for an independent internal review by contacting the Head of Corporate Information, 2nd Floor, MoD Main Building, Whitehall, SW1A 2HB (e-mail CIO-FOI-IR@MoD.uk). Please note that any request for an internal review must be made within 40 working days of the date on which the attempt to reach informal resolution has come to an end.

If you remain dissatisfied following an internal review, you may take your complaint to the Information Commissioner under the provisions of Section 50 of the Freedom of Information Act. Please note that the Information Commissioner will not investigate your case until the MoD internal review process has been completed. Further details of the role and powers of the Information Commissioner can be found on the Commissioner's website, http://www.ico.gov.uk.

However, you may wish to contact the Historical Enquiry Team, to see if they are able to provide any information in respect of your request. They can be contacted at:

Historical Enquiries Team
4 Ravernet Road
Sprucefield
Lisburn
County Antrim

BT27 5NB
Northern Ireland
Telephone: 028 9258 9258
Email: het@nics.gov.uk'

Stevie continues:
A few presumptions spring from this: all military records have been destroyed or were passed to the HET; the family have had their assumptions addressed and/ or confirmed by the HET report, and want to draw a line under what happened. Having seen the report, perhaps before the family did or during its compilation, the MoD has asked for a copy under these terms so as to deny access to anyone other than the family. What this 'specific purpose' may have been is open to interpretation. 'Cover your arse' is my best guess; they don't do anything like this out of goodwill. Perhaps they did not want a story of someone being left behind, to dilute the current climate of popularity that the public now hold the Armed Services in; who knows? Sorry I couldn't extract more from them. It's hard to know what the other members of the patrol feel about this; confusion, perhaps – or maybe some will be ready to vent their feelings as, with all such traumas, there are some parts which remain hidden longer than others.

After each and every soldier's death in Northern Ireland, there was shock, grief and ultimately, anger as his comrade's came to terms with the news that 'Yorkie' or 'Geordie' or 'Taff' had been shot or blown up. Given the very high number of fatalities caused by PIRA (Provisional Irish Republican Army) terrorism, it is all the more comforting that the British demonstrated their famous fair play and conducted themselves with professional restraint. In earlier wars, that sort of fair play was certainly not in evidence by the soldiers of different countries. The infamous 'Pinkville massacre' when elements of the US 20th Infantry Brigade murdered up to 500 innocent and unarmed civilians at My Lai, South Vietnam is but one example. On 16 March, 1968, undisciplined and outraged US soldiers, allegedly with the tacit compliance of two of their officers, raped, tortured and killed between 350 and 504 civilians. In an earlier war, the German 2nd SS Armoured Division 'Das Reich', having had one of their officers killed by the French Resistance committed one of many unspeakable atrocities at Oradour-sur-Glane in western France. On 10 June, 1944, SS soldiers killed 642 French civilians in retaliation and later destroyed the village and bulldozed over the remains.

The British were not blameless and in an earlier conflict, in Palestine between 1945-8 when the Jews murdered and dynamited their way to the birth of Israel, soldiers of 6th British Airborne reacted badly to some of the Jewish atrocities committed by both the Stern and Irgun terrorists. On or around 29 July, 1947, two British undercover soldiers – Sergeants Clifford Martin and Mervyn Harold Paice – having been held for 17 days in an airless and pitch black underground tank in Netanaya, were hanged in a disused factory. Their corpses were then hung from trees in a eucalyptus grove and the area underneath them was booby-trapped. When they were discovered, a searcher detonated the device and the men's' bodies were terribly mutilated.

Norman Rose in his excellent book, *A Senseless, Squalid War: Voices from Palestine, 1945-1948,* describes what happened in one incident. The British 6th Airborne – who some 20 years later would also find themselves as the 'meat in a sectarian sandwich' in Northern Ireland – suffered 169 fatalities in a little more than three years.

> Twelve hours after the bodies [of Martin and Paice] were found, a Palestine Police (British) armoured car-load of avenging British angels let loose hell into a bus load of ordinary Jewish civilians in the middle of Tel Aviv. Five innocent people (including an eight-year-old girl) died and 70 were seriously injured.[4]

Interestingly enough and not for the first or last time, Briton's enemies were shamelessly supported by the Americans; during the Troubles, it had been the Irish-Americans; on this occasion, it was the Jewish American lobby.

The Provisional IRA was always portrayed by the Irish-Americans as an 'army of liberation' and it is certainly true that this major section of US society saw them as 'freedom fighters'. Perhaps it was the anti-colonial or anti-imperialistic instincts of our 'cousins across the Atlantic,' but there was a gross hypocrisy about their actions. The Americans always like the world to see an image of themselves as nurturers of liberty and as anti-Colonialism, and yet their 'claiming' of the Philippines, Puerto Rica et al show them for the naïve, two-faced nation that they are. Their support for Jewish terrorism in Palestine in the mid to late 1940s was mirrored by their support for Republican terrorism in Northern Ireland during the Troubles. This support was demonstrated both at Government level where the US State Department was famed for its anti-British meddling, and also at grass roots level where ordinary Americans were able to influence matters on a less grand scale.

One seriously wonders just what the Irish Americans, willingly dropping their dollars into proffered collection tins in a myriad number of Irish bars throughout eastern America, actually thought about where that money was going. Did they, for instance, ever think about the consequences of their actions? In places of Irish-American concentration such as Chicago, Detroit, Boston, Philadelphia and of course, New York City, every 'Shamrock Bar' or 'Paddy's Bar' would have its NORAID supporters, always eager to use the patrons' cash to buy Armalites and Semtex etc. Did they ever stop to consider the mayhem, murder and heartbreak that they were funding? Indeed, did they really care about the innocents amongst the 'folks back home' being killed and maimed by the very organisation which professed to be the 'guardians of their long left behind communities?

How would they, for example, have greeted the information that members of PIRA would enthusiastically gather around TVs and radios on Northern Ireland's early morning news, awaiting the death tolls among the security forces as a consequence of the jobs they had staged the previous night? Were they aware that every 'Volunteer' listened avidly to find out how many widows back on the British mainland that they had created; how many soldiers or policemen they had killed or wounded? Raymond Gilmour in *Dead Ground: Infiltrating the IRA* writes:

---

4   Rose, Norman, *A Senseless, Squalid War: Voices from Palestine, 1945-1948*, (London: Random House, 2009) p. 165.

The bulletin always gave a catalogue of all the previous night's bombings, shootings, hijackings, knee-cappings, riots, arrests and arms finds. It was like the football results on a Saturday afternoon.

In the days and weeks after the lone soldier was 'executed' by PIRA, *Lost Lives* records no instances of 'controversial' deaths at the hands of the Army. The killing of Edward Sharpe on 13 March was the only one in which the circumstances might said to be 'disputed' but then even this august tome generally uses such emotive language when describing the deaths of PIRA or Irish National Liberation Army gunmen. There is no evidence that the British Army sought retribution for the death of the young QLR soldier.

Some four weeks before Barlow's murder, units of the Green Howards arrived in Welland Street, close to Newtownards Road, where the Army had been battling with the Loyalists for several hours. The Loyalists were protesting the internment of Protestants, no doubt convinced that only Catholics should be interned. As Private Raymond 'Tapper' Hall got out of the vehicle, a member of the UVF shot him in the back. Hall, so named because of his habitual 'tapping' (borrowing) of cigarettes from comrades, died of his wounds on the same day as the horrific and cowardly murder of Private Barlow of the QLR. Private Hall was 22 from Hornsby-on-Sea; he died with his parents at his hospital bedside.

The day after, units from the Coldstream Guards were patrolling routinely on the Ballymurphy Estate. There was already tension in the air because with a vital referendum on the Province's future less than a week away, other units were tasked with ensuring that the event would pass without violence. As a consequence, the notorious Republican enclave was being searched for arms and explosives. Guardsman Anton Brown (22) from Coventry and father of a tiny baby was shot and killed by a gunman in the Whitecliffe Crescent area; he became the fourth 'Coldcreamer' killed in the space of just two weeks.

Less than 36 hours later, a routine foot patrol from the Parachute Regiment was attacked by a gunman in Armagh City and returned fire. During the firefight, in Navan Street, they confronted two gunmen and hit one of them, Peter 'Jake' McGerrigan (18) of the Official IRA. It is worth noting, that the Official IRA, known by their Republican rivals the Provisional IRA as 'stickies' had been in a ceasefire with the Army since the previous year. Public opinion on the Creggan Estate in Londonderry had turned against them after the brutal slaying of a local man who was home on leave from the Army. The death of Ranger Best is covered in several books by the same author. McGerrigan died shortly afterwards.

The day after the McGerrigan killing – polling day in Northern Ireland – the Provisional IRA took the war to England and exploded two car bombs in London, killing one person and injuring more than 200. One of the bombs had been planted at the 'Old Bailey' court in London.

The bombers chose a day when thousands of commuters were forced to drive into central London because strikes had hit public transport services. Miraculously only one man – Frederick Milton (60) a caretaker from Surrey – was killed. But scores of office workers were cut down by flying glass or hit by falling bricks. The blast and the screams of the wounded alerted staff from nearby St Bartholomew's Hospital, who ran to the scene to attend to the injured.

Keith Page looking relaxed in Belfast (Keith Page)

Two other car bombs were defused and after Police swoops at the major airports, the bombers were arrested. Nine people were found guilty of the bombings on 14 November 1973. Among those found guilty was Gerry Kelly. Kelly was later to become a leading member of Sinn Féin and played a role in the negotiations that led to the Good Friday Agreement on 10 April 1998.

LENADOON NEAR MISS
Private Dave Sherlock, Cheshire Regiment

As last light was descending over the estate, the patrol ambled its way along Glenveagh Drive road heading towards the Suffolk road. We patrolled in those early days in six man teams; later this was to change to four man teams called a 'brick.' I happened to be one of the back men with my mate Steve; taking turns walking backwards to offset the threat of being sprayed from the rear by a gunman. I noticed a car with its headlights on full beam and it was just not acting correctly. It's that sixth sense that seems to be with you on those streets; something that saved my life on more than one occasion. The car passed as we shouted to the driver to lower its headlights. In the next instant it had swerved from the main road, mounted the kerb and into a side road hitting 'Mick', the section commander and took him along with him splayed on its bonnet. We were in shock for what seemed like ages, but was only a split second before we reacted. What did the yellow card say? Was the car not stopping a terrorist act? Fuck; no time to debate that! The Section Commander was injured and being carried away by this Car. Once he had rolled off the bonnet, 20 yards up the road, all the members who could, let rip at the car and did so until it sped around the corner.

The section 2IC John, picked up the Pye radio microphone off the floor and gave the initial 'contact' report, giving enough detail quickly to alert other Patrols in the Area. Pete Newman was the closest, and having got the description of the vehicle saw it passing the top of the road he was in. He also sent a few 7.62mm 'messages' towards the fleeting Car. Because he was on high ground, his bullets flew over a static small base off the Suffolk road, who immediately thought they were being attacked. Consequently, they returned fire back up the hill towards Pete. With all that happening, your mind works overtime and you soon realise that war is utter chaos! The full report was relayed and Mick was taken back in the PIG to be treated for shock, and injuries. Not only had he just been run over, but it must have seemed the whole of his team were out to shoot him!

Within the hour a vehicle was stopped at a routine checkpoint, and quite by accident, one of the lads noticed the car had three bullet holes in the back screen. The driver did not have a clue, as he was pissed up. Later on it was established that one of the rounds was still lodged in the metal part of his seat directly in line with his spine. He was later fined for motoring offences; was he a lucky dude!

ARDOYNE: BERWICK ROAD OP
Mick Dexter 3 LI

In March 1973 I was a young soldier on my second tour in the Ardoyne, and we were based in a bus depot. We had a permanently manned OP in a fortified house looking down Berwick Road towards Brompton Gap.[5] The inside of the house was lined with sandbags and there was an extension on the side upstairs so we could see right down the road. Outside we were protected by a high mesh fence. To our front we had Catholics and behind Protestants and they were kept apart by a high corrugated barrier and concrete blocks; we would spend between five and seven days in this section OP.

Once while we were there a man came out of the darkness in front of us intending to throw a bomb over the barrier. As he drew back his arm to throw the bomb it exploded and he disappeared. Next morning all we could see was a mark in the snow where he had been stood. On another occasion we came under fire one night. It was estimated that about 230 rounds were fired at us from various positions. None of us were injured but my mate Ed, who was stood beside me, had a lucky escape when one of the bullets fired by the IRA went into the muzzle of his SLR and shattered the flash eliminator. I still have a newspaper cutting of him with his smashed rifle; I recently learnt that the SLR is on display in Winchester.

A few months earlier, during the previous December, at this OP an unfortunate tragic accident happened. We were filling sandbags in the back yard when shooting started. We ran upstairs and took up firing positions. From behind a chimney to our left what looked like a rifle barrel appeared, then a man. One shot was fired and the man fell back through the roof. Another man burst through the

---

5   This was close to where Private Tommy Stoker of the same Regiment was shot and fatally wounded by an ND (negligent discharge) in July of the previous year.

Looking down Berwick Road towards Brompton Gap (Mick Dexter)

roof tiles and was shot. We ran round to the house and found one man dead and one wounded. It turned out they were two innocent workmen who were doing repairs and what we thought was a rifle barrel was lead piping. The wounded one later denied there was any lead piping but we saw it lying beside the dead man at the top of the stairs. Mrs Bell, the dead man's widow was very understanding and said she didn't blame us but blamed the IRA for shooting at us. Mrs Bell had a baby daughter who would grow up without her father, another innocent victim of the Troubles.[6]

The Northern Ireland sovereignty referendum of 1973 (also known as the Border Poll) was a referendum held in Northern Ireland on 8 March 1973 on whether Northern Ireland should remain part of the United Kingdom or join with the Republic of Ireland to form a united Ireland. The Unionist parties supported the 'UK' option, as did the Northern Ireland Labour Party and the Alliance Party of Northern Ireland. However, the Alliance Party was also critical of the poll. While it supported the holding of periodic plebiscites on the constitutional link with Great Britain, the party felt that to avoid the border poll becoming a sectarian head count, it should ask other relevant questions about the future of the Province.

On 23 January 1973, the Social Democratic and Labour Party (SDLP) called on its members to completely ignore the referendum and reject this critical decision by the British Government. Both the British and Northern Ireland governments were prepared for violence on polling day. Mobile polling stations could be rushed into use if there was bomb damage to scheduled poll buildings

6   Reference can be found to this incident in *The Bloodiest Year: Northern Ireland 1972* by Ken Wharton.

Ardoyne's grimness captured by a soldier's instamatic (Keith Page)

Ardoyne area, Belfast (Keith Page)

Crumlin Road shops at Woodvale Junction. Locals get out of the way
as youths gather for a riot, January 1973 (Mick Dexter)

The result was an overwhelming majority who voted to remain in the UK. The nationalist boycott led to a turnout of only 58.1% of the entire electorate. In addition to taking a majority of votes cast, the UK option received the support of 57.5% of the total electorate. Less than 1% of the Catholic population turned out to vote.

As expected, the IRA tried to wreck the day; there was much intimidation of Catholics who wished to vote and scores of Army units were attacked up and down the country. Two soldiers were killed by the IRA – one of whom had been shot earlier – and Loyalist murder gangs killed a Catholic man in a purely sectarian killing.

A gang from the UFF abducted a Catholic security guard and, having tortured him, murdered him, leaving six children fatherless as they continued their contributions to misery throughout Northern Ireland. David Glennon (45) was abducted, possibly in or close to Belfast city centre and his body was found close to one of the sectarian interfaces in the Oldpark area.

Shortly after the discovery of David Glennon's body, the IRA attacked a polling station at St Joseph's Roman Catholic school in Slater Street, Belfast and shot one of the sentries. QLR Private John 'Johnnie' Green (21) died within seconds after being hit several times in the chest, despite the immediate attention of his comrades who were desperate to save his life. The school sits just above the Grosvenor Road and is surrounded by streets as notorious as Servia Street and Leeson Street, scenes of many shoot-outs between the Army and the IRA. Just a few hundred metres away from where Green was killed, Corporal Joseph Leahy (31) of the Duke of Edinburgh's Royal Regiment (DERR) lay dying after a fight for life lasting several days. The Swindon soldier had been badly wounded by an IRA booby trap in a house close to Forkhill, in the area which would become known as the 'bandit country' of South Armagh. Attached to the Royal Hampshires, he and another soldier had been caught in the blast and he succumbed to his injuries shortly after the IRA shot the QLR Private at the nearby St Joseph's school.

Mystery surrounded the killing the following Saturday, when Dennis Eccles (25), a member of the Loyalist UFF, was killed by other Loyalists in one of their own clubs at Silverstream Road in North Belfast. It was alleged that the shooting was carried out by a UDR man but the charges were later withdrawn.

On the 13th, the UFF proved that when it came to 'own goals', anything that the IRA could mess up, so could they. Alan Welsh (16) was handling an explosive device in a building in the Protestant Woodstock Road area of North Belfast when it prematurely detonated. On the same evening, in what the Army claimed was "… a case of mistaken identity". An innocent Catholic (and former British soldier) was shot dead by a member of the Parachute Regiment. Edward Sharpe (28) was standing outside his house in the Ardoyne, Belfast, when a soldier watching from a nearby OP claimed that he saw a man with a rifle. Mr Sharpe's family was later awarded compensation for the tragic error on the part of the soldier involved.

Crossmaglen, the very embodiment of 'bandit country' has a chequered history going right back to partition. On 13 January 1921, during the Irish War of Independence, the fledgling IRA shot dead an Ulster Special Constabulary (USC) constable in the town. He was the first member of the USC to be killed whilst on duty. Labour Party MP Clare Short – considered by many to be both an embarrassment to the Labour party and an apologist for Republicanism – once famously said: "It is ridiculous that British troops are here in Crossmaglen. The claim is that they're in Ireland keeping the peace between the two communities. But there is only one community in South Armagh, so what the heck are they doing here?" During the Troubles, around 182 soldiers and policemen were killed by Republicans in the South Armagh area, many of whom were killed in and around Crossmaglen.

A border patrol of the Royal Hampshire Regiment was crossing a bridge close to Crossmaglen the same day, when they triggered an IRA bomb placed under it. The explosion killed Private John King (22) of Portsmouth and seriously injured two other of his comrades.

The UVF then targeted a Catholic businessman, Larry McMahon (42), and shot him at his home in Jordanstown, Co Antrim and then immediately destroyed one of his business premises. It was a major step up by the Loyalists as they escalated their war against innocent Catholics. The IRA continued their war of intimidation against the Ulster Defence Regiment (UDR), targeting Private William Kenny (28). Having staked out his address near York Road, Belfast, close to the scene of the earlier Fusco killing, they abducted him en-route to Girdwood Barracks. As he drove towards the barracks, a car, hijacked earlier by the IRA forced his vehicle to stop and he was bundled out and taken to a house on the Catholic New Lodge Road. For several hours he was interrogated and, before being shot, was almost certainly tortured by the IRA.

Private Kenny was the fourth member of the UDR to be abducted and then murdered by Republicans that year which was only its tenth week. Small wonder then, that off-duty UDR soldiers would not only have their PPW (personal protection weapon) loaded and cocked, but generally very close to their bodies as they travelled throughout the Province. One former UDR man told me: "Wherever I went, see, wherever I was going, my pistol would have one up the spout and it would be wedged between my thighs as I drove; ready for immediate use should the occasion arise."

On the same day, Driver Michael Gay (21) of the Royal Corps of Transport (RCT) was driving through Balleygawley, Co Tyrone on what the Army termed as routine administrative duties. An IRA landmine was detonated as his vehicle passed and he was killed instantly by the massive blast. The Cambridgeshire boy's funeral was held at Tydd St Giles Cemetery in his hometown of Wisbech.

March continued on its bloody path and another Loyalist 'own goal' occurred when an attempt to bomb a Catholic pub inside the Irish Republic. The intention was to drive a car packed with explosives and leave it outside 'Kirk's Lounge Bar' in Co Donegal on, appropriately enough, St Patrick's Day. Unfortunately for the driver, Lindsay Mooney (19) of the UFF, but fortunately for the drinkers in the packed pub, the device exploded prematurely. Mooney was immortalised in Loyalist songs and by having a Flute band named after him, when in reality, he was simply a failed mass murderer.

Throughout my writings, I have always ensured that I do not reserve my opprobrium just for the killers in the IRA, but rather share my contempt equally between them and the Loyalist paramilitaries. On March 18, two young Protestants, neither with any paramilitary connections, strayed into the Catholic Ardoyne, en-route for their home in the southern part of Belfast. In the daytime, the delineation lines between the Republican Ardoyne and the Protestant Shankill or Crumlin could be witnessed by the change in the colour of the flags being flown; as one stepped into the Ardoyne, the Union Jacks would be replaced by the Irish Tricolour. Lost and confused, they asked for directions outside a club and were unlucky enough that the person they asked was almost certainly a member of the IRA. He and three other IRA men bundled the two teenagers into a car and took them to a place where they could be interrogated before being tortured and killed.

One of the young men, after being tortured with a cigarette lighter managed to escape but his friend, Robert Collins (18) – who was shortly to leave Northern Ireland in order to join the Royal Navy – was shot, fatally wounded and dumped in the same area. He died in hospital on 20 March. On the same day, the bloody game of tit-for-tat continued and UFF gunmen in a stolen car shot and killed a young Catholic boy, Bernard McErlean (16) close to the Grosvenor Road. Several of the people he was talking with were also wounded and as there was an Army armoured vehicle close by, the IRA seized the opportunity for a moment of propaganda and spuriously accused soldiers of shooting the boy.

Friday in the UK is traditionally the start of the weekend and it is a reason to go out on the 'razz', to have a 'piss-up', and just to have a good time because tomorrow was always 'Saturday!' Belfast, indeed the whole of Northern Ireland, even in the Troubles, was no different, although with sectarian murder gangs roaming around looking for drunken victims, some measure of care had to be taken. On this particular Friday night – the 23rd – an incident so shocking and sickening occurred that, even by the murderous and sickeningly low standards of the Provisional IRA, plumbed the very depths of immorality. A group of Army Sergeants based at HQNI (Headquarters Northern Ireland) in Lisburn hit the pubs of that very well guarded Army garrison town. However, drawn to the wilder, more exciting pubs of Belfast, just five or six miles away, they took a taxi into the city. Somewhere in the safety of Belfast City Centre, they met some

Wrecked Saracen driven by Private Dixon (1LI) after an IRA
landmine explosion at Crossmaglen (Brian Sheridan)

Another view of the Saracen driven by Private Dixon (1LI)
after explosion at Crossmaglen (Brian Sheridan)

women – whom they had met on a previous occasion – and were invited to a party on the Antrim Road. What the four NCOs didn't know was this was an IRA 'honey trap', not dissimilar to the one which had lured three young soldiers from the Royal Highland Fusiliers to their deaths at Ligoniel two years and 13 days earlier.

When the men arrived at a flat in the Antrim Road, Belfast, they saw candles burning and a table laid with food and drink. One of the women left, promising to bring back a fourth 'hostess.' The men were then lured to a bedroom and as they entered, armed gunmen burst in and at gunpoint, ordered the soldiers to lie down on the bed. It was a carefully laid plan and the flat had been rented some time earlier – but left unlived in – awaiting the opportunity to murder off-duty soldiers. All four of the NCOs were searched and then each was shot, cold-bloodedly, in the head. Sergeant Richard Muldoon (25) from the Royal Army Dental Corps was the first to die, killed instantly, and followed by Sergeant Barrington Foster (28) of the Duke of Edinburgh's Royal Regiment. The third soldier, Sergeant Thomas Penrose (28) of the Royal Pioneer Corps, died in hospital within hours. I am not prepared to name the fourth soldier who miraculously survived his dreadful wounding. The killers were never caught, but one of the women involved – Margaret Gamble (35, at the time of the murders) was stabbed to death a little over three years later; ironically on the Antrim Road, close to the scene of the debauched murders.

On the long and glorious Roll of Honour of the Royal Artillery, the name of Gunner Ivor Swain (26) who was attached to 42 Commando is included and dated 23 March

Departing chopper seconds after dropping Light Infantry
soldiers near Crossmaglen (Brian Sheridan)

Roof sky high and spare wheel doing 100mph: IRA bomb Kilkeel (Brian Sheridan)

1973. The MoD honours his name but only under the statistics for road traffic accidents (RTA).

It is a tradition in my native country of England, and no doubt through a myriad number of other western countries in the world, after a night on the tiles to purchase a takeaway meal and dash home, though unsteady on ones feet, to consume it before it gets cold. On the night of March 24, John Huddleston (28), following an evening's drinking was indeed hurrying home in order to share such a meal with his mother at their home in Durham Street in the Catholic Grosvenor Road area. As he reached his front door, no doubt feeling the safety of home, a car pulled up containing a Loyalist murder gang and they opened fire, killing him and seriously wounding his brother. The car was later found abandoned in the Loyalist Sandy Row area close to Belfast centre.

The day after, policeman Ronald Macauley (43), who was shot and seriously wounded on 27 February, died from those injuries. In the same incident his colleague William Wylie had been killed at the scene.

On the 27th, three people were killed in separate incidents; one was a civilian shot by the Army by mistake, another was IRA member and the third was a soldier. Samuel Martin (33) was shot by a soldier from the Royal Hampshires who was later charged with manslaughter but acquitted by a Judge. Mr Martin was shot outside his home in Newtownhamilton by a soldier who mistakenly believed that he was armed. Under the British Army's strict rules of engagement, a soldier can fire without warning if he believes that his life is in danger. In this instance the soldier concerned clearly felt so, and in empathising deeply with the Martin family, the author understands the tensions and confusion created by the IRA in choosing urban settings as their battleground. Later that day, a soldier from the Parachute Regiment shot and killed a member of the IRA Fianna (Youth Wing). Patrick McCabe (17) was observed walking along Holmdene Gardens in Belfast's Ardoyne area with a known 'player' who was armed and the soldier opened fire. He hit McCabe who died at the scene whilst the IRA man who was armed, ran off into the Ardoyne.

Some miles southwest lies the Omagh to Aughnacloy Road and it was there that the IRA planted a landmine, cleverly camouflaged to fit in with the rural surroundings, hidden in a pipe underneath the road. A two armoured vehicle mobile patrol from the 16/5 Lancers whose battle honours include the 1943/5 Italian campaign, headed towards Omagh. The device, said to contain 500 lbs (227 kgs) exploded and completely wrecked the leading armoured vehicle and killed, absolutely instantly, Second Lieutenant Andrew Somerville (21). Unbelievably the driver was only slightly injured and curiously, it was an ambulance from the Irish Republic which attended the scene and took dead and injured to the nearest hospital.

March 28 was a day of embarrassment and a major setback for the IRA and Colonel Gaddafi, the Libyan leader who was one of their great supporters. A massive arms shipment, bound for Ireland and the IRA was seized by the Irish Navy. *Claudia*, a Cypriot-registered coaster, was seized, and the following were captured: 1,000 rifles and anti-tank guns, 100 cases of landmines, 5,000 lbs of explosives and 500 hand-grenades sent from Libya. The *Claudia* was intercepted off Helvick Harbour in Waterford. A total of five tonnes of equipment and explosives was seized from the ship.

Displaying uncanny arrogance, IRA Chief of Staff, Joe Cahill who, amazingly was on board, was captured. He was later sentenced to three years in jail. He told the Special Criminal Court his only crime was in " ... not getting the contents of the *Claudia* into the hands of the freedom fighters ... " He was convicted along with four other men. This was not only a major setback but it was also incredibly embarrassing for the Provisionals. However, weapons continued to pour in from their Irish-American well-wishers as well as the more conventional of Britain's enemies.

The day after the embarrassing loss of arms and explosives and the arrest of its Chief of Staff, the IRA extracted quick revenge and killed a soldier in Belfast's Andersonstown district. Private Michael Marr (33) a career soldier was shot by a sniper whilst on a routine foot patrol and died soon after reaching hospital. Private Marr (23546324) was a native of Aberdeen a strong traditional recruiting ground for his regiment the Gordon Highlanders.

ANOTHER BLOODY TOUR OF ULSTER
Steve Norman, Royal Anglian Regiment

The year 1972 had been for us, 3rd battalion the Royal Anglian Regiment, a baptism of fire. We had spent four months in the 'Hells kitchen' of the Lower Falls, Belfast, which had cost us four dead and numerous seriously injured. It had been our first time in Ulster but we knew it would not be the last. As a mechanised infantry battalion stationed in Paderborn, Germany the New Year 1973 was just around the corner, and the 'rumour mill' was in full swing. The optimistic among us said we would soon be off to Cyprus or Hong Kong but most of us realised we had been blooded, and the MoD were bound to send us back in the New Year. That Christmas had been celebrated in the normal way by us squaddies; just one big piss up really, but with an added element as it could be our last.[7] As the New Year dawned we found out in the usual way, via dodgy orderly clerks etc., that we had been earmarked for the Creggan Estate in Londonderry. We knew this was going to be big trouble. Only the previous year the infamous event known as 'Bloody Sunday' had taken place in the Bogside area of the city and many of the dead that day had come from the Creggan, which sat on a hill overlooking the Bogside; we knew what to expect when we got there. Eventually our CO got us all together in the gym in Alanbrook Barracks and revealed the name of our destination (to which we all looked suitably surprised) and the date 29th of March. He then went on to give us a very gung ho pep talk along the lines of: 'We are not prepared to suffer the losses of our last tour'. So with that in mind we are going to give them a very hard time. I mean aggressive patrolling; meeting them head to head if they start rioting, and lots of cordon and search operations. You will be given a book with mug shots of local players to take on patrol with you. Starting today you will all familiarise yourselves with the streets and area layout so that you will know every inch of the Creggan as well as the locals do. This time we WILL be prepared and we are going to flush the buggers out and get them off the streets.

The next few weeks saw us practising patrolling around the camp with all the names of the Creggan street names displayed on walls everywhere. They selected NCOs to act as the bad guys, they fired blanks at us from windows, corners etc. and on one occasion in the cookhouse while we were eating. This was done to test the speed of our reaction and although it was great fun we realised it would not be long before we would be doing it for real. We also paid several visits to a special training camp called 'Tin City'. This was a mock up urban firing range where we patrolled and reacted with live rounds at targets that appeared at windows alleyways cars etc., to achieve a sense of reality. Some of the targets were not terrorists but children with a plastic gun or grannies holding a rolling pin; you had to react and make an assessment in an instant. Was it a gunman or someone that just looked like one? Of course many a kiddie or granny bit the dust there and one of our lads shot a mock up granddad holding a pipe. He was thereafter known as the 'pipe killer'!

There was also mock riot training where we were kitted up for a riot with shields and helmets, and members of another unit dressed as civilians would stage a riot and throw bricks bottles and petrol bombs with the odd thunder flash to simulate a nail bomb. It was bloody good training and boy, were we grateful for it when we finally got to the Creggan because we soon had to do it for real. As the clock ticked down towards our departure the atmosphere became tenser, especially among the married men as they were acutely aware they may never see their wives or kids again. Two of our dead from the first tour had been married men with children, and for the rest of us it was a case of what would be would be. One of our platoon lads, Tony organised a last night out for us all a few days before we

---

7   For three of Steve Norman's comrades it would be their last.

left. The tragic irony of that party was that it was Tony the organiser of it who never came back with us but more of that later.

Steve is referring to Private Anthony Goodfellow killed whilst manning a Vehicle Check Point (VCP) on the Creggan in late April; his death is dealt with in the next chapter.

During the course of March, in addition to the mysterious death of Royal Marine Ivor Swaine, there were five further deaths, at least four of which were mysterious. On the 9th, the Royal Regiment of Fusiliers lost Corporal Derek Napier (23) from Bolton in an RTA. Whilst that at least was explainable, no public reasons have been given for the following four soldiers: Sergeant David McElvie, Royal Corps of Signals; Corporal David Brown (29), REME; Captain Harry Murphy (47) Royal Army Medical Corps and Corporal Patrick Davidson (46) of the UDR, but on attachment to the Royal Corps of Transport. In the case of Captain Murphy, the author has, quite unofficially been led to believe that it may have been an accidental shooting.

Spring had arrived and a quarter of 1973 had passed. March was another bad month for violence, with 39 people dying. Twenty one of the dead were soldiers, including poor Gary Barlow with the IRA responsible for at least 14 of those deaths. Thirteen civilians had been killed, with the Loyalists having been responsible for eight deaths and the IRA three. One policeman died at the hands of the IRA and the terrorist losses were two Loyalists and one IRA member.

Chapter 4

April

The conveyor belt of slaughter began early and, like many things in Northern Ireland during the Troubles, there was mystery attached to the first victim, David McQueen (28), who had been shot and his body dumped on the Ards Peninsula. He died from multiple bullet wounds and, other than his rejected application to join the UDR, had no connections with either side. He went out on the evening of his death and was later found lying dead on the coastal road close to Ballyhalbert on Northern Ireland's eastern coast. No paramilitary organisation ever admitted responsibility for the man's murder.

The 7 April was a Saturday, four British soldiers would die this day; two as a consequence of terrorist activity and two in an RTA. Two more names would be added to the MoD list of the fallen but the other two would only be acknowledged at the beautifully run Palace Barracks Garden of Remembrance and in the NIVA ROH. However, CVOs would still be appointed from the Duke of Wellington's Regiment and the Parachute Regiment and the news which they delivered to four separate families would still be equally as devastating. To a simple soldier-scribe such as myself, there is no distinction.

On that day, Private Brian Oram (23) and Corporal David Timson (26) were involved in a dreadful accident which caused both their deaths. The two soldiers belonged to what other units refer to as the 'Duke of Boots' and were both Yorkshiremen; Oram was from Huddersfield and Timson was from York.

There is absolutely no disrespect intended here to the memory of the two dead Paras, in mentioning their names after the two 'Duke of Boots' lads but one wishes to stress that due honour and recognition should be shown towards all those of the 1,294 who fell, howsoever they fell.

On the evening of that same day, a mobile patrol of the Parachute Regiment was driving in the area of Tullyogallaghan, in South Armagh, as part of a three vehicle set up. As the lead vehicle passed over a culvert, a concealed IRA landmine, estimated to be 300lbs, was detonated from close to the border with the Republic. The massive explosion killed Birmingham boy Corporal Steven Harrison (24) and his comrade Lance Corporal Terence Brown (24) and a native of Perth. A third soldier in the vehicle miraculously escaped with just a broken arm. Survivors and back up troops apprehended a suspicious man who was shot and wounded as he tried to escape. Later forensic evidence linked him to the attack and he was later jailed for 30 years. Other members of the IRA firing team melted away across the border and were never charged, with these murders at least. One of the members of the dead men's unit later recalled washing down blood-soaked stretchers in the shower block at Bessbrook Mill.

Ironically, only five days earlier, the then Prime Minister, Edward Heath, had cabled Liam Cosgrave, then *Taoiseach* (Irish Prime Minister), seeking further cooperation between security forces in Northern Ireland and those in the Republic of Ireland. For many years of the Troubles, the *Gardai Siochana* (Irish police) rather gave the impression of an 'After youse, sor' policy of conveniently ignoring fleeing IRA terrorists as they crossed into the Republic.

In January, the Royal Regiment of Fusiliers had been involved in a gun battle with the IRA after being ambushed near Lurgan in Co Armagh. In the firing, Fusilier Charles Marchant (18), like many of his 3rd Battalion comrades, from the North East of England, was badly wounded. On the day after the attack on the Parachute Regiment, Charles Marchant died from those wounds.

His grieving mother wrote these words:

> *Eighteen summers was all he had*
> *Eighteen winters not so bad*
> *A boy was in his youthful bloom*
> *A boy made into man so soon*
> *On patrol to guard a people*
> *Without a soul or scruples*
> *When a sniper's bullet*
> *Gunned him down.*
>
> Reproduced with kind permission of the mother of Charles Marchant

On April 9, a routine foot patrol from the Royal Regiment of Fusiliers (RRF) was patrolling on the Republican Culdee estate in Armagh City. Previously the Army ran patrols like clockwork, which enabled the IRA to plan attacks almost to the minute. By 1973, much of the earlier naivety displayed by the Army had gone and times, places and routines were varied. The Republicans therefore relied on the 'dicker' system, where sympathisers or 'dickers' would stand around, apparently innocently on street corners, or outside shops and report on the presence and movement of soldiers. Often they would follow a foot patrol on several occasions and try to spot a weakness in their routine. On this occasion, the RRF soldiers were not seen and chanced upon terrorist activity in Culdee Terrace.

Three men were seen carrying weapons from a house to a car and under ROE (Rules of Engagement) soldiers were allowed to shout a warning and then open fire. At least one of the men, Anthony Hughes (20) who was a member of the Official IRA, pointed weapons at the soldiers and all three were hit. A crowd quickly gathered and all three wounded men were spirited away and the RRF foot patrol seized several abandoned weapons. Two of the wounded men were never traced, but Hughes' body was recovered from an un-named hospital.

FIRST BLOOD ON THE CREGGAN
Steve Norman, Royal Anglian Regiment

Our first patrol on the streets of the Creggan saw us zig-zagging out of the back gate of Bligh's Lane over the Eastway Road and up a steep grassy bank and through to the Creggan Broadway. This was no mean feat, as we were all laden with riot gear even though there was no riot, but it sent out the message to the locals that we meant business. The Broadway was the main shopping area and the usual hanging out place for the local yobs who eyed us with suspicion and contempt. It was to be one of the main battle areas and known to us as 'sniper's alley.' It is true to say the whole population of the Creggan hated us with a vengeance partly because of what had gone on before we arrived ('Bloody Sunday' the year before) and by what they perceived as the ongoing occupation by the British army.

This was a community that had murdered one of its own; Ranger William 'Billy' Best. Although having never served in Northern Ireland, he was abducted after he left home in Rathkeele Way while on leave visiting his family. His body was later found in William Street, shot in the head, his body bearing the marks of a beating before being executed. He was just eighteen years old. The Official IRA admitted to his murder which, to give the locals some credit, caused such uproar that the Officials called a ceasefire.

But we were up against the Provisionals; hard men, seasoned in murder and no fools. It did not take the yobs long to accept our tacit invitation for trouble, and within days, serious rioting broke out in the Creggan. Day after day saw us facing the mob, with our riot shields and wearing crash helmets and respirators. The respirators were supposed to give us protection from the CS gas canisters we had thrown at the rioters but like most MoD issue were useless! We just had to grin and bear it with the rest of the rioters. The whole area was soaked in the gas which got into your clothes, your skin and your hair; it hung around for ages. If you took a shower after its use, the water would activate it again and much cursing and laughter could be heard in the showers back in camp. Of course its use and the use of Rubber bullets enraged the locals even further. The rubber bullets, or as we officially called them, baton guns, and baton rounds, were American-made and called FRGs or Federal riot guns. These weapons had already blinded a school boy from the Creggan after being hit in the head and later on in our tour would cost the life of a local youth; more of which later.

Strange as it may seem, and despite all that was going on, we had a sense of humour that only squaddies can understand. Call it gallows humour if you will but I recall during one riot a member of my platoon called 'Starry' (after his love of the song 'Vincent') received a direct hit from a half house brick. It impacted with his nose and top lip, just as he was shouting: "Look out lads; the bastards are behind..." He never got to complete his warning, as the exploding nose trick sent him into frenzy. We were in hysterics, which just made him worse; the angrier he got the more we found it funny, despite being in the middle of a riot. He was taken to hospital later on, to have his top lip stitched back together. The irony of this tale is that any injuries sustained in Northern Ireland were subject to compensation from the criminal injuries board. 'Starry' duly received a nice little lump sum for the facial scarring, but what the board did not know was that he was born with a cleft pallet and already had a substantial operation scar before he even joined the Army! I guess that 'Starry' had the last laugh in the end, though he refused to buy his tormentors a drink out of it.

This was the funny side of things but our first fatality was just around the corner and we didn't know it at the time.

The Creggan (Irish: *An Creagán*, meaning stony place) was, and still is, a large Council estate in Londonderry. It was the first housing estate built in the city specifically to provide homes for the Catholic majority. According to the 2001 Census, Creggan Central was the 11th most deprived area in Northern Ireland, whilst Creggan South is ranked 15th. The Creggan is situated on an old pig farm – hence the term 'Piggery Ridge' – in the north-west of Londonderry and was described by a soldier as 'not a place of happy memories.' It is but a stone's throw from the border with Co Donegal in the Irish Republic or 'Mother Ireland' as it is known to those who long to live within its territory. Raymond Gilmour in *Dead Ground: Infiltrating the IRA* described it thus:

The streets were filthy and there were rusting iron beds and burned out cars in the alleys at the back of the houses. Every morning there were ashes blowing through the streets and the smell of smoke on the wind……..The gardens behind the disintegrating concrete fences were mostly unkempt, and the public spaces, like the stretch of grass across the road….were minefields of broken glass and bits of scrap metal, further scarred by the burned, bare circles left by countless fires. Some of the houses were as filthy as the streets. There was one in particular, Ogie Barrett's, on Rinmore Drive, which stank like a public toilet. It reeked so strongly it would make your eyes water when you walked past. [1]

Gilmour also wrote: "The Creggan was windswept and dirty, the people shabbily-dressed, pinched, poor and grey-faced."[2] One former member of 2RGJ told the author:

West Belfast – the 'Murph, Falls etc – was a real shithole and I often wondered how people could live like that. But when I toured Londonderry, or Derry as the Catholics called it, I had my eyes opened on the Creggan. The walls were a dirty orange and there was always rubbish free flowing in the street and overturned metal dustbins. Everywhere smelled like stale piss. The Creggan actually made the Falls Road look like a bleeding Palace!

The action then turned to the Bogside area of the city and a Royal Artillery patrol was attacked in the notorious Bogside. Only 15 months had passed since the 1972 killings on 'Bloody Sunday' when 14 unarmed civilians were shot by elements of the Parachute Regiment and feelings amongst locals remained extremely tense.[3]

An IRA sniper shot Royal Artillery Gunner Idwal Evans (20) in the head, the young man from South Wales died almost immediately. The soldiers had just passed Blucher Street when the shot rang out. Gunner Evans who was from the Rhondda is now commemorated on the War Memorial at Tonyrefail, alongside the town's fallen of two World Wars and other conflicts. He was attached to the Royal Marines at the time of his death.

The day after the Welsh boy's death, the Provisional IRA lost one of its members after soldiers opened fire on two known 'players' in Cape Street in Belfast's Fall area.

1   Gilmour, Raymond, *Dead Ground: Infiltrating the IRA*, (London: Little, Brown & Co, 1998) pp. 9-10.

2   *Ibid*, p. 25.

3   See *The Bloodiest Year: Northern Ireland 1972* by Ken Wharton for a more detailed account of the events of that day.

Edward O'Rawe (27) was shot after he had climbed over a garden wall in Garnet Street and entered Cape Street. When soldiers witnessed O'Rawe's words and actions that he was going to shoot, they shot first. O'Rawe died at the scene. Later forensic evidence failed to link either man with the handling of firearms and explosives but one wonders what the IRA would have done with an unarmed soldier. The reader must forgive the author's rhetoric, because enough unarmed soldiers were sent to early graves at the bloodied hands of the IRA.

SQUADDIE JUSTICE
Mick Dexter 3 LI

One Saturday night we had the usual riot. The next afternoon we had a VCP outside the bus depot on Estoril Park. We stopped every car going in and out. In one car which we stopped, I recognised the passenger as the ring leader of the previous night's riot and arrested him. He was taken to an RUC station and held. I was to give evidence in court but before that I had to go to Lisburn for a day to learn about court procedure and how to deal with defence lawyers questions. The rioter came from Dublin and was found guilty of rioting and inciting others to riot. The judge bailed him to await sentencing but needless to say he never returned. He didn't get off scot-free though. As we left court he made a lunge at me and his head collided with the butt of my SLR which had just been returned to me. One of the lads who had escorted me to court hit him on the side of the head with his rifle butt. We stepped over him and left; he wasn't going to complain. Squaddie justice felt good.

One of the most heinous crimes which a soldier can commit is the negligent discharge (ND) when he accidentally or carelessly discharges a loaded weapon. Sometimes, the ND leads to the death of a soldier such as the case of Tommy Stoker (18) of the Light Infantry, who was fatally wounded by an ND at an Army OP in the Ardoyne in July 1972. Such an event was also common amongst the terrorists of both sides of the sectarian divide. In what was a somewhat mysterious death, Joseph Adair (17), a Protestant was shot dead by his 'best friend' as they larked about in a pub in East Belfast. His 'best friend' was jailed for three years.

As students of the conflict, known euphemistically as the 'troubles' will be aware, the IRA was a Nationalist and ergo, a Catholic organisation. It was not sanctioned by the Roman Catholic Church, but there is sufficient documentation to suggest that many Catholic priests either openly supported the IRA or sought to obstruct their arrests. The IRA operated in Catholic areas and was supported by Catholic people. A Republican who was also a Protestant was, therefore, something of a rarity. Robert Millen (23) was such a rarity and was linked with Official Sinn Féin, the political wing of the Official IRA. He was shot dead close to his home in South Belfast by gunmen from a Loyalist murder gang thought to be the UVF on 14 April. Their rationale, if indeed they ever needed one, was that he was not only a Republican but he was also a 'traitor' to the Protestant faith.

FATE LENDS A HAND ON THE FALLS
Private Dave Sherlock, Cheshire Regiment

'C' Company' were camped in a makeshift old warehouse right on the end of the M1 motorway. Our main area of patrolling took place in the New Beechmounts and Springfield Road areas, which linked up with 'Support' Company in the Whiterock. Together with 'B' Company in the Protestant area on the bend in the Springfield road area, this formed a triangle. It was always a hard slog up that hill which sapped your energy on warm summer days. Having made our plan and chosen the five letter word for this patrol. The patrol map area was split into five parts, so we picked a five letter word and put it on the map in the Operations room. This was used to indicate to the other bricks which area we were in. Simple, and it worked as anyone could nominate the word of the day; no Enigma code was needed here!

My four man brick led the way up the Broadway, ready to cross the Falls Road and into the Beechmounts. You know that sixth sense, that instinct which keeps you alive? Well 'the little man in my head' told me to stop, so I stalled my patrol just before the top of the road. This was to allow the other brick to move to Fallswater Street, on my left. At that time we moved as a multiple, in what was referred to as 'paralleling.' The other team was in the PIG and had yet to deploy. I had to guess when the other brick would be about the same distance up his road, before I started moving again.

He must have gotten about five yards ahead of me, before I started to move again. Those five yards saved my life, because at the top of Shiels Street, an IRA

Berwick Road OP Looking down Berwick Road towards Brompton gap from standby room, February 1973 (Mick Dexter)

gunman was kneeling in the 'aim' position with an Armalite rifle. He was waiting for me to show and give me a burst at a distance of no more than 50 yards. At that range I would have taken more than one round and the chances were that I would have been killed outright. Mac, the guy to Pete's left saw him first and shouted, alerting the rest of their patrol and sadly also, the gunman. He had been let down by his 'dickers' as they not seen the other patrol moving up that road. The gunman fled, with Pete in hot pursuit. He managed to get away. If only Pete had been where Mac was, the gunman would have been destined for a permanent plot in the Republican plot of Milltown Cemetery. Pete was an excellent shot and would have fired without warning, as he believed it was saving life. We had already discussed this scenario.

Once again, the thin gossamer thread of fate had spared a soldier's life and he would live another day or longer. Throughout this author's works, that same thread of fate has been illustrated again and again. Mostly capricious it works sometimes with a positive effect and sometimes it doesn't. The 9mm round which killed RGJ soldier Bob Bankier in February 1971 would have merely wounded him had it not flattened and torn through his femoral artery. A Light Infantry soldier was about to shoot a 'gunman' in Belfast City Centre in 1972 and had taken up first pressure on the trigger, before he spotted that the 'rifle' was a spade. A Gloster soldier was about to shoot a man with a rifle, before he realised that the man was holding a tool. That same thin gossamer thread of fate on this occasion worked, to Dave Sherlock's profound relief, in his favour.

Flax Street Mill, March 1971. Left to right: Snowball, Jock, Mick
Millard, Mick Dexter and Alan Dowling (Mick Dexter)

In a period which contained much mystery as well as controversy, the Troubles account for a time when one had no idea where the next killing was coming from. However, there was generally no mystery why, say a soldier or a terrorist had been killed and there was generally some sort of sick, perverted 'rationality' and justification provided by the sectarian killers. In the case of the death of Margaret Miller (59) who was shot dead at her home in South Belfast there was neither. She went to answer a knock at her front door and was hit by a hail of bullets and died immediately. She had no connections with either of the paramilitary factions, no connections with the Security Forces and no apparent political opinions either way. *Lost Lives* states that is was probably a case of mistaken identity.[4]

On 16 April, there was an accidental discharge of a weapon at Flax Street Mill, Ardoyne, when Lance Corporal David Alan Forman (23999960) (24) of the Parachute Regiment, was shot and killed. At the time of publication, I cannot obtain any further information other than this.

Brompton Park stands on the edge of the Catholic Ardoyne area in Belfast and is located the other side of the Crumlin Road which is fiercely Loyalist. The Parachute Regiment were deployed there with some elements in Flax Street Mill, an old disused linen mill which dominated the whole of Flax Street before it was demolished. A Para foot patrol entered Brompton Park and stated that they observed a group of armed men near Etna Drive. Locals claimed two of the men, members of the IRA, were not armed. The soldiers opened fire, killed Brendan Smyth (32) and seriously wounded a second man resulting in a permanent disability and slightly wounded a third. Local supporters stated the killing was 'indiscriminate' but the Army stated otherwise. The controversy deepened 24 months later when a disaffected soldier who shortly afterwards left the Army, claimed that he had lied in order to justify the shooting of the three men. The case was re-opened by the RUC and an Ardoyne man accused at the time of handling weapons was found not guilty and released. A measure of justice was achieved in the end, but more hatred was added to the simmering pot of existing hatred in that part of Belfast.

On April 19, in the same street that Smyth had been killed, a child was tragically killed in crossfire between the Army and the IRA. Anthony McDowell (12) was hit by a high velocity round of the sort which the Army used, as well as the IRA on occasion.

In Dublin, on the 22nd, an incident occurred in which it is alleged, IRA sympathisers in *Gardai Siochana* turned a blind eye to illegal activity. One of the leaders of the IRA, Dáithí Ó Conaill, addressed a public demonstration to commemorate the 1916 Easter Rising in Dublin. Following the speech, close to the City Centre, he somehow 'managed' to avoid arrest.

Previous publications mention Lenny Murphy and the notorious Loyalist murder gang the 'Shankill Butchers.' However, on 24 April, Murphy surfaced whilst on remand in Crumlin Road jail. As a suspect in a murder case, he confronted, almost certainly with some collusion among Loyalist prison officers, one of his UVF cohorts, Mervyn Connor. Both Murphy and Connor (20) had been charged with a sectarian murder in September of the previous year. The two had shot Edward Pavis (32), also a Protestant, the result of an arms deal gone sour. Murphy was aware that Connor was about to turn

4   McKitterick, David et al, *op cit.*, p. 350.

'Queen's evidence' and implicate him. Connor was forced to write a letter, exonerating Murphy of the murder. Murphy then forced cyanide down Connor's throat, silencing him permanently, and the authorities somewhat naively assumed that it was suicide. Eventually the leader of the 'Shankill Butchers' was set free to continue his evil role as a sectarian murderer.

Throughout my works, I have often referred to places as either a Protestant/Loyalist area or their counterparts as a Catholic/Republican area. To the uninitiated, this may well conjure up a mental image of strict delineation or demarcation lines. There was, of course, no such line and other than a multitude of Irish Tricolour flags or IRA graffiti which would mark a Catholic/Republican area or conversely a similar plethora of Union Jacks or Loyalist graffiti, one might be clueless as to ones location. In the dark hours, when the sectarian murders generally took place, it was not easy for a stranger, unsure of his location and lost in the gloom, to know on which sectarian territory he was. I refer to the North Belfast suburbs of Shankill, Crumlin and Woodvale as Loyalist and to the Ardoyne and New Lodge as Republican. However, if one peruses a map of that part of Belfast, one can see that there are no obvious sectarian interfaces which mark the change from 'friendly' territory to 'enemy' territory. For example, examine the Ardoyne and Crumlin Road areas; both are on opposing sides of the sectarian divide but it is so easy to cross from to the other without being aware. It is little wonder then, that some of the sectarian abductions, which almost always led to murder or a severe beating, took place when a drunk or unsuspecting citizen accidentally crossed the divide. It was often the very last mistake they made upon this Earth.

I mention this to the reader to emphasize not only how dangerous it was to be a Catholic in a Protestant area and vice-versa, but how problematic it was to know exactly where one was. A glance at the monthly figures of sectarian murder at the end of each chapter, adequately demonstrates the author's points.

In November 2008, I re-visited Belfast for the first time in over 30 years and found myself with a King's Regiment comrade on Stewartstown Road, Woodbourne just off the B102 in south-western Belfast. It was and still is a Republican area and one which would have presented intense and imminent danger to myself if I was still a soldier. I walked around the former RUC station, now still an active unit but rebadged PSNI and was surprised to see that it was still well fortified with strategically placed bricks to prevent car bomb attacks, with high, reinforced steel walls to repel all potential terrorist activity. As I gazed at the high, metal walls, I remembered it was here, one warm summer's evening in 1979 that a crazed soldier had shot a comrade dead before being killed himself by his grieving comrades. RIP Eddie Maggs and John Tucker.

Woodbourne is one of the five major Nationalist areas in West Belfast and sits below Ballymurphy, Turf lodge and Andersonstown and above Poleglass and is still a hotbed of Republican opinion, if no longer one of violence. I stood alone whilst soldier 'A' – who, all these years on, still does not wish to be identified – parked the car over in Ringford Crescent, across from the busy B102. I reflected on what it must have been like for a lone, late night drinker, staggering home from a few 'sherbets' as we somewhat euphemistically referred to beer in my native Yorkshire, back in those dark, dark days of sectarianism. I imagined what it would be like for a lone man wandering down Stewartstown Road, an obvious Catholic in a Catholic area, with predatory murderers such as Lenny Murphy of the 'Shankill Butchers' on the rampage and it totally unnerved me. After a while, I crossed the road onto a newish, certainly post-war, housing estate with its red brick Council houses and well kept gardens, spotted our hire car and hurried towards it. I thought, silently to myself, that the last time I had been in an area like this in Belfast, I was a well-armed, flak-jacketed soldier and, although permanently on edge, knew at least that I had equally well-armed comrades at my side. This time, in 2008, I was alone and as I entered Ringford Crescent on a cold, grey and miserable late Autumn afternoon, a man, wrapped up against the cold, seemed to rush toward me as though to confront me. I was, after all, a stranger on a Republican estate, where memories of nightly sectarian murder are still etched in the psyche. Lenny Murphy and his mad dog, Loyalist killers were active in West Belfast not that many years ago and memories die hard.

Did I use the word 'confront'? Perhaps it was much more prosaic than that and he was just rushing for a bus or to get out of that icy, biting cold. Anyway, I muttered "What about ye?" in the best Belfast brogue that I could muster and thought: 'What a shit undercover soldier you would have made!' The man ignored my pathetically inadequate attempts to 'blend in' and hurried past me. I breathed a sigh of relief, thanked God that Lenny Murphy was rotting in Hell and rushed over to the car.

FROM CUPS OF TEA TO BULLETS AND BOMBS
Rifleman, 1st Bn, Royal Green Jackets

I served several tours of the Province and I can honestly tell you that I served with some of the best geezers in the world and the best regiment in the Army. We were called 'Donkey Jackets', 'Black Mafia' Cockney barrow boys' and such like but there wasn't a unit to touch these lads. I am proud and honoured to have been a Rifleman and worn that beret which the 'Arfers'[5] called a 'war memorial hat!' Most of our major battle honours are on that cap badge and we all used to joke that if we'd had more, the badge would have been too big for our berets!

The author of this book wrote another book some years ago, called *Bullets, Bombs and Cups of Tea* which to many people might sound a bit daft, until you realised that our early days in Ulster were typified by cups of tea, given to us by grateful civilians; Catholic and Protestant alike. Then it was bullets and bombs and if you weren't there – and I don't give a shit how many documentaries or TV newsreels you've watched – then you couldn't begin to understand what this meant. I don't want to give Ken too much publicity, but his books about what he calls a 'forgotten war' have given many of the lads the courage to talk about what happened, what we saw and what we did and hold our heads up because we did nothing to be ashamed about. Can civvies begin to understand what it was like to face daily riots, daily abuse, daily petrol bombs and daily shootings and bombings? No, course they can't because they never had to do it; but they all had their opinions, like the woman who asked why we had to shoot the IRA! Bleeding hell, Missus; why did we have to shoot them? Because they were shooting at us! Her next question: Why didn't we shoot the weapons out of their hands? You are having a tin bath, missus![6]

I served at various bases including the RUC station at Springfield Road, the Mission Hall in the Markets, Albert Street police station and North Howard Street

5   Light Infantry.
6   Cockney rhyming slang for 'you are having a laugh!'.

Mill and I got to know that area very well indeed. Irish tricolours everywhere, green and orange paint, IRA slogans; you name it. It was like being in another country, only it wasn't another country; it was part of Britain and we had geezers from England, Scotland, Wales and Northern Ireland in the Regiment and going to Belfast was no different to going to help the police in Cardiff, Glasgow or London. The accents were different that's all! The houses looked like the slums of the East End, like the slums of Leeds, like the Gorbals in Glasgow and no doubt like the back streets of Cardiff or Swansea. We had to fight to keep order and stop terrorists in another part of Britain. My Grandad was a sailor and he served the war in the Far East, thousands and thousands of miles away from England and Britain and home. We were about 60-odd miles from England for Christ's sake!

I also remember the early days and the tea stops where we could get a cuppa Rosie Lee, a biscuit or a piece of cake and a chat and be told by the lady of the house 'God bless youse, lads; God bless yez!' I can also remember on a later tour, the same people spitting at us, throwing shit at us and screaming: 'Fuck orf, yez English gob-shites!' From Custard Creams and cups of Brooke Bond to shit sarnies! Only took a year or so, but talk about fickle people!

I remember having to search a house around Cromac Street and knocking on the door, with a mob starting to gather outside and fat old housewives banging dustbin lids and blowing whistles. Nobody answered, so a couple of lads booted in the door with their size nines and in we went. Jesus Christ; the stink hit you like a wall; stale piss, soiled nappies, rotting food. I worked on a council refuse tip for a few months after leaving school ('on the dust' as we called it) and the smell was the same; fair made your eyes water. I was concentrating on staying alive and doing a professional job but years later it crossed my mind: how can people live like this?' Anyway, there was no-one home and we had to do a search and we made a real mess of the house, tipping up stinking and dirty beds, pulling out drawers, pulling paintings of the Virgin Mary (and I do mean plural) off the walls and tipping out the contents of cupboards. I'm not bleeding proud of what I did and what we all did, but by this time, we'd had one of our Full Screws[7] killed near here a couple of years before and several lads had been injured. One of the geezers in my platoon was badly injured by a brick and the crowd jeered and spat at his prostrate body before we dragged him behind a PIG. Looking back I can see now that whilst some of the lads (not just Jackets but other units also) hadn't exactly covered themselves in glory by their actions, but IRA/Sinn Féin propaganda painted us as jack-booted fascists and Nazis. Trouble was, the locals believed every bit of that propaganda shit they spouted.

I was involved in a couple of firefights with PIRA gunmen in Belfast and whilst I have vivid memories of the second time, I have no memories of the first time I had to fire at another human being, in terms of emotions that is. I just remember that it wasn't like firing at number nine targets at the ranges; there you had a crack as the round was fired, but when you are firing on an urban street, it is 'crack' as the round goes and 'splat' as it hits a brick wall or something solid. When the rounds are incoming it is 'zip' as it flies over your head, 'crack' as you (hopefully) hear the

---

7   Corporal Robert 'Bob' Bankier was killed on 22/5/1971.

round being fired and 'splat' as it hits a house or brick wall behind you. They say that you never hear the one which hits you, but I was never shot, so I will happily take their word for that!

I realise now, 30-odd years later, looking back, that the Catholics were very put upon by the Prods and that the discrimination and prejudices would have made me angry too. I still cannot believe that they fell for all that Provie crap though and they believed all the stories they were told. I bet if Gerry Adams had gone on TV and stated that British soldiers threw babies into the air and caught them on their bayonets, the old biddies on the Falls and the rest would have swallowed every word; hook, line and sinker! I have one lovely memory of an old lady who would have been in her 80s and looked like my old Grannie. I was on my haunches on a street corner and was looking down my SLR barrel at the rooftops of a row of houses down the road. She whispered as she walked by: "May God keep you safe for your Mammy, son!" I smiled at the time, but later when I attended my Gran's funeral, I remembered those words and I still cry when I think about them. The Micks weren't all bad, but I'll never forget that little, old lady. I wish now that I could have said: "Thank you, missus." Too late now; RIP all the 'Black Mafia' who never came home.

The author knows this writer well and was happy for me to refer to him by his first name of 'Mickey' although he didn't wish to have his surname used. This decision relates to his Irish background – although he is as Cockney as they come – and to his fears over security. I am happy to respect his request and at the same time, associate myself with his eloquent words.

REFLECTIONS FROM THE WOODBURN HOTEL 1973
Private David Sherlock, Cheshire Regiment

Life was basic on those early tours. Our homes were in caravans and we slept six men in them. The smell of six men in hot sweaty clothes, living together has to the worst odour known to mankind. We sometimes slept in full uniform; boots denims, puttees, and woollen shirts which were like sandpaper. All that and the old US flak jacket that had been dragged out of some old surplus stores smelling of moth balls this was further compounded by us sleeping in camouflage cream on the night stags.

Yes, our home, in the Woodburn Hotel was everything a tramp could wish for. Sleeping was done two ways, mostly on the top of your bed in a hot smelly sleeping bag, sometimes boots on sometimes boots off. This was due to the guard duties around the camp, two hours on four off. During that four hours off, you had to clean weapons, do ammo checks etc. These guard periods could last for up to ten-day stretches at a time. Only on rare occasions when you were on complete stand down, and had over six hours to sleep, would you finally get into clean white sheets.

The only light relief from our soldier's routine was to spend your money in the 'choggie shop.' This was a shop ran completely by Asians who lived within the camp for their own protection. They sold you everything like a little grocer's store, with some basic boys' toys like radios and other Items to try to extract your money from you. As a great example of marketing, they gave you credit which you paid up at the end of each month. I have often wondered should I have reported them to the monopolies commission! We needed them, as the NAAFI could not get into these temporary bases for obvious reasons[8]. They were quick to get the their money back; I recall the Sergeant Major getting us on parade as two bills were outstanding for that month; 'Would Corporal Gerry Adams and Lance Corporal Martin McGuiness, please step forward, as you have a huge outstanding choggie Bill to pay!' We roared, but I don't think they ever discovered who had knocked up those bills! Needless to say, the nominal rolls and ID cards were soon brought into play.

On a break from patrol, I stripped off and rolled my denims down, exposing my white legs to the sun; leaving my boots on in case I had to react. I had bought a cheap little radio with an earpiece, and was lying next to the caravan, listening to Roberta Flack singing 'Killing Him Softly with his Song.' Just then, the news came on and I went white as a sheet as the newsreader said: 'There has been a shooting in the New Barnsley area; a soldier had been shot and seriously wounded.' Our 9 Platoon had been tasked to go down there for the day to help cover some elections for the Light Infantry. I felt sick as my mate Les Duckers was in 9 Platoon. He was with me when we made our way from Birkenhead to join up. We served in the IJLB at Oswestry together. Throughout that Patrol, all I could think about was who had been shot.

On return from patrol, I soon found out it had been Les! The IRA had sniped at this new platoon patrolling, what was them an unknown area. He was hit by an Armalite round which entered his right arm, passed through his rifle butt, tore open his abdomen and then went through his left arm. He was so lucky, and I heard the stories from the other guys in his patrol. They were actually holding his insides inside as he was so badly hit. Fortunately, their quick reactions saved his life, and he was finally evacuated to Hospital. Les was shot on the 25th of April at 1:06pm.

I have often thought about that, who in their right mind would send a new platoon into an unknown patch? The dickers would have seen them looking at maps to get around the area. Pretty soon, the news would have got to the IRA' and it would have been too good an opportunity to miss. The local IRA could activate a shooting within a few minutes at that time. The weapons were close and the gunmen were all local men. Les was presented that rifle butt, with its bullet hole mounted on a stand and still has it to this day; a reminder of his lucky escape.

On the 27th, the Troubles claimed two more victims. Amongst one of the less lethal pastimes of the IRA was the public humiliation of those whom they accused of anti-social behaviour. The deemed behaviour often came in the form of those who had robbed people in their own communities, dealt in drugs or tried to muscle in on the IRA's own illegal activities. The preferred punishment was coating a victim in hot tar and feathering as in medieval times with a mass of feathers which clung like glue and

---

8   See Appendix II for a list of improvised Army bases.

serving to publically humiliate them. The IRA had a more 'humane' method and the accused – never the 'guilty' always the 'accused' – would be covered in a syrup or oil and then covered in feathers and forced to parade around their home streets, bearing placards which detailed their alleged 'crime.'

One such person who attracted the IRA's attention was a local girl in the Lower Falls area. She was unfortunate enough to be spotted befriending a soldier from the Royal Anglians. As punishment, and no doubt as a salutary lesson to others thinking of 'straying', she was tarred and feathered and both her and her family were warned of future dire consequences. The soldier, Private Anthony Goodfellow (26) from Northamptonshire had helped her to move to London where there was talk of future nuptials. Sadly this never occurred as he was shot by an IRA sniper whilst manning a VCP in the Creggan in Londonderry. Was he targeted because of his connection with girl? One will never know and only the 'Godfathers' of the IRA Army Council could answer that one.

DEATH AT A VCP
Steve Norman, Royal Anglian Regiment

Hindsight is a wonderful thing but with good foresight hindsight is an irrelevance. We lost a member of our platoon at the Tesco Vehicle checkpoint in the Creggan to a well planned IRA sniper attack. This checkpoint was permanently manned by the Army and was a source of deep resentment by the locals. It was a main entrance to the Creggan and situated at a crossroads with a small Tesco shop opposite hence the name; it consisted of a raised sangar with one sentry and a couple of bollards to act as a sort of chicane. The idea was for a section at a time to man the VCP with a parked up Saracen and check all vehicles coming and going into the area. This was achieved by stopping them asking to see the licences; if the occupants got stroppy, we would make a thoroughly prolonged search of both the vehicle and the people in it. Of course this upset the daily flow of life for the residents and caused many confrontations.

They saw it as a symbol of Army occupation and a breach of their civil rights, whilst the IRA saw it as a target, too good to be true in both a military and propaganda sense. We will never know how long they waited for the right conditions; perhaps weeks, months or maybe just on the day. It happened on the 27th of April 1973; in the afternoon. Tony Goodfellow was a well liked and much respected member of my platoon. At 26 he was somewhat older than most of us and had been a Queen's scout and a valued member of his local Rugby club in Rushden, Northants. On that day it could have been any member of the sections turn to step out and check the licences. It was just the luck of the draw that it was Tony. As he stepped forward, two shots rang out. He was hit in the chest and fell; he never knew what hit him. He was given the kiss of life by one of the lads – Andy – but he died within seconds. Fire was returned by members of the section as one of the shots appeared to come from a roof. This was probably a diversionary shot by the IRA team to lead us away from the real sniper, and we claimed no hit.

It was later established that the fatal shot may have came from a derelict house just up the road, and was fired, in all probability, by the same 'one shot sniper' who claimed the life of a young royal Artillery soldier Kerry Venn. This shooting took place in the Carnhill and Bloomfield Estates in the same area the next day; he was just 22 years old. The VCP was then subject to a re think. Too bloody late for Tony and I still can't help feeling angry at those above us for their lack of military foresight into the planning of that checkpoint; it was all so avoidable. The IRA's next target was to be the Bligh's Lane camp itself and yet again the result was also avoidable, but more of that later.

When the reader and serious student of the Troubles encounters the name of Londonderry, they could be forgiven in thinking that the only four troubles spots were the Republican Bogside, Creggan Estate and Gobnascale and the Loyalist Fountains area. There were, however, other trouble spots in the city and Bloomfield Park and Carnhill – two estates on the north-eastern outskirts of Londonderry – were such places. The two estates are very similar, comprising new, two storey council houses, gentle grass slopes and lots of open grassed spaces between blocks. As April drew to a close, a foot patrol from the Royal Artillery was fired at by an IRA sniper concealed in Carnhill flats. One soldier was hit and died very quickly afterwards on the open ground he and his patrol were crossing. Gunner Kerry Venn (22), the father of a young child, was the second soldier to be killed that weekend in Londonderry. He was from Weston-Super-Mare in Somerset.

The month was almost spent, but the killers in the IRA wanted to ensure that there would be further misery in more British households before it was over. In Belfast, a mobile patrol from 42 Commando of the Royal Marines entered the New Lodge area and the two vehicles of the patrol had just entered the New Lodge Road. Unknown to them, the IRA had taken over a house and as the leading vehicle appeared, gunmen manning an automatic weapon opened fire. Marine Graham Cox (19) from Hampshire was hit in the chest by a burst of gunfire and mortally wounded. He died within a few seconds of the attack which also wounded a comrade. He was the third soldier to be killed in as many days, as the IRA's toll on the Army continued to grow exponentially.

Of the 12 soldiers killed in April, there were two deaths for which I have no information; other than the fact that both soldiers – from the UDR – died, nothing further is known of their cause of death. Private Alexander Martin McConaghy (21) and Private Samuel Noel Beattie (31) died on the 10th and 14th respectively. I have no further details at the time of publication.

In all, 21 people had lost their lives in April; of these, 12 were soldiers and four were civilians. The paramilitaries lost men also; the IRA lost three, all shot by the Army and the Loyalists lost two, both killed in internecine feuds. It is worth noting that the IRA were responsible for at least eight of the fatalities. During the month, there no sectarian murders and the fact that Lenny Murphy was incarcerated for much if not all of the month may have been a significant factor.

Chapter 5

May

In May a total of 17 soldiers lost their lives due to a variety of causes, but all inextricably linked with the on-going troubles, including the 50th to die in 1973. May was also the month of the IRA atrocity at Knock-na-Moe Hotel when four soldiers were killed; the worst incident involving the SF to date. However, where the IRA was involved there was scope for much worse.

The Loyalist murder gangs had lain low in April, or at least there had been a shortage of victims. Perhaps as the attractive pastime of late night drinking, and the associated stagger home, suddenly lost its powerful allure for obvious safety reasons. There were times when my eldest son, Jonathan, would stagger home in such a fashion but never, for a second, was the prospect of him being murdered in North Yorkshire, simply because of the church in which he chose to worship ever in my thoughts. The cruel pattern of sectarian murder began with a renewed violence and on 2 May Liam McDonald (19) was killed after an innocent night out with his equally young girlfriend. The pair had spent the evening at Whitewell, Co Antrim, some three or four miles north of Belfast City Centre and he was returning to his home on the Catholic Ballyduff Estate in Rathcoole. He was abducted and shot by UFF; his lifeless body was discovered the following morning.

Further north, an IRA sniper – rumoured to be the same one who had murdered Anthony Goodfellow and Kerry Venn a few days previously – shot Sergeant Thomas Crump (27) whilst he was on foot patrol with the Royal Artillery in the Creggan Heights. The Pontypridd boy was the sniper's third soldier victim in seven days. The father of two young children clung to life, despite being hit twice in the head, but succumbed to his wounds some 12 hours later. The toll of military fatalities continued as the IRA stepped up its attacks in an effort to make the death toll soar. Sergeant Crump was the 48th to die this year and it meant that, in a period of just over 16 months, a staggering 220 members of the British Army had died in the Province.

48 hours later the forces of evil were at work again, this time at Moybane, Armagh, close to the heartland of 'bandit country,' Crossmaglen. It is only half a mile from the border with the Republic and a short dash to safety for the terrorists. An IRA unit had laid a landmine on a track that they had previously seen soldiers use and indeed, had found military detritus from other units – used ration packs etc – on the well-trodden patrol route. This would also be a factor in the death of Lance Corporal Simon Ware of the Coldstream Guards in 1991, when dickers had spotted the same type of military rubbish and had used this information in order to plot the deaths of the SF.[1]

A routine foot patrol of the Parachute Regiment was passing through Moybane when a remote control command wire, linked to the bombers over the Irish border, was triggered and WOII William Vines (36) was killed by the massive blast. Unknown

---

1   See Ware, Darren, *A Rendezvous with the Enemy: My Brother's Life and Death with the Coldstream Guards in Northern Ireland,* (Solihull: Helion, 2010).

to the searchers, the IRA unit, who were aware that a follow up unit would be in the area within hours, had placed a secondary device. This was a ploy which they used successfully over the years but none with as much devastation as that which killed 18 soldiers within an hour at Narrow Water, Warrenpoint in Co Down on August 27, 1979. In this incident, the command wire for the device was concealed along the ground leading into the Republic, and was fired by cowards hidden within their 'safe sanctum' operating with impunity. WOII Vines was hit by the full force of the 400 lb blast and as his widow later commented: "I didn't even have a body to bury" The soldier's funeral was yet another sand-filled coffin affair, where what few remains of the body were left were ballasted with sand, in order to give the illusion that the man's comrades were carrying his body and that the family had mortal remains to inter into the ground.

Follow up units arrived less than three hours after the first blast. But, whilst a unit from the 17/21 Lancers was close to the seat of the original device, a second bomb exploded. Corporal Terence Williams (35), a father of three, from Canterbury in Kent and Trooper John Williams (24) from Edinburgh were killed instantly. The two soldiers became the 50th and 51st soldiers to be killed in Northern Ireland in 1973. The 17/21 Lancers whose predecessors charged with Cardigan in the vainglorious and ill-fated charge of the Light Brigade in the Crimea in 1851 were amalgamated with the 16/5 Queen's Royal Lancers in 1993, to form the Queen's Royal Lancers. As Cavalrymen, their motto is 'Death or Glory' and their cap badge is the skull and crossbones. Sadly for the two soldiers, a wood near Moybane, South Armagh became their 'valley of death'. Trooper Williams left a baby son and who, at the time of writing, will be around 38 years of age. He grew up without the presence of his father, thanks to the IRA.

In Northern Ireland, even during the Troubles, farming was still of crucial importance and the work of a farmer was never-ending on both sides of the Irish border. It was backbreaking work with very long hours, often starting long before the dawn. It was doubly hard for a Protestant farmer working his land in dangerous border territory and unimaginably difficult if you were also a part-time member of the UDR. Franklin Caddoo (24) was all three and his farm was located at Rehagy, Aughnacloy in Co Tyrone some two miles from the border with the Irish Republic. On the evening of Thursday, 10 May, he was stacking milk churns prior to morning collection, when he was attacked by IRA gunmen who shot him at close range as he tried to escape and left him for dead. The UDR Corporal left a young pregnant widow.

The same day, an IRA member was killed when a landmine, which he was planting on Cloughmore Road, Mullinahinch, Co Fermanagh, exploded prematurely and he was blown to pieces in a classic IRA 'own goal.' Anthony Ahern was just 17 when, in the words of an RUC man he "was killed doing the Devil's own work!".

Two days later, a four man 'brick' from the Light Infantry (LI) were patrolling in and around the old match factory on Donegall Road, Belfast, having received a tip that arms might be on the premises. A booby-trapped device, left by the IRA exploded and terribly wounded Corporal Thomas Taylor (26) and Private John Gaskell (22). Both men were from England's North-East, like so many from the LI's 2nd Battalion and were rushed to the RVH for emergency treatment. Corporal Taylor died the day after and his critically wounded comrade died on 14 May. The other two men in the brick were seriously injured and it is thought that at least one of them was later medically discharged from the Regiment.

Martin McGuinness, now a 'respectable' politician

On the same day that the LI's John Gaskell died from his wounds, the UDR shot and killed Kevin Kilpatrick (20) an IRA member from Co Tyrone when he refused to stop at a VCP at Ardboe. An IRA unit nearby also opened fire on the soldiers but thankfully none of the men were hit. Later forensic evidence proved that the IRA man had been involved with the firing of a weapon. The UVF re-commenced their violent traits three days earlier. They shot and seriously wounded John McCormick (34), a father of four, as he returned to his home in the Falls Road area. He died from those wounds in the RVH. The sectarian murderers were back on the streets after a short break and piously claimed that the murder was a retaliatory measure for the murder of UDR man Frank Caddoo on 10 May.

In a measure of supreme irony this was also the day on which the Irish authorities chose to release the 'Londonderry Butcher' Martin McGuinness, the Londonderry IRA commander, from prison. He had served six months for membership of an illegal organisation, but he was fit and raring to return to the 'armed struggle'.

The 17th of May dawned and four people lost their lives that day leaving not only four more families distraught with grief, but also leaving the already overstretched RUC another four deaths which they would be unable to investigate thoroughly. On that day, the IRA made plans to attack the SF in the Portadown area. A device was planted in a farmland cottage close to the hamlet of Selshion as it was expected that an Army patrol would very likely enter or inspect the apparently derelict property. A farm labourer, Robert Rutherford (33) for reasons unknown, tried the door of the cottage and triggered the device, killing him instantly.

Cumann na gCailini was a Republican scouting organisation which attracted young girls from the nationalist area, imbued with the spirit of the IRA and Republicanism; in reality it is, or was, the women's section of the IRA youth. Eileen Mackin, who was 14 and a resident of the Ballymurphy Estate in Belfast, was a member of this organisation. On 17 May, an armoured vehicle patrol was in Springhill when the IRA opened fire and the young girl was hit by a round from an Armalite, used exclusively by the Provisional IRA. The American manufactured Armalite fired a high velocity 7.62mm round – the same as the British Army used in its SLR with a muzzle velocity of 3,200 feet (975 metres) per second. It was capable of inflicting a phenomenal amount of damage on a human being. Armalites were smuggled into Northern Ireland for IRA use, either singly or multiple shipments. Many were brought in, disassembled by IRA sympathisers among boat crews, including Cunard Ship Lines, or part of larger arms shipments. NORAID was an organisation of Irish-Americans who hated the British with a passion, with their members citing incidents going back to Oliver Cromwell's pogrom against the Irish in the 17th century. Under the guise of raising money to help dispossessed families back in the 'old country' these self absorbed and over romantic Irish-Americans funded the IRA's terror campaign for over 30 years. Eileen Mackin was standing close to where the Saracen armoured vehicle had come under fire and she was hit by a round fired by an IRA gunman – 'protectors' of the National communities – and died a few hours later in hospital.

Later that day, an obviously embarrassed spokesman for Provisional Sinn Féin, the so-called 'political' wing of the IRA, tried at first to blame the Army. Subsequently they accused Loyalist gunmen from the neighbouring Protestant area of Springmartin. Yet again, the IRA had chosen to make the Ballymurphy Estate – for all of its social faults – into part of their battlefield against the British Army.

The day was still not over, when a Loyalist murder gang attacked the Jubilee Arms pub at Lavinia Street close to the southern arterial Ormeau Road. A UVF gunman fired several shots into the pub, a known drinking haunt of Catholic men, hitting and killing Thomas Ward (34). The fleeing gunman then left a bomb in the doorway before rushing off. A very brave soldier picked up the device and threw it over a wall onto a railway line where it exploded, fortunately causing no injuries. Shortly afterwards, an earlier victim of a Loyalist attack, Joseph McKenna (24) died from his wounds inflicted nine weeks earlier after being shot close to the RVH in Belfast.

On the afternoon of the following day, inside a derelict house on Butler Street, in Belfast's Crumlin Road area, a covert unit of soldiers from the Parachute Regiment observed two men with firearms. As one of them aimed an Armalite rifle at the house, one of the soldiers shot and killed IRA member Sean McKee (17). A crowd of sympathisers gathered and attempted to remove both the body and the incriminating rifle, but the soldiers fired several warning shots and the Armalite rifle was recovered.

Omagh in Co Tyrone is a town of three rivers; the Camowen and Drumragh flow into Omagh from the south-east, and the Strule eventually flows through Londonderry city as part of the Foyle River. The Sperrin Mountains are within sight to the north and the town nestles in an agricultural hollow in the centre of county Tyrone. Omagh is the largest town in the county and is 70 miles west of Belfast and 40 miles south of Londonderry.

The town was relatively sheltered from the Troubles, although a number of IRA bombs severely damaged the town centre in the 1970s and 1980s. Two incidents – one of which is beyond the scope of this book – was to change all that. On Saturday 16 August, after the 'ceasefire' a bomb planted by the so-called Real IRA (RIRA) exploded, killing 28 people including several children and a pregnant woman. In the typically cowardly fashion of the RIRA, no warnings were given and the quiet market town was turned into Hell on a sunny Saturday as townspeople shopped. The incident that is within the remit of this book took place on the night of 17/18 May 1973, when five off-duty soldiers were killed by an IRA bomb placed under their car at the Knock-na-Moe Castle Hotel in the centre of Omagh. On a warm May evening, four soldiers from various regiments, but all on secondment to the Army Air Corps (AAC) socialised over a few beers in the best pub in Omagh, the Knock-na-Moe Castle. That evening, there was the usual Thursday dance and social activities spilled over past midnight. At around 1:00am, the four soldiers returned to their car left in a car park close to the hotel. IRA Intelligence had spotted the car before and, having identified that it had belonged to an RUC officer, targeted it for an attack. The car, however, had been sold to one of the soldiers and the number plates had not been changed for security purposes. The IRA under vehicle booby trap (UVBT) was placed with the intention of killing policemen but instead killed five soldiers.

The device, which had been planted by women members of the IRA, exploded as soon as the car began to move with the five men inside. The blast hurled one of the men some 150 yards away and killed four of the soldiers instantly and dreadfully wounded the fifth. The car park had been empty of people when the bomb went off, but shortly afterwards the planned exodus of drinkers would have resulted in a packed car park, and thus utter carnage. No doubt had dozens been killed and maimed, the IRA's 'Department for Pious and Meaningless Apologies' would have wheeled out a spokesman regretting the loss of innocent lives as they had aimed the blast at 'legitimate' targets.

The soldiers killed were: Sergeant Sheridan Young (26), Royal Military Police, from Buckinghamshire; Staff Sergeant Barry 'Pip' Cox (28), Blues and Royals, from Manchester; Colour Sergeant Arthur Place (29), Prince of Wales' Own and from York; and Sergeant Derek Reed (28), Royal Marines and also from York. Sergeant Frederick Drake (25) of the Royal Inniskilling Dragoon Guards was very badly injured and died of those injuries on 3 June. The IRA attack on five off-duty soldiers had devastated the area, widowed five women and shattered the lives of five separate families.

In its later editions of 18 May, the *Daily Express* managed to put the incident on its front page under "4 am: 4 Men Die in Ulster Car Blast." The front page of that day's edition involved lurid stories about 'society' novelist Barbra Cartland and singer Dorothy Squires. On the day of the blast, the Provisionals had also publically warned that they intended to blow up Aldergrove Airport in Belfast and thus further cripple the economy of that besieged city. However despite these warnings and death threats against pilots and other airline staff, the Airport authorities refused to close their doors and courageously airline staff refused to boycott the airport. Only two round trips – from Glasgow to Belfast – were cancelled and a BALPA (British Airline Pilots Association) stated: "We are not worried by people who go round with old socks over their faces frightening old ladies and children!"

Instead, the IRA turned their attentions to two of the Province's railway stations. A bomb was placed in a toilet in Great Victoria Street, Belfast station and the surrounding area was badly damaged. A warning had been given and there were no casualties. Another bomb caused some damage to the Co Down station in Queen's Quay, also in

Belfast. The Provisionals were absolutely determined to shut down the city and destroy its commercial heart thus making Northern Ireland's position within the UK totally untenable. This was just another day in the battle of 'Bloody Belfast'.

On the same day, Sinn Féin activist Caroline Reneham was jailed for five years in Edinburgh for the possession of large amounts of explosives, including sticks of Gelignite and detonators. The Civil Servant was convicted following the discovery of an explosives cache at a Roman Catholic Church at Possilpark, Glasgow. Scottish police were also seeking, at the time, the Curate, Father Bartholomew Burns who was allegedly involved and was thought to have fled to the Irish Republic.

Robert McIntyre (24), a member of the UVF, had earlier tried to hijack a car on the Shankill Road. Unfortunately for him, a UDR soldier in the car at the time shot and fatally wounded the Loyalist. McIntyre died in hospital the day after the Knock-na-Moe Castle outrage. About the same time, two UFF gunmen who specifically targeted their Catholic victim, shot and killed Edward Coogan (39). He had driven from the Falls to the Antrim Road in Belfast and was hit by rounds fired by the Protestant terrorists shortly before midnight. Tragically, his partner, Margaret Hyrkiewicz (24) was stabbed to death in nearby Adela Street, off the Antrim Road just a week later. She had suffered multiple stab wounds, and it is widely considered that she was killed by the same UFF gang who had shot Coogan.

On the day before the Knock-na-Moe killings, a resident of the Creggan Estate in Londonderry had been hit by a rubber bullet fired by the Army. Serious rioting in the Piggery Ridge area – the Creggan was formerly a pig farm – was ongoing when Thomas Friel (21) was spotted, apparently orchestrating the rioting. A soldier fired a rubber bullet

Steve Norman, third from left, Blighs Lane, Creggan, Londonderry, July 1973 (Steve Norman)

Nose Cap of RPG-7 found at Blighs Lane, Londonderry after
an IRA attack, 4th July 1973 (Steve Norman)

at the man and it struck him in the head. Friel, who was not known to be a member of any Republican organisation, died 48 hours later in hospital. His death resulted in two-three days of savage rioting and protests in the Creggan and several soldiers were badly injured from petrol bombs and flying bricks.

DEATH ON THE CREGGAN
Steve Norman, Royal Anglian Regiment
Rioting had now become a daily ritual in the Creggan, especially as the kids came out of school; it needed no special incident to kick things off. On May 17 1973, however one riot ended in the death of a rioter. Thomas Friel aged 21 from Creggan heights was struck on the head by a rubber bullet and died six days later in hospital, having never regained consciousness. As usual, the circumstances regarding the nature of his death were contested by both sides. The Army statement said he was one of the leaders of the riot on the estate that night, and had been struck on the head from a distance of 25 to 30 yards by a rubber bullet. The locals denied this and said he had been hit from a distance of only two yards away. The incident happened at 11:30pm, with the locals again claiming that Thomas and a friend were on their way to the Piggery ridge Army camp. It was because they had been told the soldiers were beating up a young boy that they knew, and wanted to help him.

Whatever the truth of the matter, it was yet another tragic waste of life. No doubt his family and friends felt his death, as much as we had for Tony Goodfellow and truth be known we had no sympathy, at that time for this young man's death. Our hearts had become hardened and indifferent as a consequence of the constant abuse and hatred shown to us; an unspoken feeling of Tony's death somehow being avenged, prevailed among us. For the next two days after his death, the Creggan became a battleground of serious rioting, with the rioters upping the ante by throwing nail bombs at us.

On one patrol out of Bligh's lane, my section were cut off by a huge mob of rioters; we had no choice but to head for the Piggery ridge camp at the top of the estate for safety. As we ran up the hill towards the camp, the mob was close on our heels with bricks, bottles and anything else they could throw at us, whistling by our heads. As the camp metal gates slammed shut behind us, we gave a sigh of relief but were soon pressed in to action, as the rioters were now outside and trying to get in. The camp perimeter was made up of corrugated sheets that made it look like a tin fort; along the length of it ran a platform upon which now stood all available baton gunners, including me. We were all crouched down so the rioters could not see us and at the given signal we all stood up, took aim and fired; the look on the yobs' faces was priceless! Added to that, someone had got our Pompadours' flag on a long pole, and was waving it at them whilst we all shouted: 'All the 4444444s; the Pompadours,' which was our clarion call.

It gave us great satisfaction and was treated as a huge joke by both the men and officers, but in the back of our minds we knew there was bound to be a more serious response from the Provos of Derry. And that day was close at hand; the 4th of July, American Independence Day.

The Parachute Regiment, who had already had three of their number killed in South Armagh, were to lose another man and their fifth so far of this particular tour. On 24 May, a woman living in the village of Cullaville was warned by a neighbour, as she returned from the local Roman Catholic Church not to enter her house. A masked gunman was observed forcing his way into her house and reportedly had left a bomb.

Point of impact from an RPG-7 at Blighs Lane, Londonderry, 4 July 1973
(Now with wire mesh, added after the event!) (Steve Norman)

She contacted the RUC and the matter was passed on to the Army after a cursory inspection of the property. Two soldiers then attempted to enter the house to conduct a further inspection for booby traps. One of the soldiers was with part of the search team in the back garden and one in the front. All of a sudden, a massive explosion occurred and caught most of the men.

Sergeant Major Ian Donald (35) of the Royal Engineers, from North Yorkshire was in the rear garden and was killed instantly. Acting Sergeant John Wallace (31) of the Parachute Regiment, a Somerset boy, died very quickly afterwards from the blast. The Coroner's words condemning the killings as "cowardly and brutal" fell on deaf ears in Republican circles.

Another sectarian killing took place much further north, in Belfast, where the UFF abducted a Catholic man – Joseph Matthews (30) – from the Falls Road area who had drunkenly and unfortunately, entered a Loyalist bar in Donegall Pass. He was seized, taken out of the pub to another place and tortured before being shot and killed. His body was dumped at the Giant's Ring, at Ballynahatty, a prehistoric Henge type castle some three miles or so, south of where he had been abducted.

Finaghy Road North in Belfast sits south of Kennedy Way and close to Riverdale, Andersonstown in the Riverdale area and today, the modern M2 motorway thunders past. It, like many parts of the city, has a clear view of the Black Mountains, the feature which dominates Belfast. On a bright May day in 1973, little Paul Cromie (four) was playing in his garden. It was an innocent pastime for a young child to whom the Troubles meant nothing. Nothing that is, until the irresponsibility and callousness of an IRA active service unit that opened fire on a foot patrol from the Gordon Highlanders. The child was standing only feet away from a targeted soldier and was hit and killed by an IRA bullet, a victim of the Republican's choice of battlefield. A distraught relative said: "There is no doubt the IRA was to blame. Now all we can do is give the boy a decent, dignified funeral."[2]

The month ended with two additional killings, both as a consequence of murder gangs from the Loyalist side. Although a captain in the Merchant Navy, Thomas Curry (50) was technically a civilian; it was his misfortune to be drinking in Muldoon's in North Belfast. The UFF chose that night to launch a gun and bomb attack on three bars in the city, including two which were Catholic-owned. Thomas Curry was killed when the bar was attacked by automatic weapons and dozens of rounds were fired, injuring several patrons. Within hours, another bar – McGlade's in Donegall Street – was attacked as a large device was thrown at the front door. It exploded and killed Gerard Barnes (31) a Belfast man who left a young, pregnant wife and injured a dozen more people. There was yet another gun attack on a third bar that night which was also carried out by Loyalist paramilitaries, but thankfully, there were no more fatalities.

THE CREGGAN NATIVES
Steve Norman, Royal Anglian Regiment

Our high profile patrol and search in the Creggan was now doing exactly what our CO had intended; we had indeed stirred up an ant's nest. We did our searches at night, which had the inevitable result of the whole area turning out onto the

---

streets with scores of women blowing whistles and banging dustbin lids to warn any IRA players in the area, they were affectionately known by us as the 'Bogside Bags' and were the meanest, most foul mouthed-women I have ever had the misfortune to meet. They would spit in your face, throw urine over you, and on one occasion one rather stupidly slapped one of the lads round the head; this particular soldier was not the sort to take that from anyone and felled her with the quickest right hook I have ever seen. It wasn't big, it wasn't clever, it was just instant reaction and it was a fair bet she would not try that again. There was even a local dog that hated us more than the locals. It would go berserk at the sight of a patrol; snarling barking slobbering and running at the back of your legs to take a bite. We called it 'Bonzo the Provo'. This canine crackpot was finally cornered by a patrol and gaffer-taped from head to toe and its bollocks were left with a neat imprint of a DMS boot then thrown at its owner's front door. This broke its spirit and the scabby mutt ran a mile thereafter when it spied a patrol.

Again, unnoticed in all of the mayhem this month, a further four more soldiers were killed; three to RTAs, but the fourth death cannot be accounted for. On 20 May, Corporal Alistair Roderick Lane (33) of the Royal Military Police was killed in an RTA, the details of which are unknown to the author. Four days later, the UDR lost Lance Corporal Hugh Watton (45) and sadly, there are no further details available. On the same day, Private Joseph McGregor (30), Duke of Wellington's Regiment and from Scarborough, East Yorkshire was killed in an RTA, "somewhere in Northern Ireland." Finally, on 30 May, another RTA for which the author has no specific details claimed the life of Corporal Richard John Roberts (21) of the Royal Military Police. He was the third 'Red Cap' to die in Northern Ireland in the month of May.

In all, the month had claimed 34 more lives; 17 were soldiers, 13 of whom were killed by the IRA. The IRA lost four members, including two to 'own goals' and irresponsible shooting and the Loyalists lost one. Of the 12 civilian deaths, Loyalists were responsible for ten sectarian murders and the IRA and Army for the other two. It is worth noting, that the British Army, much maligned by the Irish Americans and the Irish Lobby, championed by Senator Edward Kennedy were responsible for four deaths in the Province during the month, and the Provisional IRA, the doyen of the bleeding heart, Brit-hating Irish Americans caused the death of 17 people.

Chapter 6

June

June was a light month insofar as the Security Forces (SF) were concerned, with the numbers killed decreasing to three, including the death on 3 June of Sergeant Frederick Drake, from the injuries he had received in the Knock-na-Moe Castle bomb blast. There was, however, no decline in the slaughter of civilians and June included the outrage at Coleraine.

Even by the Loyalists' own bloody sectarian standards, the death of Samuel McCleave (25) was remarkable. In true sectarian fashion, he had been spotted by a Loyalist murder gang, as he reeled through the streets after a night of drinking. His route towards the Catholic Unity Place clearly betrayed him as a Catholic. He was abducted in Skipper Street and taken to an unknown location where he was beaten and strangled to death. What was both offensive and bizarre was the fact that his killers then suspended his lifeless body from metal railings in nearby Hill Street, some 300 yards from Queen Elizabeth Bridge.

Loyalists were then responsible for a double murder in the Oldpark area of Belfast. Though shocking by any civilised standards, the killings in Drew Street failed to create even a ripple in a country which had lost its capacity to be shocked, as the Troubles edged towards their fourth year. Sadie McComb (41) was a Protestant and in the eyes of the Loyalist bigots, she had committed an unforgiveable crime; she lived with a Catholic man, Alfred Acheson (48). She was stalked by a Loyalist murder gang: gunmen burst into a neighbouring house, shot them both dead and wounded the neighbour. Apparently, the Loyalists were intent on introducing and administering their own version of 'Sharia Law'.

The Provisional IRA too, were not averse to resorting to their own tribal punishments; those of knee-capping, punishment beatings and of course, public humiliation. According to RUC records, between 1973 and 1979, there were 756 knee-cappings; 531 of them on Catholics and 225 of them on Protestants. The actual number of victims is around 700; however, some people had shown themselves to be slow learners and had been kneecapped twice or even three times. The author has personally seen the shocking after effects of a knee-capping injury and many of the victims are rarely able to walk properly again, without a limp afterwards. Dr. James Nixon, an orthopaedic surgeon in Northern Ireland, wrote a dissertation based on a study of punishment shootings occurring between September 1974 and January 1975. He wrote of the victims: "Some of them suffer from residual paralysis of muscles in the lower leg." One Royal Green Jacket said, of a knee-capped youngster on the Turf Lodge: "His ballroom dancing days were over!"

Raymond Gilmour in *Dead Ground: Infiltrating the IRA* wrote:

Two or three Provies held the victim face down on the ground while another put a gun barrel behind the man's knee. When he pulled the trigger, he blew the victim's knee-cap off. For obvious reasons, people would never obligingly hold still while this happened and it wasn't unusual to hear of victims of knee-capping who had been shot anywhere from the calf to the thigh. If they were very lucky they got away with a flesh wound instead of a shattered knee-cap, but people also died after botched knee-cappings. One Derry man bled to death after a shot went through the artery in his thigh.

Other than death, there was one further IRA punishment shooting which was even worse than the 'traditional' knee-capping that was used exclusively by the IRA; this form of punishment could render the victim almost completely immobile for the rest of their lives.

One of the IRA's major worries was that of informers, or 'touts' as they referred to them, adding a new expression to the lexicon of the English language. Those members suspected of being either a police informer or having been recruited by the British Army could expect very short lives, ended by a bullet in the back of the head. At first, they would be lured to the house of a Republican sympathiser, a 'safe house' in other words and one which had not yet come to the attention of either the RUC or the Army. The suspect, or dare one say, without adding legitimacy to this terrorist organisation, the 'accused' would meet at some pre-arranged spot and then be blindfolded 'for security reasons' and taken to the aforementioned 'safe house.' Once there, they would be taken upstairs to a bedroom which had been stripped of furniture other than several chairs and forced to sit with their chair facing a blank wall. The room would have been blacked out with almost wartime-like dark curtains.

This 'kangaroo court' would ask question after question, sometimes repeating the same question endlessly, so confusing the suspected tout and this could go on without breaks for hours. (Two excellent books which deal with this type of interrogation are: *Killing Rage,* by Eamon Collins and *Unsung Hero* by Kevin Fulton.) If it were clear, that is in the twisted logic of the 'Court', that he was guilty, the man would be handed over to the 'nutting squad' who would then be responsible for his execution. Often, if they were unsure, they would placate the man and 'request' that the case be resumed at a later stage, thus adding to the fear and heightening his or her apprehension. Fulton writes of the sadistic nature of both the 'Courts' and the 'nutting squad' who had already pre-determined the outcome and simply like to stretch out the agony. This author is not a psychiatrist nor has he had any psychiatric training, but the people who carried out these insidious tasks clearly derived emotional and possibly even sexual pleasure from their work. It made them feel all-powerful giving them a 'high' from both beatings and executions. These sociopaths and psychopaths would have been child molesters, rapists and sadistic killers, even if the Troubles had not happened in order to bring out the sadistic beasts inside themselves.

Any 'deeper' interrogations would be carried out by the IRA's 'internal security' squad and unless the alleged tout was prepared to admit, at once, that he was guilty, the physical would soon replace the psychological. Torture implements – according to those who have spoken publically about such IRA methods – would include: sharpened screwdrivers, knives and the pointed edge of a claw hammer. The 'claw' would be driven into the suspect's thigh or arm. The naked and bound man would be subject to the most demeaning of torture and it was not unknown for the interrogators to wire the

Body of an informer murdered by the IRA, Whitecross, South
Armagh; a victim of the 'Nutting squad'. (Brian Sheridan)

man's testicles up to a 12 volt battery and subject him to immense pain. If all else failed, however, the 'security' squad would take it in turns to beat the defenceless man with their bare fists, ensuring that the pain of broken teeth, broken noses and gouged eyes would accompany the man to his death. A former soldier in the Army Air Corps described how a lifeless corpse found on the border had been burned with electrical steam irons as the squad sought to extract a confession.

After the body had been discovered, there would be the incredibly pathetic sight of the victim's mother or father speaking in public, flanked by 'caring' Sinn Féin officials. Sickeningly, the grieving parent would state that he or she felt no anger towards the IRA as they had acted in the 'best interests of Republicanism' and they were not to blame. They would sob out that their son was at fault for betraying their community and their friends and that the responsibility lay at the feet of the security forces.

Fulton also writes of men who had been led to believe that they were safe and were being escorted home, only to be cold-bloodedly shot in the head whilst almost within sight of the sanctuary of their own front doors. During punishment beatings, the leader of the 'nutting squad' would sneer at the victim: 'Which road do you want to close?' This was a reference to the automatic closing of roads by the Security Forces, when a dumped, and generally hooded, body was found at a deserted spot. Because the IRA often cynically booby-trapped the bodies, the authorities had to close off areas or stretches of roads in order to ensure that no-one else would be killed or injured.

One such IRA 'nutting squad' was in action on June 5, when, following the usual 'kangaroo court' a man suspected of being a tout was shot dead and his body dumped on a road between Clogher and Monaghan on the Irish border.

Terence Herdman (17), an Irish-Canadian, was shot by the IRA having being suspected of informing. Up to the time of his death, he had been living in the Andersonstown area of West Belfast.

Although the British Army never fully defeated the Provisional IRA – neutral observers would possibly describe it as score-draw – nor was the converse true. After the heady but bloody days of PIRA ascendancy and much 'success' in the early to mid-1970s, the British Army through superior and less naïve tactics, sheer weight of numbers and improved intelligence gathering managed to neutralise their threat. The Provisionals' leadership was constantly aware of the threat of informants, whether it was for pecuniary or ideological reasons. 'Touts' ruined many a PIRA operation, saved lives and led to a major reduction in the number of terrorist threats. The author has dealt with the subject of touts in earlier books, but the paranoia it produced certainly was a major cause in curtailing the activities of the IRA.

Northern Ireland was undoubtedly a 'dirty war' – although one might argue what war isn't – but as dirty wars go, that fought between the British Army and Republican terrorism was undeniably so. Many IRA cells or ASUs were clearly infiltrated by the security forces. It was a dangerous, often short-lived and highly tense task and many undercover agents 'closed roads' with their bodies. A perusal of undercover autobiographies by men such as Raymond Gilmour, Marty McGartland, Kevin Fulton and Sean O' Callaghan to name but a few, amply demonstrates this.

The agencies responsible for placing these men, protecting them and for extracting precious intelligence were as ruthless as the IRA, and simply could not be trusted as Gilmour and some of the others claim. Raymond Gilmour writes in *Dead Ground: Infiltrating the IRA*:

> There was always a thought in the back of my mind that someone in the RUC might decide that it was too much trouble or expense to look after me, and so they'd throw me to the wolves or betray me in order to divert attention from another, more highly placed agent in the IRA. This wasn't just paranoia – they'd done it before and would do it again, with an agent called Joe Fenton, who was told to finger two other informers, Gerard and Catherine Mahon to divert attention from himself. That ploy bought Fenton time, but in the end, in an attempt to conceal yet another agent, he himself was sacrificed by his handlers and executed by the IRA.

Catherine Mahon (27) and her husband Gerard (28) were executed on 8 September, 1985 in the Turf Lodge by the IRA after they admitted working for British Intelligence for the previous 18 months. They had been betrayed by Joseph Fenton. Joseph Fenton (35) was executed by the IRA, in the Lenadoon area of West Belfast on 26 February, 1989 after he admitted to spying for the RUC.

Once the interrogation was over, the condemned man – or woman – would be dressed in a boiler suit, in order to leave no forensic evidence in the car in which he or she would be conveyed to a place of execution. Once they had arrived in a remote field, the executioners would force the hooded and bound victim to kneel, read him the appropriate sentence from the IRA's 'Green Book' and, having had a 'tame' priest read the last rites, would then shoot the victim in the head. Sometimes it would be one shot, sometimes two and the shot or shots would obliterate the face, making identification extremely difficult. As Raymond Gilmour writes: "There was no way that there would be an open casket at (the) funeral, for the funeral director had not been born who could put a face back together after two .45 rounds had exited through it."

The executioners would then stuff a large denomination note (often £20) into the dead man's hands as a symbolic sign that he had been touting for money. Wires and batteries might then be attached to the body giving the impression of being booby-trapped and the final humiliation might be that the bomb disposal experts would tie a rope around the dead man's ankles and tow the body to set off any explosives. If they were tied up on other jobs, the body might lay there for some time, rotting in the sun and covered by flies. This was the image that was never shown to the Irish-Americans in their 'Shamrock Bars' drinking green-coloured Guinness on St Patrick's Day and digging deeply into their pockets to support a terrorist organisation.

On the same day as Herdman's execution, the IRA attacked two policemen as they walked, on patrol through the town of Enniskillen, Co Fermanagh. The town was the scene of an IRA bomb attack on Remembrance Sunday in 1987 when, on that most sacred of days to the British, 11 innocent civilians were killed as they remembered Commonwealth war dead. As the two officers walked along East Bridge a car pulled up alongside them and a gunman with a Thompson sub-machine gun, the IRA's preferred weapon, opened fire and between 20 and 30 rounds were fired. Constable David Purvis (22) was mortally wounded and died as he was rushed by helicopter to hospital; he was the 38th member of the RUC to be killed during the Troubles.

Daniel O'Neill (36) a Catholic, living in Glen Road, Andersonstown had been out in North Belfast with his wife, before they separated after a fall out. Somewhat worse for wear after drinking, Daniel walked off alone. In the early hours, as he made his way south through the staunchly Loyalist Deepark close to Crumlin Road, he was sighted and shot by a roaming UFF murder gang. Despite the sounds of gunfire, local residents ignored the situation and he bled to death when prompt action by the locals could have saved his life. Later that day, the UDA were involved in a firefight with the Army in the area of the Albertbridge Road and Woodstock Road in the east of Belfast. Samuel Rush (50) a bus driver, was on a routine journey that day, and by chance, his bus ran straight into the crossfire between the two sides. Tragically, as he drove along, a stray round hit him and he crashed into an Army vehicle and died at the scene.

Some 55 miles north-east of Belfast and 30 miles east of Londonderry is the town of Coleraine. The name comes from the Irish *Cúil Raithin*, meaning nook of the ferns. Twelve people were killed in the town over the long course of the Troubles, half of whom were killed on a single late Spring day in 1973. On June 12, two cars stolen in the south Londonderry area were used to carry bombs to Coleraine. At 3pm, a 100lb bomb – hidden in a stolen Ford Cortina – exploded outside a wine and spirits shop in Railway Road. Six old age pensioners were killed and 33 others injured. The casualties included a number of children returning home from school. Five minutes later a second car bomb exploded in a garage at Hanover Place, and although no one was injured in the explosion, it added to the overall confusion and panic.

A telephone call claiming that another bomb had been left in Society Street, proved to be a hoax. Although a warning had been given for the Hanover Place bomb there was no warning given for the Railway Road bomb. This led many to speculate that the bombers' intention was to draw people towards the bomb in Railway Road and inflict as many casualties as possible. However the death toll could have been much worse. What saved even more carnage was that, if the bomb had exploded 15 minutes later, schoolgirls from the nearby high school would have been leaving school and walking along the street.

The Irish News, in an editorial under the headline "Horror in Coleraine" two days after the outrage, stated:

> Those who engineered or committed the Coleraine slaughter do not give a damn about the most basic of all rights: the right to life itself. After Coleraine we are faced again with the terrible pathology of human beings who see nothing in the routine of destruction by methods which can so quickly mean death and indescribable injury to innocent people.

The bombing was never claimed by the IRA or Irish National Liberation Army– for a variety of reasons, not least was the public opprobrium – but it had all the hallmarks of a Republican attack on a soft target. One of those convicted of the outrage was Sean McGlinchey, brother of the founder of the INLA Dominic McGlinchey. He allegedly said: "Youse know I done it and that's it. There are six people killed but we never meant that. I am up to my neck in it. I didn't intend the bombs to injure anyone."[1] As stated previously, all were old age pensioners and a glance at the following list and their advanced ages demonstrates the softness of the IRA's target, if indeed it was them. This author cannot prove that it was the IRA, but he believes fully that the cars and the explosives were taken to Coleraine and detonated at the behest of the Provisional IRA. One also wonders how the bigoted Irish-Americans in bars in Detroit, Boston, Chicago, New York and Philadelphia would have greeted this appalling slaughter. As the pulses in their foreheads throbbed with pride, listening to the words of songs from 'back home' did the knowledge that the shredded bodies of old people was paid for out of their donations disturb them? One thinks not!

The dead were: Nan Davis (60); Francis Campbell (70) and his wife Dinah Campbell (72); Elizabeth Craigmile (76); Elizabeth Palmer (60) and Robert Scott (72); all the dead were Protestants. Additionally scores were injured, some terribly in the initial blast.

A seventh person died that day, but some 55 miles south of the town in an incident involving a domestic disturbance and the Army. Strictly speaking, the incident although worthy of inclusion is not, in my opinion connected to the Troubles, although one might argue that the associated tension probably did contribute towards the fatal shot. Some readers of my earlier works might recall a similar incident at Springfield Road, some two or three days into the start of the Troubles involving a 'domestic.' On that occasion, a soldier was forced to threaten to shoot a drunken, enraged husband who was trying to kill his wife with a carving knife.[2] This latter incident however, ended in bloodshed as a soldier felt that he was going to be fired upon and fired first. Anthony Mitchell (38) and his wife, parents of five children had argued after he had become drunk and she was forced to run the 500 yards to Springfield Road police station in order to seek protection. He attempted to gain access to what the locals called 'the barracks' and as he climbed

---

1   McKitterick, David et al, *op cit.* p.367.

2   Wharton, Ken, *A Long Long War: Voices from the British Army in Northern Ireland, 1969-98* (Solihull: Helion, 2008) p.50.

one of the security fences, armed with a chair leg, he was shot. A soldier from the Light Infantry saw what he thought in the gloom was a weapon, and opened fire, killing Mr Mitchell. The soldier was charged with manslaughter, but was later acquitted.

One has previously written about the Loyalist murder gangs and they were very prominently featured in three killings over the period June 15-17. The UDA saw itself as the Loyalist equivalent of the Republican Sinn Féin (RSF) and just as RSF was the 'political' wing of the IRA, so too were the UDA the 'political' wing of the Ulster Freedom Fighters (UFF). Another two major Loyalist paramilitary gangs must also be noted here, the UVF and the 'Red Hand Commandos'. Taking its name from the 'bloody red hand of Ulster' the RHC was very closely associated with the UVF. It was formed in 1972 in the Shankill area of west Belfast by John McKeague, and membership was high in the Shankill and Sandy Row areas of Belfast, in Newtownabbey, as well as in parts of county Down. In 1972 the RHC agreed to become an integral part of the UVF. It kept its own structures but in 'operational' matters agreed to take its lead from the UVF and share weapons and personnel. The organisation was declared illegal in 1973.

Late in the evening of Friday, 15 June, several men knocked on the door of a house in Ravenswood Crescent, in the Loyalist Braniel Estate in East Belfast. Asleep in the house at the time, was Michael Wilson (18) who was related through marriage to UDA leader, Tommy Heron. Heron would himself be shot dead later that year (15 September) in a Loyalist feud. The men, members of the UFF, threatened Wilson's sister – Heron's wife – before going upstairs where they shot Wilson in the head as he lay in bed, mortally wounding him. He died before the ambulance arrived and by which time his cowardly killers had melted away into the Braniel. In what bore all the hallmarks of a Loyalist feud – it is said that the only people that they hated more than the IRA were themselves – they later accused Wilson of being an informer in the pay of the Official IRA.

The UFF were again involved just a few hours later when they turned their sick attentions to their 'other' enemies: any Roman Catholic. Daniel Rouse (17) was walking towards Riverdale in Andersonstown along Finaghy Road – close to the scene of the shooting of four-year-old Paul Cromie the previous month – when he was abducted by a Loyalist murder gang. He was bundled into their car and taken to a derelict part of Upper Dunmurry Lane where he was shot and killed. Upper Dunmurry Lane is a little over a mile as the crow flies. The route taken by the killers to the place of Rouse's death was along the Upper Lisburn Road into Dunmurry. It would have taken at least five minutes. Driving within the speed limits so as not to attract the attention of either the Army or the RUC might have taken even longer and one can only imagine the terrified thoughts of the young Catholic boy as he was driven to his death.

In the early hours – what the Belfast folk call 'the wee hors' – of the following day, a former part-time British soldier, James Kelly (25) from Larne was abducted and murdered by the UFF. Larne is approximately 21 miles north east of Belfast and Kelly was attempting to hitch hike back to Larne after visiting his girlfriend in Belfast. His battered and murdered body was found around midnight at Corr's Corner on the Belfast-Larne Road near Ballyclare; he was half way home. The UDA, taking a pious lead from the IRA, claimed that they had shot Kelly, claiming that he was a member of the IRA, in retaliation for the killing of Michael Wilson. Their claims were treated with the contempt which they deserved by the Security Forces and in truth, in all probability, their own community itself.

The 'long walk' is how the Army's EOD soldiers describe the lone trek to a suspect device in order to defuse it. Also nicknamed 'Felix', the men of the Royal Army Ordnance Corps were the bravest of the brave and their attrition rate was understandably high. Captain Barry Gritten (29) from Co Durham in England's north-east was tasked to inspect a suspect device at Lecky Road, Londonderry on 21 June. Together with three other comrades, Gritten approached the device and as he started to examine it, it detonated, killing him instantly and injuring the others, one of whom was blinded in one eye. A telephoned warning that a bomb had been left in a hut on waste ground was clearly an IRA 'come on.' A 'come on' is a means by which the IRA, generally through an 'innocent bystander' calling in the Army, in order to shoot or blow them up with booby-trapped devices. Captain Gritten was the first EOD operative to be killed in 1973 and he would be one of four killed in a three month period from late June to early October that year.

Strabane in Co Tyrone is a town on the very border with the Irish Republic and its western suburbs, particularly Castletown, are less than 800 feet from the actual border. Any IRA gunmen or bombers striking at the SF in the town itself were always aware of how close to safety they were in the post-strike period. They were acutely aware of two factors: Once they crossed the border the Army and RUC were forbidden to chase them; and the Irish police (*Garda Siochana*) and Irish Army would generally turn a blind eye to their presence. The Ballycolman Estate was on the eastern fringes of the town, but still roughly only a mile from the border. It was Republican estate and as such, drew the attentions of the Army which regularly patrolled the area. A routine foot patrol from the Royal Welch Fusiliers (motto: *'Ich Dien'* which is German for 'I Serve') was searching some reportedly unoccupied houses for arms and ammunition stores, when a booby-trap device exploded. The house was almost totally destroyed. Much of the roof vanished as debris showered on nearby houses and injured three children playing outside. The blast killed a Cardiff boy, Corporal David Smith (31) and injured several of his comrades. Again the Provisional IRA showed scant regard for the safety of their own community and no doubt would have had a readymade apology prepared, indicating regret at the loss of innocent children, but at the same time, blamed the British Army for being there in the first place.

On 20 June, after taking part in the pursuit of a stolen car which was considered to have been taken for terrorist purposes, Reserve Constable William John Rea (58) collapsed. Moments later, he died from a massive heart attack, sustained in the course of his duty.

On that first day of the British summer – if one forgives the oxymoron – the Official IRA shot a man whom they claimed, without proof or justification was a member of the UFF. David Walker (16) was a Protestant with learning difficulties who had no paramilitary connections whatsoever. The IRA abducted him in the south of Belfast, took him to the Falls/Divis area and cold-bloodedly shot the boy dead. The Official IRA though never as murderous or as psychopathic as their hated rivals in the much larger Provisional IRA, was able at times to emulate their rivals' bloody handiwork.

The Loyalist paramilitaries were as equally paranoid about touts in their midst as were the IRA. In this regard they were much alike in that guilt or innocence was not the issue. The issue was whether or not the punishment had a salutary effect on any waverers within the ranks. Joseph Cunningham (36) was born a Roman Catholic, and he converted to Protestantism and as such, was labelled a possible tout. Although he, like the innocent David Walker, had no paramilitary connections, the UFF shot him at his home in the Oldpark area of North Belfast. Their pathetic excuse: He was suspected of passing information to the IRA which was entirely spurious and his death was in 'retaliation' for the IRA's murder of the aforementioned David Walker.

This latest sectarian murder also saw the emergence of the mythical 'Captain Black' of the UFF and whose name was always given as their spokesman when calling the Press, Radio or TV to claim responsibility for a killing or other outrage.

Somewhere in the middle of the political spectrum in Northern Ireland, between the Loyalists and the Republicans is the SDLP and one of its prominent members right from the early days of the civil rights movement was Senator Paddy Wilson who was 40 at the time of his death. He was its first General Secretary and was also a Belfast city councillor and a constant thorn in the side of the extreme Loyalists.

On 25 June, Senator Wilson and his Protestant girlfriend, Irene Andrews (25), were found stabbed to death at a quarry on the outskirts of north Belfast. The pair had been abducted near Upper Donegall Street in Belfast City Centre. Wilson, shot and stabbed multiple times, had his throat cut in what was, at that stage in the Troubles, possibly the bloodiest, most savage attack so far. The Belfast Coroner noted that in the frenzied attack Wilson had received 32 stabbing wounds and Ms Andrews 19. The author frequently uses the emotional term 'Loyalist murder gangs' and invites the reader to propose a less emotive expression to describe these people.

Although John White, who was a prominent member of the UDA/UFF, was arrested and questioned about the killings the next day, he was not charged. However, some three years later, he was questioned in Castlereagh RUC centre, about other offences and admitted his involvement. He claimed that the UDA had decided to try and sicken the nationalist community after six Protestant pensioners were killed by the IRA in Coleraine and White said that a decision had been taken to murder the prominent nationalist. He was quoted as saying:

> We felt the SDLP was supporting the concept of a united Ireland, therefore giving some support to the armed struggle, to pursue that through violence. We felt that (killing) someone like Paddy Wilson, someone of that calibre, would be seen as someone high up within the nationalist community. That would send a powerful message and strike fear into Catholics." When asked why they had also murdered Irene Andrews, he replied: "We didn't know she was a Protestant; we just thought she was a Catholic to be honest.

Sentenced to life imprisonment, White started the sentence in 1977, four years after the killings; he was released in 1992 having served only 14 years for his part in the frenzied murders.

On the same day as the double murders, an IRA unit was en-route to Lisanelly Barracks close to Omagh. As they drove in their stolen car packed with explosives along the Omagh to Gortin Road, the bomb exploded prematurely. (And who said there was no justice??) In what was another classic IRA 'own goal' three members of the IRA were killed. The three terrorists were: Sean Loughran (37); Dermot Crowley and Patrick

Carty (26). *Lost Lives* state that the last man, Carty was a suspect in the killing of UDR man, Frank Caddoo in April.

The British Army has always used civilian workers throughout the world in its thousands of barracks; every UK camp on which I was based as a young soldier used a myriad number of 'civvie workers' and Northern Ireland was no different. Soldiers since the time of Empire have always referred to those employed as catering workers by the epithet 'wallah' and in India there were 'char wallahs' (tea) and 'choggie wallahs' (sandwiches etc.) The term in Arabic means a person who is associated with a particular work or who performs a specific duty or service. Noor Baz Khan (45) was one such 'choggie wallah' and he was well known around the Army units based in Londonderry. Originally from Pakistan, Khan was proud to serve his Army customers and at a time when the IRA had no compunction in murdering other contractors for supplying the Army, he would have known of the threat to his life.

Based at Fort George Army base in Londonderry, he regularly used to collect catering supplies from all over the city and was on a re-stocking trip on the day that he was murdered by the IRA. As he drove along Celtic Park, he was stopped by two men, one of whom fired a single shot into his head before running away. Khan was murdered by a coward and the coward's comrades later claimed that the 'choggie wallah' was a member of British Intelligence, a charge so lamentably and outrageously inaccurate that I will not comment further.

THE MURDER OF NOOR BAZ KHAN
Steve Norman, Royal Anglian Regiment

Life inside the camp at Bligh's lane was a mixture of Guard duties, patrolling or on standby; our only comforts were the TV and we watched *Top of the Pops* as all young men did, plus the occasional film show. We had the obligatory 'Choggie Shop' run by the 'Choggie man' who for some reason, were all called 'Muckergee.' Every camp had one; it was usually a little four-walled cabin in which 'Muckergee' ate, slept and lived. He sold us just about everything, from tiny transistor radios to burgers of dubious origin plus fags and dirty magazines. Our own 'Muckergee' was foolish enough to allow us to run up a slate which all went down in a big book he kept by his side at all times. He would often say in his thick Indian accent 'You bloody squaddies; I know you and if I no careful you nick it for sure!' The poor bugger had no idea that our names were just nom de plumes that only squaddies could think of. Such as 'Private Hugh Janus'; 'Corporal Ramsey Tupper' and 'Lance Corporal Pat T. Cake.' The last few days of the tour saw 'Mr Muckergee' wandering around asking 'Who Ramsey Tupper?' to which everyone replied: 'All of us if we get the chance!'

I am sad to relate that the local Provos did not think the Choggie men funny, and as far as they were concerned in their own warped minds they were legitimate targets. On the 26th of June, 1973 the 'Choggie man' from Fort George Londonderry, Noor Baz Khan was stopped with his brother along Lone Moor Road near Celtic Park after going to fetch groceries by two men. One of whom pulled out a gun and shot Noor Baz Khan in the head. The IRA claimed he was a member of the British Intelligence but later admitted he was murdered simply because he served tea to the Army. That really summed up the kind of mindset we were up against. But now through a different kind of mindset, one of our own making, we were to lose one of our own platoon members. We were naïve enough to set up an unscreened static vehicle checkpoint at the edge of the Creggan. With hindsight, what happened later was bound to happen.

As the month drew to an end, there was another death caused by soldiers which has never been satisfactorily explained and until or unless the true circumstances are revealed, a stain will sadly appear over the Army's conduct in Northern Ireland. The British Army conducted itself with dignity, professionalism and restraint and behaved according to its own high standards of being the best trained – not always the best equipped – Army in the world. Its soldiers behaved with restraint in view of some of the most appalling provocation any modern Army has ever faced. It was confronted on every single one of the approximate 10,585 days during which the Troubles raged in every part of the Province. It faced physical as well as verbal abuse, daily riots and daily violence as well as injury and death. There were occasions though, when the professional mask slipped and it sometimes, regrettably resulted in the deaths of the innocent.

This author was proud to have been a soldier and will not take lessons in morality from the Republican movement – the rare lapses by the Army pale into utter insignificance when measured alongside the indiscriminate and irresponsible violence of the Provisional IRA, INLA or any of the Loyalist paramilitaries. In the early hours of the last Monday of the month, a mobile patrol unit was on the Brandywell in Londonderry when one of the soldiers thought that a man had pointed a pistol at the open rear doors of a Saracen armoured vehicle. The soldier fired one shot and mortally wounded Robert McGuinness (20) and he died later in hospital, his death unexplained and sadly unjustified.

There was a final and somewhat mysterious death on the last day of the month. There was no mystery about the outcome; a newly married man – Robert Armstrong (31) – was shot dead at his home in South Belfast, the gunmen brushing past his new bride before shooting him three times. The mystery was that it was a Protestant terrorist – probably UFF – shooting a fellow Protestant for no apparent reason. Mr. Armstrong was positively identified by his murderer to the point of being asked if he was 'Robert Sean Armstrong' before being shot and killed.

June ended as it had started, on a dreadful note, but then so did every month during the long and bloody course of the Troubles. In this month, 31 people lost their lives. The dead included three soldiers, two policemen and 23 civilians. The IRA lost three at their own hands following an own goal in Co Tyrone. It is worth noting that, of the 23 civilians killed, Loyalist murder gangs were responsible for 12 deaths, the IRA nine and the Army for two.

Chapter 7

July

"Belfast was always either bleedin' hot or sodding raining!" wrote a former Rifleman in the Royal Green Jackets of his time in that bloody city. It was now summer and a time for strolls in the warm summer sunshine, ice creams in the park and ice-cold beers outside the pubs watching the world – and the girls – go by. The seasons mattered little to both opposing forces of paramilitaries and July wasn't very old before the killing commenced. The soldiers were the meat in a sectarian sandwich.

Private Reginald Roberts, a Doncaster lad and soldier in the Light Infantry celebrated his 25th birthday on July 1 and as he stood on guard, protecting council workmen, his thoughts might have wandered about two delightful prospects. Back home in South Yorkshire, his wife was expecting twins and that very night, he would share a jar or two with the other LI lads in his platoon. As he guarded men engaged on fencing repairs on the Ballymurphy Estate, a gunman fired two rounds at him, one of which hit him and he died instantly. There was further tragedy as Mrs Roberts was shocked into premature labour and lost both her twins; the IRA had killed three Brits with one bullet and there would be celebrating on the 'Murph that evening.

The morning after US Independence Day – and no doubt a time of giving to NORAID in the Irish-American bars in North America – father of five, Robert Clarke (56) went about his lawful and respectable business in South Belfast. UFF gunmen were aware that he and his brother – a fellow Catholic – delivered to a builders' yard in Pembroke Street and a gang lay in wait for their arrival. On that morning, Mr Clarke's brother, Vincent had failed to turn up for work and cheated death as the Loyalist murder gang shot and killed Robert Clarke. His reprieve, however was only temporary as 'Death' had smiled at Vincent, and he was also shot by Loyalists, the following February in the Whiterock area. Later that day, an IRA gang hijacked a bus on Cliftonville Road, Belfast and, having robbed the driver, sprinkled petrol on the upper deck and forced the terrified passengers to jump from it. Protestant Mrs Dorothy Lynn (46) was unable to escape the flames and collapsed from burns and smoke inhalation. She died in the RVH five days later.

THE IRA TRY TO KILL ME
Steve Norman, Royal Anglians

July 4th, 1973 held no particular significance for me or my section as we began a routine patrol around the Creggan Estate in Londonderry. It was just another day nearer the completion of our tour, as far as we were concerned. But somehow things felt different! That afternoon, the locals avoided eye contact with us and did not engage in the usual 'Brit Bastard' type of abuse. Something was very wrong; this was a real 'Sir, they're taking the kids indoors' moment. The section corporal indicated to us that we were going back to Bligh's lane camp, even though we had only been out for half an hour; we needed to get back and report that something was afoot. As we zig-zagged down the hill and into the rear gates of Bligh's lane, we had no idea that just behind us was an IRA ASU, just waiting its moment to strike.

That moment came, just as we stood at the unloading bay ready to clear our weapons. There was an almighty bang, followed by what I took to be complete silence. That silence was, of course, my own ears reacting to the concussion of an explosion, created by the warhead of a Russian made RPG-7 (rocket propelled grenade) hitting the large extractor fan above our heads. Of course I knew nothing of this at that moment, so struggled to make sense of what had happened. I came to, on my back as the blast had knocked me flat, and could see people running around in what appeared to be a confused state. Vaguely I heard the section corporal shouting to us to get up and follow him back out the gates, to fire back at our attackers. But as I tried to stand up, my left leg buckled under me. I felt a stinging throbbing sensation just above the back of my knee; realising I was in no position to follow the section corporal and the lads, I lay back down. By now, a firefight was taking place up the hill where the section corporal had gone.

Someone then emerged from the ops room, and dragged me around to the unloading bay sandbags (to this day I do not know who it was). He asked if I was ok, and when I told him that my leg hurt, he pulled down my combat trousers, as he could see no blood or large hole to indicate any serious damage. I was now on my stomach; I turned my head to see the look on his face, and despite him saying: "You're all right lad; it's only superficial," I knew it was much worse. At this point two medics got to me, and as I started to shiver and go into shock, they gave me an injection of morphine which had the immediate effect of making me feel that I was walking on air, hand in hand with Jesus himself! No pain and a feeling of not caring what the hell happened to me.

After being taken into the medics room to await evacuation to the Altnagelvin civilian hospital, I was paid a visit by little Jock Robinson, one of my old platoon mates; he proceeded to fill me in about what had happened. The rocket had hit dead centre of the fan, and had had blown the lot, and sent shrapnel into the accommodation below, ripping up bedding and kit as it went in. By some miracle this just happened to be my own section's room and we had been stood outside when it hit. Just a few more minutes and we would have been in there; God only knows what would have happened. Jock asked if he could he see where I had been hit, so I told him to help himself, as they wouldn't let me see it. "Bugger that," said Jock and went off to get a mirror so i could see for myself. He held the mirror, and I then saw a hole, roughly the size of a golf ball right through to the bone, with hardly any blood and all the skin and muscle tissue missing. I had been lucky; if that piece of shrapnel had hit my head I would have been dead for sure! Such was the force and heat, it had cauterised my main arteries and saved me from bleeding to death.

That afternoon produced major fighting in the estate between us and the IRA. A total of 227 7.62 SLR rounds had been fired, along with 36 baton rounds, eight CS gas cartridges, four CS grenades and seven smoke grenades. Besides myself there had been one other significant casualty; a young man from the estate thought to be a member of the IRA ASU. He had been shot through the neck by our lads, and was now on his way to the same hospital as me. For his actions that day Bill was awarded the Military Medal, and it was to be some years before I got to meet him again; 30 odd in fact but that is another story.

Steve and I have gotten to know each other over the years, and as a consequence of his many tours, he has been a source of consistently interesting and powerful contributions to my writings. I have resisted his blandishments to 'feel his wound' and will go on resisting. His Regiment, the Royal Anglians, lost 26 soldiers to various causes between 1970 and 1986; its three (at the time) regular battalions were known as the 'Vikings', 'Poachers' and 'Pompadours'.

It was the UVF's killers who struck next, when they stalked Patrick Bracken (28) a 'Captain' in the Official IRA as he left a café close to Linden Street, in the Falls area of Belfast. The murder gang fired a salvo of rounds and hit both Bracken and a friend, killing the IRA man.

The IRA targeted off-duty UDR men and women, generally as they returned home from work or as they drove to work or actually at their desks, counters or other sites. They attacked these part-time soldiers in such circumstances, as they were 'soft targets'. Rarely could members of the IRA ever be 'tarred' with the epithet: brave; cowardly would be more apt. They also chose to kill former members of the UDR, no matter how tenuous their previous connection had been and no matter how long they had been inactive. On 9 July – the same day that Mrs Dorothy Lynn died from her IRA-inflicted injuries – Isaac Scott (41) had just left a pub in Belleek, Newtownhamilton, when gunmen approached the front of his car and shot him several times through the windscreen. He was killed instantly, another victim of a Catholic murder gang, seemingly desperate to keep the blood flowing on the streets of Northern Ireland.

July 12 is the start of the traditional Loyalist 'marching season' where parades of 'Orangemen' in full regalia, accompanied by full marching bands and the banners of their religion parade through the streets of the Province. There are two perspectives here, as the cultures of the sectarian forces collide often in bloody confusion, injury and death. To the Protestants, they are a series of parades held annually by members of the Orange Order during the summer in Northern Ireland, to a lesser extent in Scotland, and occasionally in England, and throughout the Commonwealth. These typically build up to the 12 July celebrations which mark William, Duke of Orange's victory over the Catholic, King James II at the Battle of the Boyne in 1690. To them, it is their birthright and if a few Catholics are upset by their routes through Republican areas, so what. The Catholics on the other hand, find them garish, provocative and insulting to their religion, and it is yet another manifestation of the manner in which the Protestants were able to 'lord' it over them.

The 1973 marching season began, as it often did, with a death; this time a former RAF man, Frederick Davis (29) who lived in the eastern part of Belfast. He was seen by witnesses to be drinking heavily and calling out sectarian slogans and after disappearing, his dead body was found dumped on the Newtownards Road. It is widely believed that he was murdered by Republican supporters, acting independently of the IRA. As was the case in the Province during the Troubles, his killers were never convicted.

On July 17, an ADU (Army Dog Handling Unit) was searching a field near Clogher, Co Tyrone, approximately two miles from the border with the Republic. The team had spotted a milk churn – a favourite of the IRA bombers – and went to investigate, with Corporal Bryan Criddle (34) and his sniffer dog in the lead. As he approached the milk churn, it was detonated by remote control and he was dreadfully injured; the dog, although blown some distance away, survived. Brian Criddle, BEM, died in hospital five days later. Clogher is overlooked by several hills, and it is thought that a hidden IRA team was watching the Gloucestershire boy's every movement and remotely triggered the device. One of the survivors that day, was Staff Sergeant Francis Beckett of the Royal Army Ordnance Corps; 44 days later, he too would be dead also at the hands of the IRA's bomb-makers.

Divis Tower is a 200-foot tall tower in Belfast. It has 20 floors and was built in 1966 as part of the now-demolished Divis Flats complex. It is named after the nearby Divis Mountain. The complex of 850 flats, housing 2,400 residents was designed by architect Frank Robertson for the Northern Ireland Housing Trust. Due to Provisional IRA activity in the area, the Army constructed an observation post on the roof in the 1970s and occupied the top two floors of the building. At the height of the Troubles, the Army was only able to access the post by helicopter.

Divis Tower was a flashpoint area during the height of the Troubles. Nine-year-old Patrick Rooney, the first child killed in the Troubles, was killed in the tower during the riots of August 1969, when the RUC fired a Browning machine gun from one of its Shortland armoured car into the flats. The RUC stated that it was coming under sniper attack from the tower at the time. Patrick Rooney's death took place during a day of street violence throughout many areas of Belfast. It was also the scene of the death of the first British soldier to be killed during the Troubles. Trooper Hugh McCabe of the

A car bomb explodes in South Armagh (Brian Sheridan)

Queen's Royal Irish Hussars, was killed in a friendly fire incident at the Divis on the same day as British troops went into the Province. He was home on leave from Germany at the time of his death.

A huge tower block of Council-owned flats dominates Divis Street in Belfast, just where it merges with the Falls Road. Known to many soldiers as the 'bad arse tower', it was a breeding ground for the IRA, representing as it did the worst deprivation of the era. The squalid dwelling place represented the quintessential second-class nature of Catholics in the eyes of the Protestants. It was also the scene of several killings of members of the Security Forces (SF). On July 17, a foot patrol from the Gloucestershire Regiment was carrying a search of the upper floors of the tower block. The 'Glorious Glosters; as they are known (motto: 'By our deeds we are known') took the title after their heroic stand during the battle of Imjin River during the Korean War.

The IRA had booby-trapped a large cupboard containing fuses for the entire electrical system for the flats and as soldiers searched the cupboard, the device detonated. Privates Geoffrey Breakwell (20) and Christopher Brady (21), from Staffordshire and Plymouth respectively, were killed – Private Brady instantly – by the blast. Two other soldiers were injured – one seriously and a resident of the flats was also hurt. The IRA 'claimed' responsibility. Although, several of the newspapers, in defiance of the terror group, worded it differently and reported that the IRA 'admitted' responsibility. The other two casualties were Ray Peart who was blinded for life and Andy King.

The modern readers have a myriad of high-tech programmes available to them today, with which to get an instant view of virtually any street in the world. Throughout this book, there are references to this Street or that Road etc., and readers who will immediately check out the location. The views today are, in most cases, so much different to how they looked when we tramped those streets in Belfast and Londonderry over 40 years ago. As a consequence, there is a real danger that a modern view will not be able to give the reader the correct impression of the places as they were back in the early days of the Troubles. A perfect example would be Leeson Street and a quick glance shows neat rows of new, red brick houses and well kept, albeit tiny gardens. Leeson Street which runs off the Lower Falls Road and is close to the Divis was so much different back in the day. A perfect illustration of this can be found by looking at Terence de Cuneo's painting of the major firefight between IRA gunmen and the Royal Green Jackets' 'R' Company in September, 1971. The title of which is 'Leeson Street Patrol.'

Only if there is a 'Street View 1971' would the reader be able to see for his or herself, the grim, terraced, one up-two down houses with outside toilets and witness the grey drabness of Northern Ireland when soldiers first walked the streets. New Lodge, 1971 would remind the reader why Mick Pickford of the Royal Artillery referred to that area as the 'long streets'. Finally, an Aroma guide to the area in 1971 would allow the reader to smell the omnipresent boiled cabbage, stale urine and burnt petrol which pervaded everywhere.

Crumlin Village in Co Antrim is eight to ten miles away from the city of Belfast and it gives its name to one of the main arterial routes out of the city and is one of the loosely defined borders between Loyalist and Republican areas. It is a quiet place and one in which the Loyalists chose to 'retaliate' for the two Gloster deaths earlier that day. The UFF placed a car, packed with explosives outside the 'Silver Heel' bar in Crumlin which was very busy with early evening drinkers. The car bomb exploded, injuring almost 20 people – some terribly – and killing a local Catholic, Owen Ruddy (60) who was in the pub with his wife who was also injured.

The words 'horrifying, callous and cowardly' are epithets which, in the opinion of this author and former soldier, adequately describe the conduct of the Provisional IRA. When they killed another off-duty UDR soldier on 20 July, they were the very words used by the Coroner to describe his murder. Private Sydney Watt (36) lived with his wife and four children in Ballintemple, Co Armagh and just over two miles from Narrow Water where the IRA would later kill 18 soldiers in two connected bomb blasts. Private Watt had just returned home in the very early hours, when an IRA murder gang who had lain in wait in his garden opened fire with automatic weapons mortally wounding him. As they made good their escape across the Irish border, some 13 miles away, his distraught wife dashed from the house to find him dying.

Later that same day, the IRA struck again in Co Armagh when they killed one soldier from the Royal Engineers (RE) and injured several others at a bomb blast in Keady. A unit of the RE was searching derelict buildings at Crossdall, which are less than 1,000' from the Irish border and some 13 miles from where Sydney Watt had been murdered earlier that day. Major Richard Jarman (37) from North Yorkshire was killed instantly by a large booby-trapped device and another soldier was very badly wounded. Major Jarman was alerted by one of the accompanying sniffer dog's behaviour a few seconds before the explosion, but this was sadly too late.

On July 21, an IRA ASU was transporting a bomb in the region of Newcastle, Co Down to an unknown target. The three members of the team included two men and a woman and as they passed along Causeway Road, Newcastle, close to Dundrum Bay, the explosives detonated prematurely. In the 'own goal' explosion, Pauline Kane (21) and Alphonsus Cunningham (21) were killed and the third IRA man was injured.

The cowardly murder of a German national, Paul Linauer (24), a merchant seaman demonstrates the earlier points about the dangers of Belfast in the Troubles of being in the wrong place at the wrong time. Linauer had been drinking in the city centre before being invited to a party in the Cliftonville area. He left in the early hours of the morning in order to walk back to the city centre and as he crossed from a Catholic area and entered the Shankill Road, he had the misfortune to stumble into a Loyalist murder gang from the UVF. Despite the fact that he spoke very poor English, his murderers had seen him emerge from 'enemy' territory and assumed that he was a Catholic. For that crime, he was shot three times and his body dumped close to the Shankill Road. At his inquest, the Coroner described it as a "…motiveless killing." This however, was Belfast during the Troubles and motiveless murders abounded.

The UVF were again involved on the 21st when they attempted to rob a bar on the Shankill Road. The owner of The Horse Shoe, Leonard Rossborough (38), saw the masked men shortly after closing time and confronted them. Realising that resistance was futile, and despite offering the gang the night's takings, he was shot and died in hospital three days later. Witnesses stated at the trial of one of the publican's killers, that the men removed their masks as they came out of the pub and were laughing and joking after killing a fellow Protestant.

THE ARMALITE
Sergeant Major Haydn Davies, Royal Regiment of Wales

It was July 1973; we were based in Londonderry and it was the time of the 'Apprentice Boys march' which was one of those stupid Prod marches through Nationalist areas that intentionally upset the Catholics. As I remember at the time, we saw a US Sailor all dressed in 'Whites' and on leave from his ship, walking through the Bogside. We were at a loss how to handle that, as I thought he may be mistaken for a British sailor and murdered by the IRA. However, it turned out that he had 'ancestors' in the Bogside![1]

We were a reserve company and were laying on our packs in the sunshine on the square at Ebrington barracks on the Waterside. The Resident unit was an Anglian battalion and on this particular day, the RSM of the Anglians walked past our command vehicle carrying an Armalite rifle. We asked to see it and he was quite proud of it and gladly showed it off! On the rifle were several labels, one in particular was marked 'United States Department of Justice' and various typewritten remarks on the label. One in particular was marked: 'Case number' plus some numerals. The rifle had been completely 'disarmed' by a system of welding most of the parts. It had been found or captured by the Anglian battalion during a 1972 tour. The RSM remarked that the rifle had been 'gone' for eighteen months.

Was this evidence of collusion between the US legal system, in that a captured weapon found its way back into the hands of the IRA? Could it have been some Irish-American court worker or policeman who felt that he was helping the cause 'back home? Perhaps we will never know.

On the long and glorious Roll of Honour of the Royal Marines, the name of Marine John Joseph Shaw (19) of 40 Commando is included and dated 26 July, 1973. The MoD honours his name but only under the statistics for road traffic accidents (RTA). He was in plain-clothes and it seems likely that he was acting as an undercover soldier at the time of his 'accident'. That the Marines consider his death as not only mysterious, but as a death on active service is good enough for this author to agree and include him on the ROH as such. Marine Shaw, from Manchester, on duty and in plain clothes, was either in pursuit of or being pursued by another vehicle on the M2 motorway when his car crashed. He was killed at the scene but officially at least, no further details are available. This will be rectified in a further book should those details be forthcoming.

Steve Norman of the Royal Anglian Regiment was injured when the Provisional IRA fired a Russian-made RPG into his base in the Creggan Estate.

He takes up the story after his initial operation.

AFTER THE ATTACK; FAMILY AND MY MEDICAL CARE
Steve Norman, Royal Anglian Regiment

I awoke the next day in a small ward of the Altnagelvin Hospital in Londonderry; this was the same hospital as the dead from 'Bloody Sunday' had been taken, and the attitude from the nurses towards me was professional but very cool. Right

---

1   See also the section on the alleged 'Saturday night sniper', thought to have been an off-duty US soldier in the author's previous work *The Bloodiest Year; Northern Ireland 1972*.

Recce Platoon, 2RGJ West Belfast (Charles Heyman)

beside me, in a chair was an Army plain clothes SIB man complete with Browning pistol in a holster. The implication was clear, that this was not a safe place to be; the IRA was not above shooting injured military personnel in their sick beds. He spoke first to ask how I was feeling. I said that I was ok, but all I wanted to know, was had my family been informed of what had happened, and what was going to happen next? He told me not to worry about anything, as it had all been taken care of; he told me that my family had been told and sent their love. He also told me that I was staying there for about a week, before they took me to Musgrave park military hospital in Belfast for another operation.

I remember telling him that I had just had one here, and I didn't understand? To which his reply was: "Oh that was just a clean-up operation; they have not taken anything out the shrapnel is still in there; they want to do the proper job with an Army surgeon who knows how to deal with gunshot wounds!" He then added that they needed the metal inside my leg for forensics! As it turned out, the latter part of the conversation was true, but the former part about my family was a downright lie. What had actually happened was that a policeman and a Corporal from my local recruiting office had turned up at my mother's front door, and informed her that I had been injured. They also told her that, although not life threatening, it was serious enough for another operation to take place. My mother lived on her own; no brothers or sisters or husband to comfort her. With that, one of those two bearers of bad news gave her a scrap of paper with a phone number on and left her in complete shock on her own; typical bloody MoD!

Fortunately she had great neighbours who knew that I was serving in Ireland and one had spotted those two 'care bears' leaving out the front door. They had put two and two together and went to her aid. My mum now went through what must have happened to so many families of killed and injured soldiers, after being given the bad news. She said it was like being in a bad dream that you cannot wake up from, and a sense of unreality and fearing the worse. A neighbour then rang the number Mum had been given, and was told that she could not come over to visit me as it would be inadvisable and dangerous. This, of course was MoD talk for: 'We are not going to pay for you to visit!' It was several days before I got to speak to her on the phone, and of course I did what any son would do: I made light of things and told her I would be back before she knew it. At least she had the comfort that I would be back; for so many other mothers, there was no comfort and their sons never did go back.

For the next week or so, I was guarded around the clock by my minders. Then, one afternoon one said to me: "Sorry, mate; I have to go to the toilet. Here, stick this under your pillow; you know how to use it if you have to!" To my amazement, he slipped a Browning pistol, fully loaded, under my head and headed off for a fag! Meantime, right on cue, in came two nurses who had been particularly cold and distant to me and proceeded to change the bed sheets and pillowcases. How I kept a straight face, I will never know, but sure enough when she got to remove the pillow, she let out a howl of anguish saying: "Oh my God; he's got a gun here! It's a bloody gun I tell you!" With both of them holding their hands to their mouths, they recoiled in horror as if they had seen Satan himself tucked up in the pillow!

Again right on cue, in came my hero: the minder who quickly sized up the situation, he just sunk down in the chair and said: "Oh bloody hell; I'm in for it now!" As ill as I felt, I had tears coming into my eyes and a lady visitor at the next bed came over, and put her arms around me and said: "Oh my dear; don't cry, it must be awful for you it's not your fault!" She suddenly realised that I was not crying because I was upset; these were tears of laughter. It did wonders for my spirit and every time these two nurses came into view thereafter, it sent me in fits of giggles even though they scowled at me at every opportunity.

On my last day there, Major 'W' turned up with his minders to see how I was doing; to his credit he made a great fuss and had brought fags and mags and a bottle of Lucozade and wished me well and speedy recovery. I thanked him for the visit and he replied in typical 'Rupert' mode: "Ah well, it would have been bloody well rude not to have done!" That afternoon, I was told that I was being taken to Musgrave Park Military Hospital. I had been expecting that, but what I did not expect was an Army helicopter, landing in the grounds to pick me up and take me! Wow; this was travelling in style. As I was being loaded on to the helicopter, I looked up to the windows of my ward, to see lots of people waving me goodbye; including the two nurses who had found the gun. Maybe I had misread them after all. I was now airborne and on my way to a whole new experience at the wonderful Musgrave Park.

July came to an end and the death toll was 18; of these eight were soldiers, seven were civilians and three were members of both wings of the IRA. Of the civilians, the Loyalists killed three and the Republicans the other three. The year was now seven months old and a total of 202 people had already been killed. The death toll was made up of 75 soldiers, seven Policemen, 88 civilians, 20 members of the IRA and 12 Loyalist paramilitaries. It cannot be compared to the bloodiest year of 1972, when almost 100 people lost their lives in the month of July alone, but it was still unacceptable.

It is worth noting that, in 1968, the murder rate in Northern Ireland was 0.33 per 1,000 of population, but in 1972 it leapt to 24.58 and the following year it reached 13.1. In other words, the rate of murders in the Province had increased by c. 750%. Furthermore, in seven months 75 soldiers had lost their lives; add to that those who died in the previous year, and there had been 247 military deaths in the last 548 days. The IRA boast of killing a soldier a day was looking less and less like idle Republican rhetoric.

Chapter 8

August

In the author's previous work on the Troubles, *The Bloodiest Year: Northern Ireland 1972*, the tragedy of the 'disappeared' is dealt with in minor detail. Principally, it considered the case of Jean McConville, a Catholic resident of the Divis flats, who was accused of passing information of IRA movements to the Army, and of the murdered undercover soldier, Captain Robert Nairac of the Scots Guards.

To the new reader, the basic concept behind the 'disappeared' – the phrase was coined by relatives of the dead and missing – was that it reduced the IRA's embarrassment, it also left loved ones guessing and further 'mystified' the name of the IRA. There was a further sick 'rationale' in burying the bodies secretly. This was allegedly done in order to cause less 'distress' or embarrassment to the families of the those murdered. This was so in the case of well-established Republican families who would not wish their standing in the Republican community to be tarnished. This 'thoughtfulness' did not apply to the death of Nairac, a soldier on undercover duty, and his death will be dealt with in a later book.

During August, 1973, an IRA 'nutting squad' picked up Peter Wilson (21) from his Belfast home on the Falls Road. He was taken away, presumably interrogated and then shot. His body was buried in an unmarked and shallow grave beneath sandstone cliffs in the Glens of Antrim.

Wilson's body was located and exhumed on November 3, 2010, after a tip-off was received by the Independent Commission for the Location of Victims' Remains, a body established by the British and Irish governments a decade ago in the wake of Northern Ireland's peace settlement. Wilson was one of the 'disappeared'. These were 16 people who, at different times during the Troubles, were killed and buried secretly; 11 of them by the IRA. Wilson's sister Anne Connolly said the news was doubly distressing because her mother, who had died three years earlier, often sat on the beach during warm summer days. There are still more of the 'disappeared' who lay in shallow graves and on unconsecrated ground. This author has often discussed the collusion between Catholic priests and the IRA, and nowhere was this more borne out than when at least two of the murdered members were allowed to be confessed to a Priest at their place of 'execution?' What in God's name possessed these Priests to have allowed themselves to be used in order to make these murders 'respectable' is beyond the simple comprehension of this author.

Mr Wilson's family believes the IRA was responsible for the murder although the organisation's leadership has never officially admitted the killing. A spokesman for the Wilson family said:

This is a special day for our family – Peter has been missing for 37 years. For 37 years, we have missed him and have often wondered what happened.' Sinn Féin President Gerry Adams said: 'The reports that remains have been found at

Waterfoot, Co Antrim, where the Commission have been searching for St James man Peter Wilson, is welcome news. 'My thoughts are with the Wilson family at this time and I would hope that confirmation would be speedy to ease the burden of the final wait the family will endure. 'I again would repeat my appeal that anyone with any information which might help other families locate remains, and find closure should bring that information forward.

Another of the 'disappeared' Jean McConville, a mother of ten, went missing from her home in 1972. She was taken across the Irish border, shot as an informer, and buried on a beach in County Louth.

Gerry Adams, whose Sinn Féin party was the 'political wing' of the IRA and which shares power with the Democratic Unionist Party in the Northern Ireland Assembly, has denied that he was involved. In an interview in 2010, he told Ulster Television (UTV): "I reject absolutely any accusation that I had any hand, act, or part in the killing and disappearing of Jean McConville."

His former comrade in the IRA, Brendan Hughes, claimed during a tape recording in 2008 that Adams had been involved. Hughes has been interviewed by Dublin journalist Ed Moloney for his book *Voices from the Grave*. He confirmed what many people already knew, that Adams was the IRA's Belfast Brigade Commander; the architect behind the 70s bombing campaign and principally 'Bloody Friday' when 21 bombs were exploded in Belfast city centre, killing nine people. Hughes, formerly a close friend of Adams, alleged that a British Army transmitter was twice found in McConville's apartment in the nationalist Divis Flats in west Belfast, and that she was murdered by a secret IRA unit dubbed the 'unknowns,' which he claimed was controlled by Gerry Adams. The McConville children have always denied that their mother was an informer.

One bloody and successful IRA tactic had been to target off-duty UDR soldiers at their homes and places of work. Although any UDR member was a 'legitimate' target, there were easier ones, and they clearly preferred those who lived in the rural areas and especially those close to the Irish border. Part-time soldiers who were also farmers were clearly the most vulnerable and many lived and worked close to the aforementioned border where it was easy for the killers to cross and slip away. The Loyalists appear to have taken a leaf out of the IRA's book and although both the UVF and UFF claimed responsibility for a killing on 5 August, the real killers were never caught. On this occasion, Francis Mullen (59) and his wife Bernadette (39) farmed land at Dungannon, in Co Tyrone.

To the sick and depraved killers of the Loyalist murder gangs, the Mullens, and it seems, their toddler son, were 'legitimate' targets in the sectarian war. Late on the evening of Sunday August 5, they burst into the Mullen's remote farmhouse. The masked gunmen opened fire indiscriminately and hit all three of the family, killing the husband and wife and wounding their toddler son. The two adults and their wounded child, drenched in his parents' blood were discovered later that evening by their teenage son. This was another 'satisfactory' result for the Loyalist murder gangs and two more Catholics were dead.

Four days later the UVF were back at work, killing Catholics, although there was an element of mystery about the killing of a young Protestant, who may not have been the intended target. Four days after the attack on the Mullen's farmhouse a coach taking workers home from Glengormley to various locations around the Carndonagh district, inside the Republic, was attacked from a bridge by gunmen from the UVF. Carndonagh is somewhat of an enigma, as it is located in the far north of 'Southern' Ireland and is actually further north than Northern Ireland.

The gunmen opened fire from a bridge in Co Antrim and hit the coach with at least 14 rounds, hitting six men in all and killing Henry Cunningham (17) who lived in Collon in Co Donegal. The gunmen had assumed that all on board would be Catholics, but the young man killed was in fact a Protestant.

The ever paranoid IRA had suspected that one of their supporters – Patrick Duffy (37) and a father of seven children – was 'touting' (informing) for the RUC. He had been tried and sentenced *in absentia,* and the 'nutting squad' was dispatched to abduct and execute him. On the night of the 9th, he was on a night out with his wife in Buncrana inside the Irish border, and he went for food whilst she waited in a pub. He simply disappeared and was never seen alive again. After being shot, his body was, bizarrely by IRA standards, placed inside a coffin in a car, which was dumped close to the border between the two countries. The killing for once, was condemned by the Roman Catholic Church but this had little effect on IRA support and none whatsoever on the killers themselves.

The day after it was tit-for-tat again, the UFF attacked a man, his pregnant wife and her mother as they returned from a hospital visit at the Musgrave Park Hospital. The MPH, as it is known, has a military wing and was the subject of an outrageous and appalling attack by the IRA some years later in November 1991. Two soldiers were killed by a bomb which was primed and then, unbelievably carried whilst live, through a children's ward to the soldier's rest area.

A Loyalist murder gang had abducted a taxi and as they cruised along Kennedy Way, Belfast, they spotted the three people walking in the direction of Andersonstown. Andytown, as the soldiers referred to it, is solidly Republican and the three were deemed to be Catholics and were attacked. In the eyes of sectarian killers just the possibility that their targets 'might' be of the 'wrong' faith is enough to confirm a sentence of death. Joseph Murphy Jnr (22) attempted to escape but was cut down by the Loyalist bullets and, despite his pregnant wife's courageous actions in trying to shield him with her body, was shot in the head as he lay helpless. The gunmen sped away leaving Murphy dying and his wife and mother-in-law totally distraught. There is one tragic postscript to the murder. That evening, his father Joseph Murphy Snr – believed to be in his 50s – collapsed and died of a heart attack on hearing the news of his son's brutal murder.

There were those in Northern Ireland who tried to bridge the sectarian divide and refused to be governed by sectarianism. One of those brave souls was Norman Hutchinson (17) the son of a Belfast policeman. He had chosen a Catholic girlfriend and was also known to be friends of other Catholics. In the perverted eyes of the Loyalists, this was a heinous crime and he was shot close to the Ormeau Road by a gunman from the UFF. The gunman, who was 15, was jailed for ten years for manslaughter because the Judge refused to believe that the crime was premeditated.

The IRA's bomb makers occasionally killed themselves in the early days of the Troubles due to their lack of both knowledge and professionalism, through premature detonations. These 'own goals' were largely cheered by the Security Forces, because as one former Light Infantry soldier told the author: "So long as the fuckers were killing

ATO fires an SSG shot into building in a border town where
a bomb has been placed (Brian Sheridan)

themselves, that saved us a job. Did I grieve for the bastards? Not a bit of it!" On 11 August, two members of the IRA were en-route to a Customs Post at Kilclean, close to Castlederg. The two members of the gang were Seamus Harvey (23) who had been found not guilty to a charge of IRA membership, by a tame Judge at a Dublin Court a week earlier, and Gerard McGlynn (20). The bomb exploded prematurely and the two terrorists were killed instantly. One trusts that the supine and pusillanimous Irish Judge choked on his Corn Flakes when he read of Harvey's death.

The RUC was awarded the George Cross for its courageous and meritorious conduct in the face of terrorism during the course of the Troubles. It lost over 300 officers – men and women – during the period of 1969 to 1998 as they struggled to carry out their work in the face of daily terrorism. The population of Northern Ireland is 1.5 million and on average, ten policemen a year were killed whilst the Troubles raged. In order to put this into some kind of perspective, take a country like Australia with a population of 21 million. On a strictly pro-rata basis, this would mean the equivalent of 140 of their officers being killed every year and would create a world-wide stir, not the least amongst the Australians themselves. In terms of a world-wide 'audience', the carnage in Northern Ireland was noted only by the British as they viewed the deaths on their TV screens. The exception was that it will also been noted in countless Irish-American bars in the USA though, as they wiped the Schlitz beer from their lips and reached into their hip pockets to find another donation for NORAID.

William McIlveen (36) was a member of the RUCR (RUC Reserve) and as such, a part-time policeman. He also worked at a factory in Armagh City as a security guard. It was there that the IRA targeted him and he was lured over to a parked car containing an IRA murder gang and, as he approached, they shot him dead. His brother Wilfred was a member of the UDR and he was also killed by Republicans, this time the INLA (Irish National Liberation Army), in August, 1982 by a booby trapped bomb underneath his car.

Another IRA 'own goal' occurred on the 14th when an explosion at a house in Elaine Street, close to Belfast city centre, fatally wounded two IRA bomb-makers. Francis Hall (29) and Anne-Marie Pettigrew (19) both from the Ballymurphy Estate received dreadful injuries and were taken to hospital where they died of their wounds. Hall died on August 30 and Pettigrew died two days later on September 1.

Captain Nigel Sutton (30) from the Dorset area and an officer in the Duke of Edinburgh's Royal Regiment was killed in an accident on the 14th. Other than the fact that he is buried at Tidworth Cemetery on the Tidworth Garrison, the author – sadly – has no further information.

The month wore on and, on August 15, the UVF planted a car bomb outside the Sportsman's Bar in York Street, Belfast, 800 metres north east of the Shankill Road. Edward Drummond (49) and described as a 'well known character around the markets' was unfortunate to have just left the pub as the 200 lb device exploded. He was killed instantly, and others were injured in the late night blast. The UVF chose the 'Sportsman's' because it was a well known haunt of Catholics.

The following day, another classic 'own goal' by the IRA meant its ranks were thinned by two. Patrick Quinn (16) – the IRA had a penchant for using children – and Daniel McAnallen (27) both from the Brantry Estate in Dungannon attempted to fire a mortar bomb at an RUC base. The attack at Pomeroy, Co Tyrone went disastrously wrong and the mortar exploded on the back of the lorry from which they were firing. Both man and boy were killed instantly.

Portadown in Co Armagh is approximately 16 miles south west of Belfast and is close to historic Hillsborough Castle. There is a large Orange Hall there and major disturbances broke out there during the early evening of August 17 and the RUC were called out. It is not suggested that William Holland (36) a local Protestant was involved, but the incident attracted the attention of the IRA. At around 1:00am on the 18 August Mr Holland was standing near a café on the Edgarstown Estate when a car containing members of the IRA approached. The car halted and several shots were fired hitting and fatally wounding him. He was rushed to hospital, but he died shortly after arrival.

On August 20, there was again cause to use the word 'motiveless' when a Catholic man, for no apparent reason was targeted by the mad dogs of the UFF. Charles O' Donnell (61) was sitting in his home in Grampian Avenue, close to the Newtownards Road in East Belfast when he and his wife heard the sound of breaking glass. One of the Loyalist gang had thrown a grenade-like device through a window and it is thought that Mr O'Donnell picked it up to throw it outside in order to protect his wife. The device exploded and the man who had no political or paramilitary connections was killed instantly. 'Motiveless' was gradually becoming a superfluous word.

Captain Black, the mythical spokesman for the UFF was making statements again on the 22nd after the abduction and senseless murder of Charles McDonnell (20) from Belleek, Co Down. The young man had just returned home with his fiancé after a night out and was chatting with her in the car. Masked gunmen dragged him out and then bundled him into their car and drove off at high speed, taking him a few hundred yards. They stopped and then riddled him with him 11 bullets in a frenzied shooting. It was claimed that it was in retaliation for the murder of Isaac Scott who was killed by Republicans on July 9.

Two days later, the IRA set out to kill a Tullyvallen, Newtownhamilton, UDR man but killed instead a local farmer, Rita Meeke (53), firing over 60 rounds at her car in the ambush at McGuffin's crossroads. Mrs Meeke, a widow, was unfortunate enough to be driving an identical car to that of the intended victim and the gunmen opened fire as she stopped at the crossroads. She died instantly.

The day after, another IRA 'kangaroo court' had sat in judgment of a Catholic who lived just off the Grosvenor Road, Belfast. Owen Devine (24) was accused of theft. His family made a statement just over 33 years after the 'nutting squad' had carried out their evil task. The family accused the Official IRA of the murder, stating: "He was taken to a house on McClure Street off the Ormeau Road. He was interrogated and threatened with an M1 carbine, but he stood up to this gang so they shot him dead." Mr Devine was not killed outright and the SF found him dying at the house in McClure Street and he died shortly afterwards.

The sickness which prevailed throughout the Province in these years manifested itself in many different ways and different degrees of what was essentially, the same evil. That men could take the step of ending another's life was one thing; in wartime it becomes not merely a necessary act, but becomes, depending upon ones perspective, a righteous act. However, these people took the step of prematurely ending another man's life, destroying his family emotionally and often financially, with the same amount of thought and consideration that one would give to swatting a fly. The utterly amoral men of the UVF carefully planned their next murder with precision but executed it with the same capriciousness that one would give to a spider's life; to crush or to take outside.

Sean McDonald (50) and his brother Ronald (55) ran a car repair shop close to Cliftonville Road, Belfast in the Mulhagnacall North area close to the Republican New Lodge. Shortly after they opened for business on the morning of Saturday, 25 August, armed men burst into the work area, hurling blast bombs and spraying the three men inside with automatic fire. Both brothers were killed and their young apprentice, Tony McGrady (16) also died with them. He was nothing but a child, in his first job and with his entire life ahead of him. The cowardly murder of the McDonalds left nine children fatherless. The sad thing about this entire matter is that many of the Loyalist – and Republican – murderers still walk the streets of Northern Ireland today. Some were spirited away to Australia, Canada and New Zealand and others were given new lives by Irish-Americans supporters in the United States.

The same day as the senseless slaughter at the repair shop, outside the RVH in the Falls Road and Grosvenor Road, a soldier was shot and fatally wounded by the IRA. Private Richard Miller (21) from Co Durham in England's North-East was apparently targeted by an IRA gang and as he walked along the Falls Road, he was shot from a passing car. There is speculation that he had been seconded to a specialist unit. He died of his wounds 24 days later.

On 27 August, a bomb warning was phoned through to the RUC in Armagh City, and a joint UDR/Police patrol was sent to the Culdee Estate. The warning turned out to be a hoax, following two earlier explosions and whilst a suspicious vehicle was cleared, Private Kenneth Hill (24) and other members of his unit stood guard. Several IRA gunmen, in what was clearly a 'come on' opened fire, hitting one other soldier and a policeman but fatally wounding Private Hill who lived near Loughall. He died shortly afterwards.

Staff Sergeant John Beckett (37) a bomb disposal expert in the Royal Army Ordnance Corps, had narrowly avoided death the month before in the incident where Bryan Criddle of the ADU was killed. This time he would not be so lucky. An IRA gang had crossed into Northern Ireland from Pettigo in the Republic and had placed a 20 lb bomb in the post office at Tullyhommon, before seeking out a UDR man who lived close to the village. They went to his place of work and lined up several men and identified the part-time soldier who made a dash for safety in order to grab a weapon.

The un-named soldier collected his weapon and began firing at the terrorists. The gang then fled the scene and the Army was alerted and an EOD team, which included John Beckett, arrived. He quickly realised that the device in the Post Office was due to detonate and he bravely dragged it outside in order to minimise damage but it exploded and the Hereford soldier was killed instantly.

The Royal Tank Regiment's own regimental newspaper, *The First Edition*, reported the incident as follows:

> Eight armed IRA members raided the border village of Pettigo in late August, taking hostages and lining them up outside the customs post there. They then blew up the post and a nearby garage and shot and wounded a 13-year-old boy and soon afterwards, S/Sergeant Ronald Beckett of the RAOC was killed defusing a suspect device.
>
> The armed men drove into the village from the Irish Republic and immediately seized and lined up hostages – including women and children – and asked their names and religion; at the same time, other terrorists were placing suspect devices. When one of the hostages, in giving his name, inadvertently identified himself as a member of the UDR, was threatened, he knocked the pistol in the hand of a terrorist and the shot went high. Another shot was fired as he ran away and then a 13-year-old boy was hit in the arm, and later taken to hospital.
>
> The UDR man managed to reach his house and grabbed his SMG, returned and opened fire on the IRA gunmen who fled the scene and escaped over the nearby border. Within a few seconds, the bomb detonated and the customs post was destroyed, with the people escaping injury.
>
> Very quickly, both RTR [Royal Tank Regiment] men and RUC officers were on the scene where they were informed that there was a suspect device inside the village's post office. Ronald Beckett inspected the device and then tried to detonate it with a controlled explosion; tragically, when he went back to inspect it further, it detonated and he was instantly killed.[1]

Over on the British mainland, an IRA ASU and known as the 'England Team' planted two bombs in Solihull and incendiary devices inside Harrods in Knightsbridge, London, there was no loss of life in these explosions.

---

1   The author is indebted to Keith H for kindly loaning a copy of the RTR newspaper for reprinting in this book.

Moyard Crescent, Belfast (Mike Sangster)

Moyard Parade, Belfast (Mike Sangster)

The month ended with somewhat of a coup for the Army and two known Provisional IRA members, including the most wanted man in Northern Ireland were shot on the 'Murph. The Ballymurphy Estate is located in West Belfast and rests in the foothills of the Black Mountain. The Greater Ballymurphy area is a cluster of housing estates based at the foot and lower slopes of both the Divis and Black Mountains; it is to the west of Belfast's city centre. The area is approximately one square mile in size and it consists of such housing estates as Ballymurphy, Dermott Hill, New Barnsley, Moyard, Springfield Park, Sliabh Dubh, Springhill, Westrock and Whiterock. Within this, is the Ballymurphy Estate which is the centre piece of the larger area; sometimes known as 'God's Little Acre.' Kevin Myers, a Belfast journalist, wrote of it:

> Ballymurphy was built just after the war and was a miracle of forward thinking. Intended to be a slum from its first day, it had instantly realised this heroic ambition … it imitated in meanness and misery the conditions in the horrific Victorian slums its new residents had come from.

Jim Bryson was one of several IRA men who had made an audacious, and admittedly, daring escape from a prison ship moored in Belfast Docks and was wanted for six murders of both soldiers and policemen. James Bryson (26) from the Ballymurphy Estate was shot near the Bull Ring on the 'Murph by soldiers on August 31, 1973; dying of his wounds on 22 September. He was described by a senior British officer as "an evil looking man, who joined the IRA to indulge in his homicidal tendencies" He was, nevertheless regarded as a hero to the locals. Certainly, no member of the Security Forces mourned his passing. Patrick Mulvenna (22) was shot and killed in the same incident on 31 August. Both men were seen driving around the Ballymurphy Estate and were observed to be heavily armed. Soldiers from the Royal Green Jackets in a covert OP saw the men along with two others and eventually opened fire hitting Mulvenna and Bryson. Mulvenna died close to the scene.

The actual incident was blessed with some farce, as the two soldiers were in a roof space near the Bull Ring on the estate and observed four armed men in a car behaving somewhat erratically. Bryson considered himself the 'Cock o' the 'Murph' and was often observed carrying weapons in public around the warren of streets. One of the soldiers accidentally dislodged a roof tile and as it crashed to the ground, Bryson is said to have whirled around and aimed his weapon at the roof. The two soldiers were then forced to open fire and hit three of the occupants of the car, and the men, wounded and unwounded drove off. However, the car returned and the soldiers opened fire again, this time hitting and fatally wounding Bryson. The car drove off a second time but crashed and two IRA men were able to escape.

The death of Bryson, an IRA mass-murderer, was a grave blow to the Provisionals and it was a major coup to kill both him and Mulvenna. Bryson was a friend of 'respectable' politician Gerry Adams of Sinn Féin and the bearded one described him as: "a dear friend of mine." His death from his wounds will be covered in the next chapter.

Lost in all the turmoil of this month were the deaths of two other soldiers. Sergeant Major Peter Lindsay (36) of the Duke of Wellington's Regiment was killed in circumstances unknown on the 28th. He was from Hightown, near Bradford in West Yorkshire. Corporal Andrew Hinds Gilmour (30) of the Royal Corps of Transport was

The morning after; two weary soldiers following another riot in West Belfast

killed the following day in a vehicle crash whilst on duty. He was from Kilmarnock in Scotland.

August came to an end and the death toll was 28. Of these five were soldiers, 15 were civilians and seven were members of the IRA. Interestingly enough, six of the IRA dead were killed in 'own goal' explosions. Of the civilians, the Loyalists killed 12 and the Republicans the other three.

Chapter 9

September

S eptember dawned, and with it the end of summer and the long light evenings which we British have always loved. Throughout the United Kingdom, in the months of June and July, with the longer days, children could play out later, neighbours returning from work could chat in the streets and there would be an all pervading air of safety. Everywhere that is, except in Northern Ireland.

Three more soldiers would die this month from circumstances unknown and their deaths would not be recorded in the MoD Roll of Honour; in total six soldiers' families would receive the dreaded knock at the door from an Army Casualty Visiting Officer (CVO). The IRA would bomb two London rail stations and an officer would become the first bomb disposal man to die on the British mainland during the Troubles.

A BURGLAR ON THE FALLS
Private, Light Infantry
I want to tell you an about an incident which doesn't involve shootings and bombings or riot control; God knows, I had enough of that, but this was different. It might not be 'glamorous' enough for your books, but I would like you to consider it for publication.

We were out on search duties with the RUC, and we wanted to hit some houses close to the Falls Road. We were round the back somewhere near the Beechmounts. We had gone firm behind this wall and were fairly spread out, covered by this fairly high wall and of course the night shadows. I was next to the Sergeant and we were whispering about the task in hand which involved searching the house of a player who was what the PIRA called OTR (on the run) and our INT boys had received some info that there was an Armalite hidden in one of the kiddie's bedrooms.

All of a sudden, an object came flying over the wall and landed with a crump at our feet with a tinny, rattling noise. We were all gob-smacked and then something else came flying over; the toe-rag who had thrown the object, which we saw was some sort of haversack. He stood up after the jump and then saw us and sort of pissed himself; eight men, faces all cammed-up, pointing SLRs straight at him. He started crying and he was shaking like a leaf; he was aged about 18 or 19 and before he had any notions of legging it, two of the lads grabbed him and pulled him down to the pavement. We had our gloved hands over his mouth so that he couldn't shout and one of the lads looked in the bag and there were the proceeds of a burglary which this little toe-rag had just carried out.

We couldn't be compromised but we knew how few possessions the Catholics had and we were incensed by this piece of filth's actions. For his trouble, he got my rifle butt between his legs and, let's put it this way, after his legs had had a bit of attention from us, he wouldn't be doing much boogying down the dance halls for a year or two. No more dancing to the local Showbands! He was led away, painfully, by the RUC, and we went firm again, ready for the raid. About ten minutes later, we did the raid and found nothing; just the usual smell of dirty nappies, piss and fried food. We left behind another Catholic family hating us but the consolation was that in a cell somewhere, probably Springfield Road Police Station, there was a very sore burglar!

The month started with the death through injury of IRA bomb team member, Anne-Marie Pettigrew (19), who had been badly injured in an 'own goal' detonation the previous month. The IRA were also responsible for the death of a farm worker, Patrick Duffy (19) at a farm close to Belcoo, Co Fermanagh; the victim of an IRA landmine.

One of PIRA's favourite tactics was to leave large explosive devices at roadsides in rural areas, either hidden in fields and hedges or buried in culverts beneath the roads. As an Army mobile patrol drove over or past a device, it would be triggered by a command wire – and later, as technology improved, by remote control – from a hill overlooking the spot. Generally, these attacks were on the border with the Republic, or actually inside the 'safety' of the Irish Republic. Belcoo is close to Greaghnaglera and the town itself is a mere 200 yards from the border, ill-defined as it is. Looking west from the centre of Belcoo one can see the hills of the Republic which are ideal for concealed bombers.

The IRA had done their homework, and they planted a 100lb device in a field in order to catch unawares either a foot patrol, or, more likely, a mobile patrol and ensure slaughter. They had earlier placed a suspicious looking box in the middle of the road which had been attended to by the RUC and cleared. Shortly afterwards, Patrick Duffy, quite innocently drove over the landmine and was killed instantly. The author has tried to trace whether or not the IRA made an apology for the death of a local Catholic but has been unsuccessful in doing so.

It is highly likely that the same IRA unit which caused the death of the Greaghnaglera teen a few days earlier were also responsible for the murder of a UDR soldier at Kellagho. The village is only a few miles and a few minutes away from Belcoo and tragedy re-visited the area only 48 hours after the explosion at Greaghnaglera. Matt Lilley (54) was a part-time soldier and a Private in the UDR. His full-time job was as a milkman and the IRA knew that his rounds took him to several very remote areas. They had reconnoitred his route and arrived at one of his delivery points in advance, tied up the staff there and awaited his arrival. As he arrived and started his tasks, gunmen came out of hiding and shot him dead. The murder left four children fatherless and this no doubt, was cause for extra celebration amongst the gang members and their sycophantic supporters throughout the Irish-American communities, 3,000 miles away in the eastern United States.

The 17/21 Lancers had previously lost two of their soldiers to an IRA bomb; on the 14th, they lost another but this time to a 'training accident.' The words taken in any context appear so prosaic, but the end result was anything but as both the man's comrades and his loved ones had still lost a friend and relative. Trooper Adrian Kenealy (19) was killed in what was euphemistically referred to as " … a training accident …" at Gosford Castle, Co Armagh. The author understands, however, that the young soldier was engaged on a telephone call in the Company office when he was hit by a negligent discharge (ND) fired by a comrade in the Loading/Unloading area. Back in 1973, it was the base of the Lancers; today it is abandoned, but nearby there is a tourist attraction and conference centre. The advertising blurb reads:

> … hidden, almost lost, in a forest in County Armagh, stands Gosford Castle, one of the most remarkable buildings. This is a truly exceptional opportunity to enjoy the grandeur and opulence of 1800s period living in one of the most awe-inspiring properties in Ireland.

GOSFORD PARK GHOSTS
Alex, Royal Tank Regiment

Six years ago, I returned to Gosford, now once again abandoned and asleep. Nothing has changed; the place is now boarded up, but still casts its brooding countenance over the surrounding parkland. The old car park is unchanged, and I was captivated with the place, somehow unable to drag myself away. We left as night was falling, and as we walked to the car, I heard the strange, unmistakable sound, of a Saracen APC starting up; a sound unforgettable. I turned around quickly, in surprise, expecting once again to see the Regimental 'Sarry, standing on its once familiar spot. The sound ceased; there was nothing there. Just the ghosts of my youth; or was it?

The IRA's 'England Team' struck again on Monday 10 September with two bomb attacks at train stations in London. At 12:24pm, a small bomb exploded at King's Cross Railway Station when a 3lb device was thrown without warning into the station by a youth who escaped into the crowd and though passers-by chased after him, he was not caught. Just minutes later, the Press Association received a phone call warning of a further bomb at Euston Railway Station. Less than ten minutes later, it exploded outside the Rail Bar at the station; whilst there were no deaths 12 people were injured in the blast. As stated previously there were, thankfully, no fatalities, but the IRA was demonstrating a capacity to carry the war to the mainland and many tragedies were just around the corner. That 'corner' was only a mere 13 days away and 100 miles further north.

Thomas 'Tommy' Herron was a founder member of the Ulster Defence Association (UDA) and undoubtedly pulled the strings of its 'military wing, the UFF (Ulster Freedom Fighters). There are many that will deny that he had any influence over the actions and activities of these Loyalist murder gangs, but an equal number will cite him as its guiding light. Tommy Herron, then vice-chairman of the UDA, was found shot dead at Drumbo, near Lisburn. Various claims were later made about who was responsible for his killing, with some people suggesting that he may have been killed by elements within the UDA because of his alleged involvement in racketeering. Others suggested that a branch of British Army intelligence may have been involved. Whoever killed him and whatever the motive, his body was found with a single bullet wound to the head. There is some speculation that he had finally recognised the futility of the sectarian killings and was engaged in a dialogue with the Official IRA for either a ceasefire or for loose alliance. If this indeed was the case, both the Provisional IRA and their hated enemies in the UFF would have been almost literally 'queuing up' to kill him. No paramilitary organisation ever claimed responsibility. It is not beyond probability that the earlier killing of his brother-in-law Michael Wilson was an earlier disguised, albeit bungled attempt at a dress rehearsal for Herron's eventual demise.

Edgbaston is a suburb of England's Second City, Birmingham and is to the south-west of the city centre. It is also the home of Warwickshire County Cricket Club and the site of the Test Match ground where England have enjoyed and sometimes, not enjoyed cricket clashes with the 'old enemy' Australia over the years. The rationale behind the IRA's choice of venue for the next bombing attack by their 'England Team' is however, lost on this author.

On the 17th, a GPO employee who was delivering mail to an office block in Highfield Road, Birmingham, close to the very busy A456 Hagley Road, noticed a suspicious looking object and immediately dialled 999 and alerted the police. Given the heightened tension of the IRA bombing campaign, the Army bomb disposal squad were called. A unit attended which included Captain Ronald Wilkinson (30) of the Royal Army Ordnance Corps. The Hereford-born soldier approached the device. As he reached it, it exploded and he received the full blast and was dreadfully injured. Captain Wilkinson died of those injuries in hospital on the 23rd of the month.

On that same September day, Sapper Malcolm Orton (24), from Walsall, was killed in Northern Ireland. His cause of death is unknown. Lance Corporal Richard Miller (21) had been shot and fatally wounded by the IRA on 25 August; on 18 September the Light Infantry soldier succumbed to those wounds.

John Hume MP described it as "Another callous murder in the name of Ireland", he went on to describe the murder of James Brown (26) who was executed by an IRA 'nutting squad' on 21 September. Brown lived in Londonderry and the local Provisionals suspected him of being a 'tout' and he was *tried, found guilty and executed.*[1] An Army patrol found his hooded and beaten body on Foyle Road in the city, close to the river and directly opposite the Republican Gobnascale Estate. Being an informer and being caught, was an automatic death sentence for an IRA member, a sympathiser, or just being an ordinary civilian in the eyes of the Provisionals. Being only an 'alleged' informer was enough also to warrant the bullet in the back of the head.

A day later James Bryson (26), who had been wounded in a shoot out with the Army on the Ballymurphy Estate, died in hospital. It is thought that he was responsible for the murders of at least six soldiers and policemen over the previous few years and his death was a huge blow to the Provisional IRA. On the last day of August, Bryson and Patrick Mulvenna and two other IRA gunmen had been doing the rounds on the Ballymurphy Estate, armed and posing for the community. Close to the Bull Ring, where the Ballymurphy and Glenalina Roads meet, two undercover soldiers, concealed in a roof space were on observation duties. These types of operations involved the covert insertion of two or more men, usually into derelict houses, at the dead of night or under the cover of a riot. Armed with not only their SLRs and Browning handguns, there would be rations for several days and the ubiquitous 'piss bucket' for their personal 'comfort'.

Bryson, Mulvenna and two unnamed IRA men, unsuspectingly, stopped outside the house where the covert OP was taking place. One of the soldiers – thought to be Royal Green Jackets or Paras, moved a roof tile for a better look and it dislodged and crashed to

---

1   Author's own italics.

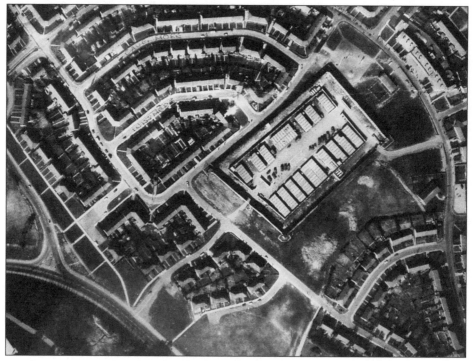

The Ballymurphy Estate, Belfast.

the street below. Under threat of their lives, they fired at the men, hitting Mulvenna and possibly wounding another. The hijacked car took off, but returned almost immediately and a brief firefight saw Bryson badly wounded and the car left a second and final time, crashing nearby. Two of the men, one of whom was possibly wounded, ran off, leaving Mulvenna dead and Bryson critically injured. A little over three weeks later, he died also.

The Provisional IRA in their roll of honour death notices eulogised Bryson as follows:

> Shortly after internment was introduced, Jim joined the ranks of Oglaigh na hEireann. He was arrested on 29 December 1971 and interned on the 'Maidstone' but with six comrades he escaped to freedom only 19 days later, on 17 January 1972. Living a life on the run, yet constantly engaging in actions against the British, Jim remained free until September 1972, when he was arrested, charged with possession of a handgun and remanded to Long Kesh. However, within six months of his capture he had devised an escape plan. On 20 February 1973, whilst he and a fellow POW were being taken along the tunnel which links Crumlin Road Jail with the courthouse, they overpowered their prison warders and stripped them of their uniforms. The plan was to coolly walk through the court building and escape by commandeering a car on the Crumlin Road. Only Jim was successful. Once out of the building he disposed of the borrowed uniform and headed for the Shankill Road, where he stopped a car and asked for a lift to the Royal Victoria Hospital saying his wife had been taken there. The occupants of the car obliged, dropping him off at Divis Street, from where he walked to a safe house. After the news of his

second escape hit the headlines, it was revealed that the two occupants of the car had been armed UDR men.

Free again, Jim was soon active as an IRA volunteer. Jim and three comrades were travelling in a car in their native Ballymurphy on 31 August when British soldiers in a secret observation post opened fire on them. Vol. Paddy Mulvenna died instantly and Jim and another Volunteer were badly wounded. Jim died of his wounds on 22 September 1973.

Although the Official IRA had remained largely dormant since their ceasefire of the previous year there was still much going on under the surface. The waters of Irish Republicanism run deep and are rarely calm, as was further illustrated by their killing of a former member on the 25th. James Larkin (34) had been a member of the Official but had fallen out with the leadership and had been 'expelled' from the country. He moved to England for his own safety but he returned, it is thought, at the behest of his family and, having been sentenced to death, foolishly returned to Newry. Newry in Co Armagh is a predominantly Catholic and Republican town and he visited the Derrybeg Estate which is rabidly pro-IRA. He was abducted on the Derrybeg on the evening of the 24th and was beaten and then shot in the head and his body was dumped close to the border with the Republic.

The Loyalist murder gangs had been quiet by their own murderous standards this month, but that changed on the very last day, a Sunday. Tragically for Eileen Doherty, a 20-year-old Catholic from the Republican Andersonstown, the Taxi office into which she walked on that Sunday night contained two UVF gunmen. She had reached the Ormeau Road after a night out visiting friends and the two men overheard her asking for a taxi to a Catholic area. They offered to share the fare with Miss Doherty and she willingly agreed; there may have been the constant threat of sectarian murder, but in Belfast, especially amongst the poorer Catholics, every penny counted. The taxi had only travelled less than a mile when one of the two men pulled out a pistol and instructed the driver to stop. The taxi driver bravely grabbed the girl and they ran off on foot, but the Loyalist drove after them and caught and shot Miss Doherty dead before fleeing in the vehicle. The young woman had been killed merely because she was a Catholic woman and had been heading in the direction of a Catholic area; sickeningly, she had signed her own 'death warrant' by agreeing to share the taxi ride home.

During this month, the Royal Anglians who were based on the Creggan in Londonderry lost one of their comrades and to date, the author has not been able to ascertain an official explanation. Private N. Marwick died on 12 September and although his cause of death is unknown, I received the following from a member of his Regiment.

Soldier, Royal Anglian Regiment

I was in two Royal Anglian on that tour; based at Bligh's Lane and Private Marwick was in Creggan Camp. It is not known what happened but it was rumoured that it could have been an accidental discharge, but only a few people really know. Down in Bligh's Lane we had a parcel bomb go off in our Ops Room and to this day it is not known how the IRA got it into the camp, never mind the Ops Room.

September came to an end and the death toll was 13; of these six were soldiers, four were civilians, two were members of the IRA and the Loyalists lost one as a result of an internal feud. Of the civilians, the Loyalists killed one and the Republicans the other three.

Chapter 10

October

Summer had gone. Northern Ireland entered the autumn season, ready for colder days and shorter evenings. Unfortunately the commensurate increase in the hours of darkness gave the sectarian killers much more scope and time in order to carry out their murderous deeds.

The IRA, ever fond of the soft target, had clearly marked for death any former member of the UDR, no matter how long ago he had resigned membership. On the morning of Wednesday, 3 October, one-time soldier, Ivan Vennard (33) was collecting mail in the rabidly Republican Kilwilkee Estate in Lurgan, Co Armagh. A postman, he had left the UDR some nine months earlier, but had been targeted by the IRA for murder. He was shot in the head several times and died more or less instantly from the terrible wounds. An IRA spokesman claimed that he had been 'executed' for being connected with the TA, Britain's part-time soldiers.

Later that same day an incredible lapse in security at an Army base in Londonderry led to the death of one officer and the maiming and blinding of another. A letter or parcel was delivered by hand to the sentry at Bligh's Lane, where the Royal Anglian Regiment was in occupation. It is not for this author to apportion blame, but this was close to the Republican Creggan and Bogside Estates, both of which were rabidly anti-Army and fanatical breeding grounds for the Provisional IRA. The troubles had been raging for over four years and over 250 soldiers had been killed in this period. To accept anything, delivered by hand, with no vetting, no searching and no sort of quarantine is simply incredulous. There is no doubt that, in addition to the dispatching of a CVO after the explosion, urgent questions were raised at HQNI in Lisburn.

The parcel was being handled by Captain Ray Hazan when it exploded, killing Second Lieutenant Lindsay Hamilton-Dobbie (23) instantly. Captain Ray Hazan was also badly injured. He was totally blinded, suffered severe hearing loss and lost his right hand. He recently retired after working for 34 years as a member of staff of St Dunstan's, the national charity caring for blind ex-Servicemen and women, he was elected their President in 2004. The dead officer was in the RAOC and was on attachment to the Royal Anglians. Another soldier, Corporal Tom Wesley, the duty signaller, had a lucky escape as he only just left the room in order make a cup of coffee. The thin gossamer thread of fate had spared one soldier and killed another.

Captain Ray Hazan wrote the following words:

My first tour of duty in Ballymurphy, Belfast commenced six weeks after I got married in September 1970. I found the situation unreal, patrolling a suburban estate, no different from the mainland, but with a loaded rifle, or Christmas shopping in Marks & Spencer with a pistol on my belt. The second tour in Londonderry in 1973 was even harder; I had left a pregnant wife behind and, if anything, the situation in Northern Ireland had worsened. One questioned the purpose and efficacy of our presence there. Sadly, I was never to see my son; losing my sight five months before his birth.

On Friday 5 October, William Whitelaw, the then Secretary of State for Northern Ireland, chaired a series of talks at Stormont Castle, Belfast, on the question of forming an Executive to govern Northern Ireland. The talks involved representatives of, the Ulster Unionist Party (UUP), the APNI, and the SDLP. The parties disagreed on issues related to internment, policing, and a Council of Ireland, but did manage to make progress on other less controversial areas in the social and economic spheres. That is, if anything during this period of turmoil, could be considered 'less controversial.'

Rather as the Loyalist murder gangs both assumed and demanded that their supporters hated Catholics, so the Provisional IRA required the same feeling amongst their 'community.' However much the IRA protested that they were not sectarian, they were certainly not averse to killing Protestants in the deadly game of tit-for-tat murders. There were still decent people in the Province whose emotions and behaviour transcended the sectarian boundaries; one such person was Raymond McAdam (20) and it tragically cost him his life.

On 12 October, the IRA targeted a Protestant-owned shop in Glebe, Newtownbutler, Co Fermanagh. A stolen car drove up the shop frontage and a man hurled a bomb at the entrance. Mr McAdam, who was Catholic, went to attempt to warn the Protestant owner – a 68-year-old woman – when the blast detonated. He was killed instantly, and the owner received severe injuries. The Provisionals tried to absolve themselves of responsibility but given the other attacks by the IRA in the town that day, culpability almost certainly rests with them.

Four days later there was no question of who was responsible when a young RUC Reservist was killed whilst patrolling with another officer on the Antrim Road in Belfast. William Campbell (27), a part-time Policeman, was checking the outside of business premises when gunmen fired three shots at him, despite the closeness of a young girl who was walking past at the time. RUCR Campbell was fatally wounded and died in hospital; the young girl was hit in the leg and was taken to the same hospital. *Lost Lives* comments that neither of the officers was wearing body armour.[1]

It was the turn of the UFF next to make a cowardly attack; this time on a Catholic-owned bar on the Newtownards Road in East Belfast. Wilson's was frequented by Catholic drinkers, in the main from the Republican enclave of the Short Strand which was a little over a mile away. A Loyalist gang left a device in the doorway of the bar and then escaped by car, leaving bar staff in a quandary; move the device or evacuate? They had cleared most of the drinkers from the bar when it detonated and an innocent passer-by was buried in the rubble. Ronald Fletcher (46) and ironically a Protestant, died at the scene. Shortly afterwards, another Catholic-owned pub very close by – the Ballyhackmore Arms – was also attacked, but an Army EOD unit safely defused the bomb.

One common theme amongst the many contributors to my books on the Troubles, are complaints from soldiers of a lack of recognition. It wasn't for individual acknowledgement and it wasn't for personal glory; it was merely for someone on the

---

1   McKitterick, David et al, *op cit.,* pp. 395-396.

ATO team prepare for 'the longest walk' in Newtownhamilton (Brian Sheridan)

mainland – Government, media or civil populace – to even recognise the dangers and pressures under which soldiers were operating in Northern Ireland. One such soldier articulates below the frustration felt by many.

DID ANYONE KNOW OR CARE?
Mike Sangster, Royal Artillery

The Army's PR department has to shoulder a lot of the blame for giving the public the false perception that NI in the early 70's was all tea, cakes and discos. The only official access that the media were given was reporting rights on community projects, soldiers at rest and soldiers posing with some piece of 'crumpet' who'd won some obscure beauty contest. I know from personal experience that the lads on the ground were banned from speaking to the media unless it was a staged event which would be heavily censored before being allowed in print. A new job was created for Ruperts called the PRO (Public Relations Officer) which was usually given to some oxygen thief who was useless at anything else. Any real interviews which related to loss of life or some major atrocity were given by either the Commanding Officer (CO) or the 2IC.

There were countless acts of gallantry performed during that time, which nowadays, would have resulted in some form of official recognition coupled with good media coverage, but they were usually rewarded by a pat on the back and 'I owe you a pint for that mate.' The award of the GSM only came into being May/June 1971 and I can only recall one gallantry award, – the military medal – being awarded prior then and that was kept quiet. The posthumous George Cross (GC) awarded to Sergeant Willets of the Parachute Regiments for his selfless

1st Bn Light Infantry: Crossmaglen Square, no time to hang about (Brian Sheridan)

actions at Springfield Road RUC station was the first time, in my memory, that an act of bravery was given widespread media coverage.[2]

A typical action which went unrewarded was that of a Sergeant of my regiment. In January 1971, his unit was based at Bessbrook when a telephone warning came in of a bomb having been planted at the Fathom Mountain UTV mast. He was dispatched with a mobile patrol to investigate. When they got there, they found what was the then largest bomb planted in the Province; 48 lbs. of gelignite with an alarm clock initiator. The nearest ATO was ages away, so he decided to deal with it himself. He disconnected the battery and as he disconnected the alarm clock it went 'Brrrrrrr.' He escaped death by seconds. When the ATO arrived, he got a right old bollocking. Although HQNI gave the story to the media, I think it was only the *Daily Express* which gave it a few lines on one of its inside pages. He was given no official recognition for his actions that night. As far as he was concerned, he was fulfilling part of his remit which was to defend civilian property. Even today, very few soldiers, let alone civilians know of

---

2   Michael Willetts, GC, was killed on 25 May, 1971 and was awarded a posthumous George Cross for his heroism in saving lives during the IRA bombing which claimed his life. The Harvey Andrews song 'Soldier' commemorates Willetts' sacrifice. Willetts was killed in Springfield Road RUC station as a result of a bomb attack by the Provisional IRA. A man in his mid-twenties emerged from a car and threw a suitcase containing a blast bomb into the lobby of the station. Willetts thrust two civilians into a corner and stood above them as the 30 lbs of explosives detonated, fatally injuring him. Seven RUC officers, two soldiers and 18 civilians were injured in the attack. Willetts was fatally injured by a chunk of metal from a locker which had struck him in the back of the head. As he was being removed by ambulance, he and the injured officers were jeered by local youths who screamed obscenities at them. Willetts died two hours later as medical staff tried to save him at the nearby Royal Victoria Hospital.

this incident, and years later, I have only seen it mentioned in print once which was in the book 'The British Army in Northern Ireland' written in 1985 by Mike Dewar.

The Gaelic Athletic Association (GAA) is an amateur Irish and international cultural and sporting organisation focused primarily on promoting Gaelic games, which include the traditional Irish sports of hurling, Gaelic football, handball and rounders. The GAA also promotes Irish music and dance, and the Irish language. Francis McGaughey (35) was a farmer in Glassdrummond, Co Tyrone and as such, innocent. Innocent that is to any sane, decent human being other than the Loyalist murder gangs. As a prominent member of the GAA and a Catholic to boot, he was guilty of promoting Irish culture in Northern Ireland; accordingly, he was marked for death.

Early on the morning of 28 October, he was working in one of his cow sheds, when an explosive device detonated, leaving him terribly wounded. He died of those injuries 11 days later. The UFF claimed responsibility for the device, piously declaring that it was in revenge for the earlier killing of UDR man, Frank Caddoo. Whilst it is generally accepted that the Loyalists murdered Mr McCaughey because of his membership of GAA and his active promotion of Irish culture, another factor comes into play. The device might have been designed to kill and maim soldiers on rural patrol and may have been planted by the IRA. However, given the location of the device, in the cowshed/dairy and given that the farmer would enter there, at least once a day, it is more likely that he and not soldiers, was the target.

Crossmaglen (or 'XMG' as it was known to three generations of British soldiers) has often been described as an Irish Republican town inside of Northern Ireland. It was once considered the most dangerous place in the world to be a British soldier and even today, an English accent is most unwelcome; in short, it is a place to be avoided. It nestles – surely an oxymoron when considering the decades of hatred which fuels the soul of the village – in an area a little over half a mile from the border with the Irish Republic. It is a short trip down the A29 New Road in the most picturesque countryside. Caveat emptor for the scenic views masks the loathing and detestation for anything British on which this place thrives. On 28 October, the IRA engaged the Army in a firefight in order to try and prevent repairs to the Army base there. Patrols from the Light Infantry were mounting a constant guard on a detachment of Royal Engineers who were engaged in the repairing the aftermath of a recent IRA bomb attack.

Bristol boy, Private Stephen Hall (27) was hit by a burst of automatic fire and fell, mortally wounded in the village square. He died within seconds and it is thought that the soldiers hit and wounded one of the IRA gunmen. No traces were found, and with a dozen or more medical sympathisers just a few miles away in places such as Farrandreg or more likely in Dundalk, treatment was at hand. The treatment would be discreet and, even if the Garda Siochana were aware, nothing would filter back to the British authorities.

Private Hall was one of three people to die that day, in three separate locations in the Province, as October which had been relatively quiet by Northern Ireland standards ended with violence.

John Doherty (31) was a member of the RUC's CID branch and as such, had been directly involved in investigations into and prosecutions of the Provisional IRA. He had been marked for murder and gunmen had staked out his parents' house in Lifford, Co

Donegal inside the Irish Republic, north-west of Strabane. He was based in Omagh and made the 15 mile trip to the border as a matter of routine. On this occasion, gunmen from the IRA were waiting and shot him as he drove his car close to the family home; he died at the scene. *Lost Lives* note that he was the first RUC officer to be killed inside the Irish Republic.[3] It is open to speculation whether or not he was killed for religion (he was a Catholic in a predominantly Protestant force) or as a result of the ease of attack as he had no back-up.

The killings on that day – a Sunday – ended in the late evening when a Loyalist murder gang killed a Catholic man at his home in Banbridge, Co Down. They calmly knocked at the front door of Patrick Campbell (34) and a father of three and politely enquired of his wife if he was home. When he came to join her, they shot him down in cold blood and left him dying in his own hallway. The killings were claimed by both the UVF and the UFF, though it is more likely it was the former. One of the men who was rumoured to have killed Mr Campbell was Wesley Somerville, a known member of the UVF. Somerville was himself killed by his own bomb on 31 July 1975 along with another accomplice when they stopped a bus containing members of the popular Irish musicians, the Miami Showband. Several of the band's members were killed by the UVF as they masqueraded as UDR men at a fake VCP. This will be dealt with in more detail in a later volume by this author.[4]

The following day the IRA used a hijacked helicopter to free three of their members from the exercise yard of Mountjoy Prison, Dublin, in the Republic. One of those who escaped was Séamus Twomey, then Chief of Staff of the Provisional IRA. Twomey remained at liberty until he was recaptured in December 1977. The Mountjoy Prison helicopter escape took place on the last day of October, when three PIRA members escaped from Mountjoy Prison in Dublin. Several men on board a hijacked helicopter landed in the prison's exercise yard and, having distracted the guards, the prisoners dashed to the helicopter which lifted off. The escape made headlines around the world and was an embarrassment to the Irish coalition government of the time, led by Fine Gael's Liam Cosgrave. A manhunt involving over 20,000 thousand members of the Irish Army and *Garda Síochána* (Irish Police) was launched for the escapees. A popular song celebrating the escape called 'The Helicopter Song,' topped the Irish popular music charts despite being banned by the Cosgrave Government.

At this time, the Republic of Ireland in what was seen as a 'too little, too late' gesture was attempting to curb IRA activity. Both contemporary observers and historical writers felt that this was a hollow, platitudinous action, designed to show that they could get tough. There are, however, too many examples of border chicanery, with both Irish Army and Police, turning a blind eye to IRA activity. The Dublin Courts also, like their Supreme Court counterparts in the USA, did little to help bring known and convicted

---

3   *Ibid* p. 397.

4   This was a bombing and shooting attack in Northern Ireland on 31 July 1975, against five members of the Miami Showband – one of Ireland's most popular cabaret bands – who were travelling home to Dublin by minibus. They were stopped at a bogus military checkpoint on the A1 road, at Buskhill, Co Down, seven miles north of Newry. UVF gunmen dressed in British Army uniforms ordered them out of the minibus and to line-up by the roadside. Although some of the gunmen were members of the UDR, all were members of the UVF. Whilst two of the gunmen were placing a time bomb on the minibus, it exploded prematurely and killed them both. The remaining gunmen then sprayed the band members with automatic weapons, killing three and wounding two.

terrorists to justice. Fine Gael had come to power on a law and order ticket, and several 'suspected' IRA members were arrested and accused of IRA membership. This was a crime under the Offences against the State Act. They were tried at the juryless Special Criminal Court in Dublin, where the traditional IRA policy of not recognising the court resulted in a *fait accompli* as no defence was offered and IRA membership carried a minimum mandatory one-year sentence.

In September, 1973 the IRA Chief of Staff, Seamus Twomey, appeared at the Special Criminal Court charged with IRA membership, and shouted "I refuse to recognise this British-orientated Quisling court." He was found guilty and received a five-year sentence, joining some very senior PIRA men such as JB O'Hagan and Kevin Mallon in Mountjoy Prison.

The IRA's GHQ staff approved a plan to break out Twomey, O'Hagan and Mallon, and arrangements were made to obtain a helicopter. A man with an American accent calling himself 'Leonard' approached the manager of Irish Helicopters at Dublin Airport; with a view to hiring a helicopter for an aerial photographic shoot in Co Laois. 'Leonard' arranged to hire a five-seater Alouette II for October 31. On the day of the escape, he met Captain Thompson Boyes and instructed him to fly to a field in Stradbally, where after landing two armed, masked men approached the helicopter. The pilot was held at gunpoint and told he would not be harmed if he followed instructions. One of the heavily armed gunmen climbed aboard the helicopter and it took off towards Dublin. As the helicopter approached Dublin, Boyes was informed of the escape plan and instructed to land in the exercise yard at Mountjoy Prison.

In the prison's exercise yard, the prisoners were watching a football match. Shortly after 3:35pm the helicopter swung in to land, with Kevin Mallon directing the pilot using semaphore. A prison officer on duty initially took no action as he believed the helicopter contained a VIP visitor. Prearranged fights then broke out as the officers realised an escape attempt was in progress. As other prisoners restrained the officers, Twomey, Mallon and O'Hagan boarded the helicopter. In the confusion, as the helicopter took off, one officer shouted: "Close the gates; close the fucking gates". The helicopter flew north and landed at a disused racecourse in the Baldoyle area of Dublin, where the escapees were met by members of the IRA's Dublin Brigade. The escapees were transferred to a taxi that had been hijacked earlier, and transported to safe houses.

During the course of the month, in a four day period, three UDR soldiers were killed or died in unknown or uncertain circumstances. The cause of their deaths of course meant little to their grieving families, only that they had lost their loved ones. The soldiers were: Private Thomas Forsythe (41) from Aghalee, Co Antrim whom it is thought was shot accidentally. Private Colin McKeown (18) died in a tragic RTA and there are no public explanations for the death of Private William Magill who was 22. As always, this author invites any reader who has information about any unexplained deaths to contact him at the email address to be found at the end of this book's Roll of Honour.

The death toll for October was 11, marginally down on the previous month. Of these, six were soldiers, three civilians, and two policemen. Of the civilians, the Loyalists killed two and the Republicans the other one. The number of sectarian killings had fallen, and during the early part of the following month, the UVF declared, what would turn out to be a 43-day ceasefire.

Chapter 11

November

Twelve soldiers lost their lives in this month, three of whom under circumstances which the MoD termed as "death by violent or unnatural causes". My own understanding, based on my personal experiences and from speaking with other soldiers who were there, leads me to three possible explanations. The first is the tragedy of suicide; the second is being accidentally killed by another soldier in an unintentional firing incident, or 'candy-coated' as a negligent discharge. The third is somewhat more unpalatable; that of one soldier practicing upon another, the pastime which Cain made popular in Biblical times when he slew Abel; murder. There is absolutely no inference as to the cause in the following three deaths and it is not within this author's remit to attribute causes.

On 2 November, Lance Corporal Roy Grant (29) of the Royal Anglians died in the Londonderry area, and his passing can only be described as death by violent or unnatural causes. He was killed in an accidental shooting in his barracks at Londonderry. He was one of 12 siblings, and had been serving in the Army for ten years at the time of his death. He is buried at Saffron Hill Cemetery in Leicester and irrespective of in what means this soldier died, a CVO still had to deliver the tragic news to his grieving family.

48 hours later, Private Thomas Nelson Beatty (31) of the UDR also died; the cause of his death is officially listed as 'unknown.' But what does that mean? Was it a violent death; did he die in a training accident; was it from a negligent discharge or was it a 'natural' death albeit at the young age of 31?

Twenty two days later, Rifleman Nicolas Alejandro Allen (22) of the Royal Green Jackets – almost certainly of Greek extraction – died in mysterious circumstances; I am reliably informed that he died as a result of a negligent discharge and that he is laid to rest at the Aldershot Military Cemetery. Furthermore, I have been informed that his family were living in the London area. This author would like to pay a more fitting tribute to these three soldiers and in the fullness of time one can only trust that this will be possible.

We must backtrack to the beginning of November and to the first day of the month and to the Loyalist heartland of the Shankill Road. The Shankill is derived from the Irish word *Seanchill,* which literally means 'old church.' It is a main arterial road and leads through a predominantly Loyalist, working-class area of Belfast; known simply as the Shankill. The road stretches westwards for approximately 1.5 miles from central Belfast and is lined, to some extent, by shops. The residents live in the many streets which branch off the main road; the area is marked with graffiti which screams out: "No Surrender!" The territory is marked by a profusion of Union Jacks. As such, it is an area which is 'verboten' to Catholics and it is unwise to be in the area if one is of the 'Roman' persuasion. 'Fuck the Pope' was an alarming and disturbing piece of graffiti which this author recalls as a young soldier on the Shankill.

Dave Smart (Parachute Regiment) on sangar duty, Shankill area

Daniel Carson (29) was, by all accounts, a decent Catholic with no paramilitary ties who chose to work at a Hardware Wholesalers in the land of 'No Surrender.' He paid for his temerity with his life, having been marked down for murder by the UVF. On the afternoon of the first, he was driving home and had turned off, near St Peter's Hill when a gunman fired three shots from the pavement into his car, mortally wounding the father of one whose pregnant wife was left a young, grieving widow. He was rushed to the nearby RVH where he died shortly after arrival.

On the evening of the same day, the UVF continued their deadly trade and left a stolen car, packed with explosives outside the Revue Bar in Union Street, Belfast. Hours earlier, Daniel Carson had been shot after his car had turned off the Shankill Road, down Boundary Street and had entered Greenland Street. The Revue Bar was a mere 500 yards away from the scene of his shooting and it is entirely possible that the same UVF unit was responsible. Clearly, some paramilitaries were sociopaths with psychopathic tendencies but there must have been some who had not killed before and were reluctant to do so. However, once a terrorist had pulled the trigger of a handgun whilst pointing directly at another human being's head and taken a life, then the boundary of decency had been crossed. The late Eamon Collins describes in his autobiography of an IRA man, *Killing Rage,* how a hitherto inoffensive man turned into a psychopathic killer. After a while, it seems, it becomes second nature, even pleasurable and killing becomes addictive.

That was what possibly motivated the gang who planted a car bomb in the aforementioned bar which exploded and killed an innocent passer-by, Francis McNelis (65), who simply was in the wrong place at the wrong time. Mr McNelis was killed instantly and for good measure, in the sick, perverted logic of the Loyalist murder culture, he was also a Catholic.

Earlier that day, Jamie Flanagan replaced Graham Shillington as the Chief Constable of the Royal Ulster Constabulary. Flanagan was the first Catholic to hold this post. On the morning of the 2nd, one can only speculate if Flanagan sat in an office in Castlereagh and looked at the files on his desk which would have contained details of the two murders of the previous day. Those two files might well have only contained a page or two, but it is certain that both were several inches thick within a short space of time. As he did so, the enormity of his task, if he wasn't already aware, must have loomed very large.

Newtownhamilton, Co Armagh is located in beautiful countryside, a mere two miles, as the crow flies, from the border with the Irish Republic. Like Crossmaglen to the south, it is a Republican town inside the United Kingdom; as such it was a dangerous place for members of the SF. There are many roads which lead into Ireland from the town, some of which are mere dirt tracks and other unclassified roads along which both arms and explosives could be smuggled into the North. Accordingly, Newtownhamilton (or NTH in Army speak) was an important place to both the Army and to the IRA. It was regularly patrolled and there was a permanent military presence in the area.

On 6 November, a unit of the Royal Corps of Signals ('scaleybacks') used in the foot soldier role was guarding the courthouse in the town. Unknown to the Army, an IRA unit had taken over a nearby pub, holding the staff hostage and had set up a firing point overlooking the Town Square. Corporal John Aikman (25) from Midlothian, Scotland, was hit by a burst of automatic fire. He died at the scene, and the gunmen escaped from the building which was being refurbished after an earlier bomb attack and scuttled back across the border; presumably to a 'nod and a wink' to any patrolling *Gardai Siochana*.

Robert McCaffrey was an 18-year-old apprentice and worked for Mackies' Engineering in Belfast. In 1973, James Mackie & Sons was a textiles' machinery engineering plant, and one of the largest foundries in Northern Ireland. The company closed in 1999. Latterly called Mackie International, at its height James Mackie & Sons was one of the largest employers in Belfast. Mackie's, as they were known locally, were a major supplier of munitions during the Second World War. Unlike many other Protestant-owned businesses at that time, Mackies employed Catholics but many of their Catholic workers were subject to some terrible sectarian intimidation from Protestant co-workers. Young McCaffrey had not been there long and had been at a training depot close to the Springfield Road on the day of his death. As he walked down Springfield Road with a group of workmates, they were approached by an armed gang from the UFF who opened fire, hitting the young Lenadoon boy. As he lay wounded, he was shot again at close range and died at the scene.

In 1979, his murderer faced court, apparently unrepentant, and received a Life sentence. Amongst the comments he made, was the admission that it had been done " ... for a bit of a laugh." Within those few words lay the reasons behind why quiet, unassuming people can be transformed into cold, passionless killers.

FIRST TIME ON THE BOGSIDE
Alan, Mac, Royal Artillery

I had only just turned 18 in the October before we were deployed to Londonderry in the November of 1973. Being from the province I had to get special clearance to serve there. We landed at Aldergrove and piled into the Bedfords waiting for us and set off for our TAOR in Derry. We arrived at Hawkins Street in the wee, small hours. It was a matter of getting gear stored, weapons and guard duties sorted and the fortunate few catching a few 'Z's. There was no time to think about where we were but we had been trained well, trusted each other and were ready to go.

The first few days were fairly run of the mill; getting to know the areas, because as Reserve Troop, we had to know our Regimental TAOR plus our neighbouring Regiment's area. The DWR (Duke of Wellington's Regiment) had responsibility for the Brandywell area, which was a hardline Republican area. Saturday was 'bomb patrols' in 57 Battery's area of the Strand Road, but more of this later. Sunday was 'Bogside day' and it would be hard to say how we felt when we left the comparative safety of Hawkins Street. Excitement certainly; not so much fear as apprehension; I mean, this was the world famous Bogside and we were about to go into for the first time. For most of us, even some of the senior NCO's it was our first Op Banner tour.

We duly arrived at the Knicker factory on Bligh's Lane; got our gear stashed away and, like true squaddies went to find the cookhouse. Then our time came and we had our first briefing. I don't remember much about it; basically we were to patrol from one side to the other, look for bad guys and get picked up again; simple really. Leaving the Knicker factory was an experience in itself! You didn't just drive out; oh no. Because of the threat of RPG-7 attack, the gates would be flung open and two PIGs would roar out, followed by about 12 crazed squaddies trying not to fall over each other' They would then scramble into the back of said PIGs and away we would go, hoping we hadn't left anybody behind. After driving round just to check out the area and what 'faces' were about – highly trained soldiers squealing like schoolgirls if we recognised one – we got dropped off and began our task.

I have absolutely no idea what we were supposed to do as the next thing I remember was 'going firm' and the PIG being radioed to come and get us. We were driving along when the Op's room came on the air, politely requesting to know what we doing on our way back. Well I wasn't the radio op so I assume that it was polite. Anyway some surprise was expressed that a patrol that should have taken at least an hour had been done in seven and a half minutes. We had gone out so fast that the 'Bog Rats' at 'aggro corner' didn't even have time to pick up a brick or stone, never mind throw it. They got even more annoyed when, naturally, we were sent back to do the patrol properly and, they were on their way home when we passed them! Not one of them had a brick or stone handy.

Who says Gunners can't move? That was our introduction to the infamous Bogside. Nothing to worry us here; we were young and invincible. That attitude was to change soon.

FIREFIGHT ON THE BOGSIDE
Mike Sangster, Royal Artillery

We had been deployed to Londonderry on the 14 November 1973. By coincidence, it was Prince Charles' birthday and also the day that Princess Anne married Captain Mark Philips. As we were in the reception area of Aldergrove airport waiting for our kit, we watched it on TV. My troop acted as Regimental reserve so we had to familiarise ourselves with the whole TAOR (Tactical Area of Responsibility) of Strand, City, Brandywell and Bogside. Our base was in Hawkin Street in the Loyalist Fountain area. As we were basically on permanent standby, base duties, such as guard etc were carried out by rear echelon lads. Suited us, as I am sure it did them as it was a cushy number in a fairly safe area.

Sunday, and it was the turn of the Bogside to get the privilege of our presence so we hopped aboard our PIGs and made our way to the Saracen factory in Bligh's lane. This base was located slap bang between the Bogside and the Creggan and used to be a textile factory which made underwear. Needless to say, it inherited the name the 'Knicker Factory.' Right next door was the 'Essex' factory which was occupied by a company of infantry who worked the Creggan. Quite often the front of both bases came under attack from RPG and small arms fire. When we got there, the local tour guides pointed out the various bullet strikes on the walls which were a reminder not to hang about too long in full view of the locals.

After a fairly thorough briefing in the ready room, we set off on our first foot patrol. It was far too dodgy to exit from the base on foot, so the way it was done was that the patrols were dropped off by PIGs. At that particular time, the tactic was to use two parallel six man patrols. The two pigs would drive around and at a signal from the boss, the back doors would be opened and the six lads would exit the moving vehicle to cover positions; the doors would be shut and the vehicles would carry on swanning around the area until pick up time. It was quite a sound tactic as it kept the local bad boys guessing. This particular patrol went off without incident. It only lasted about half an hour and to be honest, none of us learned a thing as we were far too hyped up to take in any of the surroundings. I had a SUIT (Sight Unit Infantry Trilux) sight on my SLR which was originally issued to the better shots in the Troop' However each time I tried to have a good scan through it, the patrol would move off.[1]

We were tasked with another 'footsie' at about 3:30pm. We were told that this one would be a bit dodgier as we would be on the ground just as the light was fading; the IRA's favourite time for an attack. Originally, I was not to go on this one, but one of the lads from another section was suffering from the runs (yes, I thought that too) so this stupid Jock Lance Jack did what you should never do. When we left the base, I was in the back of the leading PIG, sitting second in on the left from the rear door. We went down Bligh's Lane, crossed the Lonemoor

---

1   SUIT was the forerunner of the SUSAT designed for use originally for the American M14 then adapted for use on the SLR. It first made its appearance on the streets in 1972. It had a 4X scope with pre-set ranges of 300 and 500 metres. The sighting mechanism was a downward facing pointer with a built-in trilux which glowed in the dark for night shooting. It was not as robust as the SUSAT and if dropped, tended to lose a bit of its zero, but very good for both shooting and for scoping out an area.

Road and went down to the bottom of Stanley's Walk. We turned left and as we reached the Bogside Inn, we turned left again into Westland Street. As we passed the Bogside Inn, we noticed that the CO's Rover group was parked there. What the old man was up to I don't know. Both our PIGs continued up Westland Street which was a fairly steep hill so we slowed down to a crawl. We had just about reached the junction with Cable Street on our left, when we came under fire from a gunman with a rifle. I could hear the rounds striking the PIG and both the lads at the rear sensibly got their heads down. Like an idiot, I decided to have a look using my SUIT sight. By this time, the driver was throwing the vehicle about, but as we passed Cable Street, I spotted something on the upper walkway of Meenan Flats.

Through the sight, I clearly saw the bastard, kneeling with his rifle balanced on the bars and I swear to this day that I saw the shock wave as he fired again. All I managed was one quick snap shot as the PIG was rocking and rolling, but it had an effect as the shooting stopped. I shouted to the section commander and told him where the fire position was, but as he was giving the contact report; he was overruled by the booming voice of 'call sign niner.' This call-sign was the CO, who insisted that his Rover Group had been the target and the fire position was behind the Bogside Inn. We knew this was rubbish, but what could a mere NCO do when the CO gives an order? We were told to turn into Elmwood Road, debus and set up a blocking position and await further orders.

The more experienced among us voiced thoughts of a possible IRA 'come on' but orders are orders. As we turned left into Elmwood Road, we opened the back doors and I legged it across the road, and took up a fire position on the edge of Garten Square facing Westland Street. I glanced behind and saw that a lad called Dave Tobin was positioned about ten feet behind me. I started scanning the area of the wood yard which leads down to Glenfada Park. We'd only been there about 30 seconds, when there was the typical CLACK-CLACK-CLACK of an M1 Carbine, missing me by not a lot! I had not seen where it had come from so I decided it was time to move to some better cover and the PIG parked opposite looked just the job.

As I moved off, I saw Dave lying on the pavement. Our Troop 2IC, 'Nosher' saw him at the same time and both of us grabbed Dave by the flak jacket and dragged him to the back of the PIG, and unceremoniously dumped him in the back. Dave started to come to, with blood coming from the area of his eye, so the Troop boss shoved a lit fag in Dave's mouth and a field dressing over the wound, and gave out the 'Crash Call' for the ambulance. By now, lots of kids had gathered around us so it was obvious that it was all over.[2]

Shortly afterwards, 'Burke and Hare' (our humorous name for the medics and named after the infamous body-snatchers of 19th century Edinburgh and London) with the 'Sarry' turned up.[3] They bundled Dave onto a stretcher and

---

2   Although the IRA were often unconcerned about hitting passers-by in their murderous crossfire, children from the Republican areas had an uncanny knack of knowing that it was safe to come out. Whether or not this is a unique awareness inside children in warzones or, more prosaically, they simply observed gunmen vacating the area is a moot point.

3   Saracen armoured vehicle.

spirited him away. Not long after, we were told to mount up and head back to Bligh's Lane. I was standing next to 'Nosher' at the unloading bay. We checked each other's rifles then he told me to check as he unloaded Dave's weapon. He took off the mag but as he tried to pull back the working parts, they were jammed. We then both noticed the bullet strike on the dust cover. It was now obvious what had happened. One of the rounds which missed me had hit Dave's rifle and he'd caught some of the splinters in the eye. What a lucky lad. The REME armourer came out, and using his number four iron, hammered the working parts back so that the live round was ejected.

When we got to the patrol room, the CO was there already. He was still claiming that he had got it right. My boss told him that I had seen the gunman in Meenan Flats and fired at him but he wouldn't accept this. The debate was settled when the RCT lad who was driving our PIG walked in carrying his vehicle rear number plate. It had two bullet holes through it and he said that you could also see three more strikes on the rear and left side of the armour. End of argument. The CO sort of sniffed, muttered to me: 'well done' and walked out. We were not happy bunnies! Because of this muppet overruling the contact report and sending us to Elmwood Road, Dave Tobin had been needlessly shot. Despite the fact that we suffered three fatalities, the tour was a success judged by the number of arms and explosives finds and the arrests of many wanted men. My whole Troop was awarded a GOC's commendation, but guess who didn't get the OBE that most COs got? As for Dave Tobin, his 'lucky' escape was not so lucky after all. Some of the splinters had pierced his eye and he unfortunately lost the eye completely. As was our lot in those days, he was given the medical boot, a few quid a week pension and a couple of grand compensation from the Northern Ireland Office. Years later, I saw him on TV being interviewed for one of the many programmes about OP Banner. He'd got himself a job at a Central London Post Office as a Postman!

The three fatalities Mike refers to are: Gunner Joseph Brookes who was shot in the Bogside; Bombardier Heinz Pisarek who was killed in the same incident in November, 1973. John Haughey was killed by a bomb which had been placed behind a telephone junction box at the top of Stanley's Walk near the Lonemoor Road in the Creggan Estate, in January 1974.

On 8 November, Francis McCaughey (35) the farmer badly injured in a Loyalist bomb attack the previous month died of those injuries after an 11 day fight for life. The following day, the UVF struck again and left an explosive device outside the Sunflower Inn, in Corporation Street, Belfast. The bar, though Catholic-owned and in the main, patronised by Catholics was in an area not definably Republican. Located some 250-300 yards from the Victoria Channel of the River Lagan and the docks, it was a working class area and reasonably mixed with families from both sides of the sectarian divide. Like poor Francis McNelis – killed a week earlier by a UVF car bomb – William Wallace (62) was an innocent passer-by, simply walking past the pub in the wrong place at the wrong time. The device exploded and the retired Docker was killed instantly.

Today Corporation Street, albeit different, is still standing, but the terraced houses which adorned either side of the road are now gone. The church at the bottom near the aptly named Tomb Street still stands as does the Victorian architecture of the Royal Institute of Chartered Surveyors. Of the pub outside of which the explosive device was placed, there is no obvious sign, other than the Direct Wine Shipments whose premises resemble a pub frontage. On an evening and on Sundays, it will resemble a ghost town as the workers and delivery people to the industries which have replaced the houses stay well away. How different it was on that fateful night in November 1973 when an innocent retired man walked past and for his troubles, was killed instantly.

On 9 November, the UVF declared a ceasefire which was to last for a total of 43 days. They did not kill again until 9 January, although there were some attempted killings which have been attributed to them. Their 'brothers' in the UFF neither declared nor observed any such ceasefire.

On 13 November, an IRA unit had abducted twin brothers from a youth club and taken them away for 'questioning' that euphemistic IRA term for a kangaroo court trial and then being taken away by the 'nutting squad.' Bernard Teggart (15) and his brother were interrogated and then one of them was released and given money for his bus fare home. Bernard, however, was shot and his body was dumped near Bellevue with a label marked 'tout' pinned to his corpse. The IRA justified his death by stating that he had brought about the arrest of IRA men attempting to hijack a lorry some days earlier. Apparently the young boy had witnessed the incident and in his child-like innocence, shouted to the gunmen that he would inform the police. A passing patrol of soldiers arrested the men, but even though it was a mere coincidence, held the boy accountable. This was yet another example of how the Provisional IRA protected their 'community' and one shudders at the prospect of what would have happened had they succeeded in driving the British out and forming a Government.

On the same day of the Teggart murder, the many tentacles of the IRA were again in evidence, as they forced the issue with the Army and presented their community with the *fait accompli* of being an integral part of an urban battleground. This time the battleground which the Republicans forced upon their supporters was that of the Short Strand.

The Short Strand (Irish: *an Trá Ghearr*) is a solidly Republican area in the east part of Belfast, surrounded by a mainly-unionist area and is located on the east bank of the River Lagan. Even today, a peace line stands, separating its southern boundary of Madrid Street from the Loyalist area. Like many parts of Belfast and largely as a platitude to the Nationalists, the English street names have their Irish equivalents italicised underneath. Harper Street is *Sraid Harper*; Mountpottinger Road is *Bothar Thulach Phoitinseir* and so on. Many of the old terraced housing still remains but are now interspersed with newer, neater town houses and looks nothing like the Short Strand of old.

The Army had built a sangar in Moira Street – now long demolished – and gunmen from the IRA opened fire on soldiers manning its entrance. Their supporters, sympathisers and the like generally cheered every round fired at the Army and gleefully applauded every hit and, as Kevin Myers wrote in his quite excellent *Watching the Door*, celebrated by dancing in the blood of a fallen soldier. One wonders how much celebrating was done, when an IRA bullet struck John Lundy (61) and killed him. Their sycophantic supporters would, no doubt have roundly condemned the Army for the killing, whilst conveniently forgetting that it was the Provisional IRA which had turned Madrid Street and Moira Street into battle zones.

Jim, Argyll & Sutherland Highlanders

On the 12th November 1973 at 1:00pm the battalion took over from the 2nd Battalion Grenadier Guards. This tour was a complete culture shock from last year's tour in Crossmaglen. I was part of the continuity team and as such, arrived in the Oldpark area of Belfast a couple of weeks before the main battalion. All we did were patrols; no guard duty or standby, simply patrolling. The job of the continuity team was to get to know the area and the personalities. The Guards guys did a good job in passing on all they had learned, and, when they arrived, we in turn began passing our knowledge on to the rest of our company. It paid off within the first few days. On a pubs and clubs tour, I pulled the patrol commander aside and told him there was a wanted man in the 'Hole in the Wall' club. I showed him the photo and we went back in; the patrol had a quick look and as he passed the man, grabbed him and dragged him outside. The rest of the patrol blocked the entrance to stop people pouring out. Transport was arranged, he was taken away; good result to start the tour.

Apart from that, although the area bordered the Ardoyne, it was relatively quiet. There were a couple of incidents that stand out though. A wanted IRA man was expected to try and visit his mother in the Cliftonville area just before Christmas. An OP was set up to watch him and one night a car sped up towards the house; stopped and then a machine gun opened up and sprayed the front door and windows. The guys in the OP tried to get out and stop the car, but they were unable to do so; in fact, it became a threat to them that they put fire down in an attempt to stop it. We heard later that two UVF men, in the car had been wounded.

Another incident concerned, I am sure, 'Basher Bates' (of 'Shankill Butchers' fame.[4] He was drunk, and had armed himself with a machine gun on the Shankill, and was heading for our area. We went out to look for him near the bottom of the Oldpark Road. Then, in a side street we came across a UDR patrol grouped round a figure on the ground; they were laying into Bates and when they saw us, they headed off, saying he was all ours; so hospital first stop then.

Running off the Oldpark road was Ardilea Street, and halfway along was what we knew as the 'Green Hut' an Official IRA club. I was taking a patrol in there one night, and was stopped by a civvie guy who asked me if our new orders had come down from Lisburn yet. I was puzzled, but passed the info on when we returned to base and then forgot all about it. Now, if you read Ed Moloney's book *Voices from the Grave* (p. 173), Brendan Hughes tells the story of bugging HQNI, Lisburn.

---

4   The Shankill Butchers was the name given to a particularly vicious Loyalist murder gang, many of whom were members of the UVF. The gang conducted paramilitary activities in Belfast, during the 1970s. It was most notorious for its late-night abduction, torture and murder by throat slashing of random Catholic civilians. The Shankill Butchers killed at least 30 people, including a significant number of Protestants in sectarian attacks, paramilitary feuds, and personal grudges and bombing raids. Despite extensive RUC resources channelled towards their capture, a wall of silence created by a mixture of fear and respect in the Shankill community provided few leads that could be followed. Bates was shot and killed in the Upper Shankill area on 11 June 1997 by a relative of the UDA man he had killed in a bombing attack at the Windsor Bar in Belfast.

About 100 metres from the green hut, was the 'Red hut' which was a PIRA drinking den. Going in there was something else; it could be packed with way over 100 people on a Friday or Saturday night and the atmosphere was definitely anti-British. All these drinking dens were illegal but I guess they were tolerated, since it might have been easier to keep tabs on who ran about with whom.

All in all, a pretty quiet tour and we were relieved by 3rd Battalion the Parachute Regiment at the end of February 1973. A few of us stayed on for a couple of weeks to show the Paras around. God they had a different style and approach. Suffice to say, we would not wear red berets preferring to wear our Glengarries.

On the same day as the Old Bailey bomb trial, there was yet more evidence that the IRA cared very little about the dangers of using suburban streets as shooting galleries. Seeking a spectacular in order to get their 'England Team's impending heavy jail sentences off the front pages; they attacked an Army patrol in Londonderry's Bogside. Lecky Road is situated less than 500 yards from the River Foyle and close to where Derry City's Brandywell Stadium is located. Close to the Bligh's Lane Army post, it is thought that the soldiers on foot patrol were from the Duke of Wellington's when it was attacked. As the soldiers walked along Lecky Road, there were plenty of children playing in the street when suddenly, several blasts from a whistle were heard and the children began going indoors. No doubt the immortal words of "Sir, they're taking the kids indoors" were heard and the soldiers knew that an attack was not only likely, but also imminent.

Within minutes, a single shot rang, proven later to be an American Armalite and a young child, Kathleen Feeney (14) who lived a few streets away was hit in the head and mortally wounded. Despite the best efforts of a soldier who placed himself back into the firing line in an effort to save her young life, she died at the scene. It was known in INT circles, that the attack was the work of the Brandywell unit of the Provisional IRA and they promised 'retaliation' for the death of the young girl, in a statement dripping with hypocrisy.

In typically despicable and hypocritical fashion, the IRA's 'Department of Pious and Meaningless Apologies' made a statement blaming the Army for the tragedy. They stated: "We say categorically that the shooting of young Kathleen Feeney was the work of the British Army and not of the Republican movement."

It took them 32 years before they made the following statement:

We found, as the Feeney family have always believed, that Kathleen was hit by one of a number of shots fired by an IRA active service unit that had fired upon a British army foot patrol. The IRA accepts responsibility for the death of Kathleen Feeney. Our failure to publicly accept responsibility for her death until now has only added to the hurt and pain of the Feeney family. The leadership wishes to apologise unreservedly to the Feeney family for the death of Kathleen and for all the grief that our actions have caused to them.

On Wednesday 14 November, at the Old Bailey in London, eight people were found guilty of planting bombs in the city, earlier in the year on 8 March. Eight of those found guilty received life sentences, of whom six admitted to membership of the IRA. A ninth defendant, 18-year-old Roisin McNearney, was acquitted. One person died and almost 200 were injured in the two bombs. One blew up outside the Old Bailey criminal court, while the other went off outside Scotland Yard.

The ten-week trial at Winchester Crown Court had witnessed some of the strictest security precautions in British legal history. The court was heavily guarded throughout, and as the verdict was delivered, four rows of plain-clothes detectives sat guarding the dock and at least 15 prison officers surrounded the defendants. All doors to the court were bolted.

First, the jury returned a not-guilty verdict on Roisin McNearney, a known IRA activist who was believed to have helped the police identify the other conspirators. As her verdict was handed down, the other defendants began to hum the 'Death March' from *Saul*, and one of the bombers threw coins at her, shouting: "Take your blood money with you!" as she left the dock in tears. Threats had already been made to members of her family and she stated that she was unlikely ever to be able to return to her native Belfast.

As the eight guilty defendants were led to the cells below the court, several gave clenched fist salutes to relatives and friends in the public gallery, who shouted Republican slogans in defiance.

The following day, 15 November, there was an attack on the Papa 15 checkpoint located at Butcher's Gate. This leads directly from the city to the Bogside. A lone IRA gunman, covered by some locals (whether they knew that is not known) walked up to the checkpoint and opened fire with a pistol. He shot the sentry in the sangar then proceeded to shoot randomly at the other members of the checkpoint, narrowly missing the WRAC girl (Women's Royal Army Corps) who was tasked to search females. It was little short of a miracle that nobody else, army or civilian were hit. The gunman escaped into the Rossville Flats complex followed by a couple of rounds fired by the checkpoint commander. The wounded soldier was hit in the face but happily made a full recovery. The author is aware of the identity of the wounded soldier, but acting on the advice of a friend and comrade for whom I have the utmost respect and affection, will not name him. The troops manning the checkpoint were from 47 Regiment, Royal Artillery, doing their last duty before going home.

The gunman, who cannot be named for legal reasons, lived in Cable Street in the Bogside. He was about 21 years old at the time, one of three brothers, one of whom was also involved in PIRA. He also had a sister who was thought to be a leading member of the Bogside bombing team. The gunman's name also came up in regard to the shooting of Bombardier Heinz Pisarek and Gunner Brookes at Rossville OP on 25 November. As a postscript, the unnamed gunman was arrested, in February 1974. He refused to speak during screening and was interned in Long Kesh. He was released in December 1975 when the Northern Ireland Secretary, Merlyn Rees ended internment. The unnamed Brandywell man was allegedly shot dead in June, 1976.

Unfortunately, four months later, the Brandywell terrorists did have a success. This one was claimed by the Brandywell IRA as being in revenge for the killing of the Feeney girl. This involved the death of Leeds boy Michael Ryan and will be dealt with, later in the book.

Mick Hollowday (Royal Green Jackets) on patrol in Belfast (Mick Hollowday)

MEETING THE GALLAGHERS
Alan Mac, Royal Artillery

I was due to go on leave but due to operational commitments I was tasked to do a house search in the Creggan area the morning I was due to depart. The family concerned (the Gallaghers) were well known to the security forces as hardened Republicans so we weren't expecting much co-operation.

However and somewhat surprisingly, they were quite friendly, which made us even more suspicious. However, it turned out it was the start of what is called the 'Derry Fortnight' and they were going on holiday. Anyway nothing was found, so we all went our various, merry ways and I finally got starting my leave. That night my mates and I went to one of our locals in a seaside town in Co Antrim. As soon as I walked in the door, there was Ma and Pa Gallagher; complete with the whole family sitting there. I don't know who got bigger shock but you should have seen the look on their faces; it was priceless. It was even more so, when after half an hour with them continually glancing at me, one of my mates went over and asked if there was a problem. There was a lot of stuttering, and trying to explain that I looked like somebody they knew, but couldn't think where from. They left about ten minutes later, and strangely I never saw them again. That is, until the next time I searched their house of course.

Keady in Co Armagh is located a mere three miles from the border with the Irish Republic. Like so many of the border towns and villages, it was key to the IRA's movement of men, arms and explosives. The RUC station there was a heavily fortified joint Police and Army base; as such, it merited the attentions of an IRA bombing unit.

The station was described as a " ... symbol of the British forces of occupation" by a Sinn Féin spokesman.

A large unit of the IRA crossed the border on unmarked roads in a stolen car and parked near to the RUC base. Led by Michael McVerry (23), the unit placed two devices against unguarded walls and retired to a firing point, intending to shoot police and soldiers when they came out to investigate. One device exploded, but thankfully the second did not. As soldiers and police came out, a fierce firefight broke out and in the course of this, an RUC officer was wounded. McVerry was hit by fire from a Sterling Sub Machine Gun and dragged into the car and driven to the border. They paused long enough at a Customs Post to set it alight before skulking into the 'safety' of the Republic. The mortally wounded terrorist died shortly before reaching hospital in Co Monaghan. McVerry was something of a cult hero in Republican circles, having tunnelled out of Curragh Jail – described by a senior IRA man as a 'concentration camp' – and also lost a hand and a part of an arm in an 'own goal' explosion. One soldier told the author: "After his death, we remarked that he [McVerry] had gone to Hell to join the other parts of him. We heard that he was a singer of some note; hope that they have a choir where he went!"

Proving yet again, that 'own goals' and premature detonations were not the sole province of the IRA, the Loyalist paramilitaries lost one of their men to the 'clumsy hands syndrome.' Charles Logan (26) and described as a 'Major' in the UVF was handling a device in a farm building at Desertmartin, Co Londonderry, close to the A2 road in the vicinity of Magherafelt. It exploded in his face, killing him instantly, injuring several others and demolishing the farmhouse. Demonstrating that the IRA were not the only hypocrites, their statement eulogising the dead man could have been taken

Corporal Brian Sheridan and Dave Hawkes (1LI) take it easy after a
search of a scrapyard in South Armagh (Brian Sheridan)

straight out of the IRA's own book of cant. Logan was described as having been killed on 'active service' and the prominent Loyalist family on whose property he was assembling the device were apparently being held 'hostage.'

On 20 November, two UDR men, Corporal William Martin (25) and Private David Spence (27) were in a dreadful car crash (RTA) whilst on duty. Their deaths are noted in this author's extensively research ROH, but to the Mandarins in the MoD in Whitehall, they are deemed, apparently, not worthy of inclusion on the ROH of the Troubles. In common with most milestones reached at any stage of the Northern Ireland troubles, this was a tragic one. The two became the 99th and 100th soldiers to die in 1973 in or as a result of the Troubles.

On the 23rd, Lance Corporal Edmond Crosbie (25) from Newtownabbey, Co Antrim was killed in a tragic RTA. Crosbie who was a member of the Royal Corps of Transport (RCT) was a native of Northern Ireland.

The following day a unit of the Welsh Guards, whose motto is: *Cymru am Byth* (Wales Forever), were tasked to a rural patrol in Crossmaglen, South Armagh. The first Northern Ireland Secretary of State of the next Labour Government (1974-9) was the late Merlyn Rees, MP. Later, during his tenure of office, he was to describe South Armagh as 'Bandit Country.' Never were a politician's words so apt or accurate. Guardsman David Roberts (25) from Holywell in North Wales was part of a foot patrol that was walking along Carlingford Street in the town. A concealed device was detonated by radio remote control and it exploded and killed the Guardsman instantly. The *Flintshire Chronicle* reported: "Shops, hotels and pubs in Holywell closed for the afternoon on the day of his funeral, with 500 people attending the service." The town later dedicated a Cadet Service building in his name and amongst those who attended the reopening of the centre were members of David's family, including his father Tom.

On the same day, an Army foot patrol came under attack in the Divis Street area and it resulted in the loss of an IRA 'volunteer.' Michael Marley (17) threw a grenade-like device at the soldiers from the Royal Green Jackets from the balcony of flats in Whitehall Row. The flats, part of what soldiers dubbed 'the Zanussi' were a seemingly haphazard, zig-zag design of drab, grey and soulless tenements. So-called because the residents threw whatever they could at soldiers patrolling in the streets below. Televisions, washing machines and even refrigerators were hurled over the balconies in the hope of killing a soldier. On the morning after, the area resembled a Zanussi white goods showroom and one soldier remarked to the author at the time: "I wonder if that lot's insured!"

The Jackets shouted a warning and when Marley failed to stop, he was shot dead which the soldiers were entitled to do, under ROE (Rules of Engagement). Soldiers testified that, in accordance with the 'Yellow Card' conditions, three warnings had been shouted before shots were fired at the fleeing man. The soldier who fired the fateful shot gave first aid treatment to the dying IRA man (a member of Fianna, the youth wing) and desperately tried to stem the bleeding. Later forensic examination showed that Marley had traces of explosives on his body and a search of his pockets turned up bomb-making parts.

Earlier in the year – on 12 July – the Loyalist marching season had commenced with the killing of Frederick Davis, apparently by the IRA and allegedly for shouting sectarian slogans. On Sunday 25 November, Francis Benson (25) was shot and killed, it is thought,

Mick Hollowday (Royal Green Jackets) (Mick Hollowday)

by the IRA. His body was found in a derelict house in the Republican Markets area of Belfast, in a badly mutilated state. As *Lost Lives* records he was stabbed 13 times with two separate implements, he had been bludgeoned with a blunt instrument and kicked and punched repeatedly. His body was in such a mess, that he could only be identified by distinctive tattoos; he had no known paramilitary connections. It is widely considered that he and another man, later killed by the Official IRA in March of the following year, had been responsible for the murder of the aforementioned Frederick Davis. Although the Officials denied responsibility for the death of Francis Benson, it is one which will be forever attributed to one or even both wings of the IRA.[5]

One of the most famous landmarks in Londonderry was the Rossville Flats which dominated the Republican Bogside. The Rossville Flats were built by the former Northern Ireland Housing Trust as part of the Lecky Road/Rossville Street redevelopment scheme; first tenants moved in from other demolished areas of the Bogside, in 1966. The flats complex originally housed some 109 families. Some of the three main blocks were six stories high and another was ten stories high and the complex was a hot-bed of Republicanism and the source of many killings and attacks on the SF.

That bloody weekend was not yet over and two people were yet to die, both of whom were soldiers; comrades from the same Regiment. The Army had decided to use the roof of the flats, overlooking the Bogside as a permanent OP under the call-sign T2. Late on that Sunday evening, the OP was manned by two soldiers with satellite four man 'bricks' patrolling the floors of the complex as well as the streets below. Access to the roof was gained via a trap door from the lift machine room. This room served as the rest and

---

5   McKitterick, David et al, *op cit.*, pp. 403-404

Mick Hollowday (Royal Green Jackets) (Mick Hollowday)

cooking area for the men on duty and access to the roof was forbidden to the residents. From this room, a narrow stairway led down to the top corridor of the flats right next to the lift. This area was guarded by another two soldiers, whose job was to ensure no unwanted characters got access. One was to watch the lift and the other guard the stairs which ran all the way down to the ground floor. Their positioning meant that they were quite close to each other.

As both soldiers were killed in the attack, it is not known precisely what happened, but it is thought that an IRA gunman had sneaked up the stairs and waited just out of sight of the sentry. A second gunman, hidden from view by others, exited the lift and immediately opened fire on the two Royal Artillery men. This was the signal for the other one to make his appearance and he also opened fire – neither soldier stood a chance. At the same time, a third gunman opened fire at the actual OP, shooting from the area of Glenfada Park. This tactic was thought to have been to divert the attention of two foot patrols who were on the ground at the time so as to prevent them blocking off the exits from the flats so allowing the murderers to escape.

The two soldiers killed were Bombardier Heinz Pisarek (30) from the Hanover district in Germany and Gunner Joseph Brookes (20) from Staffordshire were both rushed to Altnagelvin Hospital. Sadly, both soldiers died in the ambulances taking them there. The two soldiers were also the 27th and 28th Royal Artillery soldiers, respectively to die since the start of the Troubles.

A former soldier in the Royal Artillery told the author:

As it happens, I was on one of those foot patrols and Alan Mac was on the other. The tactic worked because we followed up on the gunman who was shooting from outside. By the time we had finished chasing our own shadows, the whole Rossville complex was covered with troops who had crashed out from Bligh's Lane but far too late to catch the gunmen

AN 'OUTING' TO THE ROSSVILLES
Alan Mac, Royal Artillery

The Section was on foot patrol and passing Rossville Flats when Stevie and Heinz were gunned down and we heard the shots. The 'contact' had barely come over the air, before we had the flats sealed off. We knew that the gunmen were still inside and nobody was getting in our out. However when the patrol commander radioed through that we had the flats secure, in a very short space of time, we were told to back off to the Dove Gardens area and observe. I couldn't understand why; that was, until many years later, when I read a book about an IRA informer and some things just slotted into place. Orders from Higher Authority had been issued; it wasn't a military decision but political. Even back then talks were taking place between the Government and the IRA. We were expendable, and when I think of the lives that could have been saved it makes me so angry.

I was on R&R when John Haughey lost his life, and when I found out the details I was quite shaken as I had taken cover behind that junction box more times than enough.[6] For those unfortunate to have missed out on service in Londonderry, it's quite a beautiful city with a history that would stand against anything on the mainland. However when it rained it was the most miserable grey damp place on the planet. It was just that type of day when one of those incidents that gave us simple pleasure took place. Saturdays was 'bomb patrol' day on the Strand Road. This consisted of two men, one armed with an SLR, the other with his riot baton. The idea was to do random searches on people, most of who had already been searched at the main checkpoints. Originally the man with the SLR carried his magazine in his flak jacket pocket but the regional RUC inspector soon put a stop to that. The word 'edjit' (idiot) was one of the politer words used.

This particular Saturday, Fred 'H' and I were on patrol and the weather was crap; constant heavy rain and overcast. Neither of us could be bothered doing searches; we just wanted to get back in for a 'banjo' (sandwich) and cuppa. Anyway none of the attractive 18 to 20-year-old females ever seemed to have anything worth arresting them for. I recall that we were standing in a shop doorway at the junction of Little Patrick Street and Strand Road, when two of the local females pushed out past us commenting about the smell of 'pig.' We couldn't resist the opportunity, so suggested she didn't smell that bad but it could be the rain keeping the smell down. That started the whole thing off. So, trading insults, we followed them up the street. The usual niceties were being swapped; it being suggested that as Brit Bastards we might consider going home, whilst I reminded them that, as they had probably been born in Altnagelvin hospital they were Brits as well! And as I was older than them it had been my country longer than theirs.

There was a bit of a problem working that out, but the 'craic' was good. Then I realised where we were! Williams Street with the notorious Rossville flats in front of us! We had, unwittingly gone the whole way up Strand Road through the 'F1'

6   For more information see Chapter 13, January 1974.

checkpoint and down Williams Street. Oh fuck! Fred was still giving the females 'pelters,' so I shouted to him and he went white! He suddenly realised where we were. Quick about turn and scurry back to the checkpoint, as we were getting a crowd round us.

Luckily for us, the 'F1' commander sent half his guys to help us as the sentry in the coffin saw what was going on. Was I ever glad to see them? We got the mother and father of bollockings but looking back, it could have been so much worse, as not only had we put ourselves in danger but the lads sent to get us. Bomb Patrols were never quite the same again.

In June 1989 demolition work began on the remaining two blocks of one of Derry's most noted landmarks, Rossville Flats. Block one had been knocked down three years previously.

Sectarian murders were and remain a despicable characteristic of any society, ancient or modern. The history of the British Isles is littered with Catholic pogroms of Protestants and of Protestant pogroms of Catholics. In the 12th century, English and Normans killed Jews; Hitler compounded that with the Genocide of 5.7 million Jews in the 20th Century and today in the volatile Middle East, Jew kills Arab, Arab kills Jew on a depressingly regular basis. For 500 years or more, sectarian hatred has been etched into the very psyche of each Protestant baby and the same is true of the Catholic baby. The Prods hate the Taigs and vice versa.

Sectarianism, albeit mistaken sectarianism, reared its vile head on the last Monday of November, only this time with a difference. Anthony Braden (58) and a father of 5 children was stopped at an illegal VCP (IVCP) in Jamaica Street, Ardoyne, Belfast as he drove home from Flax Street, also in the Ardoyne. Mr Braden was a Catholic and might well have assumed that, despite the inconvenience, he was at least in his own community and the IRA were, after all, the 'protectors' of the Catholics. Tragically for him he was confronted by a 17-year-old psychopath with a loaded pistol, who mistook him for a Protestant and shot him dead. In a court statement, the teenage killer explained without a trace of irony, that the killing was a " … morale booster for the Provisional IRA … after those sectarian killings … " He was jailed for life.

The very next day, November 27, the Army was involved in a fierce firefight with the IRA in the small town of Coalisland, Co Tyrone. The small market town is some three miles west of picturesque Lough Neagh and 20 miles due west of Lisburn. A British Army foot patrol disturbed an IRA gang attempting to hijack a car in the town and came under fire. They engaged the armed IRA men and shot and killed Desmond Morgan (18) who was found dead at the scene, although his accomplices escaped in the direction of the Irish border. Morgan had taken part in an all-day IRA operation to block almost 100 roads throughout the Province with hijacked vehicles. This operation not only cost the life of a terrorist but also claimed other lives as well.

The final two deaths in November were innocent civilians, killed because of the IRA, and though classed as an accident, their deaths can be laid firmly at the door of both the IRA 'Army Council' and the Commander of the Provisionals' Co Tyrone Brigade. Two Dungannon men, Protestants and friends, were driving home from Ballygawley when their car came around a blind bend – immediately on the other side of the bend was a lorry, abandoned by an IRA gang. The driver had absolutely no time so see the vehicle, let alone stop, and both men were killed instantly. Ivan Charlton (19) whose wife was pregnant at the time and Cyril McCaul (32) were both killed instantly in the smash. The Provisional IRA was absolutely guilty of causing their deaths; before and after the fact.

November had finally ground to a halt and the death tally was 26 – more than twice as many as the previous month. Of these ten were soldiers (five were killed by the IRA) 12 were civilians, three were IRA members and one was a Loyalist paramilitary. Of the civilians, the Republicans killed eight and the Loyalists the other four. In total, the Provisional IRA was responsible for the loss of 13 lives during the course of November. What was sadly overlooked was that by the end of 1973, 278 British soldiers would have died in, or as a consequence of the Troubles over the two worst years: 1972 and 1973. The IRA was still not beaten and soldiers were dying at the rate of almost three per week; this at a time when Britain was not officially at war. More importantly, the Troubles still had another 24 bloody years to run and a second and third generation would be involved.

Chapter 12

December

In any civilised State, the murder of a policeman is treated as a heinous crime, as it quite rightly should be. It is a cause of shock, often disgust, but it is an event which is newsworthy and one which, thankfully, happens rarely. In Northern Ireland during the bloody path of the Troubles, it was an event which, if not a daily occurrence, happened too many times for it to completely shock. Between 1969 and 1998, over 300 members of the Royal Ulster Constabulary (RUC) – men and women – were killed in a country which is geographically smaller than the Australian island state of Tasmania.

Lurgan in Co Armagh has been described variously as a "Republican cess pit" and also as a "green hell" It is located a little over 20 miles from the Irish border and 15 miles south west of Belfast, and as such was of strategic importance to both the Security Forces (SF) and also the IRA. A small unit of the IRA had taken over a derelict house close to Sloan Street and Edward Street. Today, the modern visitor will find that quintessential aspect of the 'American invasion' a McDonald's fast food outlet, close to the very spot where, back in December 1973, an RUC mobile patrol was driving past. Gunmen opened fire on the police vehicle with automatic weapons and over 20 rounds were fired. Constable Robert Megaw (29), a father of three, was mortally wounded in the attack; he died shortly after being admitted to hospital. One of his colleagues, Constable Cyril Wilson was killed almost four months later, in exactly the same place. The IRA had left three more children without their father and created yet another widow on an endless list. It is all well and good for the apologists of Sinn Féin to apologise now for 'Bloody Friday' the Abercorn bombing, the killing of the little Feeney girl et al, but those people still lie dead. Some lie cold in their coffins, others their dust scattered to the four winds and yet others lie in unconsecrated ground; no amount of apologies and contrition will restore their victims back to their loved ones.

A little over three years after the Lurgan attack, an IRA member was jailed for conspiracy but it wasn't until the summer of 1993, almost 20 years after the murder, that one of the actual gunmen was convicted. He had fled shortly after the killing to the 'land of the free' (and presumably of Irish terrorists) and was only back in Northern Ireland facing trial, because the American legal system, it seemed, had finally grown a pair of testicles and deported him. The IRA man bitterly complained to the Judge that he had been thrown out of the US simply because he failed to declare a conviction on his visa application form. This speaks volumes about the disproportionate influence of the Irish-American lobby, in that he was deported on a technicality and not for the crime of murder!

POLITICIANS HAVE NO SENSE OF HUMOUR.
Mike Sangster, Royal Artillery

One of the young Gunners in the Reserve Troop, Dennis, had the misfortune of sharing the same surname of the then Northern Ireland Secretary, William

Whitelaw. This was December 1973, and the minister was about to change jobs so decided on a farewell tour of army bases. This particular night, the Reserve Troop was at the Saracen factory giving a helping hand to the Bogside Battery. Two of our sections were on foot patrol whilst unbeknown to us, Willie Whitelaw, accompanied by our much hated CO was inside the KILO OP observing our movements. As the parallel footsies[1] reached Westland Street, as was SOP, one went firm to cover the other across the road. My section went firm. The first couple of lads crossed the road, but the third one, young Dennis got half way over when he tripped and went arse over tit. I remember having a bit of a giggle about it. Meanwhile, in the OP, this mishap had been seen and somebody asked who it was that fell. The bloke manning the high powered binoculars replied in a loud voice: 'That stupid bastard Whitelaw!' A very flustered CO had some very rapid explaining to do to a very unamused politician; that story did wonders for our morale.

On the 3 December, a taxi, hijacked earlier the same day on the Creggan Estate in Londonderry was involved in a shooting incident at Central Drive when shots were fired at a passing foot patrol. The soldiers returned fire and three people in the vehicle were hit and the car abandoned several minutes later. Amongst those wounded was IRA member Joseph Walker (18) a Creggan resident. The IRA's mouthpiece, Provisional Sinn Féin denied that Walker had been involved and there was a suggestion in some circles that he was not a member of the IRA. Interestingly NORAID, the funders of Republican terrorism, name Walker on the Derry Brigade Roll of Honour.[2]

On the same day Francis Pym succeeded William Whitelaw as Secretary of State for Northern Ireland. Many people were critical of this particular change given that the talks on the crucial issue of the Council of Ireland were scheduled to begin on 6 December 1973. One other criticism of the appointment was that Pym had comparatively little knowledge of Northern Ireland. He was soon in the thick of things the next day, when he held a meeting with Ian Paisley, then leader of the DUP. Paisley stormed out of the meeting having been told that Loyalists would not be invited to participate in the Sunningdale conference but could come to put their point of view.

Whilst the tentative UVF ceasefire was happening, one of the other Loyalist paramilitaries, the UFF felt under no such constraints, and on the second Saturday of the month shot dead a Catholic in South Belfast. James Gibson (42) and a father of five who ran a small shop in Stranmillis Road, some 1.5 miles slightly south east of Milltown Cemetery, selling Grocery items. A UFF gunman fired several shots into his head from point blank range, mortally wounding him. A passing RUC officer rushed to his aid, and found Mr Gibson dying but was unable to do anything other comfort him. His wife was heavily pregnant with their 6th child at the time of the murder. A member of the UDA was later charged with murder, but after severe witness intimidation, the case was dropped.

The Civil Service Staff College at Sunningdale in England played host to a conference to try to resolve the remaining difficulties surrounding the setting up of the power-sharing Executive for Northern Ireland. Sunningdale was the first occasion

---

1   foot patrols.
2   Available at: www.noraid.org/roll_of_honour.

since 1925 that the Prime Minister of the (UK), the Taoiseach (Irish Prime Minister), and the Northern Ireland Government had attended the same talks on the future of Northern Ireland. Edward Heath, then British Prime Minister, and Liam Cosgrave, then Taoiseach, and senior ministers attended in addition to representatives of the Ulster Unionist Party (UUP), the SDLP, and the APNI.

The participants discussed a number of matters but the main item of concern centred on the unresolved issue of the 'Irish Dimension' of any future government of Northern Ireland. Proposals surrounding this 'Irish Dimension' were finally to be agreed in the form of a proposed Council of Ireland. The elements of the proposed Council were that it would consist of a Council of Ministers and a Consultative Assembly. The Council of Ministers was to be comprised of seven members from the Northern Ireland Executive and seven members of the Irish government. This Council would have executive and harmonising functions and a consultative role. The Consultative Assembly was to be made up of 30 members from the Northern Ireland Assembly and the same number from the Dáil. This Assembly was to have advisory and review functions.

THE LADIES OF LONDONDERRY
Tim Francis, Royal Artillery

It would have to be said that the Londonderry of 1973/74 was one of the most unpleasant cities on the face of the earth, an opinion which, on two subsequent visits in 2001 and 2009, has not really changed, despite superficial improvements. There was however, some compensation in 1973/74 in that many of the good ladies (?) of Londonderry saw the influx of fit healthy young men into their community, in the shape of the army as not just a supply of boyfriends, but an opportunity for self-improvement in the shape of possible marriage rapidly followed by emigration. Sadly for them, most were to be disillusioned of this theory as they found themselves discarded or let down and, often, shunned by their own communities as a result. My own battery's experiences when based at Victoria Barracks at the back of the Strand Road Police Station are probably a good example overall.

It has to be borne in mind that any encounters with the opposite sex had to revolve around a working pattern of, typically six hours on, six hours off followed by 12 hours on, six hours off and then potentially followed by 18 hours on, then six or maybe 12 hours off if one was really lucky. For some people this resulted in very complicated, confused lives, but clearly where there is a will there is a way and a lot of guys did find a way. Sangars were possibly not the best of places for romantic interludes but the term 'sangar bangers' became legendary, although not, I might add from personal experience! Names that spring to mind immediately are 'Diane' and 'Heather' and it is really difficult to see what they, 'Diane' in particular, got out of their series of one night stands.

Even one of our very young and somewhat naive officers was to attempt to unravel the mystery of this female, but found himself totally without a frame of reference; she was clearly not a type he had encountered in his sheltered upbringing. 'Heather' was a slightly different matter, as during our 1973/74 tour she had the misfortune to fall in love with a member of my troop; probably the most unsuitable individual she could have chosen but sadly amongst many who did so over the years, all destined to the same fate. She was certainly brave with it, on one occasion even visiting the British Legion club with him, very much a no-go area to anyone from her side of the sectarian divide; despite our cynicism it was difficult not to feel sorry for her. There was also 'Alice', again associated with a member of my troop; again doomed to heartbreak as he had a wife and children elsewhere.

There were other distractions too, as the last remaining shirt factory abutted our area, albeit on the other side of fences. Many a soft patrol was interrupted near there for a chat to whichever girl happened to be nearest the window, responses tended to vary from: 'Fuck off, you British bastards!' to the other extreme, eventually leading to yet another member of my troop became attached and then marrying the lady in question; sadly not for very long.

The British Legion club in Waterside, although somewhat staid at face value, had a somewhat dubious reputation as there were often girls from the Loyalist community here looking for a good time. Some of them were temporarily free of their husbands for the evening which seemed to encourage them into wild behaviour. A position on one of the row of dustbins at the back of the club was much prized late in the evening for illicit encounters in the dark.

As Londonderry was still a fairly busy port in those days, this brought merchant sailors to the city and inevitably girls came looking for a good time. There were various checkpoint incidents as 'ladies' handbags were searched and somewhat unusual items found, which certainly kept the guys on the checkpoints amused if not the ladies. I can also recall an occasion where two members of my troop were invited to a highly illicit drink on a docked ship one evening, and met a couple of ladies there who assumed they were sailors and therefore fair game. They were to be rather annoyed the following day to bump into them, this time in uniform on bomb patrol on Strand Road. The reaction of the 'ladies' in question was fairly blue to say the least!

We were warned on many occasions that girls were likely to be used as 'honey traps', intended to gather intelligence about on-going activities or possibly to set up an attack. However, with what we knew it is very hard to see what they could have gained of any use whatsoever to anybody in IRA circles. The only possible exception to this was an instance where yet another troop member made the acquaintance of a young lady, arranged a date, left our base, breaking every rule in the book in the process and went to the cinema just around the corner with her. He returned safely to base having arranged to meet her two nights later according to his work pattern. In the meantime a security alert appeared about a young lady working for the IRA, complete with photo. The response of my mate was a whispered: "I shagged her last night!" So ended that relationship and possibly extended his wellbeing.

Leeson Street in Belfast is located off the Falls Road and is a popular cut through for traffic intending to turn left into Grosvenor Road at the traffic lights by Dunville Park. Cars seeking to avoid the long delays at these lights can go down Leeson Street, turn right into modern Servia Street and then enter the Grosvenor Road. Back in 1973, Leeson Street, before the 21st Century redevelopments, ran directly into Grosvenor

Road. On 10 December, a foot patrol from the Queen's Own Highlanders had reached the point where Leeson Street reached Grosvenor Road, when a shot rang out. A lone IRA sniper, using an Armalite rifle fired a single shot and hit Private James Hesketh (21); the Clydebank soldier died very shortly afterwards.

One of the 'selling points' of the US-made (and no doubt US-smuggled) Armalite is that it has a folding stock and can be instantly reduced in size. In the seconds after any shooting, a fallen man's comrades are in state of shock, and try desperately to remove him, give him medical aid and at the same time, locate the sniper. Whilst Private Hesketh's comrades were reacting instinctively, the well-rehearsed IRA tactic of spiriting both gunman and weapon out of the area was put into practice. The gunman located somewhere on the Grosvenor Road or Leeson Street passed the stripped down weapon to a waiting woman with a baby and pram and then disappeared into the maze of streets and to a 'safe house'. Meanwhile the woman walked the length of Leeson Street, past the soldiers and possibly even glanced over at the sight of where the young Scot lay dying, surrounded by his comrades fighting to save his life. At the top of the street, she crossed the Falls Road and into Sevastopol Street and the murder weapon was deposited in yet another 'safe house'.

SHOOT OUT ON DUNMORE GARDENS!
Steve Norman, Royal Anglian Regiment

After Tony's death, our attitude hardened towards the locals, and at least our Platoon officer Lieutenant 'G' had the good sense to keep us confined to camp on guard duties for a few days before letting us back on the streets. But eventually, we were back on patrol and looking for revenge; we wanted to get even. If this meant stopping people and searching them with the inevitable result of a riot then so what? Bring it on; it gave us the chance to fight the buggers back and if it brought the gunmen out into the open so much the better.

Our chance came sooner than we thought. Whilst patrolling at night along Beechwood Avenue, we were heading towards the infamous Broadway. I saw a young female whom I recognised as belonging to a republican family; she was standing under a street lamp watching our every move. As 'tail end Charlie' my alarm bells were ringing and just then, a motorbike with a pillion passenger drove slowly by us and then accelerated away. It turned right into Dunmore Gardens, the next junction up from us. I told the next man up from me to take over tail end and I leapfrogged up to Bill, the section NCO. I was going to tell him what I had seen, but before I got to him, two of our lads had crossed the junction to cover the rest of us as we crossed over. As the next man ran across, a burst of automatic fire came seemingly from nowhere, and our reaction was instant. Every one of us cocked our weapons and fired at where we thought the shots had come from. In my own case, I saw shit being kicked up from the alley behind the shops on the Broadway and what appeared to be a figure. I put two well-aimed rounds in that direction, whilst others thought that the shots had come from the direction of Dunmore Gardens and let fly in that direction.

For a few seconds, it was deathly quiet then all hell broke loose. Whoever fired that burst at us obviously had second thoughts and buggered off as soon as he saw our reaction, but the locals came out screaming and shouting. They were asking us 'what the fuck did we think we were doing? We explained that 'what the fuck we were doing was returning fire at one of their own local heroes.' We explained none too gently, that he had just put their lives on the line as this was a built up area, at night and we sure as hell were going to fire back at him. The crowd got bigger, the mouths got louder and eventually we were ordered to bug out and get back to Bligh's lane as the nice men from the SIB wanted a little word with us.

Back at camp, standard procedure kicked in and once we had unloaded our weapons, they were taken from us and the investigation began, one on one. I was taken into a room and two SIB men began to question me; it went as follows:

'How many rounds did you fire?' Answer: 'Two.' 'What did you fire at; was it an identifiable target? Answer: 'I saw a target behind the shops in the Broadway. I saw dust kicking up at the same time as the gunfire.' 'Did you hit anyone?' Answer: 'Don't know, but the shooting stopped!' End of interview. This happened to all who fired and when we compared notes afterwards, it appeared half had fired in one direction – i.e behind the shops – and the other half had fired up Dunmore Gardens. The problem was that the houses up Dunmore were the old prefab style and as thin as a 'Primark T shirt.' Several rounds had gone through the whole lot, as the houses were staggered, one by one in an uphill direction. No wonder the locals went loopy! But at the end of the day the onus was on the gunman he had the drop on us and knew the area and knew the risk he was putting his own community at. The local Provos also knew now that we were not the sort who would baulk at firing back and we would react in the same way each time we were attacked; the ball was now in their court.

Over the next few days we heard from our intelligence cell that a local Provo by the name of Charlie had indeed been hit behind the shops on the Broadway but ironically had nothing to do with the shots fired at us. We never knew if that was verified, but by God wouldn't that be poetic justice if it was true?

On 11 December, the day following the murder of Private Hesketh, another well-laid and executed IRA plan to kill policemen took place. Three separate ASUs in Co Down, placed devices under the cars of three off-duty RUC officers. One of the devices was discovered, in another, the officer concerned had a leg amputated after being severely injured in the explosion, but a third led to the death of DC Maurice Rolston (37). A UVBT (under vehicle booby trap) placed under the officer's car exploded and killed him instantly. His wife and three children were actually in the house at the time and had just bid him goodbye after their evening meal.

A NORMAL DAY?
Alan Mac, Royal Artillery

One particular day, we were driving through the Bogside in a convoy of two PIGs, then the lead PIG turned off whilst we continued along Rossville Street towards Stanley's Walk. Dennis 'W' and I were the rear doormen that day, and as this was a favourite time for attacks, I suppose we were more tense and alert. The CO's rover group were also on the ground for no particular reason other than to make a nuisance of himself, something he was exceptional at. 'A' Section had just turned into Stanley's Walk when the first shots were heard.

If you have ever been inside a PIG you would understand, but these metal coffins were hot, stuffy and noisy; difficult to hear what was happening outside. Inside the Pig it was impossible to say where the shots had come from, but the Contact report from 'B' Section gave us the general area. However call sign 'Niner' came on and insisted that his Rover group was the target; simultaneously our PIG came under fire, and if it was chaotic before, it just got ten times worse. At first I thought we were being stoned, but it was a different sound altogether. I remember looking over at Dennis and him looking at me; the realisation that we were under fire suddenly dawning on us. The strange thing is, while all this chaos was going on I have this everlasting impression of silence. I know it was anything but, but that is my abiding memory. We shouted to the patrol commander that we had 'contact' only to be told to shut up as he was trying to listen to the 'contact' reports from the other Section and CO's Group.

For some reason, this officer didn't realise that we were telling him about the shots which were being fired at us! Thankfully we had an RCT driver who was on the ball; he slammed his foot down, and weaved his way up Stanley's at top speed, which in a PIG wasn't very fast. He did manage to keep the local panel beater in work for the rest of the year though, as I saw three or four cars he sideswiped, and in that area I doubt if many had insurance. I think we were onto Lonemoor Rd or possibly Westland, before we got it through to the officer concerned, that we had been in Contact as well. Call sign 'Niner' still insisted that he was the target.

Even this doesn't finish the story, as back in camp the CO was still insisting that he was the target, until the driver of the first PIG brought in his rear number plate and showed the bullet holes in it plus strike marks on the vehicle. This was followed by our driver who also reported strike marks on the rear of his vehicle. None were found on the CO's vehicle; funny that!

On 15 December Jim McGinn (20) was killed in another IRA 'own goal' when a device which he was either transporting or preparing exploded prematurely. The device exploded at Clady Bridge, inside the border with the Republic and a later follow up between the RUC and the Gardai drew the attention of IRA gunmen. The policemen from the two countries were attacked from firing points on the Irish side of the border, but there were no casualties. It is thought that the bombing team, prior to McGinn's premature demise had planned to attack Strabane RUC station. He is eulogised amongst Republican sycophants as somewhat of a 'sartorial' terrorist.

Another member, or rather former member, of the RUC was murdered by the IRA either just on the border with the Republic at Monaghan or actually inside the border with the North. The sanctimonious killers then tried to justify the man's death with a series of audacious and attention diverting claims. Ivan Johnston (34) had been a member of the RUC Special Branch but had resigned in order to take up a job as a lorry driver. He was abducted close to Monaghan and was tortured and then shot. In some sort of sickening self-justification, the IRA claimed that he had photos of suspected terrorists and had 'admitted' to working undercover for the police. The unit which murdered him had stated that they had been trying to kill the man "for quite some time."

Throughout the long and bloody course of the Troubles, there were men and women who were shot in the crossfire, shot because they were in the wrong place at the wrong time or killed through mistaken identity. Rodney Fenton (22) had the tragic misfortune to be killed in a combination of all three. He was a bank worker and worked in the Antrim Road branch of the Northern Bank; together with three other fellow employees, he had been out for pre-Christmas drinks. One of the four was an RUCR (part-time policeman) and it was thought that it was he, and not Fenton who was the target. As they walked along the Antrim Road, an IRA gunman fired shots at the group from very close range, hitting the RUCR man before then shooting Rodney Fenton. The young man died at the scene. The IRA's sick justification was that they had warned people, not to be seen in the company of members of the 'occupation forces.'

Christmas Eve in 1973 was celebrated throughout the country in various ways. In Scotland, England and Wales, the revellers danced, drank and sang their way through the night. Their only worries would have been the cost and availability of taxis home, or even whether they should risk driving home after a few 'sherbets.' In Ulster, the collective concerns of the drinkers there would have been much the same, together with the fear of a bombing or a shooting. On that night, in the season of goodwill to all men, the IRA launched a bomb attack on a packed pub in Monaghan Street, Newry.

A three man unit consisting of Edward Grant (17) from the Republican Derrybeg and Brendan Quinn (18) from Bessbrook and a third, unnamed man entered Malachy Clarke's Bar armed with a rifle and a bomb. Holding the staff and customers at gunpoint, they told them that they had two minutes to clear the bar. Immediately, there was a huge explosion which killed both terrorists and an innocent member of the public. The blast injured over 20 drinkers and many passengers on a passing bus were caught in the explosion. The third IRA man was also injured, but managed to escape. Aubrey Harshaw (18) had business in the pub and was killed instantly along with Grant and Quinn.

NORAID in their roll of honour of IRA dead acknowledges that the pair belonged to the Newry Brigade.[3] Their deaths are attributed to their being on 'active service.' The third IRA bomber was brought to court several years later but never convicted.

There were no troubles-related deaths recorded on Christmas Day, but Boxing Day brought renewed violence, this time inside the Long Kesh Internment Camp, known to all simply as the 'Kesh.' Her Majesty's Prison, Long Kesh was used to house paramilitary prisoners during the Troubles from mid-1971 onwards. It was situated in the former RAF station of Long Kesh, on the outskirts of Lisburn. This was located in Maze, about nine miles southwest of Belfast. Despite the close proximity of two sets of paramilitary prisoners, both seething with hatred for each other, there were surprisingly few cases of murder inside the wire. In what bore the classic hallmark of an internal feud, George Hyde (19) and a member of the UFF was beaten to death by fellow Loyalists. As no-one was ever charged with his murder, it is unknown, other than among the perpetrators, whether or not he was killed by fellow members of the UFF or the rival UVF. In Loyalist circles, there was a spurious tale circulated that Hyde had informed the warders of an impending breakout.

Three days later, with the clock ticking down towards the New Year, soldiers were involved in a fracas with Shankill Road residents at the Bayardo Bar. In the incident, a

---

3   Avaliable at: www.noraid.org/roll_of_honor.

foot patrol from the Queen's Own Highlanders had stopped at the bar and, against all the 'rules and regs' had entered for a drink. Inside, one of the QOH NCOs had been assaulted or threatened by drinkers and gone outside and had fired his weapon, killing a passerby. Alexander Howell (36) and father of four died at the scene. The soldier was later charged with, and acquitted of, manslaughter.

Mobs began to gather on the Shankill and barricades were thrown up to prevent troops entering. At nearby Agnes Street, Loyalist gunmen fired several shots at an Army foot patrol and in other parts of the Province, buses were hijacked and set alight.

Loyalist gunmen then attacked an RUC patrol which was investigating at a shop in Forthriver Road, in the Protestant Glencairn area. As their patrol car arrived at the premises, they were ambushed by several gunmen and one of the RUC men, Constable Michael Logue (21) was shot and died at the scene. It was a joint UVF/UFF attack and broke the ceasefire – if indeed it ever existed – that the former had put in place. Apparently, the ceasefire did not include the SF and they did not carry out any sectarian murders again until the second week of the New Year. The Loyalists offered an outrageous excuse for the murder of the policeman – a Catholic incidentally – claiming it to be in retaliation for the earlier shooting of Alexander Howell.

In the middle and late sections of the 20th Century, Italy experienced a wave of kidnapping-for-profit when the Mafia or Cosa Nostra would abduct anyone for whom they thought they might extract a ransom. The IRA attempted this but once and it ended disastrously badly and they emerged with even more stain upon their collective character. Thomas Niedermayer (45) was a German industrialist who ran the Grundig plant at Dunmurry, in the western part of Belfast. He was a man not only prepared to try and bring economic prosperity to war-torn Belfast but also served as the honorary consul to Northern Ireland.

Niedermayer was abducted on 27 December 1973 at around 11pm by two men who lured him outside his house on the pretext that they had crashed into his car. The incident was witnessed by his 15-year-old daughter Renate who had answered the door to the kidnappers and by a neighbour who worked at the Grundig factory. Niedermayer was never seen alive again and it would be over six years before a breakthrough in the investigation of his disappearance led to the recovery of his body. The investigation revealed that he had been pistol-whipped and then buried face down in a shallow grave under a rubbish dump at Colin Glen. Niedermayer's funeral took place at Dunmurry in March 1980, where he was interred in the churchyard. His wife Ingeborg returned to Ireland ten years after her husband's funeral and booked into a hotel at Bray, County Wicklow. She later went for a walk along an isolated stretch of beach and committed suicide by walking into the sea.

It is thought that he was killed on or about December 30 and if the IRA hoped to turn his abduction into some sort of 'cash cow' their execution of the plan went terribly awry. Some six days or so after his kidnapping, the British Government was issued with a ransom demand. Whether or not the Republicans thought that they might extract funds from the West German, the British Governments, or from Grundig themselves or perhaps even the rich man's family is not known for certain.

Other than the tragedy of the death of Mrs Niedermayer, there was one other postscript; at a trial of some of the kidnap gang in 1981, it was revealed that there might have been one other motive. One of the gang claimed in court that the plan was to obtain the release of the Price sisters, Dolours and Marion who had been jailed for the Old Bailey bombings earlier that year. At that time the two, along with Gerry Kelly another of the convicted bombers, were on hunger strike in a mainland prison. The plan had already failed because the kidnap gang had already killed the German. Somewhat sanctimoniously, one of his killers revealed in court, that after they had buried his body in Colinglen, they: "…said a prayer for him".

1973 was limping towards its bloody end, and there was one more CVO to be dispatched, one more set of loved ones to grieve and two more children to be left fatherless. December 31 fell on a Monday and in the early afternoon, an armed gang of IRA thugs burst into a house on Beechmount Avenue. They held the family there at gunpoint and set up a sniper rifle in one of the bedrooms overlooking the point where Islandbawn Road joins Beechmount Avenue. The location was some 130 yards north of the Falls Road and any Army vehicles coming up Islandbawn Road would have to slow down before entering Beechmount Avenue.

As a mobile patrol from the Scots Guards reached the point where they had to slow down, one of the IRA men in the house fired a single shot which entered the observation panel in the PIG and hit Guardsman Alan Daughtery (23). The young Guardsman who lived in Co Durham was killed instantly. The gunmen and his accomplices made good their escape into the back streets of the Beechmounts and left the abducted woman in fear of her life if she gave evidence. The IRA proved yet again, that when it came to shooting their own supporters or blowing up their own people or even terrifying the very communities that they professed to protect, their hypocrisy was matchless.

The Scots Guards, whose motto is *Nemo Me Impune Lacessit* (no-one assails me with impunity), lost 22 of its soldiers during the course of the Troubles, and Guardsman Daughtery was the 10th to die in Northern Ireland. This proud Regiment, formed in 1642 boasts battle honours as diverse as Egypt, Waterloo, South Africa, Mons retreat and the battle of the Reichswald in 1945.

It fought with bravery and distinction on Tumbledown in the Falklands and it spilled its blood at the junction of Islandbawn Road and Beechmount Avenue.

For the Army, a total of 278 soldiers had lost their lives in exactly 24 months, but the old naivety was fast disappearing, training and intelligence methods were improving and both the Army and the RUC were now taking the war more directly to the IRA. 1973 had ended; 1974 was about to begin.

December ended, and the death tally was 16, or one every other day. Of these two were soldiers (both were killed by the IRA), three Policemen, six were civilians, four were IRA members and one was a Loyalist paramilitary. Of the civilians, the Republicans killed four and the Loyalists one and the Army shot one civilian. In total, the Provisional IRA was responsible for the loss of half of the lives during the course of December.

1973: The Final Tolls

Over the year as a whole, beginning with the brutal murders of Oliver Boyce and Briege Porter and ending with the shooting of Guardsman Daughtery, a total of 297 people had lost their lives in, or as a direct consequence of the Troubles.

The tolls were as follows:

British Army	106
RUC	12
Civilians	128
IRA	36
Loyalists	15

Further, it is worth noting, that of the 128 civilian deaths, at least 74, or c. 60% were killed in sectarian murders.

Part Two: 1974

Preamble

As with the previous year, I have chosen to include amongst the military deaths three former members of the Ulster Defence Regiment and one former member of the Royal Green Jackets. I believe that the Provisional IRA deliberately targeted civilians who had at some stage been a full or part-time member of the UDR. It mattered little to the Republican killers that these men had resigned and were now trying to lead normal lives. Normal that is, in the context of a troubled and dangerous Northern Ireland. The sickening hypocrisy of the IRA was revealed – again – after they murdered UDR Private Robert Jameson on 17 January. They warned that members of the UDR, on or off duty, would be targeted unless they resigned. If this was the case, why did they murder three former members through the year? I have also included a former soldier in the RGJ, Bryan Shaw (21 July) because his abduction and murder was guaranteed once the Provisionals had learned of his military past; his English accent was his death warrant.

During the course of this year 74 serving, and five former serving, soldiers were killed in, or as a consequence of, the Troubles. The total of 79 was down on the 106 killed in the previous year and half of the slaughter of the bloodiest year, 1972. It reflected several changes in military tactics and as more soldiers returned for a second, third or even fourth tour of duty, there was a solid core of men, street wise and experienced in dealing with the terrorists.

The New Year of 1974 may well have brought new hope to all those who first-footed at the 12th peal of the churches at midnight, but disillusionment was just around the corner. February would witness the slaughter of soldiers and innocents alike on an Army bus in West Yorkshire; the first women soldiers would be killed at a pub in Guildford and 33 civilians would be slaughtered in the Irish Republic, in a bloody two hour spate of four bombs. It was also the year of the Birmingham pub bombings, which killed 21 young drinkers on a cold Friday evening. Despite all of this, bigoted, irrational Brit-haters in the Irish American community, through their mouthpiece, the offices of NORAID, continued to fund the bombings and the murder. Without the 'mighty dollar' the killings would have ended much sooner.

1973 had ended with the New Year's Eve murder of Guardsman Alan Daughtery in Belfast's Beechmounts area, 1974 would continue in the same vein. For the Provisional IRA, it was business as usual, as it was also for their Loyalist counterparts, the UVF and the UFF. There was, however, another grouping which would come into play, albeit later in the year; the INLA. Originally the PLA (People's Liberation Army) it would soon try to bloodily oust the other terrorists off the front pages and at times it made even the Provisionals look 'moderate.'

The Irish National Liberation Army (INLA) would prolong their campaign from late 1974 until 1998 and one will examine their late entry onto the terrorist scene later in this book. For now, innocents feared to walk the streets at night because of the threat of sectarian killers and soldiers and police alike had to walk the streets of Ulster to keep the peace; and stay alive.

INLA came into being as a result of the more militant members of the Official IRA finally losing patience with the organisation who wished to talk peace rather than commit murder on the same scale as the Provisionals. The period of INLA's campaign was punctuated by the bitter internecine struggle with the 'Stickies' but once that was dealt with, they would be finally strangled to death as they waged war against the Provisional IRA.

Chapter 13

January

The New Year was only 40 minutes old when the IRA began their killings. They attacked an Army mobile patrol on the Ormeau Road in South Belfast. At least three gunmen opened fire on an armoured land rover; all the shots missed, but did hit an innocent civilian out with his father and searching for a family friend. John Whyte had celebrated the New Year with his family and friends and was out trying to find his brother who had also been out to a New Year's Eve party. Sadly for Mr Whyte (26), he was hit by one of the rounds fired from an American M1 carbine and he died at the scene. Local protests were made against the IRA for endangering locals as they yet again made a battleground of Belfast's residential streets. That the killings continued for more than two decades afterwards, demonstrates the scant regard that the Provisionals had for 'their' community or its feelings.

Some mystery surrounds the next killing, which took place at a house in Ravenscroft Avenue, Belfast close to the Upper Newtownards Road. A gang, very likely from the UFF, were looking for a Catholic man called McCullagh although for what reason, is unknown. His father answered the door and the men demanded to know of the whereabouts of the man they were seeking. At this point, Leo McCullagh (44) was shot at close range and died very shortly afterwards, in the arms of his distraught wife.

On 9 January, the UVF abducted a Catholic, John Crawford (52), from where he worked, close to Milltown Cemetery and opposite the then RUC Station at the point where the Glen, Andersonstown and the Falls Roads all converge. He was taken away, beaten and tortured before being shot in the head and dumped close to the cemetery. In 2008, the author returned to the scene of the old RUC station, crossed the busy road and walked amongst the myriad number of gravestones; some poignant, some garish and some, sadly simple. One wondered just how many of these graves contained the earthly remains of the thousands whose lives had been ended prematurely, through either terrorism or as a consequence of the sectarian madness.

There are many things which all take for granted in life; shopping, partying, relaxing and even the household chores. Who could have foreseen that giving a friend a simple driving lesson, would end in two more deaths? On 11 January, two friends, both civvie workers at Ebrington Barracks in Londonderry set out for a driving lesson; teacher and pupil. The Official IRA – although it took them exactly 25 years before they admitted responsibility – had marked the pair down for execution because they worked for the 'occupation forces'. A large UVBT (under vehicle booby trap) was placed under the car which contained John Dunn (45), a father of six, and Mrs Cecilia Byrne (51) and it exploded in the Waterside district; both were killed instantly. The Official IRA not only denied categorically that they were involved, but the Derry Brigade even sent a note of condolence to the families! *Lost Lives* notes the words of Mrs Byrne's husband; he said: "They say that time is a great healer but it's not really true. We had planned to retire a few months after she was killed. We had no children so it meant the end of my home and my family. I lost everything."[1] As stated, it took the Official IRA a quarter of a century before they owned up; one can only conjecture that they were either a) ashamed of their actions b) were not willing to be seen breaking their 1972 truce or c) that they were disappointed that the UVBT had not exploded inside Ebrington Barracks and killed soldiers.

THE BRITISH ARMY 'HIJACK A BUS'
Tim Francis, Royal Artillery

'Papa 9' was a very large permanent vehicle checkpoint situated on the quayside of the Rover Foyle. As part of the then one way traffic and security system, all vehicles and their occupants in the three lanes of traffic headed down towards the Foyle Bridge were checked to varying degrees at the discretion of the guys manning the checkpoint. Traffic here consisted of cars, buses – mainly from the Shantallow area – and many lorries, in varying numbers, depending on the time of day. In order to man this checkpoint efficiently it had a contingent of nine men manning it, 24 hours a day. Generally these were rotated so that three guys usually had their feet up in the hut or, in the depths of the night six could be resting whilst at rush hours, all hands were on deck to keep the traffic moving without compromising security. In addition, pedestrians passing down the quayside were also checked, often with slightly hilarious consequences as there were often ships moored there overnight, predictably often visited by local ladies of a certain type looking for a little distraction on board with the sailors, also equally interested in distractions.

Stags here consisted of six hours at a time but often extended to 12 hours from 8pm to 8am for at least some of the guys. It could be a very long night indeed; hours spent dozing in an extremely unpleasant, gas heated hut with a bucket in another hut for facilities and a reinforced sangar for the sentry on watch. This was also used occasionally for other rather dubious activities with the opposite sex. It was a strange existence, toasting bread on the front grill of the gas heaters, drinking horrible tea from the flasks sent out on each stag; a constant fog of cigarette smoke together with the assorted odours of half a dozen guys too long on duty and smelling accordingly. In simple terms, if you started at 8 in the morning this would be a frantic and very busy period; keep the traffic flowing for an hour or so and then slightly more relaxed until changed over at two. However, with a constant flow of Shantallow buses full of gobby youngsters all day, one can imagine all the fun that went with that.

From 2pm until 4pm would be the same, which was then followed by a couple of hours where we were very busy again before tailing off down to change over at 8pm. The later evening could be relatively lively as assorted drunks made their way to and from wherever they were going, not to mention the girlies headed to and from the ships, also often not very sober. From about midnight this would tail off, with another change over for some at 2 while others stayed and then the morning traffic build up from between 6 and 7.

There was however a serious reason for our presence at 'Papa 9' and in early 1974 the eagle eyes of the guys there were to discover a car containing over 100lbs of explosives, subsequently disabled by a controlled explosion. This was to be the largest quantity of explosives found by our regiment in any single search on this tour and was the only find of its type during the four years that 'Papa 9' had been operating up until that time.

There was also another more amusing occasion when one of our sections coming off duty in the morning, boarded a passing crowded bus, telling the driver they were having a lift and that he should drop them off opposite our base which he complied with after much moaning. Unfortunately he took his moans to the local press and our guys were accused of hi-jacking the bus at gunpoint, contravening all sorts of laws by carrying firearms on a public vehicle not to mention non-payment of fares. Of course, in their tiredness our guys had overlooked just how delicate were the feelings of the locals.

This incident was, of course, front page news and the author is very grateful to Tim Francis for reproducing a copy of the local Londonderry newspaper. They reported that:

There's no transport of delight for the Army in Londonderry. Troops are in trouble with local folks over buses. For a Republican club in the city has accused the Army of 'virtually hijacking a bus.' The James Larkin Republican Club at Carnhill said an Army patrol recently boarded a bus at Strand Road and travelled on it until it reached a military checkpoint. The Republicans say that the soldiers refused to pay fares and caused a public danger by carrying loaded weapons on a crowded bus.

Presumably, the soldiers should have made themselves an easier target for PIRA gunmen, by unloading their weapons for their duration of the bus journey? One must forgive the author's heavy use of irony in this matter.

The Official IRA far from keeping their heads down, were involved just two days later when they shot a fellow Republican and ex-internee whom they accused of selling arms to the Provisionals. Christopher Daly (43) was shot by the Officials near to his home in the Ardoyne district. He was killed and left for dead in the most sordid of settings; an alleyway on Balholm Drive.

On 14 January the UVF were involved in abduction; they picked up Andrew Jordan (41) from near to a social club in Lord Street in Belfast city centre. He had absolutely no paramilitary connections and was a Protestant; his death was more likely the result of either mistaken identity or someone settling personal scores. One needs to remember that often a killing might be the settling of an argument, petty jealousy or any number of reasons for what might, in times of peace, be considered a 'normal' murder. He was taken to a field near Carrowdore, 12 miles due east of Belfast, where he was shot in the head and then, twice more whilst he lay helpless on the ground.

The IRA tactic of targeting off-duty UDR soldiers continued, and their recce and intelligence cells were constantly alert and aware of regular patterns in the targets' lives. They had clearly done their homework and observed the regular work patterns of Private Robert Jameson (22), and were waiting at the point where he regularly alighted his work bus at Trillick, Co Tyrone, to wait for his lift home. On 17 January, as he stepped off the bus, an IRA gunman stepped up to him and shot him in his head and chest. His distraught mother found him minutes later but he sadly died, shortly after receiving medical treatment.

Cappagh, Co Tyrone is a small town close to Dungannon and forms a triangle with Galbally and Carrickmore which was an area of major IRA activity. It is situated midway between Omagh and beautiful Lough Neagh; it also has a large Catholic majority. As such, it was bound to be the focal point of a Loyalist paramilitary hit-and-run. Less than an hour after the IRA had murdered Private Robert Jameson, retired farmer Daniel Hughes (72) walked into Boyle's Bar in Cappagh and no sooner had he done so, than two hooded gunmen from the UVF burst in and sprayed the bar with sub machine guns. The pensioner was hit and died at the scene, and three other customers were hit and wounded. His killers escaped in a stolen car and roared off towards Belfast, having changed cars and abandoned the original at a nearby quarry.

In the very early hours of the morning of 20 January, Desmond Mullen (33) left a bar in the centre of Carrickfergus, a seaside town in Co Antrim, and was abducted by a Loyalist murder gang. He had previously been the subject of threats and although a Catholic, had no links with any of the Republican movements. He was simply easy prey for the murder gangs: Catholic, been drinking, and out alone in the small hours of the morning. He was found, shot in the head and left in the town centre.

Later that same day, the IRA was responsible for the abduction and murder of a Head Master from Clogher, Co Tyrone. He was also a part-time soldier in the UDR. Captain Cormac McCabe (43) and his family had crossed the border to visit the town of Monaghan for a meal out. Monaghan, which is only four miles inside the Republic, would soon be in the news again, four months later, when the UVF killed seven people in Greacen's pub. Captain McCabe excused himself and went to speak to two men in the reception area. There was a scuffle before he was bundled into a waiting car, taken back over the border. He was hooded, beaten and then shot dead by an IRA gang; his body was dumped in Altadavin, close to his home in Clogher.

The day after the murder of the UDR man, Captain Cormac McCabe, the IRA struck again, this time in Londonderry in the TAOR of 94 Locating Regiment, Royal Artillery. The unit was based in an old factory close to Lone Moor Road and Stanley's Walk in the Brandywell district. Operating against them was the IRA's Brandywell Company, responsible the previous year for the death of young Kathleen Feeney who was playing near her home, when a sniper fired at a foot patrol. Lone Moor Road is a long thoroughfare and leads through the Brandywell, past Derry City Football Club and past the cemetery where some of the 'Bloody Sunday' victims are laid to rest. Stanley's Walk then joins it, shortly before Bligh's Lane.

Sergeant John Haughey (32), father of three was in charge of a foot patrol in the Brandywell area. As was normal SOP (standing operating procedure) he had taken cover behind a telephone junction box in order to make himself a 'hard target' and shepherd the rest of the patrol through. Sadly, these types of 'hard targeting' and 'going firm' had been witnessed too many times by the IRA's legion of 'dickers.' An explosive device had been placed in the same junction box which several patrols had been seen to take cover. As the Sergeant – from Didsbury, Manchester – crouched down, the device exploded and mortally wounded the soldier and injured several others. The Didsbury boy was rushed to Altnagelvin Hospital where he died shortly after arrival.

Following on from the killing of Sergeant John Haughey, the author spoke to a most impeccable source within the Regiment. My contact is highly reliable, trustworthy and accurate, and what he told me put a different perspective on the events leading up to the fatal explosion. We chose not to name the officer concerned.

THE LOSS OF JOHN HAUGHEY

On the subject of the murder of John Haughey there is a little known fact about the lead up, which is (I think) unknown outside of the Regiment. It was well covered up and I'm sure it did not come out in the inquest.

I'm not certain of the time frame for this; there was a guard sangar on the waste ground outside the Saracen factory base, which overlooked the Bogside. Access to it was gained by a sunken path. Just prior to the bomb going off, the sentry reported that a couple of men were messing around with the telephone junction box at the junction of Lone Moor Road and Stanley's Walk. The Ops room 'Rogered' this. A short time later, the sentry reported this again, insisting that the men were up to no good. Again the ops room told him not to bother about it as it was probably 'workmen.' The lad in the sangar wouldn't accept this and an argument started. The Ops officer then came on the squawk box and basically said that if he heard any more about this he would kick his arse. I think I'm right in saying that the guards then changed, and it was shortly after that the bomb exploded killing John and wounding another.

The lad who had reported the activity had to be physically restrained from going to the OP's room and committing murder himself. The whole thing left a really nasty taste in the mouth as the 'Ruperts' closed ranks and defended the Ops officer's actions; although in private, some of the younger ones voiced their disgust. Lucky for him, as ops officer, he never went out on the ground; otherwise I'm convinced he would have met with an 'accident.'

He wasn't seen again, but he was an obnoxious little fucker who got under everyone's skin because he thought he knew everything. Although about 5' 6" in height and weighing about nine stone dripping wet; he was a real bully boy who hid behind his rank. Some years later, I made up with an officer who was around at the time that John was killed and we had a good old chin wag and of course the Op Banner tour was one of the main topics. Up front, I asked him why the incident concerning the sentry and the ops officer was covered up. He said that when John Haughey was killed, it was one of the worst days of his life. He explained that the regiment had had too many losses which could be due to bad leadership and one more would have been disastrous for their reputation. It doesn't take a genius to work out whose arse was being protected.

If it hadn't been for the stupidity of the very few, we could have come away from that tour, basically unscathed apart from some minor wounds. Many years later, I was told that if it hadn't been for the RSM, really sticking his neck out, things could have been a lot worse for us. He went so far as to tell someone senior that the men totally detested the man we felt was indirectly responsible for John's death and that an 'accidental' shooting was not out of the question.

BOGSIDE BOMB FACTORY
Mike Sangster, Royal Artillery

The Reserve Troop had its own search team, and over the course of the tour, had its fair share of finds but none better than what we found on the 20th January 1974. My team were told to search the home of a well-known player. The cordons were set and the teams went in. The door to the house was locked so we used the DMS key on it. The building was cleared and my pair took the upstairs, second pair downstairs and the third, the back garden. Upstairs, we found a complete printing set up for terrorist propaganda sheets, batteries, electrical wire and loads of other material of INT value.

I was just examining some of it when I heard someone shout 'Bom' from up the stairs. Now in the Royal artillery, the rank of Bombardier is usually shortened to 'Bom', like 'Sarge' or 'Corp' so when I heard 'Bom' shouted up the stairs I replied: "What! I'm busy". Again the shout went up "Bom". A bit annoyed, I went to the top of the stairs and asked what he wanted. This time he shouted: "There's a bomb!" Well my partner and I took the stairs, four at a time but instead of heading for the front, I headed for the rear and came face to face with a very white faced Eric 'A' who had been searching out the back. "There's tons of it and I fell over the fucking stuff". He shouted. Looking out, I could see this big stack of polythene bags which were partially covered by a tarpaulin. The stink of marzipan filled the air.

We all got out and waited for the arrival of Felix. He was well chuffed with the explosives find. He said the stuff was brand new and amounted to 120 lbs of co-op mix HME. But on further searching, packets of detonators were found and one of them had a detonator missing and I remember Felix saying that there is a bomb somewhere in the Bogside.

The next day, we were back in Hawkin Street, still hyped up by our find. When some time in the afternoon, we heard a dull thud coming from the direction of the Bogside. We were soon told that a bomb had exploded as a foot patrol reached the junction of Stanley's Walk, and a friend of mine, Sgt John Haughey, had been caught in the blast. The bomb had been hidden behind a telephone junction box and remotely detonated when John approached. Sadly he died; Felix's words had been prophetic.

On 22 January, the man who many see as one of the major stumbling blocks to peace in Northern Ireland was again in the news. The Reverend Ian Paisley, the outspoken Loyalist politician, was among eighteen Loyalist protestors who were forcefully removed from the front benches of the Assembly. It took eight RUC officers to carry Ian Paisley, then leader of the DUP, to steps outside the Assembly building.

Two days later two Provisional IRA members, Eddie Gallagher and Rose Dugdale, in a scheme which could have come out *Boys' Own* comic, hijacked a helicopter in Co. Donegal, in the Irish Republic. They loaded milk churns packed with explosives and forced the pilot to fly over the border into Co Tyrone and over the town of Strabane. Forcing him to hover over the Strabane RUC station, they rolled the 'churn bombs' out of the helicopter and dropped them on the station. Thankfully, as posterity has recorded, the bombs failed to detonate.

Felix riddles a suspect vehicle with SSG shot close to
border with Irish Republic (Brian Sheridan)

Felix prepares to defuse IRA car bomb in Newry (Brian Sheridan)

One of the most famous of the Yorkshire Regiments is affectionately called 'Duke of Boots' or, more politically correct, The Duke of Wellington's (West Riding) Regiment (DWR). It was a fine Regiment and its many battle honours included Dettingen, 1743; American War of Independence (1775-83); Waterloo; South Africa; Ypres (1914) and many gained during the Second World War. Its Regimental motto is *Virtutis Fortuna Comes* (Latin: 'Fortune Favours the Brave') and the 'Boots' served with distinction during the Northern Ireland troubles.

In January, 1973, it was based in the Lough Neagh area, eight to ten miles west of Belfast. On the 25th, the DWR put out a foot patrol in the Toomebridge and Ballymaguigan area, following up an attack on a foot patrol the previous evening. The soldiers had found a rocket and booster; some ammunition and other terrorist paraphernalia and a young officer went to examine more finds in a nearby field. As he did so, he trod on a small anti-personnel mine which exploded, killing him instantly. Second Lieutenant Howard Fawley (19), who came from Shipley, near Bradford was the victim, it is thought, of an IRA 'come on.' The author understands that some of the equipment was deliberately left behind by an IRA ASU the night before, in order to lure the soldiers into the field. They will have then planted the landmine, in the hope of killing or maiming soldiers.

Having killed two more soldiers, the Republicans then turned their attention to the police and murdered two RUCR officers in the space of just three days. Glengormley, Co Antrim is approximately four miles north-west of Belfast city centre and is a small village in the Newtownabbey area. Constable John Rodgers (50), father of four, was a part-time officer in the RUCR, attached to Glengormley RUC station. He was patrolling the centre of the village, and had just passed a pub when a single shot was fired by a Glengormley youth hiding in an alleyway. Constable Rodgers died at the scene and it is quite likely, that the local youth who killed him, probably knew him or at least had seen him in the village; the IRA gang included two locals.

The IRA were again involved two days later as they attacked a bus carrying Airmen from the local RAF station close to Newcastle, Co Down. One of the shots which missed passed through the windows of Matilda Witherington (82) and hit her in the chest. Until neighbours noticed the bullet hole in the window, no-one had raised the alarm and the elderly widow died alone. She was a victim, yet again, of the irresponsibility of the Provisional IRA who turned Shimna Road, Newcastle into a battlefield. In the twisted logic of these terrorists, Mrs Witherington was an unfortunate but no doubt 'legitimate,' casualty of their war.

On 29 January, RUCR Constable William Baggley (43), father of three, was patrolling in Dungiven Road, Londonderry at point midway between the Republican Gobnascale, and the Loyalist Waterside. He was walking along in the company of another officer when shots rang out, hitting both officers. Constable Baggley fell and his colleague sprinted for cover; though wounded, he then returned fire and was hit again. He saw one of the IRA gunmen stand over the helpless officer and fire more shots into him as he lay on the ground. On June 2, 1976, only a few yards away from where he was killed, his daughter Linda, and also an RUC officer was shot dead by the IRA.

In a three-day period, gunmen from the Provisional IRA had killed two part-time policemen and left a total of seven children fatherless; no doubt the Republican terrorists considered this a good three days work. Clearly, if their strategy was to either kill every single member of the security forces, or to sicken the general public on the mainland into clamouring for a withdrawal, they were losing on both counts. Assuming for one second, that the British Government had abdicated its responsibilities to the 66% of the population of Northern Ireland who wanted to remain part of the UK, what then of the Loyalists who would remain? Had British troops pulled out, who then would have contained the inevitable bloodbath? Of course my words are rhetoric, but what if? What if the two diametrically opposed sectarian forces had been left to fight over the carcass of Ulster?

If a simple soldier scribe – as this author was once described – can see that, then could the IRA Army Council not see the same? Were then these killings merely representative of a blood lust with no tangible result possible, or had they simply lost control of the vast number of cold-blooded, psychopathic killers in their ranks?

Having seen seven children made fatherless by the Provisionals, it was the UVF's turn to add to that grim tally, when they shot Thomas Walker (38) and made it 12 children without their dads. The hierarchy of the UVF felt Walker, a taxi driver who lived in the Ormeau Road area of South Belfast had been informing on them; that suspicion was enough to sign his death warrant. They knocked on the door of his on the pretext that some fellow taxi drivers wished to speak to him. He was shot five times in the chest and collapsed dying, in his own hallway, another victim of Loyalist murderers.

The month ended with the sickening and cold-blooded sectarian murder of two Catholics by the UDA/UFF. An armed gang raided a work area on the Rush Park housing estate in Whiteabbey, Co Antrim on Thursday, 31 January where workmen were laying electricity cables. The gang first of all robbed the workers of their pay packets and then singled out two Catholics: Terence McCafferty (37) and his workmate James McCloskey (29) and fired automatic weapons at them, killing them both. Despite instructing the Protestants to kneel down, informing them that they would not be shot, three of them were injured in the indiscriminate shooting inside their work hut.

Earlier that month – on the 19th – Staff Sergeant James Lund (33) of the Royal Engineers, died in circumstances unknown; the author has no further information at the time of writing. His service number was 23658192 and he was from Middlesbrough, in the Teesside area of England.

The first month of 1974 had ended and the death tally was 20. Of these five were soldiers (four of whom were killed by the IRA), two Policemen, and 13 were civilians. Of the civilians, the Republicans killed five and the Loyalists eight; at least seven of the killings were purely sectarian. In total, the Provisional IRA was responsible for the loss of 11 lives during the course of January.

Chapter 14

February

The IRA's 'England Team' was particularly active during this year, as the Provisionals stepped up their bombing campaign on the British mainland. With ample supplies of explosives being smuggled in from countries like Libya and the USSR, and with supporters in the Basque separatist terror group, ETA (*Euskadi Ta Askatasuna*), there was no shortage of bomb making ingredients. If 1974 wasn't the year which produced the most actual number of IRA bomb attacks during the Troubles, it was certainly the year of the worst atrocities.

Some of the most indiscriminate bombing attacks and killings of the IRA's bombing campaign were carried out by what the British media dubbed the 'Balcombe Street gang'. This was a unit of eight IRA members, who were sent to London in early 1974. Unlike previous members of the 'England Team', they studiously avoided contact with the large Irish community in England in order to remain inconspicuous. In addition to bombings, they murdered several prominent figures, such as TV presenter Ross McWhirter who had offered a £50,000 reward for information leading to the gang's arrest. McWhirter, one of twins, was shot dead at his London home on 27 November, 1975. The group also made an assassination attempt on Conservative Party leader, Edward Heath.

They were eventually arrested after a machine gun attack on an exclusive restaurant on Mayfair. After being pursued by police, they took hostages and barricaded themselves, for six days, in a flat on Balcombe Street, Paddington. The incident became known as the Balcombe Street siege. They were sentenced to thirty years each for a total of six murders. The group later admitted responsibility also for the Guildford pub bombing of 5 October 1974, which killed five people and injured 54 and also the bombing of a pub in Woolwich, which killed another two people and injured 28. But they never admitted responsibility for the M62 coach attack.

Late on the evening of Sunday 3 February a specially commissioned coach set off from the centre of Manchester, carrying Army personnel and some of their families. The coach, which was not a regular service, was taking soldiers to bases in Catterick and Darlington during a period of industrial action by Rail workers. A few minutes after midnight, as it drove along the then new M62 Motorway which carries traffic and freight from the western port city of Liverpool to its eastern sister port of Hull, the world ended for eleven people on board. The coach reached Hartshead Moor, near a motorway service station. It was on the eastbound carriageway between Chain Bar, Bradford, and Drighlington south of Leeds, when a device in the luggage hold exploded.

Most of those aboard were sleeping or reading at the time, when the blast, which could be heard several miles away, reduced the coach to a tangle of twisted metal and threw body parts up to 250 yards across the road. The explosion killed eleven people and wounded more than fifty others, one of whom died four days later. Amongst the dead were nine soldiers; two from the Royal Artillery, three from the Royal Corps of Signals and four from the Royal Regiment of Fusiliers (RRF). One of the RRF dead was

Corporal Clifford Haughton who also lost his entire family. Numerous others suffered severe injuries, including a six-year-old boy, who was badly burned. An ambulance official, surveying the carnage said at the time: "You can't imagine a thing like this on a British road. How could it have happened?"

The author, who had left the Army by now, was en-route back to the University of Warwick from his native Leeds, and was unaware at the time of the carnage which had happened only about six miles from his home. At the University that afternoon, I learned of the outrage as the Student's Union was to debate the events. A motion condemning the atrocity was carried unanimously, but not before dissenting voices from IRA supporters in the International Marxist Group, Communist Party and other left-wing entities on the campus, supporting the bombers' actions were voiced. One person said to me in a face-to-face confrontation: "I rejoice in the deaths of those soldiers!" Only the British libel laws prevent me from naming this sick, ill-informed and blindly prejudiced individual.

The tragic roll of the dead was as follows: Corporal Clifford Haughton (23), RRF, from Manchester, his wife Linda (23) and their young children, Lee (five) and Robert (two); Bombardier Terence Griffin (24), Royal Artillery, from Bolton; Gunner Leonard Godden (22) Royal Artillery, from Kent; Fusilier John Hynes (20), RRF, from Oldham; Lance Corporal James McShane (29), RRF, also from Oldham; Paul Reid (17) Royal Corps of Signals; Michael Waugh (22), Guards Brigade, Signals, from Manchester and Signalman Lesley Walsh (19), Royal Corps of Signals, from Lancashire. Three days later, Fusilier Stephen Whalley (19), RRF, from Bloxwich, West Midlands, who was critically injured, died in hospital.

IRA Army Council member, Dáithí Ó Conaill was challenged over the bombing and the death of civilians, during a later interview, and replied that the coach was bombed because IRA intelligence (sic) indicated that it was carrying military personnel only.

The Daily Express of Tuesday 5 February – incredibly enough on page 5! – ran with the headline: 'Motorway Massacre'. They described: "how a motorway bomber put an end to an Army weekend". Their reporter described the scene thus:

> This tangled mass of metal was all that was left of an Army coach after a 50lb bomb ripped it in half yesterday. The wreckage spattered the eastbound carriageway of the M62 motorway, near Leeds for over half a mile. Said one survivor: 'It was a normal, rather boring coach ride. People were reading, snoozing or just having a smoke … Police believe that the bomb was placed in the boot of the coach at Manchester's Chorlton Street Station. Earlier the coach is believed to have been left on waste ground for 48 hours – with the boot unlocked.

The article goes on to quote the coach driver, Mr Handley as saying:

> Suddenly there was a tremendous crash. Everything blew up in front of me. I thought it was the windscreen.' The shattered windscreen fell on his head. With blood pouring from his face, he managed to pull the bus on to the side of the road 200 yards on. Scrambling from his shattered cab he shone his torch onto a scene of chaos and horror. He said: 'There was a little child laid among the wreckage. I

picked it up but it was dead. There was another body over its head. There was a jumble of bodies everywhere.

20-year-old Signalman Neville Maw of Huddersfield, who was sitting next to Mr Handley, escaped through the windscreen and frantically ran down the motorway to stop cars running over injured passengers. Then he scrambled back into the mangled wreckage to help the rescue operation. "It was a terrible sight," he said. "Those of us who were ok started to help the injured out of the bus. It was the most terrifying experience – something I will remember all my life." West Yorkshire Police Assistant Chief Constable Donald Roy declared: "It was a bloody sight. It was a dastardly and horrifying crime. People who commit crimes like this have no souls."

Other newspapers included the following quotes: "It was just a mangled wreck. I attended to a girl of about 17 who was 200 yards back up the road from where the coach had stopped. Her legs were injured. She was hysterical and kept saying: "My God! The floor just opened up and I fell through. I covered her up and tried to keep her warm." A police constable described the scene: "I have never seen anything like it and I never want to see anything like it again."

The injured were taken to hospitals in Bradford, Wakefield and Batley, and the Manchester police immediately searched at least three more coaches which had been commissioned by the Army to ferry personnel back to their camps. The security was certainly lax, and in view of IRA threats to off duty soldiers and the known presence of an IRA bombing team in England at the time, more could have been done to protect the passengers. This was certainly expected from the people who had a duty of care: the coach operators. This is in no way intended to divert from the heroics of the driver, whose skill and professionalism undoubtedly saved more lives in the seconds after the explosion.

THE M62 COACH BOMB
Phil Hutchinson, Royal Regiment of Fusiliers

When I got on the bus, I was probably sat about the second row down from the back of the coach. I had a friend who was on the coach – Stephen Whalley – and he was sat probably midway from the front. During the journey, Stephen wanted to swap places with me as he wanted to talk to another chap that he knew, so I swapped places with Stephen.

We'd just passed the Bradford turning and I remember that Barry Manilow's 'Mandy' was on the radio at the time. Then there was a sort of a 'whoosh' noise, it wasn't like an explosion, just a 'whoosh.' The coach swerved, and at this time I didn't know what had happened. The driver had actually got the coach onto the hard shoulder and when I looked back, the seat behind me was actually hanging down; the rest of the coach had disappeared. It was apparent that it wasn't a fault with the coach and we knew that a bomb had been planted and we knew that it was the IRA.

It was about a year later that I actually did my first tour of Northern Ireland and I went over there with 'A' Troop. I hated the Irish and I would have killed them and every time I met one, I was in a fight with him. It was luckily that, over the years I've grown up and I have realised that not all Irish are the same.1

THE LONG WAIT
Mo Norton, Sister of Bombardier Terence Griffin, Royal Artillery

We waited over 17 long and incredibly painful hours waiting for news and repeatedly making phone calls, and waiting for the phone to ring with news that Terence was OK. It was then that my mother made yet another phone call to the emergency phone line, in a desperate attempt to find out whether Terence was alive or injured. We knew after all these hours that he must at the very least been injured, as my father said: "Terence would have rung home and let us know he was OK if he had survived."

Terence' Battery Commander spoke to my mother, and told her that Terence had been positively identified and was dead. The absolute heartbreak; the sheer terror; the unbelievable pain experienced by my parents, my two sisters and myself, was nothing like any grief that I had experienced before nor after. The Battery Commander told my mother that an army officer and padre would be with us within the hour. We tried desperately to comfort each other, somehow trying to make the pain go away, yet knowing that it would not. I remember wanting to think that they had made a huge mistake, that Terence was unconscious and unable to identify himself. In my naiveté I kept telling myself that he would ring us, and that he would tell us that he was OK. This, after all, happens to other people's families, not ours, doesn't it?

We had just spent a lovely weekend together with Terence and his friend Len. It was only several hours since we had last seen them both, so it was hard to comprehend that we would not see them again. The grief was so painful, both physically and emotionally. I felt so desperately for my parents and my sisters seeing them so engulfed with grief. We turned the television on and the newscaster said the last two soldiers to be identified, have been named as Bombardier Terence Griffin and Gunner Leonard Godden. I knew then that it was not a mistake, and this was something that we would all have to live with for the rest of our lives.

Following the explosion, the British public and politicians from all three major parties called for swift justice. The ensuing police investigation led by Detective Chief Superintendent George Oldfield – later to be mentally and physically shattered by the Yorkshire Ripper case – was rushed and certainly botched. It resulted in the arrest and conviction of a mentally disturbed, former woman soldier, Judith Ward. She was a disturbed attention seeker whose life to date had included a short spell in the WRAC (Women's Royal Army Corps). She had gone AWOL and returned to her native Republic of Ireland in 1971. She claimed to have not only placed the device (inside a hold all) into the coach's luggage compartment, but also to have carried out several other bombings.

She retracted the statement later in Court, and the evidence against her was flimsy, to say the least. Most observers thought that her evidence was 'rambling and incoherent' but in spite of this, she was convicted at Leeds Crown Court and sentenced to 30 years

1   Reproduced from: *Soldiers' Stories: Northern Ireland* (History Channel: Point of View Productions, 2009).

imprisonment. She spent 18 years in jail, before this wrongful conviction was overturned by the Court of Appeal. At the time of her first trial, the Irish Republican Publicity Bureau issued a statement which read:

> Miss Ward was not a member of *Óglaigh na Éireann* and was not used in any capacity by the organisation. She had nothing to do whatsoever with the military coach bomb (on 4 February 1974), the bombing of Euston Station and the attack on Latimer Military College. Those acts were authorised operations carried out by units of the Irish Republican Army.

The late and unlamented Brian Keenan was spoken of as the IRA's Chief-of-Staff and the one time leader of the Balcombe Street gang that carried out a series of bombings in London in the 1970s. He was seen as one of the hardest men within the IRA. *The Scotsman* newspaper wrote of him in 1999:

> He was born in South Londonderry in 1942 and moved to England when he was 18, where he worked for a time with his brother in a television repair business. He returned to Northern Ireland shortly after the Northern Ireland Civil Rights Association took to the streets.

At the same time, the *Guardian* wrote:

> From 1972, he was a leading terrorist and was jailed briefly in the Irish Republic in 1974. He helped mastermind a coach bomb which killed 12 people on the M62 in England. He was jailed for 14 years for the bombings. He said at a Republican rally in Inniskeen, Co Monaghan [at the time of repeated calls for the IRA to decommission their arms]: I don't know where they get this word decommissioning, because it strikes me they mean it as surrender. There will be no surrender.

Mr Keenan, from Londonderry, worked for years as a television repairman in Corby, Northamptonshire. He was arrested for his involvement in a series of atrocities, including the M62 coach bombing – in which nine soldiers, a woman and two children were killed in 1974 – and the year-long bombing campaign attributed to the Balcombe Street gang. He was trapped through his fingerprint. He had smashed up a faulty cigarette machine as a young man, and the police had it on file. He was jailed for 18 years and served 14.

As a result of my first book, *A Long Long War: Voices from the British Army in Northern Ireland, 1969-98*, I became friends with Mo Norton, sister of Terence Griffin who was killed on the M62 Coach bomb. I count her as a close friend and it is my singular honour to know this lovely, warm hearted lady. In 2007, she kindly wrote me the following words:

> My brother, Bombardier Terence Griffin, RA, was tragically killed through the Northern Ireland Troubles in the M62 coach bomb blast, 4 February 1974. Upon reflection, I realised that most of us who are civilians did not know just how dangerous the situation in Northern Ireland was for those out there, trying their utmost best to keep peace. The reason I say this, is that my own brother, whilst

coming home on leave, had his stories to tell, but they were indeed much-sanitised stories. I realise that this was probably to protect us, his family from ever realising just how bloody and dangerous this war was. Upon reading many of the soldiers' stories, you get a sense of just how much the British Army and the Irish community had to go through.

After the bloody campaign of the mid 1970s, the IRA did not undertake a major bombing campaign again in England until the late 1980s and early 1990s. However, throughout the intervening period, they did carry out a number of high profile bombing attacks in England.

In 2008, I had the honour of speaking with Liz Burns (Linda Haughton's sister) and she gave me permission to use the following, which is on the headstone of the Haughton family grave: "Too precious to lose. Too young to die. Forgive us, God, for asking why."

As the events of the horror of the M62 were unfolding, the UVF were back on the streets of Belfast, doing what they did best: murdering Catholics in cold blood! Vincent Clarke (43) who lived in the Whiterock area of West Belfast had been talking to two men – Alexander McVicar and Arthur McKenna – moments before they were both shot by the IRA on 16 November 1970. Both were alleged to be petty criminals and the Loyalists believed – wrongly – that Mr Clarke was involved. They bided their time for over 38 months, before shooting him outside his mother's home on the same day as the M62 tragedy.

On the evening of 9 February, two friends who both lived in the vicinity of Leeson Street, off the Falls Road, had been drinking in a pub on the nearby Grosvenor Road. Hugh Duffy (22) who lived in Abyssinia Street and Anthony O'Connor (42) and a father of nine were walking along Grosvenor Road, with a female friend, intending to turn right into Hugh Duffy's street. Today Abyssinia Street ends in a cul-de-sac with no entrance from Grosvenor Road; back in 1974, the street was open-ended and there was direct access through to Leeson Street. As the two men prepared to turn right, two UFF gunmen opened fire, killing the two men and wounding their female companion. The motive was purely sectarian, and the three had been singled out by the Loyalist murder gang, as they had been drinking in a pub frequented by Catholics, and were walking in the direction of a Catholic estate.

Immediately east of the A1 Lisburn Road in Belfast, opposite Balmoral and north of Stockman's Lane is a small Catholic enclave called Bawnmore. It is an island in a large Loyalist 'sea.' As such, it was neither a happy nor a safe place for Catholics during the Troubles; and probably before and after if the truth is known. On 11 February, five friends and neighbors, who all worked for a meat processing company in Glenville Road, Belfast, set off for their place of employment in one car. Unknown to them, a UFF murder gang was lying in wait in a side street close to where the five worked. As they arrived to commence work for the day, Loyalist gunmen burst out of their stolen car and opened fire with automatic weapons. The five Catholics desperately tried to escape, but their car was only a two door model, and the rear passengers struggled to get out of the back. Thomas Donaghy (16) in his first job since leaving school was hit and died shortly after reaching hospital and Margaret McErlean (18) was hit and fatally wounded; she died in hospital on 18 February. The three other passengers were all hit, one of them seven times but all survived. Another car, driving behind was caught in the hail of bullets and a woman passenger was hit in the head but thankfully survived. The Loyalist murderers even ran after two of the wounded men as they ran away from the car, shooting as they ran, but gave up and raced out of the area. The RUC were on the scene within seconds as they had already been alerted by an employee of the company, alarmed at the sight of the waiting car which he thought was acting suspiciously.

On 12 February, an IRA ASU of the 'England Team' planted a bomb which exploded at the National Defence College at Latimer, Buckinghamshire, England. The bomb, which EOD experts estimated at 20 pounds, injured ten people but fortunately there were no deaths. Clearly, to the bombers, anything which had any sort of military connotations was a 'legitimate' target and scores of military installations throughout the mainland had their security measures stepped up. It was approximately at this time that the Army began to advise soldiers coming back from, or going on leave to wear civilian clothes and not allow themselves to be drawn into conversations about their profession.

Peter Carty (57) ran a petrol filling station at Balmoral, in south Belfast; he was described as being loved by both sections of the community. On 12 February, he was attacked at the station in Finaghy and shot dead by two men from the UFF who were attempting to rob him. He was a Catholic and their later trial, two Protestants blamed their actions on excessive alcohol.

One needs to go back to October 3 1972, and the murder of James Patrick McCartan by the Baker/McCreery gang who were part of the UFF. In February of 1974, McCreery was acquitted of McCartan's murder and celebrations broke out among Loyalists in the Newtownards Road area of East Belfast.[2] Soldiers were called in to quell the subsequent rioting amongst McCreery's jubilant supporters who had rubbed the Catholics' noses in it one more time. The Royal Military Police or 'Red Caps' as they are known to their less affectionate admirers in the rest of the British Army, were sent in, along with other troops. The RMP (motto: *Exemplo Ducemus*, Latin for 'By example, shall we lead') came under petrol bomb attack and other missiles were thrown at them in Belvoir Street. At this stage, they came under fire from Loyalist gunmen and returned fire, which under the 'Yellow Card' rules they were entitled to do. At least two UFF members were hit; one died at the scene and the other was fatally wounded. Kirk Watters (19) was killed and Gary Reid (17) died in hospital on 26 February.

Five days after the shooting of Watters, two soldiers from the RMP were killed in a tragic RTA and this will be dealt with in a paragraph or two.

The Royal Army Ordnance Corps are affectionately known throughout the British Army – or the 'Kate' as my late Uncle Tommy, a former National Serviceman referred to it – as 'blanket stackers.' In Northern Ireland, they were anything but and were often used as front line soldiers and took their share of the casualties. The Corps sustained 31 men KIA, including a staggering 20 killed whilst attempt to defuse IRA explosive devices. One such fatality was Doncaster soldier Alan Brammah (31) who was killed at Moybane, a small hamlet close to Crossmaglen in South Armagh. The EOD were called in to the area following a series of explosions the previous day. Earlier a major cross-border exchange of fire had broken out with IRA gunmen firing from hills inside the Republic, overlooking Moybane. Staff Sergeant Brammah had previously examined

---

2   See the October chapter of Wharton, Ken, *The Bloodiest Year: Northern Ireland 1972*, (Stroud: History Press, 2011).

wires in the field and when he returned for a closer look, a device exploded and he was killed instantly.

Between 19 and 28 February, both Loyalist paramilitary groups were involved in four murders as the month ground to a bloody end. Already the number of troubles-related dead had surpassed the 20 from the previous month.

Aughenlig near Kilmore is a small rural village inside the Irish Republic. There was one pub in the village; Traynor's Bar and the UVF selected it as an easy target for a bombing attack on 19 February. The bar was not busy and only three drinkers were in at the time of the attack. A Loyalist gang placed the device and then drove off, not waiting to see the death and misery which they were about to inflict on the hamlet. The device exploded, killing Catholic Patrick Molloy (46), father of five, and Jack Wylie (49), a Protestant from Northern Ireland who had crossed the border for a quiet drink.

On the 20th, two soldiers from the RMP were killed together in the same accident "somewhere in Northern Ireland". This is the only information which the author can elicit from the MoD; it may have been something as tragically prosaic as a road traffic accident (RTA) but there is still some sort of veil of secrecy about many of the Troubles-related fatalities. On that day, Corporal Stuart Milne (20) and Lance Corporal John Charles Mundy (19), both 'Red Caps' lost their lives.

It was the turn of the UFF, two days after the Kilmore attack, when they bombed the Spa Inn at the junction of Spamount Street and Trainfield Street, in the Republican New Lodge, Belfast. Today, there is no sign of the pub, but where it stood is close to the spot where Gunner Robert 'Geordie' Curtis of the Royal Artillery was shot dead by the IRA (06/02/71) and where Gunner Kim MacCunn was also killed (22/06/74). Sergeant Bernard Fearns would complete a trio of Royal Artillery dead, just a few streets away (30/07/74).

On that day, February 21, Hugh Devlin (82) one of the oldest men to die in the Troubles, was killed when the 30 lb device left by the UFF, exploded during lunchtime. Two men were witnessed running away from the pub and it was quickly evacuated, but tragically the old man was overlooked and he was killed instantly when the device detonated. Several other people, including children were also injured in an upstairs room and when soldiers attended to guard the rescue workers, they came under attack from a mob which had gathered. It was little wonder that the British soldier saw himself very much as 'piggy in the middle'.

Disturbances continued in Protestant areas of Belfast and on Saturday 23rd, in the Shankill Road area of Belfast, taxi drivers slewed their cabs to a halt, together with hijacked buses and sealed off roads in a protest against alleged Army harassment. There were further riots in Protestant areas of East Belfast, which was followed by a bomb explosion at the Belfast headquarters of the APNI; thought to have been the work of the UDA/UFF. The incoming Prime Minister Harold Wilson, back for his second term, must have realised exactly how much work the Troubles were going to bring him.

Sometime in either late January or during February, an Army search team found both a Rocket Launcher and ammunition in Raithlin Drive on the Creggan Estate in Londonderry. The Provisional IRA, ever paranoid about security immediately suspected that a tout (informer) had been at work and began an 'investigation.' It is possible that the Security Forces had one or more men inside the Creggan IRA and it is entirely possible that he diverted attention away from himself and pointed the finger at someone else. For whatever reason, Patrick Lynch (23) an IRA member was dragged before a 'kangaroo court' and found guilty. After being tortured – family members state that his body had burn marks and that metal nails had been driven through his fingers – he was taken away by a 'nutting squad' and shot dead. His lifeless body was dumped in the Creggan and he was denounced as a tout. His furious family denied this and stated that he was loyal to the IRA.

Sources close to the IRA always justify the killing of informers or suspected informers by stating that the Volunteer concerned had been 'Green booked'. The IRA Green Book is a training and induction manual issued to new volunteers. It includes a statement of military objectives, tactics and conditions for military victory against the British and their allies. In PIRA's understanding this military victory was to be achieved as part of "the ongoing liberation of Ireland from foreign occupiers". The Green Book is a manual of conduct and induction to the organisation and has been in existence for many decades. Before joining the IRA, all prospective members must be thoroughly coached in and understand the Green Book and what it means to them and their lives.

LONDONDERRY: GENERAL ELECTION DAY 1974
Mike Sangster, Royal Artillery

With only about a week of the tour left, the General Election on 28 February couldn't have come at a worse time as far as we were concerned. Everyone was a bit on edge as it was obvious that the terrorists would not let this day go by without attempting some outrage or another. The whole place had been relatively quiet for the last couple of weeks, and 'going home' fever was starting to take hold despite previous experience telling us that it would be fatal to switch off.

On the day, the Reserve Troop was up, dressed and fed long before the sun came up. We were on immediate standby at Hawkin Street ready to deploy anywhere in the TAOR. By late morning, boredom was starting to set in. We were getting constant reports from the ops room of minor disturbances in the area and a bus had been hijacked and set on fire in the Bogside but the whole thing seemed to be a bit of a damp squib. I decided to take a wander to the ops room to see what was happening. I was chatting to one of the signallers when this huge bang went off from the direction of the city centre. The regimental net (radio) burst into life requesting call sign 41 (us) to deploy to the Masonic base. By the time I'd ran back to our accommodation, everyone was donning flak jackets and boarding the pigs. The Masonic base was not far away and within 15 minutes we were in their vehicle park awaiting orders. A large bomb had gone off in the city, but as far as we could see, the city battery seemed to have everything under control. We de-bussed and hung around for a few minutes before being told to get some scoff at the cookhouse. After that we retired to the TV room, which was a manky old portakabin which abutted the wall overlooking the Bogside.

Again, after a short time, I got bored, so I decided to go for a walk. Just to the right of the TV room, on the wall, was an old unmanned sandbagged OP. I climbed in and had a good look around the Bogside. There was a burnt out bus on Rossville Street and a few groups of locals milling around but nothing to write home about. The large overt OP, 'KILO,' which was perched on the wall, was to the left and slightly below my position. It was permanently manned and gave a good panoramic view of the Bogside and Creggan. In the past, it had come under attack by small arms and RPG fire so it was very solidly built. There was nothing happening so I climbed out of the sangar and was stood having a chat with the 73 Battery MT Sergeants, when there was a loud whip crack and impact from outside. I put the mag on my rifle, cocked it and ran back into the sangar. More rounds were fired and it was obvious that the target was the 'KILO' OP. Despite the echoes, I could tell that the shots were coming from the Drumcliffe/ Meenan area, about 300 metres away, so I scanned that area using my SUIT sight. A couple of people lying prone at the corners had me taking up first pressure but at the last moment, I saw that they were covering their heads with their hands; narrow escape! I then started scanning the flats, looking for an open window. It was a cold day so any open window was suspect. The last round that was fired went over the top of my sangar so either I had been seen or it was a stray. I know the crack made me blink a bit.

I felt someone push in beside me and saw that it was Mac, our Troop sniper with his L42.3 Although the shooting had stopped, I told him to keep scanning as I could see the convoy of PIGs exiting the Saracen factory on Bligh's lane as the Bogside Battery QRF were 'crashed out.' We could at least give them some cover. I shouted out to the TC where I was sure the shots came from. It was then that we heard over the TC's radio the dreaded words: 'Crash call!' Someone inside 'KILO' had been hit. As I watched the stretcher-bearers entering the rear and they came out with a body, I was filled first with anger, then regret about not having returned fire. Although I had no target, if I'd fired a few rounds into Meenan and Drumcliffe, it would probably have put the sniper off and avoided this casualty. Totally unprofessional I know but you lose a bit of that when you see your own being injured. As it turned out, the casualty was not seriously hurt. The sniper had been using armour-piercing rounds. The inner wall of the OP was thick wood, and as one of the rounds penetrated, some splinters had hit this lad in the face; lucky man.

We got sent into the Bogside as part of the follow up but of course nothing came of it although the heavy presence of troops on the ground put a spoke in any other terrorist plans and the day ended quietly. It did have one effect on us though. There was no more going home fever and the boss and NCOs kept a tight hold for the last days.

On that final day of the month – a Thursday – the UVF launched their own version of 'Bloody Friday' (21 July, 1972) when a series of ten bombs detonated in Belfast city centre in the space of just 60 minutes. The attacks were designed to coincide with General Election Day throughout Britain. Scores of people were injured in the no-warning attacks including a 26-year-old woman who lost both legs. One of the bombs was thrown into the entrance way of the Red Star bar in Donegall Quay, which is close to the Lagan Bridge. The bar owner was shepherding the drinkers to safety which involved stepping past the bomb. Two drinkers were left when it exploded, killing one

---

3   A deactivated 7.62 Enfield L42 type sniper rifle. Chambered for the 7.62 NATO round and with a heavy barrel, this was a very accurate weapon.

man and severely injuring the other. Hugh Harvey (34) was the unfortunate man and he was killed instantly in the explosion.

On the same day, Trooper John Cyril Alfred Tyson (23) of the 14/20 Hussars was killed in a tragic accident; he was the thirteenth soldier to die during February. The month had been a bloody one, but May and Dublin/Monaghan was not far away.

The death tally for the month was 29. Of these 13 were soldiers (ten of whom were killed by the IRA) and 13 were civilians. Of the civilians, the Republicans killed three and the Loyalists ten; at least ten of the killings were purely sectarian. In total, the Provisional IRA was responsible for the loss of 14 lives during the course of February.

Chapter 15

March

During March, 27 people lost their lives, almost exactly the same number as the previous month. Loyalist paramilitaries were, again, prominent in a purely sectarian way, killing Catholics because they were Catholics. The Provisional IRA would again be important and the death of Joseph Hughes, a Catholic, was caused by their cowardly action in abandoning a car bomb in a Catholic residential area. It would also involve them in the murder of a senior Irish politician.

On 2 March a 14-year-old boy and member of the IRA walked up to a policeman, on duty outside a church in Upper Donegall Street, and shot him several times in the back and his head. The murder of Constable Thomas McClinton (28) bore the hallmarks of Gerard 'Dr Death' Steenson who first killed as a young teenager.[1] The policeman had his back to his killer and died at the scene. The same IRA 'child' was also charged, but acquitted of murdering a prison officer nine years later during an IRA escape.

The following day, an IRA culvert bomb was detonated by a command wire at Dunamore on the Drum Road, which connects Omagh to Cookstown, Co Tyrone. The area where the device was planted is extremely rural and there would have been no immediate back up for any soldiers caught in the blast. A two vehicle mobile patrol from the UDR was close to where the road from Dunamore village joins the main A505 and the leading vehicle was near but not on top of the landmine when it was detonated. Whether or not this was panic or simple misjudgement on the part of the firer, we will never know. However a large crater was formed instantly and the leading vehicle crashed into it. The impact of the crash caused Corporal Robert Moffett (36) to smash his head into the dashboard and he died shortly afterwards from serious head injuries.

On the British mainland, Conservative Prime Minister, Edward Heath, had contested an inconclusive general election the previous month – his party had won the most votes but Labour had more seats. Negotiations with the Liberal Party to form a coalition failed, and Heath resigned on 4 March. Heath's Conservative government was replaced by Harold Wilson's Labour minority government (confirmed in a narrow second general election in October). On 5 March Wilson appointed South Leeds MP Merlyn Rees to the post of Northern Ireland Secretary. However, due to Wilson's government's weak position, Rees was tied to Westminster rather than being in the Province. His 'hands-on' approach would only work if he was able to be in Northern Ireland. That would not change until the following October when Labour returned a small majority and were able to govern alone.

Forkhill, Co Down is situated in the most picturesque countryside imaginable but its beauty disguised the danger it presented as a Republican stronghold. Approximately one mile away is the village of Drumintee, with its one, obligatory Catholic church. It was there on 10 March, that an IRA unit abandoned a vehicle packed with explosives. It

---

1   For more information see Wharton, Ken, *The Bloodiest Year: Northern Ireland 1972*, (Stroud: History Press, 2011).

is unlikely that they intended to bomb a place, full of their supporters and sympathisers. It is more likely that they intended to target the Army base at nearby Forkhill. Whatever the reason was, no IRA spokesman ever admitted why they had abandoned the bomb where they did. Four local Catholic men – including three brothers –attempted to open the van doors; it exploded, killing Michael McCreesh (15) and injuring the others. One of the badly injured was Michael Gallagher (18) and his injuries were so severe, that he died in hospital just four days later. There is a very strong suggestion that the van was booby-trapped, intended to kill an Army search team, but the IRA singularly and spectacularly failed to notify the very community which they claimed to protect.

The very next day, the UVF targeted the Bunch of Grapes bar in Garmoyle Street, close to Belfast Docks. In February of the previous year, the bar had been attacked by the UVF and one of the customers, George Keating, had been there at the time. He had escaped unhurt on that occasion, but clearly believing the old adage that 'lightning never strikes twice', had continued to drink there. Sadly for him, lightning did strike a second time, and Mr Keating (47) and father of 11 children, was shot dead in a repeat attack by a UVF gunman. The killer sprayed the bar indiscriminately with a sub machine gun, wounding three other men.

There is some confusion surrounding the death of a senior politician on the same day as the UVF attack on the Bunch of Grapes bar. Senator Billy Fox (33) a senior member of Fine Gael's representatives in the Seanand Eireann (Irish Senate) was killed in confusing circumstance. He went to visit the home of his fiancée in rural County Monaghan, as he habitually did every Monday. A gang of armed paramilitaries had occupied the house in Tircooney, near Clones and as he arrived and confronted the gang he was forced to flee, but was followed and shot dead. The UDA/UFF claimed the killing in a depraved, opportunistic manner and the Provisional IRA made the outrageous claim that it was the work of the British Secret Service, in order to deflect attention away from their own involvement. Several years later, several men – all members of the IRA – were found guilty of his murder. This author maintains that the IRA gang had wrongly gone to Senator Fox's fiancé's house in the mistaken belief that there were arms on the premises; it leads to the inescapable conclusion that Billy Fox was killed by the IRA.

On 13 March, Gunner David Farrington of the Royal Artillery was manning security gates with three comrades at Chapel Lane in Belfast city centre. IRA gunmen, one of whom was using a Second World War German submachine gun, opened fire on the four soldiers. Three were hit and Gunner Farrington (23) from Romford, Essex was killed having been hit four times. Eyewitnesses, including civilians, observed that the gunmen had been hiding in the doorway of St Mary's church across from Chapel Lane. *Lost Lives* reported the following quotation from a Catholic Bishop, who was outraged that a Catholic church had been used as cover in the murder: "Those responsible for coupling murder with sacrilege seem to be emphasising their contempt and defiance of all that Christianity stands for."

On 15 March, the RUC received news that a lorry, almost certainly containing explosives had been parked in the centre of Magherafelt, Co Londonderry. The area around Queen Street was cleared and cordoned off. However, Adam Johnston (28), a father of four, incredibly was allowed to walk through the cordon, in the direction of the suspect vehicle. He was walking towards it, and had reached a spot some 200 yards away when it exploded, killing him instantly. This demonstrates the incredible killing range of the device and shows the IRA's scant concern for peripheral casualties. An RUC officer raced after him to save him from the blast. However, as he had almost reached him, the device detonated and he was injured; losing an eye in the process.

Later that day, two members of an IRA bomb-making team were involved in another classic 'own goal' when a planned attack on an RUC patrol on the A5 Tullyvar Road which links Ballygawley to Aughnacloy went wrong. The road that they chose is, in places, less than 4,000' from the border with the Irish Republic and as such, afforded them a short distance to safety, once they had blown up the vehicle. As one looks towards the border, west of the Tullyvar Road, there are flat, open fields and then the hills on the Irish side rise away from Ulster. The device which the two men were handling exploded prematurely, and both Kevin Murray (21) and Patrick McDonald (21) were killed instantly, with both bodies being blown some distance from the seat of the explosion. No doubt to be later eulogised in the songs of the Provisional IRA's East Tyrone Brigade.

An Phoblacht (*Republican News*) in their 30th June 2010 edition wrote of their dead volunteers:

> We honour them all equally and we extend our continuing sympathy and solidarity to their families. No one can measure the grief to loved ones caused by a tragic death and our thoughts go out to all the bereaved.
>
> Each and every one of those who gave their lives for freedom in this county and across the 32 Counties was part of a struggle that had endured through the worst that the Orange state and the British regime could throw at it. They were part of a struggle with a strategy, with a leadership and with widespread support. It was a struggle that was strong enough and resilient enough to adapt and change its strategy when required. It was a Movement that had the confidence to recognise that there was a time for war and a time for peace. And the Movement acted on that recognition and by doing so helped to transform politics in this part of Ireland and across Ireland.
>
> We owe a tremendous debt to the republicans who sacrificed so much in the past. They created the conditions which allowed the next phase of republican struggle to move forward. They fought the British Government and all its forces to a standstill. They made a new politics possible. Their legacy is a proud one and it means that today we have a peaceful way forward to our republican objectives and no young person need face loss of liberty, injury or death in the struggle.

This author finds it impossible to reconcile these pious words with the criminal and gangster-like actions of the Provisional IRA who brought violence and misery to the people of both Northern Ireland and the British mainland. Cowardly murders, punishment squads, the execution of alleged informers and indiscriminate bombings designed to kill and maim, were their watchword; one cannot in any way equate the words of the *An Phoblacht* writer with the criminal behavior of the IRA, throughout the Troubles.

However, this author does not reserve his contempt or opprobrium for the Republican terrorists and condemns without distinction the behaviour of the Loyalist paramilitaries. In the very early hours of 16 March, Noel McCartan (26) a Catholic who lived in McClure Street in South Belfast was walking home with his sister, after an evening's drinking in a bar in Cromac Street. As they walked in the direction of their homes, two masked gunmen from the UVF shot the Catholic man dead from very close range before escaping in a stolen car. Less than two weeks later, his grieving sister would also lose her husband in another UVF sectarian murder.

There was still more tragedy to come that day for families in both the London and Aldershot areas; two more CVOs were about receive the orders which they dreaded the most. A four man brick from the Parachute Regiment was patrolling in the countryside around Crossmaglen in South Armagh and had reached the Dundalk Road. The road itself is only 1,300 yards from the Irish border and continues on to Dundalk itself, inside the Irish Republic. It was a favourite bolt-hole for IRA men OTR (on the run) and a safe haven for the planning of operations inside the North. As the four Paratroopers reached the road, they came under heavy automatic gunfire. Two of the patrol were killed instantly, another was seriously injured and the only uninjured soldier was able to radio for reinforcements which arrived by helicopter. The dead soldiers were Lance Corporal Phillip James (22), killed the day after his 22nd birthday, from Plymouth in Devon and Private Roy Bedford (22), killed just a fortnight after his 22nd birthday; he was from Aldershot.

Craigavon, in the northern part of Co Armagh, is located approximately four miles south of Lough Neagh and 13 miles due west of HQNI in Lisburn. It was there, on 17 March, that an RUC mobile unit was responding to a 999 call when it passed the Rathmore Estate, along Tullgally Road in the south of the town. Constable Cyril Wilson (37) from nearby Portadown was hit twice in the chest as they were ambushed by IRA gunmen. He was rushed to hospital but died later the same day. It was exactly the pattern and place of attack that his colleague Constable Robert Megaw was killed on December 1 of the previous year.[2]

On 14 November, 1973, the IRA's Brandywell unit in Londonderry attacked an Army patrol and killed a little nine-year-old Catholic girl, Kathleen Feeney. Not wishing to admit that their own irresponsibility and their bullet had caused the death of the girl, they claimed that it had been the Army who had shot her. [See Chapter 11, November 1973] The IRA had vowed to 'revenge' the girl and on the same day that they killed the policeman at Craigavon, they attacked a PIG on Foyle Road, Londonderry, in the Brandywell district. They fired an armour-piercing bullet from, it is thought, an American Garrand rifle.

Inside the vehicle was a section of the Duke of Wellington's Regiment (DOWR) and the round hit Corporal Michael Ryan (23) in the face and he died around an hour later. He was from the author's hometown of Leeds and was laid to rest at Lawnswood Cemetery, in North Leeds. The author's late father's funeral was held here on 25 March 2009. Thirty two years after the IRA had claimed that the British Army shot young Kathleen Feeney; it finally came clean and made a grovelling apology, and admitted that it had been an IRA bullet which had killed her. The statement acknowledged that in statements at the time it had "…carried out an operation against the British Army in retaliation for the death of Kathleen Feeney." Interestingly, there was no apology for the murder of the DOWR Corporal, Michael Ryan.

---

2   See Chapter 12, December 1973.

Even when they were off duty, RUC officers had to be alert to terrorist attack; that is true even today (2011) and was even more so, back in 1974. Just two days after the murder of another policeman in Craigavon, the IRA planted a UVBT underneath a car belonging to Sergeant Frederick Robinson (45) in Greenisland, Co Antrim. Greenisland is a small seaside community which sits on Belfast Lough and is only a few miles north of Belfast. The Robinsons lived in Glenkeen Avenue and it was only a few minutes' walk from there to the Lough where the policeman's children would have been able to see the ferries steaming from Belfast to Larne and Birkenhead, on the mainland. Sergeant Robinson started his car and an explosion ripped it to pieces, killing him instantly.

In every war, probably from the Peloponnesian War, in 431 BC, to the present day conflict in Afghanistan, there have been deaths due to friendly fire, or 'blue on blue'; indeed it would seem that the USAAF during the Normandy campaign in 1944, developed it into somewhat of an art form. If it was true 2050 years ago in ancient Greece, it was still true of the Northern Ireland troubles. In the very early hours of Wednesday, 20 March, two separate incidents occurred, within 15 minutes of each other at Mowan, Co Armagh. Both incidents involved the RUC and two undercover soldiers from the 14/20 Hussars. The regiment, now mechanised fought as early as the 19th century Indian Mutiny and has battle honours which many regiments would envy.

On the morning of the deaths, RUC officers were patrolling in the Mowan area which was well known for terrorist activity. They encountered a broken down civilian vehicle and saw an armed man in civilian clothes and shot him dead, apparently after a challenge. The man was Corporal Michael Herbert (31) from Prestwick in West Scotland. What was unknown at the time was that the vehicle was waiting for reinforcements, and a second car to rescue the soldier. Fifteen minutes later, another RUC patrol observed a further armed 'civilian' outside a telephone box and also shot him dead. This time, they had killed Corporal Michael Cotton (36) from Nottingham. In the space of just 15 minutes, in what was the worst 'blue on blue' of the Troubles, two British soldiers had been killed by the RUC.

BLUE ON BLUE AVOIDED
Gunner 'C' Royal Artillery

When I saw that incident on the telly back in the 80's with the two squaddies in the 'Q' car at the Republican funeral, it reminded me of a minor gun-battle that took place there. If you recall, at the place where the car ran into the funeral procession, the main road (Andersonstown Road) was much higher up and looked down onto the estate. We had a patrol out (on foot) at almost the same spot where the car ran into the mob. At the same time a Ferret scout car was on the upper road shooting out streetlights. The patrol below couldn't see the cars – but heard the shots. They opened up, thinking that they were being ambushed. The commander of the Ferret thought exactly the same and gave a burst in the general direction with his Browning. Fortunately, there were no casualties

By the middle part of 1974, the Loyalist paramilitaries' intelligence wings were striving to be on a par with their Provisional IRA counterparts. They had made it their avowed intention to bring their own brand of terror to the Catholics and in many ways, bloodily outdid the Republicans. In addition to targeting late night drinkers walking towards an easily identifiable Catholic area, they were becoming increasingly aware of instances of Catholic employees working in predominantly Protestant workplaces. There is suggestion that they had their sympathisers, even members, working in Personnel Departments at many of the larger firms. These people would have access to personal records which may well have contained detailed information regarding individuals' religious beliefs. It may have also been a UDA/UFF or UVF member who worked with Catholics and betrayed them to the various Loyalist organisations. One such instance took place on 21 March at McCue, Dick & Co, a timber merchants based in Belfast's docks area.

The Loyalists would have been well aware of the after work departure patterns of the Catholics employed there and after work on that evening – a Thursday – a UDA/UFF gunman armed with an automatic weapon opened fire on the firm's lorry as it took workers home. Whether or not the killer thought that he was targeting a whole load of Catholics or whether he simply panicked, will never be known. However, he hit five of the workers, some of whom were Protestants and killed Gerard McCarthy (28) who was a Catholic. The gunman ran into a nearby Protestant area where he was 'swallowed up' amongst his supporters.

Very late on the evening of 22 March, a mobile patrol from the Royal Marines was driving along the A6, Antrim Road and had just reached Limestone Road, at the point where Cavehill Road takes the traffic into the Republican Cliftonville Estate. IRA gunmen opened fire on the Marines' rear land rover' firing from both sides of the road. They had situated themselves at Brookvale Avenue and Baltic Avenue. The two separate firing points were approximately 200 yards away from the land rover and the gunmen were firing at a moving target. Marine John Macklin (28) from Glasgow and a member of 42 Commando was fatally injured; he died six days later on 28 March.

During the bloody path of destruction and human misery of the Troubles, one factor which rarely gets more than a passing nod from my fellow military historians, is the IRA's deliberate targeting of civilian workers. On every single military camp in which this author was based, there was always a multitude of civvie workers, all of whom had to be addressed as 'Sir' other than the female ones, of course. Through the research for this author's books on the Northern Ireland troubles, six have been positively identified although there may be more; many more.[3] In March and April of this year, two more names were added; one of whom, Mohammed Abdul Khalid, will be dealt with in the April, 1974 chapter.

Donald Farrell, MBE, (56) was a former Major in the British Army – Royal Inniskilling Fusiliers – and as such, was entitled to carry his commissioned rank into civilian life. Living in Glebe, in the Omagh area, he was employed as an Army Careers Officer' helping in the recruitment of young men, eager to accept the Queen's shilling. He was also seen as a legitimate target for the IRA who had observed his journey patterns, to and from work and also his social habits. In the afternoon of 23 March, he had driven into the countryside in order to exercise his dog; he had been unknowingly followed by a car containing IRA gunmen. As he stopped and got out of his vehicle, a gunman opened fire, hitting him several times and also fatally wounding his dog. In normal IRA fashion, they sped off, leaving the man and his dog dying in the road. An Army patrol,

---

3   See Appendix III: Army Civilian Workers Killed by the IRA, for further details

alerted by the shooting, raced to the scene and found Major Farrell dead; a soldier shot the injured animal, sparing it any further suffering. He joined the army as a boy in 1933; was commissioned in 1941 and served in Korea, where he was awarded a Mention in Dispatches.

March, 1974 was not yet over, nor were the killings finished with March. Earlier that month, on the 16th, the UVF had shot and killed Noel McCartan near the Ormeau Road in Belfast, witnessed by his sister. Eight days later, his brother-in-law John Hamilton (46) had been visiting his wife, McCartan's sister, in hospital where she was still being treated for shock. He was widely – and possibly, wrongly – regarded as an informer, and had received death threats over the previous few days. As he stood outside his house in Spruce Street, in the Ormeau district of South Belfast, he was shot by a UVF gunman and died instantly.

The Provisional IRA have always claimed to represent their community; the multi-labelled Catholic/Nationalist/Republican community. It emerged out of the December 1969 split of the Irish Republican Army over differences of ideology and how to respond to violence against the nationalist community. It famously split from the mainstream of the organisation and formed a 'Provisional' wing and the remainder became known as the 'Official' wing or 'stickies' as they were disparagingly known. The 'young Turks', the more militant IRA members who formed the Provisionals had been stung by criticisms within the Nationalist community over their passive defence when the Catholic areas were attacked by Loyalists in 1969. Indeed, for a time, the initials I.R.A. were said to stand for "I Ran Away". This author has been consistently and persistently critical of the way that the Provisionals appeared indifferent to the sufferings of the Catholics caught in the crossfire between their gunmen and soldiers. They turned residential streets into a battleground and seemed impervious to suffering.

One fine example of this, took place on the Upper Springfield Road, Belfast on 26 March. Earlier that day, the IRA had hijacked a car, packed it with explosives and a timing device and was heading for an Army base; possibly the RUC station on Springfield Road or one of the temporary bases in the Ballymurphy or Turf Lodge estates. Given the course which the Springfield Road takes, any of the options could have been their choice of target. The gang found their path blocked by an Army VCP and panicked and abandoned the vehicle at the roadside on Springfield Road. Later that day, Joseph Hughes (22) of Crocus Street, was walking past the abandoned car when it exploded, killing him instantly. He was another tragic victim of the Provisional IRA's care and 'compassion' for its community.

BUNBEG PARK
Rab Hutton, Royal Highland Fusiliers

When you entered Bunbeg Park on a foot patrol, all the women would come out and lift the steel lids off of their rubbish bins and each and every one of them would start to bang them off the pavements and shout abuse at the same time. It was strange and we had a laugh the first few times, but then you get indifferent to it all and just think 'Stupid Irish cows.' They did it to let people know where we were. We christened Bunbeg, 'bin alley'.

Burnt out artic on Dublin Road, Crossmaglen located on a
bridge often attacked by the IRA (Brian Sheridan)

On March 29 and 30, the UVF caused the death of two Catholics and two of their fellow-Protestants. The UVF placed two gas cylinder explosive devices in Conway's Bar on Shore Road, close to the Republican Oldpark area. One of the drinkers, James Mitchell (38) and fellow-drinker Joseph Donnelly (24) bravely but perhaps foolishly, tried to remove one of the gas cylinders. Tragically, as they did so, it exploded, killing both Catholic men instantly. The following day, in what at first sight appeared to be a Provisional IRA retaliatory move, a bomb exploded in the Crescent Bar, in the Loyalist Sandy Row.

Sandy Row is a staunchly Loyalist enclave just off the main city centre, and close to one of the main arterial routes into Belfast, Dublin Road. The day after the UVF attack was Grand National Day and the bar was packed with drinkers and punters, putting a 'bob or two' on the most heavily backed event on the British racing calendar. It was not known immediately if the bomb was timed to go off or whether or not it exploded prematurely. The 20 lb device exploded in the toilets and almost demolished the ground floor area. Despite the crowded nature of the bar, only two people were killed, with a score injured. The two dead men were William Thompson (43) and Howard Mercer (37); both men were Protestants. At first glance it was the work of the Provisional IRA, playing a game of bloody tit-for-tat with the Loyalists, but it was soon discovered that they were not involved. It was apparently a UVF device being transported elsewhere and it exploded prematurely; perhaps whilst being stored.

Both the supposedly dormant Official IRA and the Provisional IRA, as posterity has recorded, were not averse to killing their own. Whereas the Provisionals' 'nutting squad' was much more prolific, the Officials too, had their men prepared to carry out the 'wet stuff.' On the last day of the month, Sean McAstocker (28) from the Falls area

1LI patrol leaving Crossmaglen RUC station on foot patrol (Brian Sheridan)

was abducted and executed by the Officials because he was 'suspected' of being a tout. Clearly the principle of being innocent until proven guilty did not apply in the IRA's kangaroo court system of 'justice.'

March had ended. The death tally for the month was 27. Of these, eight were soldiers (six of whom were killed by the IRA) and 14 were civilians. The IRA lost two members in an 'own goal' explosion. Of the civilians, the Republicans killed six and the Loyalists eight; at least six of the killings were purely sectarian. In total, the Provisional IRA was responsible for the loss of 15 lives during the course of the month.

Chapter 16

April

The month of April 1974 was a quieter month than the first part of the year, but deaths were still occurring with a depressing frequency, at the rate of one every other day. One particular death, however, stood out and that was the killing of Lieutenant-Colonel John Stevenson who was the first regular soldier to be killed at his own home; and on the British mainland to boot. The IRA was also responsible for killing an undercover soldier on a covert mission in Londonderry.

On what is traditionally 'All Fool's Day' throughout the English-speaking world, a senior UVF commander was killed because it would appear, of his links with the Provisional IRA. This author will not veer away from his firm stance of utter condemnation of the Ulster Volunteer Force (UVF) nor of its murderous 'sister' the Ulster freedom Fighters (UFF). Logic would dictate however, that there might well have been those in the organisation (UVF) who recognised that the senseless sectarian slaying had no long-term purpose. If their raison d'être was simply to intimidate Catholics into stopping their support for the IRA, then after two years of constant bloodshed, it clearly wasn't working. The history of Ireland over the last 500 years or more has been one of sectarian murder as two communities find it impossible to live alongside one another.

Senior UVF man James Hanna (27) described as a 'Brigade Officer' had talked with representatives of the Provisional IRA on several occasions with a view to discussing a potential ceasefire between the two paramilitary factions. What would seem clear is that there were those in both the Loyalists and the Republicans who didn't wish such an event. More clearly, there were also those within the UVF who followed the hard-line route who didn't wish it to happen either. On 'April Fool's Day,' Hanna had parked his car in Mansfield Street, Belfast in the Shankill area; his own Loyalist heartland. As he returned to it, a gunman fired eight shots into his head and also wounded his female companion. Hanna died instantly from massive head wounds and the gunman escaped. Much speculation surrounds the killing and it centres on an internal feud resulting from either leaked intelligence which allowed the Army to seize UVF bomb-making equipment or from his closeness to the Provisionals.

The UVF made a statement through one of its spokesman, stating that they were "appalled and shocked" by the murder. For an organisation such as this, an organisation whose murder gangs constantly bombed Catholic pubs, and randomly shot lone Catholics on the basis of their religion, to use such a term is utterly beyond belief. It actually understates the gross hypocrisy and double-standards of this paramilitary group. Perhaps they were closer to the Provisional IRA in terms of attitude and standards of behaviour than they cared to admit.

The row over the killing of Hanna rumbled on, and whilst there is still an element of mystery surrounding the killing of Ellen McDowell (21) five days later, it would appear that this was down to 'fall out' from the senior man's death. The real target and part of the ongoing feud was, in all likelihood, the UVF member with whom she walked down

Parachute Regiment on foot patrol, West Belfast

Loftus Street in the Shankill. A car, allegedly containing a UVF gunman passed the couple and opened fire; Ms. McDowell was hit in the head and died at the scene.

In the very early hours of Monday 8 April, the IRA's England Team murdered a Regular soldier in his home on the British mainland. The killing of Lieutenant-Colonel John Stevenson (53), Commanding Officer of the Otterburn army ranges sent shock waves throughout the military. An armed gang entered the garden of his home and knocked on the front door, shooting the officer as he answered. His wife and family were in the house at the time and the gang escaped in heavy fog. Less than two hours later, Northumberland police cornered two armed men in a local hotel and both policemen were shot and wounded. As most British readers will be aware, the police are not routinely armed and both officers were defenceless against the armed IRA men. Three men were later arrested, tried and convicted of the murder of the Royal Artillery officer. Nevertheless, it meant that every off duty regular soldier and not just the part-time UDR men were all now IRA targets.

Andersonstown is located in West Belfast as part of that crescent-shaped Republican area which includes the Ballymurphy Estate and Turf Lodge. The area (Gaelic: *Baile Mhic Aindréis*) begins at the tip of the upper Falls Road, where it meets the Andersonstown Road and the Glen Road. It ends where the Shaw's Road meets the Glen Road forming a large triangle. Andersonstown rapidly expanded during the 1960s and 1970s as Belfast City Council's housing authority built hundreds of houses for people who were needed to be re-housed during the redevelopment of the lower Falls Road.

It was frequently used by the IRA as a battlefield and they cared little, just who was caught up in the crossfire. On 8 April, they were foolish, or callously indifferent, enough to open fire on a land rover from a Parachute Regiment mobile patrol. Perhaps they worked on the basis that the 'British Tommy' was too noble and caring to return fire into an area where women and children were. Perhaps they felt that soldiers would not fire at these 'human shields.' Whatever their rationale, an IRA gunman opened fire on the soldiers from the car park of the Catholic Ex-Servicemen's Club and the troops returned fire. One of their rounds entered the building and hit and killed Daniel Burke (52) and a father of seven. There is absolutely no suggestion that Mr Burke, whatever his views, was associated either with the IRA or with the shooting; he was a victim of IRA irresponsibility.

We have discussed the IRA tactic of targeting former members of the Ulster Defence Regiment (UDR) on occasions *passim*. On 10 April, there was further evidence that the depravity of the Provisionals was an untapped well. Lieutenant-Colonel George Sanderson (58) had served during the Second World War in both the 'Skins' (Royal Inniskilling Fusiliers) and the Parachute Regiment. He had joined the UDR but had resigned his membership in order to concentrate on his full-time job; that of being Headmaster at Erne Junior School in Co Fermanagh. A stolen car carrying six armed IRA thugs drove into the car park of the school and went into the kitchens, where Mr Sanderson was relaxing with members of the kitchen staff. He was challenged and then shot ten times in his back, killing him more or less instantly. The pupils all heard the shots, and saw the masked cowards race off in their stolen vehicle. His crime had been to

Royal Highland Fusiliers in Belfast (Rab Hutton)

have once worn the uniform of the UDR. A senior Catholic Bishop wrote of their deeds: "by doing their loathsome work in a school [thus] sullying the name of all Irishmen."

A day later two more soldiers were killed. In Co Tyrone, Company Sergeant-Major David Sinnamon (34) a UDR soldier, was on a routine patrol in Dungannon. His patrol stopped to search an empty house and as he entered, he triggered an IRA booby-trap and was mortally wounded, and another soldier was injured. Hours later in Co Fermanagh, a mobile patrol of the Royal Tank Regiment was driving in countryside close to Lisnaskea. An IRA landmine exploded between the two leading vehicles, injuring several soldiers, and killing Driver Norman McKenzie (25) of the Royal Corps of Transport (RCT). The soldier was attached to the RTR and though the RCT is not known as a front-line Regiment, their drivers drove the units to which they were attached, directly to the trouble spots; as such, they will be regarded by this author as very much front-line.

As with many deaths of British military personnel in Northern Ireland there is sometimes, an air of mystery, an element of the unknown and the unspoken. Such circumstances surround the death of Warrant Officer David Christopher Rowat (30) of the Army Air Corps and the author cannot provide a definitive cause of death. The author understands that, on 12 April, he was killed by an IRA landmine in an unknown location in South Armagh. However, further information revealed that he was killed in a helicopter crash, flying a Scout, 'somewhere in Northern Ireland.' Some sources suggest that it was a 'wire strike' and a further source suggests that his helicopter crashed into a hilltop near to Bessbrook, Co Armagh.

Further evidence, based on the *Belfast Telegraph* of the same day, suggests however, that it was a flying accident. The newspaper wrote:

An Army pilot was killed this morning when a helicopter crashed into a hillside a few miles from Richhill in Co. Armagh. He has been named as Warrant Officer David Christopher Rowat (31), married with two children. His home was at Cove in Hampshire. Army headquarters at Lisburn said this afternoon that the crash was thought to be the result of mechanical failure. The Scout helicopter was on a routine flight from Gough Barracks in Armagh to Aldergrove and there were no passengers. The helicopter, in its downward plunge, tore a large gap in a tall hedge between two fields and then landed in two sections about a dozen yards apart. Then pilot was killed instantly and his body remained in one of the sections until the military and police carried out a thorough examination. It was later taken by ambulance to the Craigavon Area Hospital, Portadown. Mr Lewis Chapman, on whose farm the aircraft crashed, said that about 10pm he heard the crash on running to the scene he found the pilot was dead.' There was nothing I could do but return to the house and telephone the police and the hospital,' he said. Police and military from Armagh went to the scene and investigations started immediately. Mr Raymond Chapman, a son of Mr Chapman, said the helicopter seemed to be flying normally beforehand but he did not see the actual crash. Another helicopter flew to the scene shortly after the accident had been reported and a number of other helicopters were apparently assisting in the investigations.

EVENING AT THE PUB
Rab Hutton, Royal Highland Fusiliers

On the 13th of April, the Company did spots checks on the three different drinking Clubs in the area: the Suffolk Inn, the Green Briar and the LESA. I was part of the backup, sitting in the back of a PIG wearing a steel helmet with visor, armed with a large Makralon shield and a wooden baton. We were called out to the Suffolk first as the locals had started throwing bottles and glasses etc. We moved in with shields and batons, and forced the angry crowd back and helped our own boys out. Later at the Green Briar, the same thing happened and it was fun dodging the bottles and glasses, hiding behind my big transparent shield, missiles bouncing off it. Occasionally a glass would splatter off it and give you a wee jolt. Even though you were behind a large shield, you didn't feel 100% safe as your sides and legs were vulnerable to the odd missile. You could not spot everything coming at you. But it was good to get some action in to break up the monotony of patrolling.

On 14 April, an armed gang of masked men burst into the home of George Robinson (46) who lived near to Ormeau Avenue in South Belfast. Mr Robinson had no political leanings and did not belong to any paramilitary organisation. Although he was single, the Loyalists believed that he was married to a Catholic woman. For that supposed 'crime', mistaken though it was, he was condemned to death and he was shot dead in front of his elderly mother.

Mr Robinson was one of three men killed that day in Northern Ireland. There is some mystery, however, surrounding the death of Captain Anthony Pollen (27) from the Coldstream Guards (motto: *Nulli Secundus*; Second to None). Although he was a Guards Captain, it is thought that he was attached to 14th Intelligence Company (or 14 Det) and on the day of his death, he was in plain clothes and on a covert operation. In the company of two, possibly three other undercover soldiers, he was observed taking photographs at a Republican Parade in Londonderry. This was clearly for the purpose of intelligence gathering and was photographing the march at the time he was seized and then murdered. The Captain was challenged and tried to make a run for it. One of his colleagues, finding himself in a gap through which to escape, turned and saw over a dozen men seize him, wrestle him to the ground and moments later, the shots which took his life rang out. Captain Pollen is considered to have been seconded to 14th Int, commonly known as 'Det 14.' Were they trying to pass themselves off as journalists or were they trying to pass themselves off as Sinn Féin supporters? Either way, it did not take the hostile crowd long to see him and then challenge him.

'UK Elite Forces' describes the genesis of 14th Intelligence Company on its excellent website.[1]

Before 14 Company was created, undercover military surveillance in Northern Ireland was carried out by a unit known as the MRF (referred to in different sources as the Military Reaction Force, Military Reconnaissance Force or Mobile Reconnaissance Force). The MRF had some success, but its operations were

---

1   Available at http://www.eliteukforces.info/the-det/

Rab Hutton (RHF) on foot patrol in the Falls Road area of Belfast (Rab Hutton)

RHF in Belfast (Rab Hutton)

eventually compromised. Two IRA double-agents that the MRF had turned were discovered by the Provos and interrogated, spilling the details of a covert MRF operation based out of the Four Square laundry in Belfast.[2]

With the MRF compromised, it was decided that a dedicated force of highly-trained plains-clothes surveillance operatives should be established for operations in Northern Ireland. 14 Intelligence Company was to be selected and trained by a specially setup training wing of 22 SAS. Additionally, SAS officers would form the unit's command. In 1973, three Detachments, or 'Dets' were setup, each within its own sector of Northern Ireland. During the Troubles, men from the SAS and SBS would serve tours with 14 Company. It was good experience for the Special Forces soldiers, who would not only enhance their assigned Det with their particular skills, but they also would, on completing their tour, return to their units with invaluable operational experience.

The final death on that fateful Sunday occurred in hospital in Belfast; William McDonald (21) had been shot by a soldier, the previous afternoon and he died from that wound on Sunday evening. The incident took place in Cambrai Street in the Loyalist Shankill area, less than a hundred yards from the Shankill Road. A patrol from the Parachute Regiment was involved in disturbances and had tried to arrest some Loyalist rioters. A large mob had gathered and two of the soldiers, one of whom was severely beaten, were isolated from the rest of the patrol. A paratrooper stated in Court that he saw McDonald, visiting the area from Scotland, about to strike a downed comrade in the face with a piece of wood. He fired one round at the man with his SLR and fatally wounded him. Two other rioters were also shot and wounded, and nine Paratroopers were injured.

On April 16, a UVF bomb-maker, Ronald Neill (25) was preparing an explosive device at his home in Portadown. Something went terribly wrong for him; it detonated prematurely, and he was killed instantly. The blast extensively damaged three houses in the street and injured his partner. Later searches found explosives and bomb-making paraphernalia and so the incident was widely considered as a UVF 'own goal'.

Later that same day, an IRA gun attack at a VCP in Newtownhamilton left a policeman dead and two baby girls to grow up without their father. The Provisionals sickeningly justified it as a blow against "the occupation forces" Constable George McCall (33) was speaking to a colleague at the VCP close to the RUC station, when a shot rang out and the policeman slumped to the ground, dying shortly afterwards.

On April 18, the IRA had detonated a bomb outside a church in Saltersland, Co Londonderry; no-one was killed in the explosion but a secondary device had been planted in order to kill Security Force members investigating the blast. Tragically for Seamus O'Neill (32) a married father of four, the device exploded as he drove his tractor past the initial blast site. In the space of just a few hours, the Provisional IRA had left two women widowed and six children without their father. And still the money poured in from the United States as IRA apologists in the large Irish-American community continued to aid the 'war against Britain.' Doubtless, as Americans seem incapable of comprehending the concept of the United Kingdom or Great Britain, it was a war against 'England.'

2   For a more detailed account of the 'four square laundry', see the January chapter of Wharton, Ken, *The Bloodiest Year: Northern Ireland 1972.*

The West Belfast's 'D' Company of Gerry Adams was busy two days later when their 'nutting squad' abducted James Corbett (20) from his home at New Barnsley Drive on the Ballymurphy Estate. On the pretext of wanting to talk to him, the 'nutting squad' assured the man's pregnant wife that all would be well. He was taken to the nearby Turf Lodge Estate and shot dead, accused of being a tout.

On the 21st, the UVF targeted a leading member of Sinn Féin, James Murphy (42) and shot him dead at the garage and petrol station which he owned, in Kinawley, Co Fermanagh. It was already dark when he was shot and the murderers also stole his car, which was later found abandoned. His lifeless body lay out in the open all night and was discovered early on the Sunday morning by a customer.

As the month neared its end, a team from the Provisional IRA, equipped with at least one RPG-7 rocket launcher carried an attack on a unit of the Royal Highland Fusiliers in the Lenadoon area of West Belfast. The RPG-7 was a widely-produced, portable, unguided, shoulder-launched, anti-tank rocket-propelled grenade launcher. Originally the RPG-7 and its predecessor, the RPG-two, were designed and manufactured by the Bazalt Company in the former Soviet Union. Its maximum range is 1,000 yards (920 metres) and has a muzzle velocity of approximately 375 feet (115 metres) per second.

NEAR MISS AT LENADOON
Rab Hutton, Royal Highland Fusiliers

It was the 24th of April, three days before my 19th birthday. We were back at Glenveagh OP. At 9:30pm a Provo stepped out onto the top end of Lenadoon Avenue and fired an RPG-7 anti-tank projectile at the building. I was sitting in the TV room of the OP, appreciating the rest and peace of not being on patrol and the relative liberty of not being on duty. Slouched on the couch, which was against the outside wall; I was watching 'The World at War' with some of my comrades. Some were sitting around stuffing their faces with the ubiquitous egg banjos; some were asleep and the rest were staring blankly at the television. As the American plane 'Enola Gay' closes in on Hiroshima, the whole building suddenly shook and shuddered to the accompaniment of a loud explosion. I immediately hit the deck. It was immediately obvious that someone was trying to blow us up! For a split second, you freeze at the shock of it all, then your brain triggers into instant reaction mode. I scrambled to my rifle, belt order and flak jacket and threw them on with unsteady fingers. I then returned to the TV room ready for action to await orders.

I was not needed for the 'hot pursuit' follow up and was kept indoors. As I waited as back up, my thoughts attempted to recall the incident. When it happened I thought that someone had thrown a bomb at the base of the building? Now I was told it was an RPG warhead. All the thoughts go through your head after a major 'contact' like this. 'Where did he fire from? Why did the OP not see him and fire first? Where did it hit the building? How close to injury or death had I been? Did I react the right way? Do I feel scared? What's the next drill?' Many, many thoughts fly through your brain, but at the end of the day I was alive and unhurt, and the rest of the platoon were unscathed.

We were lucky that night because the Royal Engineers had been putting up fencing all around the block to prevent such things and they had just finished the last portion that day. When I looked at the building whilst out on patrol the next morning, I calculated that if the fencing hadn't caused the warhead to explode before it hit the brick wall and had been four or six feet higher, it would have hit squarely where I had been sitting. It would have probably taken out all personnel in the TV room, me included. I would have been a dead man along with three or four of my mates as we watched TV. It was lucky for us the protective fence had been completed. This was the first of a few incidents during my three tours of N. Ireland that I was lucky to survive. Boy, did that explosion ring my ears.

On 26 June of the previous year, Noor Baz Khan, a British Army 'civvie worker' was murdered by the IRA in Londonderry.[3] On 22 April, the IRA laid in wait on the Newry-Crossmaglen Road in South Armagh, intending to kill Mohammed Abdul Khan (18). He had committed the heinous crime – in their perverted minds – of working for the Army in Crossmaglen as a canteen boy. This 'crime' was compounded further by the fact that his dad was also the camp barber. His car was attacked as he drove along a stretch of isolated rural road and the gunmen opened up with automatic weapons; he was hit 17 times according to some sources. A spokesman for the Provisional IRA stated that young Khan was a member of the SAS. This was an assertion so sublimely ridiculous, so outrageously false, that one might have laughed, had the situation not been so tragic.

IRA PROPAGANDA
Rab Hutton, Royal Highland Fusiliers
On the 29th of April I started my five day R&R (Rest and Recuperation) leave. This leave, though I didn't know it, would for myself and a mate turn into one of the strangest incidents we both encountered in our Army careers. The leave started by flying home from Aldergrove Airport. I arrived home at Bishopton at 2:00pm. After a couple of days at home I went to meet Gerry Burns, who was also on R&R, at his house. He wasn't there, so I went to his sisters, he wasn't there either. I waited on him for a while, then got fed up and went home. The remainder of my leave I spent at home before catching the plane at 7:00pm on May 3rd, arriving back at Glassmullan at 9:30pm.

It was back to foot patrols, OP and mobiles. Everything was going along nicely. The first indication that something was up was when on the 6th I discovered that Gerry had not returned from leave. At the time I thought nothing of it, thinking that he must have a good reason for his absence. How right I was.

On the 11th I was sent to Musgrave Hospital, which has a Security Wing where all wounded soldiers are treated. It is our job to protect them. This was a cushy number, you did two hour stags with a four hour gap between each, and we got plenty of cups of tea from the nurses. It was great being away from the main camp. Great for me that is until the 13th, when I was taken from the hospital and driven to Fort Monagh HQ. On the way there I kept thinking that this was strange; why did HQ want me? No one would tell me anything. I soon found out! When I got there, I discovered that my mate was there before me, and he told me that

---

3   See Chapter 6, June 1973, for more information.

he had just been interrogated by the Special Investigation Branch (SIB) because Gerry Burns was in Dublin talking to some IRA personnel.

The SIB wanted to know if my mate and I knew anything beforehand as we were Gerry's best mates. They took me to a room with one of the SIB men and he fired questions at me right, left and centre. At first they told me Gerry was in Dublin and I just laughed at him because I didn't believe him. This did not please him, because my mate had done the same to him earlier. He interrogated me for half an hour, then cross examined my mate again, then back to me. I think they finally realised that my mate and I knew nothing about Gerry's disappearance to Dublin. When we left Fort Monagh the two of us still couldn't believe it. It was not until I saw 'News at Ten' that night back at the hospital, that I finally believed it. The boys in the TV room said I went all pale when Gerry came on. It showed him being interviewed by the newsmen. It was all unrealistic to me at the time; it was hard to take in that one of my best friends was in Dublin with IRA men.

I knew that Gerry didn't want to go to Belfast as he is Catholic and has Irish relations but I never knew the mental burden he must have been under. I still consider it was his mother that put him up to it; she was bitter, but his Dad was an ex- Royal Marine and didn't want him to do this. Gerry also didn't like the treatment given to some of the IRA suspects when they were under arrest. He couldn't stand the feelings in his heart and mind any longer, he just yearned to get away from it all. I believe what he did was what he believed to be right at that time. He may seem like a traitor to the rest of the army but I can assure you that he was duped into meeting the IRA people. The IRA took advantage of the situation; Gerry was just a gullible 18-year-old. Coming from the west of Scotland where religious tension is always around, Rangers/Celtic – Proddy/Catholic etc the feelings are much stronger up here I bear him no grudges at all; he still is and always will be one of my best friends.

Under a headline: "Soldier: Why I Am a deserter" the *Daily Express'* William Hunter wrote the following:

A soldier claiming to be an Army deserter appeared at a Press conference in Dublin yesterday. He claimed to be Gerard Burns, 19, of the Royal Highland Fusiliers, stationed in Belfast whose home is in Rutherglen, Glasgow. Also at the conference held in a small hotel in the Rathfarnham district was Provisional IRA leader David O'Connell who is on the run from authorities in the south. O'Connell who staged the surprise conference said that a commitment from Northern Ireland Secretary of State Mr Merlyn Rees to withdraw the British Army from the North could lead to peace overnight. He also demanded an amnesty for British troops who deserted on grounds of conscience, in addition for earlier IRA demands for amnesty for political prisoners and detainees.

On the morning of Tuesday 14 May, taking second place to "Burn Belfast: IRA 'Scorched Earth' Plan Revealed by Wilson," the *Express* reported: "Dublin Arrests 'Asylum' Soldier." "A British soldier who disappeared ten days ago was arrested by Dublin Special Branch last night soon after asking for political asylum. 19-year-old Gerrard

Burns of High Street, Rutherglen was held with Provisional Sinn Féin official Charles McGlade after they left Dublin's Department of Foreign Affairs. Both men were being detained at the city's Brideswell station. Burns, a deserter from the Royal Highland Fusiliers stationed in Belfast appeared at a Provo stage-managed press conference at a Dublin hotel. Later in an obvious IRA move to embarrass Ulster Supremo Merlyn Rees, he turned up at Dublin's Iveagh House where Mr Rees was discussing the Sunningdale agreement. Four hours earlier he appeared at a surprise press conference held at the secluded Taylor's Grange Hotel in the city's Raithfarnham district with wanted IRA leader David O'Connell."

The *Scottish Daily Record*'s headline screamed: "Scot Flees to Dublin". This author rarely comments or criticises articles written by contributors. However, and this is not a criticism of the contributor, one feels compelled to ask one question of Gerard Burns: the people with whom you spoke were from the same organisation which butchered Mohammed Abdul Khan for being an Army civvie worker; what possessed this young Scottish soldier to align himself with these people? What is even more incredulous is that a little over three years previously, the same men to whom Burns wished to ally himself were responsible for perhaps the single most cold-blooded incident of the entire troubles. On the evening of 10 March 1971, three young off-duty soldiers were lured to their deaths in an IRA honey trap. Whilst drinking near the Cornmarket in the Markets area of Belfast, two young brothers and their older cousin were picked up by seemingly Loyalist women with the offer of a party.

The three soldiers – according to eyewitnesses, the worse for drink – innocently got into a car with the women, still clutching their glasses half full of beer and set off for an evening's continued revelling. Just north-west of the city, at White's Brae, Squire's Hill, Ligoniel, on a lonely mountain road, the car stopped. Apparently the three young Scots lads got out of the car for a 'pee break' and, whilst they stood, facing away from the road, several members of the IRA who had lain in wait, approached them with revolvers. Two of the soldiers were shot in the back of the head and the third was shot in the chest as he turned. The bodies were found the following morning by children and two of them still clutched beer glasses in their lifeless hands. The three were John McCaig (17) his brother Joseph (18) and their cousin Donald McCaughey (23) and all were from the Royal Highland Fusiliers and were from Ayr and Glasgow. That Burns could act in this way after the callous slaughter of three soldiers from his own regiment simply defies belief.

Rab Hutton continues:

I have not heard from or seen him for over twenty years now. A couple of years later, after he 'left', he handed himself in and did a stretch (five years) in Colchester before being dismissed. At present I do not know where he is or what he is doing.

During the course of the month, a British soldier had died in circumstances unknown; another victim, indirectly of the Troubles. Private Louis William Carroll (19), from Scholes, Bradford in West Yorkshire, was a member of the Duke of Wellington's Regiment and "died in Northern Ireland."

April had ended, and the death tally for the month was 18. Of these seven were soldiers, or former serving soldiers (five were killed by the IRA), one policeman and eight civilians. The Loyalists lost two members due to internal feuds. Of the civilians, the Republicans killed three and the Loyalists three; two of the killings were purely sectarian. In total, the Provisional IRA was responsible for the loss of nine lives during the course of the month.

Chapter 17

May

May was one of the most significant – and tragic – months of the entire year. It saw the deadly Loyalist bomb blitz inside the Irish Republic, the UWC strike and an increase in senseless and random sectarian killings. It included the first female UDR death and the horrendous UVF bomb attack on the Rose and Crown pub in South Belfast. In all, 63 people lost their lives in May as a direct, or indirect, result of the Troubles; the great majority of whom were killed by Loyalists.

The Rose and Crown public house is situated on Ormeau Road, in South Belfast; it is located in a Catholic area and, back in 1974, was frequented by Catholics; as such, it was a more than obvious target for the Loyalist paramilitaries. On 2 May, the UVF threw an explosive device into the crowded pub; five people were killed immediately, a sixth died just three days later and two were maimed in the explosion. The excellent *Lost Lives* lists the residential streets where the victims lived; Farnham Street, Fitzroy Avenue, Curzon Street and Rugby Avenue are but four. A glance at a map of the Ormeau Road area shows that all the aforementioned locations very close to the pub, and entailed walks of no more than a minute.

On Thursday 2 May, just after 10pm, a car which had been hijacked earlier by the UVF drove up to the front entrance of the Rose and Crown. At least two men got out, and an object was hurled into the bar before the car roared off. Whether or not the cowards paused to see the results of their bloody handiwork is unknown, but seconds later, the device exploded. Eyewitnesses said that one of the men was unable to initially get into the car which moved off without him. Laughter is also reported to have come from within the vehicle. In the blast, the following people were killed: Thomas Morrissey (48), father of eight; James Doherty (53), father of seven; Thomas Ferguson (48); James Gallagher (23) and William Kelly (56), father of one. The bar manager, Francis Brennan (56) was fatally wounded in the explosion and died in hospital on 11 May. At least 16 children had been left fatherless, by the cowardly bombing and retaliation by the Provisionals was not far away.

The local newspaper reported one survivor as saying: "I was blown off my feet, and when I looked round I saw the place was full of people lying in the most gruesome positions imaginable. Some were terribly injured. One man's leg was hanging by a thread. Some were moaning in pain and others were cursing the people who had bombed the place."[1] Later, in the grim aftermath, survivors would question why the pub had been chosen because although a Catholic area, Protestants were all known to drink there. Poignantly, two of Thomas Morrissey's children from nearby Farnham Street, had heard the explosion and rushed to the wrecked pub, and were able to comfort their dying father. Hospital staff at the RVH was reported to have been in tears, at the sight of "a

---

1   McKitterick, David et al, *op cit.* p. 441.

jumble of unrecognisable flesh" in addition to the dead and dying they had more than 20 injured survivors to deal with.

Three and a half years later, two 19-year-olds were convicted of the bombing, which means that they were 16-year-old children at the time of the attack. One of them, claiming to be contrite told the court: "A fellow Loyalist knew one of the men who died and said that he was just a brilliant guy; just a normal Joe Bloggs who enjoyed a drink and a chat. My mother worked with one of the victim's brothers and she said the family were ordinary decent people, and in no way sectarian." He also stated that any doubts that he had about the bombing, " ... were drowned by hatred."

A black and white photograph, taken the day after and published in the *Belfast Telegraph*, displays the full extent of the blast. It shows the entrance blasted open, the words 'Rose' and 'Bar' are still there, but '& Crown' have been blasted away, with the '&' left hanging at an angle.

Throughout the modern world, each and every country employs female soldiers in their respective Armies; sometimes alongside the males, other times as support staff. The British Army had the WRACs, now disbanded, and women now serve alongside men. The Israeli Army too, allows women to be in the front line and the Americans are latter converts. The UDR, back in 1974, were no different, and their female soldiers were known as 'Greenfinches.' Prior to May 2, no 'Greenfinch' had been killed, but that changed just minutes after the carnage at the 'Rose and Crown' in another part of the Province.

Private Eva Martin (28) was killed when an IRA gang – believed to be 40 in strength – attacked the UDR base at Clogher, Co Tyrone, late on in the evening. Using Rockets and automatic weapons, the IRA launched a ferocious attack on the UDR men and women. Private Martin received fatal wounds and died at the scene. After the attack, the fleeing IRA men used a number of cars to clog up the surrounding roads, greatly exacerbating the post-attack chaos.

Soldier, Blues and Royals
There was an attack on the building Eva was working in and she was making her way to safety down the stairs when an RPG-7 was fired at the building. This hit the area of the stairwell that Eva was on and she was sadly, killed. She was found by her husband who was in the same unit. Eva was a local school teacher, whom I had never met but from what others told me, she was a lovely woman.

Sergeant David Henley, Royal Tank Regiment
More mortar fire was being directed onto the building and at least one RPG-7 rocket hit an upstairs wall. Sadly, just at the time when the rocket hit the building, Private Eva Martin (28), a part-time UDR 'Greenfinch' who was a school teacher in civilian life, was running down the stairs from the operations room to take shelter on the ground floor. Her husband, also a part-time UDR soldier who was a civil servant in civilian life, was descending the stairs just behind Eva. As the rocket struck, the blast knocked him onto his back and Eva took the full brunt of the impact from the debris and shrapnel. Eva became the first female member of the UDR to be murdered whilst on duty and everyone who knew her, including me,

was extremely saddened that such a vivacious and bubbly young woman should have had to die so tragically and needlessly.

The Provisional IRA's response to the Ormeau Road pub bombing was swift in coming and, three days after the attack, they attacked a partially built Protestant Social Club close to Donegall Pass. A device, planted by an IRA ASU exploded and the shock brought on a massive heart attack for a passerby, Albert Green (64). The heart attack killed him and he died at the scene. Mr Green was as much a victim, of terrorists as had been the unfortunate drinkers in the 'Rose and Crown.'

In a 48 hour period, encompassing May 7 and 8, Loyalist murder gangs were busy in both Co Antrim and Co Tyrone. They killed five Catholics, which left nine children fatherless. The UVF was involved, in the very early minutes of the 7th, with a cowardly attack which left a Catholic husband and wife dead and orphaned their children. James Devlin (45) and his wife Gertrude (44) were returning home after a night out; their teenage daughter was in the car with her parents. As they turned into their driveway at Edendork, Co Tyrone, hidden gunmen emerged and, using a sub-machine gun, sprayed their car with almost 30 rounds; both the Devlins were killed and their daughter was badly wounded but survived. The pair were members of the SDLP, and, as such were branded as Republicans and killed by Loyalists.

Around 13 hours later, the UFF targeted two 'Taigs' from Andersonstown in West Belfast and the Short Strand in East Belfast. Patrick Jago (55) and Frederick Leonard (20) were workmates on a building site in Newtownabbey and both endured the eight to ten mile journey north through Belfast's rush hour to find regular employment. This was not always easy for Catholics as many Protestant-owned businesses would simply not employ them. Some did it for reasons of pure, sectarian prejudice and others because the Loyalist paramilitaries had intimidated them.

Both men had spent the morning working away on the site at Ballyduff Road and had just stopped for lunch, when two masked gunmen from the UFF burst into their hut and began firing at the six men inside. Both Mr Jago and Mr Leonard were hit and four others inside the hut were wounded, despite the brave efforts of fellow workmen to jam the door closed. The Loyalist murder gang fired several shots through the closed door before escaping in a stolen car. One interesting aside to the sectarian murders, was that Frederick Leonard was a member of the IRA; that the UFF had killed one of their paramilitary counterparts appears to have been an added 'bonus' in their eyes. Some years later, one of the UFF killers told the court which convicted him that he had 'found' God; the Judge remarked: "It is a pity that [he] did not become a Christian before May 7, 1974."

The murder of the fifth Catholic in less than 48 hours took place at Glengormley, in the Newtownabbey area, north of Belfast. A UFF murder gang in a stolen car, attacked two Catholic car mechanics at a garage in the Ballyclare, and fired several shots at them, narrowly missing. They raced away and drove in the direction of King's Moss Road, where a Catholic family lived. Francis Rowe (40), father of four children was not a member of any political parties and had no paramilitary connections; that he was a Catholic, was enough to condemn him to death. He answered the door to his house near Ballyclare and was immediately shot several times in the chest and face. Already mortally wounded, he staggered out of the house and was shot again by the same gunman and died within minutes. His young son told the *Belfast Telegraph*: "My father did no one any harm in his life. He was not a member of any political party or group. I cannot understand why my family has been made fatherless by these people."

On 26 May the previous year, the IRA had been responsible for the crossfire shooting of four-year-old Paul Cromie in Finaghy Road North. Almost one year later, they were in action again in the same area. Two lone RUC officers were manning a VCP at Finaghy crossroads when they were attacked by gunmen from the IRA's Andersonstown unit. Constables Michael Ross (40) and Brian Bell (29) were both hit by automatic fire, and fell to the ground. One of the two policemen was killed instantly but one was seen by the gunmen to be still alive. One of the terrorists returned to the injured man and held a gun to his head and shot him dead. The stolen car was abandoned, and the gang was picked up by accomplices in a 'clean' car and whisked back to Andersonstown. The weapons would then have been spirited away and the gunmen taken for debriefing and the removal of all forensics in a 'safe house.'

If the reader refers to *Bloody Belfast* by the same author, it describes a scene in the same area, which involved the killing of a soldier and the IRA gunman's attempts to clear all the evidence. "With this, the door was kicked in and we went straight up the stairs, and there in the bath was a man fully clothed and washing himself and his clothes, desperately trying to get rid of the forensics. Laid on the sink was a loaded AK-47; 'Ah, fuck,' came the reply. He was taken away by the RUC and his house was ripped apart, looking for more evidence."

On 13 May, the Light Infantry – based at Mulhouse in Belfast's Lower Falls – were involved in an incident with gunmen from the Provisional IRA. On that day, Private Wayne Smith was a member of a patrol in Distillery Street when his patrol came under fire. The soldier saw a child standing in the road in the line of fire and dashed out into the shooting and bundled the child into a doorway out of harm's way. For his coolness and courage he was justifiably awarded the Queen's Gallantry Medal.

Between 13 and 15 May, the ranks of both wings of the IRA were thinned down by four, as two Provisionals blew themselves up in an 'own goal' incident and two Officials were shot by the Army. Eugene James (18) and Sean McKearney (19) were members of a Provisional IRA bombing team who were preparing to bomb a petrol filling station at Doneydale, close to Dungannon in Co Tyrone. The device exploded prematurely and both men, listed in NORAID's 'Roll of Honor' (sic) as 'Volunteers,' were killed instantly.

McKearney came from a staunchly Republican family which inflicted much misery on the Province, and in turn had much misery inflicted upon it. In 1987, he lost one brother, shot dead by the Army at Loughall and in 1992; another brother and an Uncle were both killed in a Loyalist sectarian attack. Yet another family member received a life sentence for the murder of a UDR soldier. The Ulster Workers' Council (UWC) started a general strike, which took place in the Province between 15 and 28 May, 1974. The strike was called by Loyalists who were naturally opposed to the Sunningdale Agreement, which had been signed the previous year. Specifically, the strikers opposed the sharing of political power with nationalists, and the proposed involvement of the Irish Republic's government in running Northern Ireland

The strike was organised and overseen by the UWC and Ulster Army Council, which were formed shortly after the signing of the agreement. Both of these groups included Loyalist paramilitaries such as the UVF and UFF; both of which helped to enforce the strike by blocking roads and intimidating workers. During the two-week strike, loyalist paramilitaries killed 39 civilians, of whom 33 died in the Dublin and Monaghan bombings.

The strike succeeded in bringing down the power-sharing Northern Ireland Assembly and Executive. Responsibility for the government of Northern Ireland then reverted to the Parliament of the United Kingdom at Westminster under pre-existing contingency measures for 'Direct Rule'. The successful strike was later described by the then Secretary of State for Northern Ireland, Merlyn Rees, as an: "outbreak of Ulster nationalism."

The strike had a slow start with many simply going to work anyway, but after a number of meetings, workers began leaving their workplaces after lunchtime. Some did so voluntarily, but there was much intimidation and as one Protestant worker told the author: "You can't work anyway, if someone breaks your kneecaps with a sledge-hammer!" By the end of the first day, the town of Larne had been sealed off by barricades made up of hijacked cars and Lorries and the occasional Ulsterbus vehicle. At the nearby Ballylumford power station, the largely Protestant workforce walked out and electrical supplies were disrupted. This had a knock-on effect and many factories and mills had to close down and lay off their employees.

Soldiers evacuate Belfast city centre after IRA bomb attack (Dave Sherlock)

A petrol tanker bomb near Newry. Felix and fire-fighters saved the day (Brian Sheridan)

SAVING MY OWN LIFE AS WELL AS OTHERS
Lance Corporal Dave Sherlock, Cheshire Regiment

May 1974 was a hectic time in Belfast, as the Unionists had brought the country to a standstill by staging an all-out strike and barricades were erected all around the Protestant communities. We were still in the Broadway, and it was ordered, presumably from the top – Whitehall – that we were to take down the barricades. I recall the unrest and saw many burning cars scattered on the Falls Road. Just where they got the petrol from, I had no idea! As a consequence, I was forced to weave my way past them, in my stripped-down Land rover making my way back to base for an operational briefing.

The briefing was given and it was decided that the whole regiment was to be involved in the operation, with only a few 'mobiles' (one per area) left to baby-sit the Republican estates. It was just my luck that I was nominated to provide the 'C' Company mobile patrol, thus missing out on the impending action. This was potentially going to be the biggest operation seen in Belfast since Op 'Motorman' which ended the Republican no-go areas in Belfast and Londonderry. The build-up was amazing and the Engineers plant was turning up at each base location to support us Infantry, who would be 'going over the Top.'

Preparations were made for the very next day. We continued with our routine patrols, and prior to deploying, chucked a dart into the map of the area to select the 'rummage' area for that day. A rummage involved a quick poke around, in someone's back garden. Being an athlete, I could run at a seven foot wall, hit the door thus giving me enough leverage to throw my arm over the rounded walled top; the momentum allowed my legs to follow through. The idea was that

I would land over the other side on my feet, ready to unbolt the gate and let the patrol in. I must apologise at this point for a number of broken washing lines in the Beechmount area; collateral damage I am afraid! Pete Newman started at one end of the back alley of Cavendish Street and me the other. After several rummages I gave one of the patrol members a clip around the ear for being lazy as he had not looked into a shed properly. In fact, I was still bollocking him as I lifted a cloth in the shed and saw something that I didn't like! He stammered out: 'That's a fucking rifle!' 'See, you deserved that clip!' I replied. It was a Swedish magazine-fed, bolt-action rifle similar to the Lee Enfield but longer, and it had armour piercing rounds in the magazine ready to go.

We had struck lucky! As a result the ambush was called off. This, we found out weeks later, was part of a four-weapon ambush set for the area of the bakery in Beechmount Avenue. The weapon I had found was going to be fired at one of our armoured personnel carriers – the PIG – and was designed to get us to debus and run straight into a 'killing zone.' As we had jumped out, the IRA would have opened up on us with several other automatic weapons. This was more than just 'luck' as I was nominated to be on patrol that day in the PIG which was to be attacked. What's more there would be no help coming, as the whole unit was involved with the UWC barricades and only the chefs and 'bottle washers' would be left in the bases. I dread to imagine what would have happened that day and how the newspapers headlines the next morning would read; had it not been for that lucky dart.

The strike rapidly began to affect the farming industry with uncollected and unprocessed milk literally having to be dumped and it also strangled the supply of other dairy and vegetable products to the food shops. Pubs were also ordered to close, though one rather suspects that the UDA and their supporters would have had their own private clubs continuing to supply their own personal alcohol needs. On the fifth day of the strike, the British Government was forced to send in an extra Battalion (500-600 men) to help restore order. It was fortunate that the warm weather traditionally associated with the British pre-summer period held out, because by the end of the first week, electrical supplies had fallen to around 30% of normal. The then GPO – prior to the Thatcher sell off and division into British Telecom and Royal Mail in the 1980s – requested that people only used telephones for emergency purposes only.

Prime Minister Harold Wilson, then in his second term as leader of the Labour Party became involved when in a Prime Ministerial broadcast, he referred to the UWC as 'spongers.' He had made a courageous decision – following weeks of vacillation and wavering – to send British soldiers to police the Province back in August, 1969. But now, he displayed the same *laissez faire*, don't-wish-to-rock-the-boat attitude he had shown at the Ford, Dagenham strike in 1968 when women workers struck for equal pay. It was of some surprise to contemporary political writers that he used such an emotional – and provocative – word as 'spongers.'

After almost two weeks of the strike, the Army was forced to take control of 21 major petrol filling stations throughout the Province. The sight of armed soldiers guarding other soldiers serving fuel became somewhat symbolic of the Loyalist-caused chaos. The uniformed 'petrol pump attendants' were instructed to supply only vehicles with permits from the Ministry of Commerce and were constantly under threat of attack by both sides.

The UWC retaliated following the takeover of the petrol stations. It announced that the British Army would have to undertake the supply of all essential services, including basics such as bread and milk. There was a call issued for workers to stop helping in the provision of essential services, such as ambulances and fire engines.

Brian Faulkner, Chief Executive of the power-sharing executive resigned on 28 May following Merlyn Rees' refusal to negotiate with the UWC and the rest of his Unionist colleagues followed suit. This marked the end of the power-sharing agreement, and direct rule from Westminster was only days away. The televised scenes of Loyalist farmers using farm vehicles such as tractors to blockade the entrance to Stormont, the seat of government in Northern Ireland was unedifying and disgraceful. These scenes brought about a dawning of realisation that the experiment had failed. Stormont fell and direct rule was imposed upon Northern Ireland.

Two days after the Provisonals' 'own goal', on 13 May, the Official IRA also lost two members who were shot by the Army at a remote farmhouse close to Newry, Co Down. Colman Rowntree (24) and Martin McLinden (23) were an IRA bomb-making unit and members of the IRA's South Down Brigade. The pair was challenged by an Army patrol which opened fire and killed both terrorists. Rowntree was the second family member of the IRA to die whilst on a bombing mission; his younger brother was killed at Newry Custom's station on August 22, 1972.[2] There were the usual Sinn Féin allegations of the Army 'cold-bloodedly executing two of their members' but Sinn Féin trotted out this line at every press conference. Generally they would take over a hall or meeting rooms and summon the sheep-like press and in an armed show-of-strength, subject the assembled journalists to several minutes of barely credible propaganda. For an organisation which specialised in cold blooded murder, these 'conferences' simply oozed with hypocrisy.

During the long and painful research for this book, I was approached by many people who had a story and wanted to tell that story. The following is from the son of a soldier. I re-tell it without comment; it neither proves nor disproves the oft-expressed allegation of shoot-to-kill. I leave it to the reader to imagine the situation and in that life-or-death moment, visualise yourself in the boots of that Para.

Brian Cunniffe, Son of a Soldier

I will preface this story by saying that my Dad is long dead and what I tell you is only my recollection of his take on events. I was eleven, my Dad was nominally based on Strategic Reserve in Waterbeach, near Cambridge, though rarely there, and my Mum, brother and I were living in Methil, Fife. He had already got one tour under his belt: the construction of Long Kesh. He was on his second, based in Newry. I was an Army brat, born into the Army (British Military Hospital, Hannover) and knew nothing else; my Dad was at that point practically a stranger. He was a full screw[3] Royal Engineers (RE) and had just got his third tape and we were once again heading for Hohne, BAOR (British Army on the Rhine) and home on leave.

On this particular day, two policemen came to the door and took my Dad away for 'questioning' and we were not a family who ever had the Old Bill call, so I was naturally curious as to why. On his return I badgered him as to why and was

---

2   See Wharton, Ken, *The Bloodiest Year: Northern Ireland 1972*, (Stroud: History Press, 2011).

3   Corporal.

he in trouble? His response was to go to a cupboard and take out an envelope packed with photographs which he let me leaf through. I can see them as clear as day even as I write. Steel drums full of batteries, coils of wire and other stuff; next a photo of two men lying on their backs, covered in blood. There were close up shots of their faces, others from a distance, showing them with their trousers down to their knees, with what appeared to be steam coming off them. I was fascinated and horrified at the same time. The two men, as I now know were Colman Rowntree and Martin McLinden, two PIRA men shot dead by soldiers whom I think were Paras.

My Dad was part of an RE search patrol who found bomb making equipment on a routine sweep. The gear was obviously stashed and was not armed. On reporting the find to REHQ, it was decided that the patrol was to leave everything as was and to withdraw. I assume that the decision was made on the grounds that whoever left it there, would eventually come back to lift it and a surveillance OP was put in place. Sure enough, two men turned up a while later and as soon as they put their hands on the drums, they were challenged once and then shot dead. My Dad was choppered in very shortly afterwards and by this time the place was swarming with Army, RUC, Special Branch, and Medical Staff. Someone asked if anyone had a camera and my Dad said he had one; loaded with black and white film. Photos were taken, many of them in fact, and the camera was taken away. It was returned later along with a set of photos which I was now looking at. Naturally, as an 11-year-old, I was fascinated and began to ask questions. Why the steam? It was a cold morning and they were not long dead. Why were their trousers down?

I received the answers to the questions I had posed. The doctor wanted to find out if they still had a pulse and the inside of the thigh was the best place to find one. What was in the drums? Bomb-making equipment. Why were they shot? They wanted to kill other people; anyone. What did you think about their deaths? Fuck them! I was totally shocked at my Dad's indifference. I knew he was a soldier and he was away a lot doing soldier stuff, but this was a cold reality. He explained to me that they were bad men who wanted to plant bombs which could not differentiate between Catholic and Protestant, young and old, innocent and guilty, so fuck them; they got what they deserved. End of innocence!

The problem was, of course, that neither was armed. At the subsequent inquiry, at which my Dad gave evidence, the officer said that he challenged them once, and they turned around as if reaching for weapons and he opened up and emptied his entire SMG into them; fearing for his own life and those of his men. The decision was upheld as self-defence. The incident, I'm sure, affected my Dad deeply, though he never spoke of it again to me. However, after a drunken Squadron do in Hameln in the late 70's, I walked home with him in the early hours and he began to talk about how his Army career was a complete waste of time. All he had trained for wasn't worth a fuck and how he'd never been able to put it all to use in any meaningful way. On entering our married quarter he dragged out the photos of Rowntree and McLinden and kept saying how this was not war; how this was not what he had joined up for and it was murder, pure and simple.

His take on the incident was that the soldiers had a solid contact with two players with no chance of civilian casualties and took it. Dad went on to do three more tours in Londonderry, Crossmaglen and Lurgan and completed his 22. Before he died he gave me his GSM and LSGC (Long Service, Good Conduct) medals with clasps for Malaysia, Borneo and Northern Ireland; my most precious possessions. The conflict affected not only my Dad but my Mum and us as well. I always got a cold chill if BFBS (British Forces Broadcasting Service) announced the death of a soldier; especially if my Dad was out there – until it was confirmed it was someone from another regiment, which then made me feel guilty about my relief, that it was not him or anyone we knew. Made you feel like shite! Even now with deaths announced in Iraq and Afghanistan I still get that feeling. I can't put it in to words, but it never leaves you. I'm not sure if this story is of any use to you, but I feel better for having put it down on paper, as it were,

'Shoot to kill' is a very emotive topic, and was the subject of a major enquiry in the mid-1980s by the then Chief Constable of Manchester, John Stalker. It is not the remit of this examination to cover this in any great depth. However, before consigning it to a future volume on the Northern Ireland troubles, let us examine what it means. Under all ROE (rules of engagement) and the 'yellow card' system of warning gunmen and petrol bombers, a soldier had the right to open fire, if he felt that his life was under threat. The standard issue rifle employed by the British Army at that time was the SLR 7.62mm. The SLR is a self-loading, selective fire battle rifle produced by the Belgian armaments manufacturer Fabrique Nationale de Herstal (FN). It was the preferred weapon of many NATO countries during the period of the Cold War and was also known as 'the right arm of the Free World.'

The SLR fires a high velocity 7.62mm round with a muzzle velocity of 2,756' per second (840 metres per second) and as such, would literally 'punch' its way through a man. It made a small entry wound, tore through flesh and bone and generally left a massive exit wound. Being hit by a 7.62mm round from the waist upwards, would cause such massive trauma, that the shot man was unlikely to survive. It had massive stopping power and the British Army, like all other armies, taught its soldiers to aim for the biggest body mass; the torso. It was almost impossible to shoot to wound and any Hollywood notions of shooting the weapon out of a gunman's hands are purely fanciful. John Wayne and Jimmy Stewart et al may have been able to do that; the British soldier in Northern Ireland had no such luxury. If a soldier opened fire on a suspected terrorist, he had only one intention; that was to kill the man before he was himself killed. Didn't the Provisional IRA also shoot to kill? Was there any effort on their part to 'shoot-to-wound'? How many soldiers were captured and treated humanely? The reader must forgive my rhetoric, but it merely serves to illustrate the hypocrisy of the terrorists who wished to play 'big boy's games' but did not wish to be governed by 'big boys' rules!'

Tiger Bay in Belfast is a Protestant area and, like its sister areas of Shankill, Crumlin and Woodvale, a fiercely Loyalist stronghold. It borders the Catholic New Lodge area of North Belfast, and it was in this sectarian interface, where much of the conflicts between the two communities took place. On 16 May, Maureen Moore (21) a mother of two very young children was standing, talking to a friend, close to shops in the Eddingham Street area of the New Lodge. A UFF gunman, standing inside the Loyalist Tiger Bay opened fire at random at Catholics; several shots were fired, one of which struck Mrs. Moore in the head and mortally wounded her; she died shortly afterwards in the nearby RVH. The attack was purely at random; any Catholic would do and the action of the UFF gunman left two small children without their mother. Eye witnesses reported that several children had been playing close to where Mrs Moore was shot, and clearly this had absolutely no influence on the gunman's decision to open fire.

Midway through the UWC strike, with all eyes in the Province on the Executive-breaking antics of the Loyalists, mass murder was committed in Dublin and in the provincial Irish border town of Monaghan on a day of infamy. The carnage in Dublin alone was only surpassed when the so-called Real IRA set off a no-warning car bomb in the market town of Omagh in 1998.

The Dublin and Monaghan Bombings

The troubles were about to return to the Irish Republic in general but more specifically to the capital. In the early evening of Friday, 17 May, in Dublin city centre, the UVF – which had, somewhat incredulously been legalised by Merlyn Rees, some two weeks earlier – took the war to Dublin, the capital of the Irish Republic. It wasn't, however, until 1993, that the UVF admitted causing the carnage inside the Republic. During the previous year, the centre of Belfast had been blitzed several times by the Provisional IRA in what was the zenith of their economic warfare and the Loyalists had retaliated with an attack on the centre of Dublin. In May 1974, there was still evidence of the bombings at Donegall Street, the Abercorn and the area around Oxford Street which the Provisionals blitzed on 'Bloody Friday.' Whilst the planning for the attacks on Dublin and Monaghan would have been laid earlier, any Loyalist glancing around the devastated centre of Belfast would have witnessed enough to 'justify' retaliation.

No warnings were given before the bombs exploded, three of which occurred in Dublin during rush hour. In the series of blasts, 26 people were killed and the dead tragically included a nine months pregnant woman and a baby in arms. An hour and a half later, a further device exploded in Monaghan, which killed five people and fatally wounded two more who would later die of their injuries. Most of the victims were young women, although the ages of the dead ranged from five months to 80 years. No-one has ever been charged with the attacks, which have been described by the Oireachtas Committee on Justice[4] as an act of international terrorism together with outrageously absurd allegations of the involvement of British security force.

The first of the three Dublin bombs went off at approximately 5:28pm, outside the Welcome Inn pub and close to a petrol station, in Parnell Street, near to Marlborough Street. Many shop fronts were blown out, business premises damaged and dozens of cars were destroyed. The cost in human life was appalling, even by the standards of the Troubles with bodies strewn about in the street. The bomb car was a metallic green Hillman Avenger which had been hijacked in Belfast that morning. Ten people were killed in this explosion, including two infant girls and their parents, and a veteran of the First World War. Many others, including a teenaged petrol-pump attendant, were severely injured.

---

4   The *Oireachtas*, sometimes referred to as *Oireachtas Éireann*, is the National parliament or Legislature of Ireland. The *Oireachtas* consists of the President of Ireland, plus the two Houses of the *Oireachtas* (Irish: *Tithe an Oireachtais*) These are the *Dáil Éireann* (Lower House) and *Seanad Éireann* (Upper house).

The second bomb went off a mere two minutes later when a car, packed with explosives, parked in Talbot Street detonated near the crossroads at Lower Gardiner Street. It had been purposely parked outside a shoe shop opposite Clery's, a major department store. Back in those days, shops did not have the longer, flexible opening hours of today, and the terrorists' plan was catch shoppers leaving around closing time. The car was a metallic blue Ford Escort which had also been stolen that morning in the docks area of Belfast. Twelve people were killed outright in this explosion, and another two died over the following month. Thirteen of the fourteen victims were women, including one who was nine months pregnant, killing her unborn baby. Buildings and vehicles on both sides of the street in the vicinity of the blast were badly damaged. People close by were struck by shrapnel, flying glass, and shattered engine parts of the destroyed car. Many of the dead and injured were hurled through the windows of ruined shop fronts. Talbot Street was much busier than usual, as the local bus company was on strike and many people were in the process of walking home from work. Several bodies lay in the devastated street for half an hour as ambulances struggled to get through the resulting traffic jams. The bodies of the victims, the majority of whom were terribly mutilated, were covered by newspapers and posters until they were removed from the scene. One young woman, who had been standing beside the bomb car when it exploded, was decapitated; the only clue to her sex was the pair of brown platform boots she was wearing.

The third bomb went off two minutes later, and four minutes after the first. A car, like the Parnell Street one was placed in South Leinster Street outside Trinity College, Dublin. It was a blue Austin Maxi which had also been stolen from outside a Belfast taxi company's office that morning. Two women who were walking past the car were killed instantly, and scores were wounded. Dental students from Trinity College rushed to the scene to give first-aid to the injured.

Many of the dead were young women, originally from rural Irish towns and employed as civil servants. It included an entire family from central Dublin. Two of the victims were foreign nationals: an Italian man, and a French Jewish woman whose family had survived the Holocaust. Most of the bodies were blasted beyond recognition, and over 300 were injured, some terribly. A Finglas man, Paddy Doyle, who lost his daughter, son-in-law, and two infant granddaughters in the Parnell Street explosion, described the scene inside Dublin's city morgue to journalists. He said that he had been inside a "slaughterhouse" and of seeing mortuary workers "putting arms and legs together to make up a body."

Reaction was swift and there was worldwide condemnation of the atrocity, though predictably, the Irish-Americans and NORAID were no doubt working on a statement accusing British agents of being behind the outrages. The *Daily Express* ran the banner headline "Bomb Carnage Hits Dublin" in its Saturday morning edition. A smaller headline stated: "A dying man was calling out for his wife…she was dead beside him." On its inside pages, somewhat incongruously placed above an advert proclaiming 'Leisure '74' and an equally disrespectfully located one for 'Brentford Nylons' were the words: "Death Stains The Fair City". *Express* Staff Reporters spoke of the terrible scene in Dublin: "A child trying to tend to an old man, plainly dead, in Parnell Street, while women ran by, carrying children bleeding from broken glass. From underneath a mini car, hurled through a shop window in Talbot Street, protruded a man's legs half buried in rubble. Blood ran in the gutters of South Leinster Street from two unidentifiable shapes draped in coats on the pavement." Merlyn Rees, the Northern Ireland Secretary, clearly shocked, as the Newspapers reported said: "Wherever this occurs is dreadful. It is a sad commentary on the situation here."

The author remembers, as though it were yesterday, the front page of the *Daily Mirror* with its graphic photos of horror screaming out from the front page. There, midway down the page was the black and white photograph – colour would have made it seem so much more disrespectful – of a severed foot. Whether or not it was a male or female was of absolutely no relevance; it merely summed up the murderous activities of the Loyalist UVF and proclaimed, shamefully without apology: "Whatever the IRA can do to our country, we can do to theirs!" Sammy Smyth, then press officer of both the UDA and the UWC Strike Committee, said: "I am very happy about the bombings in Dublin. There is a war with the Republic and now we are laughing at them." Eyewitness reports on the front page of *The Daily Express* spoke of scenes where: "A dying man with his face mutilated was lying on the pavement crying out for his wife. She was lying dead beside him. In the middle of the road an elderly woman whose right foot had been blown off was being held by a young boy. A young girl with her dress blown off was lying dead a few yards away". The *Express* reporter reported the words of a nurse desperately trying to save lives and fighting a losing battle: "I attended five people. Three were dead and two were dying. It was like a scene from the last war." One man explained that he had been blown out of a cafe with a door lying on top of him: "I saw a woman burned to death and a man around the corner who had lost both legs."

Perhaps the full horror of this cowardly slaughter should be best described by a survivor, Francis Brennan. "One woman was dreadfully mutilated. There were limbs and bits of clothing scattered around the street and things hanging on telephone wires. One woman was trying to move her leg where her foot had been. Another woman was rushing her child to a police car and I saw another man being carried away by his arms and legs with blood pouring from his face and chest. I could hear women and children weeping in hysterics." It finally portrayed the Loyalist paramilitaries in their true light; they were just as evil as their Republican counterparts, the Provisional IRA. From now on, there could be no mistaking that.

Ninety minutes later, at around seven minutes to 7, another car, like all the others, hijacked, this time from Portadown and packed with explosives, pulled up alongside a pub in Monaghan. The town is approximately five miles west of the border with Northern Ireland and some 75 miles north of Dublin. It had been parked outside Greacen's pub in North Road, Monaghan, just south of the border with Northern Ireland. The car was a green, 1966 model Hillman Minx and its placing and the timing was designed to cause maximum carnage just as the pub was packed with Friday night drinkers. As in Dublin, no warning had been given. It exploded with a devastating force and five people were killed instantly, mortally wounding two more who would die later in the month; a score or more drinkers were injured, some very badly. Forensic analysis of the metal fragments taken from the site suggested that the bomb had been in a beer barrel or similar container; the bomb team had audaciously chosen a pub only a few hundred yards from a *Gardai Siochana* station.

As the echoes of the fourth and final blast died down, a staggering 31 people were dead and two were so badly injured, that they would not survive their hospital treatment. Tragically there would be two more victims of the Dublin blasts, but these cannot be named amongst those who died during the long and bloody course of the Troubles. Colette Doherty was nine months pregnant and her unborn child died with her. Another of the victims Edward O'Neill left a pregnant widow, Martha; their baby was stillborn some days afterwards. Their other two children were also injured in the blast which killed their father. Their youngest, who was only 22 months old, was found dazed and wandering around the bomb site in Talbot Street, several minutes afterwards. Five-year-old Edward, unaware that his dad was dead and his little sister missing, regained consciousness and found his legs shattered, and pieces of metal from the destroyed car sticking out of his face and head. Thankfully a man carried him to a car and, mounting the pavement and steering around the debris, succeeded in getting him to hospital. He remained there for a full year before he was well enough to return home.

Another victim of the bombings was the elderly mother of Thomas Campbell, who had been killed instantly in the Monaghan pub bomb; the news sent her into shock, which killed her shortly afterwards.

The list of those murdered in Dublin by Loyalist paramilitaries that day is as follows: Breda Turner (21); Antonio Magliocco (37) an Italian; Anna Massey (21) who was due to be married in June of that year; Edward O'Neill (29) whose son was badly injured and whose wife gave birth later to a stillborn baby; Marie Phelan (20); Anne Byrne (25); Colette O'Doherty (21) who was 9 months pregnant and due to have her baby induced in hospital that very night; Christina O'Loughlin (51); Maureen Shields (51); Anne Marren (20) and her friend Josephine Bradley (21); Marie Butler (21); Simone Chetrit (31) a French citizen, in Dublin to learn English; John Dargle; Patrick Fay (47); Breda Grace (35); Mary McKenna (55); Dorothy Morris; John O'Brien (23), his wife Anna (22), and their baby children, Jacqueline (17 months) and Anne-Marie (five months); Siobhan Rice (19); John Walsh (27); Elizabeth Fitzgerald (59). All murdered by the Ulster Volunteer Force.

Those killed by the car bomb outside Greacen's pub were as follows: Jack Travers (29); Peggy White (44) who died two hours after the blast; Thomas Campbell (52); Paddy Askin (53) and George Williamson (73) and a soldier who had served in France during World War I. Two others were fatally wounded: Thomas Croarkin died on 24 July and Archie Harper (73) who died on 21 May.

What added a further sickening dimension to the carnage in Monaghan was that another unit of the UVF planted it as a diversionary tactic in order to allow their Dublin unit to cross the border into Northern Ireland in the confusion and chaos that their bomb had created.

THE BATTLE OF THE BEECHMOUNT
Lance Corporal Dave Sherlock, Cheshire Regiment

The last two weeks of the tour were finally upon us. This was the time when The Green Jackets were shown around our patch, and we all had to take them around, and introduce them to the key players. Even if they did not talk to us, they were being introduced to the new Regiment. The trick was to dress the new Regiment in our own cap badges and berets. This was to confuse the actual date of the takeover. We never underestimated that the opposition knew the rough date that we would extract, but this gave us a small deception plan.

The guys liked this time, as we had to stand some of them down from the patrol, but us poor Junior Commanders never got that luxury. Whilst doing the top part of the area by the Cavendish Road, we were called to cover the fire Brigade which had been called to attend a fire in Oakman Street. Firemen were always at risk during the Troubles and I think, were seen as an extension of the security forces; or it was just good crack to set the tender on fire? The Platoon multiple (three x bricks) centred on that area. The fire was in a pensioner's home and we felt very sorry for her. We all knew though, in the back of our minds, that this was possibly just one way to get us in a position for a shooting. There seemed to be almost something in the air; you feel the mood of the area change. Nothing too obvious; it just seemed different and those hairs on the back of your neck start stand up. I was talking to Bryn Jones, a bright guy in my patrol, as the rattle of the first automatic fire, clapped like the crack of several lightning strikes. The sound of high velocity gunfire in an urban area has to be heard to be fully understood.

I remember Bryn saying: "Let's go!" to which I replied: "Fuck off; they're shooting out there!" He legged it down the road and I followed, beating him to the PIG commanded by Gerry Long, which was across the bottom of Oakman Street, blocking access to the fire brigade. At this point we knew from what direction the shooting was coming from; the New Beechmount Estate. I had an Idea roughly where the firing point was and made sure no innocents were in the way, before letting go some return fire. As soon as we were in the open, another Armalite opened up and soon it was like a battle, as we zig-zagged through that crossfire. Later we referred to it as the 'Battle of the Beechmount. There were rounds flying everywhere and soon the contact reports were clogging up the net. This was so frustrating as some guys were talking for the sake of it, while others had the hottest information which could save lives or catch gunmen.

After letting off a few rounds, I crossed the open ground and together with Pete Newman, ran up into the Beechmount Grove area. He was on one side and I was on the other; running toward one of the firing points. There was rounds flying everywhere, and soon the contact reports were clogging up the net. This was so frustrating as some guys were talking over the Radios' for the sake of it, whilst others had the hottest information which could save lives or even catch gunmen and could not get through. Some shots hit the walls right next to us at right angles, smashing off chunks of concrete, but we ignored those as they had to be our own soldiers.

Later when searching, we noted that in fact, the gunman had been firing directly at us, as the marks of where his bullets had hit on either side of us were clearly visible running down the length of the walls. We broke out of the estate trying to cut off the shooters' escape route and I remember my beret fell off my head. This was almost very costly as my friend Pete Murphy from Support Company told me over a beer, saw me running along the buildings and assumed I was a gunman and fired several rounds at me. He was always a lousy shot! I lied; he was in fact an excellent shot!

We finally returned back to the Broadway. No one had been hit; us or them, and we counted up the rounds afterwards. They shot about 100, and we returned 69. The OC then asked who saw the gunman, and we all looked at each other, and although it was a firefight we did not see the gunmen. It was just another day in Belfast, in 1974. I often look back at the Widgery report which I had read early in the tour, and I know that once the first round is fired, it's so infectious; it takes a miracle to stop it! Some psychologist could probably tell us what really happens.

Seemingly, not enough blood had been spilled the previous day in Dublin and in Monaghan. And the UVF managed to fall out amongst themselves over the conduct of the UWC strike. The day following the UVF-inflicted carnage inside the Republic, Joseph Shaw (22) a member of the UVF was shot dead by two men from the UFF in an argument over the conduct of the strike. Many pubs had closed either voluntarily or less than voluntarily and Shaw got into an argument with Stephen Goatley and John Fulton; the two men allegedly shot Shaw dead in the North Star bar in the Shankill. The Italian Mafia speak of revenge as being like a dessert; best served cold. The resentment amongst the UVF over the death of Shaw was kept below the surface, but nonetheless, not forgotten. On 15 March the following year, the aforementioned UFF men, Goatley and Fulton, were shot dead by the UVF.

Shaw's death had been as a consequence of the North Star bar staying open during the UWC strike. There was a tragic recurrence of this, just under a week later, although one wonders, whether or not the deaths of two brothers had more to do with their religion than mere refusal to close their pub.

Sandwiched in between the two separate killings over support for the strike was another sectarian murder by Loyalist paramilitaries, again involving the UDA/UFF. On 21 May, Michael Mallon (20) was en-route from his home in Toomebridge, Co Antrim to Belfast where he was a student. He was picked up whilst hitchhiking by members of the UFF who took him to Belfast, but instead of Queen's University, he was taken to a UDA club in the Shankill where he was severely beaten up. He was then driven to the outer suburbs of Belfast, where he was shot and dumped at the roadside. The 'heroes' of the Ulster Freedom Fighters had struck yet another blow against an innocent and defenceless young man; the Loyalist thugs had demonstrated yet again, that their ranks were peopled by cowardly psychopaths!

Tannaghmore is a country village in Co Antrim, close to Ballymena and around 20 miles North West of Belfast. In more peaceful times, it might have been considered a 'dormitory' for the senior management of Belfast commerce and industry, for others it might have been an oasis of tranquillity, away from the violence of that bloody city. That was, until the night of 24 May, when a convoy of two buses and a taxi, full of UDA/UFF strike-breakers arrived in the village after a wrecking spree in Ballymena itself, when it had found pubs not complying with the UWC strike. The thugs arrived at the 'Wayside Halt,' a pub owned and run by the Byrne brothers, Sean (54), father of eight and Brendan (45). Their mission was to close or wreck – in most cases, both – Catholic pubs in the Ballymena area.

A mob of around two dozen or more masked Loyalist thugs, armed with pistols and heavy wooden clubs, stormed the Byrnes' pub and opened fire, at point-blank range, killing both brothers. The mob escaped in their convoy, but police caught up and arrested them very close to the scene of the murder.

On 25 May, a roving UFF gang, on the lookout for lone Catholics, was cruising around the interface areas between the Loyalist Shankill and the Republican Divis

Abandoned vehicle in South Armagh; often this meant a bomb,
other times it was an IRA 'come on.' (Brian Sheridan)

The remains of a car after an IRA attack close to the border (Brian Sheridan)

Felix riddles a suspect vehicle with SSG shot close to the
border with the Irish Republic (Brian Sheridan)

Street. They chanced upon Alfred Stilges (52), a loner, described as both a 'wino' and a 'down and out.' Apparently, when they picked him up, he was wandering around in a drunken stupor; he was taken to a building in the Loyalist Glencairn area and beaten to death. It would appear that the poor old man was not considered worthy of a bullet, and the gang took it in turns to hurl huge stones at the man's head. It was apparent, due to the ferocity of the attack, that he was smashed on the head several times, as he lay defenceless on the ground. The final blow which killed him was caused by a heavy piece of kerbstone which was smashed into his chest, rupturing his heart.

Two further deaths were caused as a direct consequence of the Loyalist UWC strike when Patrick McGirr (39) and his friend, Eileen McCrory (20) were killed, when their car crashed into a Loyalist barricade. The pair were driving from Dungannon to Ballgawley, when their car rounded a bend and there, in a blind spot was a felled tree, placed there by the UDA. The car smashed into the tree and the pair were killed instantly.

The Provisional IRA was responsible for the final death of the month, after one of 'their' community was killed and his daughter was maimed and blinded by a bomb which had been left near their house. Alfred Shotter (54) lived in Strabane Old Road, in the Republican Gobnascale area of Londonderry. The device had apparently been either left to kill and injure soldiers as they patrolled the area, or abandoned as unstable. The device was left in a dustbin at Mr Shotter's home.

A spokesman for the Provisionals later claimed that a warning had been sent to the residents and the Army, but the victim and his daughter were unaware, and when a neighbour told him, he went to the dustbin to check. The explosion killed him instantly, and his married daughter lost a leg and was blinded in one eye. The IRA, somewhat piously claimed: "Our sympathies are no consolation for this tragedy, yet we feel that if the British Army would withdraw from the North of Ireland a lasting peace would ensue." The naivety and hypocrisy of this statement is quite staggering and beyond the comprehension of decent and clear-thinking people. One wonders if the IRA actually believed its own propaganda.

CREGGAN ARRESTS
Chas Hawley, Ist Bn Grenadier Guards

It was the 27 May 1974, and we were just relaxing listening to 'Band on the Run' in the comfort of our superb digs at 'Piggery Ridge' on the hill at Creggan Heights. What always amused me was what a great, easy, target we really were, stuck on top of the hill. We had only been there a week, and the top of a sangar was blown off. Anyway, off we popped with my four man patrol led by my great leader 'Rompers' (I was just eighteen and two months at the time). About an hour into the patrol, the camp had been shot at with, thankfully no casualties, just a couple of shots at a returning land rover; we moved to the back of the shops on Central Drive.

Rompers and Harry at the front of the patrol were then approached by two young girls and a boy. A few words were exchanged and Rompers asked all to open up their coats. This they did and they were then sent on their way. They were then greeted by Gary and me, 'tail end Charlie.' I then asked them to open up their coats, and they pleasantly informed me that this they had just done. I then told them to try again and also to take their hands out of their pockets; this they did and duly dropped an Armalite, 38 pistol, clip of ammo and a comb. They were all searched and immediately placed on the deck, spread-eagled. Looking up, I could see Rompers and Harry, totally unaware what was going on and still tabbing down the street. That was funny.

We did shout to him and he then got on the radio (Pye set) and soon reinforcements arrived at our location. By this time, a crowd had gathered, as we had caused a bit of a commotion and 'Armalite Harry' (some irate IRA commander) was wondering where his gear was. Major Manners arrived, cracking Coy Commander; this was 3 Company's first find and spirits were high. One of the girls asked the Major if she could put her coat back on and he nodded, but also told her, 'Try to run and this guy will shoot you.' That remark did sink in and reinforced that this place was vile. Then it was back to the camp, made a statement and back to the room and 'Sailor Sam-Band on the Run.'

Rosemary Fisher, John Joseph Fisher and Bernadette Campbell were all arrested by myself and received three years each; they were all sixteen.

May was the worst month for fatalities in 1974, and only July 1972 saw more troubles-related deaths. It was the month that the Loyalist paramilitaries involved themselves in mass slaughter and if any further proof was required of the feared 'Protestant backlash' then this was the month in which it happened.

Lost in the utter carnage and indiscriminate slaughter, were the deaths of two other soldiers. On the 15 May, Lance Corporal Ian Nicholl of the Royal Engineers was involved in a tragic RTA, somewhere in the Province and died at the scene from the injuries which he received. On the 30th, UDR Private, Edward Gibson (21) was killed in unknown circumstances

The bloody month of May had ended, and the death tally for the month was a staggering 63. Of these three were soldiers, (one of whom was killed by the IRA), two policeman and 53 civilians. The IRA lost four and the Loyalists lost one member due to an internal dispute. Of the civilians, the Republicans killed two and the Loyalists 51. One maintains that 25 of the killings were purely sectarian, counting the Monaghan bomb as purely sectarian and the Dublin bombs were a mass terrorist outrage. In total, the Provisional IRA was responsible for the loss of five lives and the Loyalists for 52 during the course of the month.

Chapter 18

June

June, and the prospect of a few months of sunshine came around. The weather in Northern Ireland was pleasant, but the prospects for peace quickly evaporated as the violence continued. Political commentators had hoped that the carnage in Dublin and Monaghan might have witnessed the Troubles at their zenith, and that it could never get any worse. In terms of sheer numbers, their optimism was justified, as until the Omagh atrocity in 1998; those grim figures were never equalled. But 1974 was not finished, as the Guildford and Woolwich pub bombings and the carnage of young people in the Birmingham nightclub attacks were not far away.

Paul Tinnelly, 34 years old and a father of seven, was a former member of the Official IRA and had left the movement sometime earlier. He was still known, however, in Republican circles and this brought him to the attention of both his own Official IRA, who had accused him of collusion with the British Army; and also the Provisional IRA. The internecine feuds between both wings of the IRA continued to simmer which often resulted in deaths. Tinnelly was from Rostrevor, Co Down, and on the day of his death – 2 June – was at a family member's shop in the centre of the town. A gang of six or more masked Provisionals walked into the shop and opened fire with automatic weapons; he was mortally wounded, his mother was also hit. He died as he was being placed into an ambulance, a victim of not only the paranoia, but also the elephant-like memories of the IRA.

The following day, John McLaughlin (20), apparently a member, however tenuous, of the UVF was shot by members of the UFF and his body dumped in North Belfast. McLaughlin was born a Catholic but described himself a Protestant and was certainly on the fringes of the UVF, if not an active member. What is not absolutely certain is the UFF's motive for shooting him. It may have been an on-going feud with the UVF or it may have been sectarian, in that they believed that he was a Catholic, and for that reason killed him.

Michael Gaughan (21) became a member of the Official IRA through the Official Sinn Féin English wing, *Clann na Éireann,* becoming an IRA volunteer in a London-based active service unit. In December 1971, he was sentenced at the Old Bailey to seven years imprisonment for his part in an IRA fundraising mission to rob a bank in Hornsey, London, and for the possession of two revolvers. In late March, he embarked upon a hunger-strike and died from that self-inflicted task on 3 June, with less than a year to go before his release.

In many ways it was a forerunner to the 1981 Irish hunger strike which was the culmination of a five-year protest by IRA prisoners in Northern Ireland. It began as a 'blanket protest' in 1976, when the British government withdrew Special Category Status for convicted paramilitary prisoners. In 1978, after a number of alleged attacks on prisoners leaving their cells to 'slop out', the dispute escalated into the dirty protest, where prisoners refused to leave their cells to wash and covered the walls of their cells with excrement. In 1980 seven prisoners participated in the first hunger strike, which ended after 53 days. The second hunger strike took place in 1981 and was a showdown between the prisoners and the Prime Minister, Margaret Thatcher. One hunger striker, Bobby Sands, was elected as a Member of Parliament during the strike; it was called off after ten prisoners had starved themselves to death; including Sands.

WELCOME TO BELFAST
Gerry Chandler, 3 Royal Green Jackets

I remember being on the boat to Belfast and, as we were pulling into the docks, there was a huge explosion as the IRA blew up the BBC building in the city centre. I also remember feeling pretty scared; why wouldn't I be? I was a reasonably introspective lad who'd grown up on a Cornish farm, and who had joined the Army because there was no work in Cornwall. I was just out of basic training and had just turned 18. I also remember feeling proud that I was joining the Royal Green Jackets which had been recommended to me by my cousin Tony Sinclair who had only just left the year before. Tony sadly died in 2010 whilst on a fishing trip in Canada, where he had lived for many years.

I arrived in Belfast a day before my 18th birthday and was sent straight away to 'R' Company which was based at McCrory Park, Falls Road. This was close to Whiterock Cemetery, just down from the Ballymurphy Estate, which in those days was a hotbed of violence. I recall an incident where, I think it was Johnny Mann, had his rifle taken from him by and angry mob and as it was still attached to his wrist – as was standard procedure – they turned it on him and pulled the trigger. Luckily for him, it wasn't cocked and he was rescued in time. I think there were eight shooting incidents in 1974 compared to four the year before and something like 57 on the 1972 tour. I also recall one patrol coming under fire and one of the lads in the section being shot in the arm, leaving it flailing in all sorts of odd directions as he ran.

It was a cloudy, rainy day in Belfast – weren't they all – when I arrived at the cookhouse at McCrory Park, which was basically a portakabin, inside what looked like something out of a wild west fort! Instead of timbers there were sheets of corrugated iron all around the camp. I can see the sign above the door now: 'Joe's Cafe – Chips with everything!' Inside there were two squaddies playing table football and it was quite animated. The ball flew off the table and whizzed past my right leg. The next thing I know is I hear a gruff Scottish voice saying "I'll get it". There was a whoosh of air and a Bowie knife with what seemed to have a 12 inch blade is quivering in the floorboards next to my right DMS boot. He missed the ball,' I thought, 'he can't be that good'. That was my first recollection of 'meeting' Jock Barr. McCrory park was one of the few bases in Belfast which had a sauna; it may even have been the first. It was a great place to unwind when you came off of foot patrol and weren't required to be on standby, where basically you slept in your bunks with your equipment and boots on.

Out on my first foot patrol between the Rodney, a staunchly Republican area, and the Falls Road I remember squatting down on a corner next to a garden in which an elderly lady was pottering around. I recall her giving me a huge toothless grin and greeting me with the words: "It's a nice day to die you British bastard!" I think that was the first that I realised the true venom and political intrigue of the Northern Ireland troubles; I can still see her face today.

Several of my photos from the time show that I had to carry the rubber bullet gun and in at least two riots needed to use it. I don't think I'll ever forget the PIG accelerating into the vicinity, everyone debussing and sending off CS gas and baton rounds. I can never forget the smell and the effect of the gas, because the rioters tended to kick it back at us; you can never forget the stinging eyes and running nose and the inability to breathe. It is as fresh today as it was all those years ago. What also amazed me was the accuracy of the stone and petrol bomb throwing youths; some of whom must have been only 11 or 12.

On one particular occasion, we were driving the PIG slowly along the road – a very wide road – and we came under a hail of stones and milk bottles from a gang of youths on the other side of the street. I can still see this now as if it was in slow motion; I was sitting behind the RCT driver and the section commander was in the passenger seat. The problem was, as we turned the corner he had his window down and though they were quite small they were very, very heavy. As he tried to raise it up, I saw a kid on the other side of the street raise his arm in a huge arc and throw something towards us; it seemed to be in slow motion. Oddly, that's when the slow motion gets even slower. The section commander – a Lance Jack – was pulling on the handle of the window with all his might but the bottle, for that was what had been thrown, was travelling faster! It sailed straight through the window and smashed into the wall behind the driver's head showering him and me with glass. Thank Christ that wasn't a petrol bomb. Then came the clang, as the window finally shut and we all looked, open-mouthed at the youth who was by now dancing up and down in celebration.

The Green Howards were back in Northern Ireland and based around Dungannon Co Tyrone in June 1974. The Green Howards' battle honours run from Namur, 1695, through Quebec, 1759, Mons, 1914, Normandy, 1944, the Hook, Korea, 1950 and Iraq in 2003. Their regimental motto is 'Fortune favours the brave.' On June 5, a foot patrol of the Green Howards was walking through the centre of Dungannon and had reached William Street. An IRA sniper who had positioned himself in a ruined building in nearby Ann Street opened fire with an automatic weapon. Private Frederick Dicks (21) was hit several times in the chest. The commander of the four man brick had minutes earlier expressed his suspicions about the quietness of the area, and was doubtless extra vigilant as a result. The young soldier came from Park End, Middlesbrough and was due to introduce his bride-to-be to his parents on his next leave. The brick commander dragged the mortally wounded soldier to cover and he was taken to a local hospital, before being casevaced to the RVH in hospital; sadly, he died shortly after admittance.

On June 9, the UFF left a car packed with explosives in a car park at Hannahstown, between Ligoniel and Belfast, whilst a Kennel Club event was being held. Their exact motives are unclear, because although it was clearly a sectarian attack, designed to kill and maim Catholics, the club was non-sectarian and Protestants would have also been there. Michelle Osborne (13), a girl barely in her teens was with her father and sister and brother (aged six and 11) when the family car drove past the car bomb. It exploded, seriously wounding her father and siblings and mortally wounding her. Despite the prompt attentions of a British Army helicopter, the girl died.

'Captain Black' the generic codename for the UFF made a somewhat pious statement, which could have been taken from the same Provisional IRA book on pious and meaningless apologies, muttered some sort of an apology. The ubiquitous 'Captain' expressed his regret at the death of the girl and claimed that the car bomb was waiting for collection and was designed to be taken elsewhere; where it could, presumably kill or maim another equally innocent child.

On June 11, Concepta Dempsey, who was injured in the UVF bomb blast in Dublin, sadly died of her injuries after a three week fight for life; it brought the final death toll to 33. Three days later, the UFF killed Peter Meighan (37), father of four, in the Millfield area, close to the Republican Divis Street. He had been drinking and was returning home when a Loyalist murder gang who had followed him, shot him at close range, killing him instantly. Mr Meighan had been away from Belfast for some time and hadn't quite realised just how dangerous the streets were for Catholics walking alone and being stalked by murder gangs.

This author will support, almost unconditionally, the role and conduct of the British Army in Northern Ireland; he knew the dangers that they faced and wore the same uniform as them. It gives this author no pleasure whatsoever, to state boldly that the killing of John Cunningham (27), shot by the Army, can be in no way justified. The man, who was mentally retarded and, in the modern parlance, educationally sub normal, can in no way have ever been seen as a threat to the Army. His death is extremely regrettable and he was shot whilst running away from a foot patrol owing to his absolute fear of uniforms, close to his home in Benburb, Co Tyrone.

On the same day as the avoidable death of John Cunningham, a gang of masked men had attempted to rob Corrigan's Supermarket in Armagh City. Geraldine Corrigan was determined to resist and tackled the armed gang, one of whom shot her at close range. She died two days later in hospital but no paramilitary organisation came forward to admit responsibility. She was a Catholic and it might well have been Loyalists; on the other hand, had it been the Provisionals, even the most grovelling of apologies from Sinn Féin would not have sufficed and they may well wisely have kept their mouths closed.

On the 17th, a bomb exploded at the Houses of Parliament, causing extensive damage and injuring 11 people. The bomb blast – a 20 lb device – was claimed by the Provisional IRA and it detonated at 8:25am. The explosion fractured a gas main and a fierce fire spread quickly through the centuries-old hall in one of Britain's most closely-guarded buildings. Scotland Yard detectives made a statement to the effect that they feared the attack could herald the start of a new summer offensive by the IRA on Government buildings. What they could not have foreseen at the time, was the attacks which they carried out against pubs and other 'soft targets.'

At precisely 8:22am, a man with an Irish accent telephoned the Press Association with a warning and used a recognised IRA code word. Although officers were not able to completely clear the Palace before the bomb went off most of the injured were only slightly hurt. Consequently, Leader of the Commons Edward Short announced that a review of security procedures would begin immediately, but he said the attack would not disrupt parliamentary business or intimidate MPs. Liberal Chief Whip David Steel was in the building when the device detonated and told the BBC the damage looked considerable. He said: "I looked through Westminster Hall and the whole hall was filled with dust. A few minutes later it was possible to see flames shooting up through the windows."

Lurgan (Gaelic: *an Lorgain* meaning 'the long ridge') is a town in Co Armagh; it is near the southern shore of Lough Neagh and is about 18 miles south-west of Belfast. Lurgan and the associated towns of Portadown and Craigavon made up part of what was known as the 'murder triangle' an area known for a significant number of incidents and fatalities during the Troubles. Today the town is one of the few areas in Northern Ireland where so-called dissident Republicans, such as the Real IRA and Continuity IRA have a significant level of support. The legacy of the Troubles is continued tension between Catholics and Protestants, which has occasionally erupted into violence at the various flashpoint interface areas.

On 18 June, Constable John Forsyth (30) was with a group of fellow policemen (or 'Pol-is', as they were known throughout Ireland) searching for explosive devices in the centre of Lurgan, following a warning from the IRA. In the very early hours of the morning, Constable Forsyth was standing very close to one of the devices when it exploded. *Lost Lives* reports that an IRA statement called for a "just peace". Cant and humbug were two of the Provisional IRA's watchwords; it is somewhat sickening when one thinks of the Irish-American eulogising their " … heroes across the sea in Ireland…" That their spokesman could even contemplate using such a term shows the depth of hypocrisy to which all of the paramilitaries had sunk to. It was 'acceptable' for the Republicans and Loyalists to shoot to kill, but the soldiers, already burdened with the yellow card, apparently were only permitted to shoot to wound!

The first day of the British summer – June 21 – fell on a Friday; the longest day of the year was the last day in the life of Stanley Lemon (51). The lorry driver had just arrived for work in Shore Road, Belfast, when he was approached by an unnamed Loyalist gang. The masked men, from one of the three main Loyalist murder groups, assumed he was a Catholic who worked there and shot him dead; Mr Lemon was a Protestant.

The next day the IRA shot two policemen on the Crumlin Road, Belfast, killing one of them. The IRA unit had waited until Constable Joseph O'Connor (35) and father of three and another officer were standing on the corner of Agnes Street and Crumlin Road and opened fire with machine guns. There were other civilians milling around, one of whom was hit and wounded, and the other RUC officers nearby, were unable to return fire; the murderers escaped in a stolen car. Constable O'Connor was mortally wounded in the attack and losing blood rapidly; he died shortly afterwards.

JUNE 1974: THE HANDOVER PERIOD
Lance Corporal Dave Sherlock, Cheshire Regiment

The last few days of our tour were, as always, hectic. I always found it a depressing time, as during the tour you get yourself into a routine. No matter how hard you have to work and patrol, you get yourself into a mental routine which pulls you through these often traumatic tours. You know when you can relax, when you can eat, grab sleep; even when on many occasions you're on the go for weeks; doing 19 hour+ days. During the handover you were always over committed, and all your comforts were always handed over to the incoming unit allowing them to settle in, leaving you to rough it.

Finally the day arrived and most of the Regiment were already on the LSL down in Belfast docks. 'C' Company was to be the last Cheshire Sub-unit to pull out; Pete Newman and I were the final mobile patrol of the entire 1974 Belfast tour.

We were driving down Cavendish Street when I noticed two men walking down the road towards the New Beechmounts. Something was just not right! I recognised one of the guys, and he was known to be in the Provisional IRA, but he was in a 'Stickies' area (Official IRA). There had been a feud after some shooting, a few years before and they did not often move within each other's domain. My sixth sense was at it again. His coat was too long for the time of the year; he was hiding something! I was absolutely convinced that it was a rifle.

I told the PIG driver to stop, and jumped out of the vehicle and shouted to my patrol: 'Follow me' and ran after them. They saw us and one ran into the local corner shop, and I told Bryn Jones to follow get him as I chased the other. He ran around into the back alley of Oakman Street, but when I got there, there was no sign! I knew he could not have outrun me, so my contact report bracketed the houses he must to be hiding in. Pete Newman in the other mobile was first on the scene, and secured the area at the bottom of the street; trapping him. I went back in the shop and Bryn had got the other guy up against the wall inside. It did not take long to do a quick search, and soon we were in possession of his pistol, which he had hidden in the biscuits section.

Now the whole incident was getting confusing; there were no Cheshire Officers around and only the incoming unit, the Royal Green Jackets. Some of them were only half dressed, as we were that close to pulling out. Very soon the 'Jackets' took over the incident and we extracted ourselves, handed over our ammo within the Broadway Patrol base, and were on our way to the Docks to join the rest of our Regiment.

It was great to finish on that high, and that event complimented my good luck, as when I started the tour I made the Cheshire's first weapons find by uncovering a stash of ammo. This was claimed very quickly, by a young officer in the Scots Guards as they were in command. My company commander, Major Hawtrey came to see me on the sea journey back to Liverpool and congratulated me on the good work. He told me though that although the 'Jackets' had arrested the other man; they had not discovered the rifle.

At this point, I reflected on my actions and thoughts: I was on my last few minutes of the tour; I could have ignored them and played safe. If that IRA gunman had stopped, he had time to turn around stand his ground and as I came around that blind corner, could have ended my life. My family would have been gutted, how selfish I had been. Those tours were so hard for the mums and wives of soldiers. (Listen to the record 'Soldier' by Harvey Andrews and you will understand what I am talking about). The counter thoughts won! It was about earning the Queens shilling and why we all got it.

Little did I know then that that sixth sense that served me so well would still be needed on the streets of Ireland until the year 2004? There to protect me whilst I served my way through: Fermanagh, Derry, South Armagh, Tyrone, Newry; in fact every notorious province on the Northern Ireland map.

The Royal Artillery was founded in 1716; its Regimental mottos are *Quo Fas Et Gloria Ducunt* (Wherever right and glory leads) and *Ubique* (Everywhere). Its battle honours are many and varied and has served the Crown for almost 300 years. Affectionately known as 'seven mile snipers' and 'drop shorts,' the Regiment was used in a foot soldier role in Northern Ireland; their 71 fatalities dwarves most other units' fatalities. The second most fatalities were suffered by the Parachute Regiment with 56 and the Royal Green Jackets with 49 dead.

Spamount Street, Belfast is a part of the Republican New Lodge in North Belfast; it is part of what Royal Artilleryman, Mick Pickford, referred to as the 'long streets.' It was here that Leeds boy Kim MaCunn (18) was shot and killed whilst out on foot patrol with his Royal Artillery unit, on 22 June. The patrol was walking close to where the New Lodge Road and Spamount Street converge close to the A6 Antrim Road, when they were ambushed by IRA gunmen. An ASU had driven to Halliday's Road, around the corner from Spamount, taken weapons from a car boot and opened fire on the Royal Artillery soldiers.

Kim MacCunn was shot and killed, becoming the 33rd member of the Regiment to die in Northern Ireland during the Troubles. The author had the honour of meeting both his sister and mother at a book-signing in Leeds in 2008. It was a great privilege to meet with the two, very dignified ladies and it is to my regret that I never kept in contact with them.

The Ballycolman Estate in Strabane, a notorious Republican breeding ground was the scene of a tragedy caused by a mixture of hatred for the Army, and the most potent fuel of all; alcohol. The estate was where Dugdale and Gallagher had hatched their bizarre plot to drop milk churn bombs on Strabane RUC station in January 1974. Several members of the security forces were killed in and around the Ballycolman during the Troubles. On 22 June, Hugh Devine, 33 years old and a father of four, from the estate, had been drinking heavily throughout the day.

As soldiers from the Royal Regiment of Fusiliers were patrolling through Strabane a four man brick on the fringes of the Ballycolman were checking civilians entering and leaving the area. This tactic was fairly routine and, though tedious for the soldiers and irritating for the residents, it occasionally netted a decent 'catch' with either the discovering of the odd weapon, or the capturing of a wanted 'player.' On occasions, the residents might see it as an unavoidable evil and just get it out of the way, no matter how much they resented the searches. On other occasions it led to violence and arrests; on this occasion, it led to the death of Hugh Devine. Several Ballycolman residents began to argue with the soldiers, and Devine, much the worse for wear, attacked a soldier and grappled with him, trying to wrest the SLR out of the soldier's grasp.

This was a difficult – as well as dangerous – task, as soldiers routinely wore their rifle slings loose, so that they could wrap it several times around their wrist, thus securing it from being pulled from their grasp. As the two men struggled, a round was discharged and Devine fell dying. The soldier was charged with manslaughter but later acquitted, although he was severely criticised by the trial judge. Devine was over ten times the legal limit for alcohol in the bloodstream permitted for vehicle drivers in the United Kingdom.

On 24 June, an IRA bombing team consisting of Gerard Craig (17), David Russell (18) and at least two other un-named people, planted a bomb at a shop in Pennyburn,

ATO at work (Brian Sheridan)

close to the Strand Road, Londonderry. Immediately afterwards, they were carrying a second device into a nearby supermarket, when it exploded prematurely; both bombers were killed instantly. The carnage could have been much, much worse, as the supermarket at Greenshaw Road was packed at the time and several women and children were at the checkouts, in the front of the shop, close to where the bomb exploded.

On June 29, Corporal David Smith from Warton in Lancashire, close to the massive British Aerospace plant there, was on a foot patrol with the Cheshires in the Ballymurphy and Turf Lodge areas. The patrol was on the Whiterock Road which divides the two notorious Republican estates when it came under attack outside a bar from at least three IRA gunmen using US-manufactured Armalite rifles. The weapons, in all probability purchased by NORAID and smuggled into Ireland by Irish-American sympathisers, were a favourite of the Provisionals and had been so for at least three years at that stage in the Troubles. Around a dozen shots were fired and Corporal Smith – the only Cheshire soldier to die in open action – was hit several times and fatally wounded. He died in the RVH on 4 July.

NEWLY ARRIVED
Erich Modrowics, Queen's Own Hussars
We arrived at Aldergrove airport on a Hercules transporter and got into the trucks that were to take us to the camp in Armagh. I remember thinking we had no ammunition and were a sitting target; all of the way to the camp I sat and looked at a hole in the floor of the truck and imagined a bomb going off and blowing us to pieces. That was probably the scariest time I had, after I had gone out on patrol the first time, I believe my personality changed and I enjoyed the

rush of adrenaline that came with fear. It was like a drug and I craved it, and consequently I volunteered to do all the crazy things that most sane squaddies wouldn't have done. I kicked doors in that could have been booby trapped, went into buildings through windows that could have pressure pads waiting for unsuspecting squaddies; I did that and always got a buzz from that adrenaline rush. Northern Ireland changed my personality; I became more aggressive and, to this day, being an old fart still am that way inclined.

There are numerous incidents that I recall from my two tours but one that stands out was in Armagh City. It was summer time and the Irish girls all seemed to be beautiful; we spent many hours yearning for female company but the nearest we got was looking at the wank mags that were passed around. I did have a crush on a girl at one of our tea stops and we met now and again when it was safe to do so; the highlight of which was a kiss (I still remember you Dorothy). Anyway, I digress. Our brick was on foot patrol in the city, and we went down an alley to the back of a building where they were doing some renovation work inside. There was a pile of rubble and right on top of it was an Army trip flare minus the poles; just the flare itself. One of the guys (Stew Goldstone) went right over picked it up and said: 'Look at this!' The rest of us stared at him, our faces contorted in horror, as we knew through our training about the way that the IRA left booby traps. Stew realised immediately what he had done by the look of pure horror on our faces! The entire incident probably lasted a minute but seemed like hours; we told him to place it back where he found it, which he did very, very carefully. We then radioed ATO (Bomb disposal) and they came down and cordoned off the area. I can't remember what happened after that but that was one of the closest I ever came to being blown up!

During the course of the month, three other soldiers had died in Northern Ireland; the men were: Gunner Geoffrey Bernard Jones (20), Royal Artillery, from the Wirral on Merseyside, killed in an RTA on 9 June; Private Noel Seeley (50), UDR, cause of death unknown, and Sergeant Malcolm Seldon (36), REME, from Blackpool, who died from 'violent or unnatural causes' on 30 June.

June 1974 had ended, and the death tally for the month was 19. Of these five were soldiers, (two of whom were killed by the IRA), two policeman and eight civilians. The IRA lost four, to a mixture of own goals, hunger strikes and internal feuds. Of the civilians, the Loyalists killed five; at least four of the killings were purely sectarian. In total, the Provisional IRA was responsible for the loss of four lives and the Loyalists for five during the course of the month.

Chapter 19

July

In terms of the raw statistics of deaths and injury, July would be a 'quiet' month; quiet that is by standards set during the Troubles. However it would witness the death of a woman in a Loyalist 'romper room', and it would also provide more evidence of the murderous handiwork of the IRA's England Team in London, when they targeted the 'bloody tower.'

Newtownhamilton (Irish: *Baile Úr*; meaning new town) is a small village in Co Armagh. During the Troubles it was a dangerous place for the security forces, and although it was no Belfast or Londonderry or Newry or Crossmaglen, it was not a place that a British soldier or policeman could tread with absolute impunity. On 2 July, in the NTH area, as the soldiers called it, the IRA had forced a local man to drive a lorry packed with explosives and abandon it. A unit from the Royal Engineers had been called into defuse the massive bomb, before being ordered to search a derelict house at Carrickgallogly, north of the Newry Road and east of NTH. The soldiers from the Royal Engineers (motto: *Ubique! Quo fas et Gloria Ducunt* Everywhere! Where right and glory lead) began their appointed task.

One of the soldiers, Sapper John Walton (27), from the West Riding of Yorkshire, climbed in through an upstairs window, rather than risking the obvious traps of the front or rear doors. As he did so, a large explosive booby-trap detonated and he was killed instantly. He was the eleventh member of the Royal Engineers to die in Northern Ireland during the Troubles; even at this stage of the conflict, their fatalities had already passed those of several Infantry units. The forcing of the lorry driver to deliver explosives was a prototype 'proxy' bomb of the type which would not be developed for another 16 years. It would be used with devastating effect in 1990 and the reader can find out more in *Bullets, Bombs and Cups of Tea* by Ken Wharton. The book contains a harrowing interview with Kathleen Gillespie, widow of an IRA proxy bomb victim.

Two days later, on the 4th, Corporal David Smith (26) of the Cheshire Regiment died of his wounds in hospital, five days after being fatally wounded on the Whiterock Road, in West Belfast. In the attack on 29 June, a three man IRA unit had been firing at the men from a garden, inside the Ballymurphy Estate. The gunmen had attacked the soldiers, regardless of the fact that they would in all probability fire back and thus endanger the lives of the residents of the house whose garden they had turned into a firing point.

The following evening, Daniel Elmore (43) from Newtownabbey, Co Antrim, who had been drinking heavily, fatally wandered into the Falls Road area and was confronted by Catholics in Sultan Street. Sultan Street, back in 1974 was in the area known as 'the Balkans' which included Plevna Street, Raglan Street and Balkan Street. Cape Street has gone, as has Garnet and the rest. Those streets are now gone and the Lisvarnas and Sultan Square were built on the site of the demolished house; it is a far, far cry from the night when the mob who had surrounded Mr Elmore, kicked him near to death. He

Example of an IRA culvert bomb (Brian Sheridan)

Corporal Roger Hoskins (1LI) attending to injured soldier after
Newtownhamilton bomb blast (Brian Sheridan)

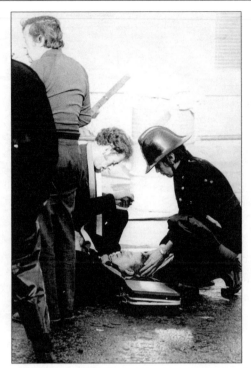

Priest attending to badly injured fireman in Newtownhamilton;
against all odds, he did survive (Brian Sheridan)

Culvert bomb placed just outside Newtownhamilton (Brian Sheridan)

Another view of Newtownhamilton culvert bomb (Brian Sheridan)

The crater of Newtownhamilton bomb blast designed to kill passing troops (Brian Sheridan)

was helped to the nearby RVH, but his injuries were so severe that he collapsed and died before the medical staff were able to help him.

Merlyn Rees MP was Secretary of State for Northern Ireland between March 1974 and September 1976, when he was made Home Secretary. For two years before the Labour government came to power in 1974 he had been Labour Party spokesman on Northern Ireland. On Tuesday, 9 July 1974, he announced that he was to end Internment; informing the Commons that it would be gradually phased out.

Exactly a week after the sectarian murder of Daniel Elmore, not that they needing the slightest excuse for 'retaliation', the UVF embarked upon a five day shooting and bombing spree, which left two Catholics dead. The violence was started by the Republicans and finished off by the Loyalists. The first incident resulted in the death of a member of the UFF; shot by Republicans in an incident in a sectarian interface area. Shortly before midnight on the eleventh, two Protestants in the Loyalist Tiger Bay area of Belfast were returning home from a night out. As they walked past Glenrosa Street, they were approached by a man who had crossed from the Republican New Lodge area. The man assured them that he was a Loyalist and, as they turned away, he shot and mortally wounded UFF member John Beattie (18) before running off, leaving Beattie dying. He died in the early hours of July 12; what is unknown, is whether or not he was shot by the IRA as a known Loyalist or whether he was simply killed at random in a sectarian attack.

Earlier on that day, a series of bomb attacks by the IRA's England Team caused injuries and extensive damage to properties in both Manchester and Birmingham. They had previously targeted the Edgbaston area of Birmingham and one of their bombs had killed an EOD officer who was attempting to defuse it. They would strike later in this month at the Tower of London, and devastating attacks in Guildford, Woolwich and in the centre of Birmingham would occur within months.

HOUSE SEARCHES
Rifleman 'C' Royal Green Jackets
I was in Northern Ireland now for the third time and although I didn't know it, I would go again but once more. Around that time we looked after part of the West Belfast TAOR, which to the uninitiated, means Tactical Area of Responsibility. A lot of the time, we were patrolling around the area of the Falls Road, Grosvenor Road and Springfield Road and around the 'Balkans.' The 'Balkans' covered a few streets close to Leeson Street and Cyprus Street; I looked on Google Earth before I gave this interview, and I couldn't find them! At first, I thought that I was going mad and that my mind was going, and then the author explained to me about how the Council in Belfast pulled them down and rebuilt them. So, they pulled down the shit-holes and they built new shit-holes?

This one particular day, we had received Intel, suggesting that a known player had come back to see his dying mother and that there might also be arms somewhere in the house. We had been told that this particular player had shot and wounded a couple of Jackets and a policeman and that he was to be lifted on sight and a rummage carried out. A rummage was a thorough look around and a search of every room; and I do mean thorough. We were kicked out of our army-issue blankets with striped pillows but no pillowcase 'beds' around 03:00

and because it was summer, we knew that we had to use what darkness we could as it was light not much after 4:00am.

I had done quite a few of these searches by now, and although I can't remember every single rummage, I can never forget the smells and the sights which we saw in these Catholic houses. In the older houses, even the ones with inside lavvies (facilities, shall we say) there was the stink of stale piss; it was in every room. It was the ammonia smell which got me, you know the way it stung your eyes? They had these old plastic buckets and even when they were empty, there was this yellowy-brown 'tide mark' around the edge. The other smell was that of boiled cabbage! I mean for fuck's sake, cabbage and nothing else! There wasn't a smell of fresh bread or spuds or meat; just bloody boiled cabbage.

Most of these houses had one room downstairs with maybe a small kitchen behind a curtain and a couple of bedrooms upstairs and there always seemed to be about a dozen kids living there at any one time. Christ, had these people never heard of birth control? There were always paintings of the Virgin Mary and Jesus himself, looking down from every wall and those eyes burned their way into my soul; they were accusing eyes and they were accusing me and I tried not to look.

Anyway, we got to the house and immediately cordoned it off and I shouldered my SLR and stood, poised there outside the front door, with my Army-issue size nines ready to kick in the door. We had been quiet; no radios, no talking, communicating by hand singles so as not to alert the 'hen patrols' with their bloody dustbin lids, clanging them fifty to the dozen and alerting all the local yobs and a gunman or two. I got the signal and wallop! In went the door, nicely off its hinges; we later sent a chippy around with an armed guard to fix it; did we get any thanks? Did we bollocks! I stood back and in went the lads and then I followed; we had a big hammer but my boots were as good as any tool!

We got the family up; one very old lady who could barely move, a younger woman of about 40, but looked older and two boys, maybe seven or eight up in their bedroom. I went into the room which the mother was sharing with the boys, and she spat at me and called me an English bastard! One of the lads got her downstairs where she started screaming the house down. I said to the lads: "Don't worry; I won't hurt you," one of them started crying and said "Youse won't hurt us mistah, will youse?" At that moment, I suddenly felt like the school bully or the school thief who has just been caught nicking the 'tuck shop' money. I can't remember my reply, but I looked around and there was an old colour poster on the wall of Georgie Best; although I was East End born and bred, my favourite football team was Manchester United and I just loved Bestie. I remember telling him that he was my favourite player and the two kids stopped crying and just at that minute, a Corporal and a woman RUC officer came and took the kids downstairs.

I just got on with it, and tipped the bedding on the floor and then looked under the beds, in the cupboards and the little wardrobe and on their book shelves and I couldn't find anything; the most incriminating thing there was a propaganda leaflet talking about 'British Bully Boys.' I can tell you; that's what I felt like. One of the other lads came in and asked me if I had found anything and

I shook my head; next thing I know, he'd smashed a hole in the wall with the butt of his SLR and was feeling inside the wall cavity for anything hidden there. We left that kids' room a real mess and I felt like shit.

We found nothing and we left, but the mother, although quiet by now, gave us such filthy looks and the older lady, the mother of the wanted player, just lay on her bed and cried. It really tore me up, it really did. I wonder what we had achieved in that rummage, except increase the hatred and resentment of another family from the Balkans. Those kids will be in their 40s now; I wonder if they still hate us; I wonder if they remember the night that they met a fellow George Best fan? I avoided their gaze when I left the house; just couldn't look at them.

I did feel bad, but every time it got to me, I remembered that the Jackets had already lost 15 lads at that stage, and every one of them there in Belfast or up in Derry. I did well on that tour and came in for a fair bit of praise, but that early morning rummage in the 'Balkans' wasn't my finest hour!

Bangor, in the northern part of Co Down, is to the north-east of Belfast and, even during the Troubles, was a relatively quiet, seaside town. July 12 is the start of the traditional Loyalist marching season and they 'kicked off' the 1974 season with a blatantly sectarian murder in Bangor. Michael Browne (16) was attending a bonfire at Bangor Castle, quietly minding his own business, when two Loyalist thugs from the UVF walked up to him and shot him dead, before making good their escape in a stolen car. Like several hundred or more sectarian murder victims, young Browne's only crime was to have belonged to the 'wrong' religion.

On 16 July, as a part of an on-going campaign of bombing pubs in Catholic areas, a UVF gang planted a bomb in the Sunflower Bar, on Corporation Street in the Ardoyne, Belfast. *Lost Lives* notes that the attack on the Sunflower was the 23rd such incident which had left many dead and scores injured.[1] Thomas Braniff (25) had survived two such incidents and was drinking with friends when the device exploded. He was mortally wounded, dying shortly afterwards and three of the survivors lost limbs, including two who lost both legs.

The IRA's England Team struck again, this time in London and on Wednesday afternoon, 17 July, they bombed the very heart of Britain's tourist industry; the Tower of London. *Visit London* describes the 'bloody tower' thus:

> The ancient stones reverberate with dark secrets, priceless jewels glint in fortified vaults and ravens strut the grounds. The Tower of London, founded by William the Conqueror in 1066-7, holds some of the most remarkable stories from across the centuries. Despite a grim reputation as a place of torture and death, this powerful and enduring fortress has been enjoyed as a royal palace, served as an armoury and for a number of years even housed a zoo!

The explosion in the Tower of London left one person dead and over 40 injured. A bomb was planted in the Mortar Room in the White Tower, detonated at around 2:30pm and killed Dorothy Household (48) and badly wounded 42 other tourists.

---

1   McKitterick, David et al, *op cit.* pp. 464-465

The Mortar Room is a small basement exhibition room, and was packed with tourists from all over the world, who took the full force of the blast. Of those injured, several suffered badly damaged and lost limbs and severe facial injuries; eight of the victims were children. The Head of the Scotland Yard bomb squad, Robert Huntley described it as an "indiscriminate attack, designed to create as much trouble and injury as possible. It is the sort of target the IRA would pick!" No plausible warning was given, other than a vague threat to an indeterminate place, just two minutes before the attack. Constable of the Tower, Major General Raeburn was contacted three days before the attack, and warned that: " ... the Tower is going up!" The entire area was searched thoroughly, but the searchers found nothing at the time. It was felt that the bomb would have been noticed by Tower staff, if it had been there for any length of time.

Mrs Household who was visiting with two young children was dreadfully injured in the explosion, catching the full force to her face and head; she died very quickly afterwards from her terrible injuries. Several schools cancelled visits by their pupils, and there was a marked reluctance from foreign tourists, particularly Americans to return, thus further damaging the British tourist industry. A former soldier who worked at the Tower told the author: "It was quite ironic, actually, that the Yanks lost their bottle and stopped coming to the Tower. They were the ones funding the PIRA (Provisional Irish Republican Army) and the first to cheer when soldiers were killed, and no doubt 'whooping' and 'hollering' when the TV news showed a building in Belfast going sky-high. It showed them as people with no bottle; big mouths and big wallets but no bottle." The source is known to the author and his words and comments are his own, though nonetheless sincere; this impeccable source still has links today with the Tower.

The Police were particularly interested in the pictures taken by a photo-journalist who described a man seen running away, moments before the blast, but later investigations revealed nothing substantial. The attack on the Tower was the second attack that day, and earlier, there was an explosion at government buildings in Balham, South London. Nobody was injured in the blast, but there was substantial damage to surrounding buildings. The Tower was closed for three days, whilst the police and Army bomb disposal units did a thorough investigation.

The *Daily Express* led the following morning with a dramatic headline which summed up the outrage suitably: "Bloody Tower. Death blast mutilates children in bomb terror." Their staff reporters wrote: "The dark medieval horrors of the Tower of London returned to haunt crowds of visitors yesterday, when a terrorist bomb exploded in an old dungeon, killing a woman and injuring 42 people, including eight children and several foreign tourists." The accompanying photograph in grainy, black and white shows two of the world-famous Beefeaters assisting sobbing women and a shocked and injured tourist out of the building. What the photograph cannot show is the human misery and carnage inside, caused by the IRA.

The newspaper continued: "With a tremendous blast in the confined space, the bomb went off, shattering armour, stone, wood and bodies. Yeomen warders rushed in and as a major alert was signalled throughout London, the injured were laid in a painful line on the outside green while traffic through the City was cleared for ambulances. Among the first into the dungeon was beefeater Joe Studham. He said: "All I could see was smoke and blood. There were women and children, lying in pools of blood around an overturned cannon. Some of the injuries were terrible. A young woman had the side of her head squashed in. I saw a boy of about ten whose leg had been blown off. Another had a piece of wood rammed into his chest. The strange thing was that the children especially, did not make much noise. They seemed to suffer very bravely." The *Express* continued with a mini-headline containing the words of a surgeon at St Bartholomew's Hospital: "We had to call in five consultant surgeons including two eye specialists, a brain surgeon and an orthopaedic surgeon. Many children are very badly hurt; many have had to have wooden splinters removed from their bodies."

Two further eye-witness survivors were quoted in the newspaper, including a 14-year-old-girl who said: "There was a tremendous explosion and as my friend and I clutched each other with fright, I spotted two youths in blue jeans running as hard as they could away from the White Tower,' Another survivor said: 'One woman with half her arm blown off was not making a sound. All around were men, women and children with torn and blood-stained clothes. I saw a little boy with his hair completely burned away. It was horrific." A Swiss student summed up the moment: "People were lying, covered in blood. After that, I passed out. I can't remember any more."

The England Team now had a string of mainland bombings behind them, some which caused injury and death, and others which simply destroyed property. But everything that they did, each action, each outrage, demonstrated to the British Government and its public, that the Provisional IRA had the capacity to transfer the terror to England. It demonstrated that they could kill British subjects, not only in Northern Ireland but even at the very heart of Parliament. The M62, Westminster Hall and now the Tower of London attacks were behind them; Guildford, Woolwich and Birmingham as well as others, still lay ahead.

BLOODY DOGS
Erich Modrowics, Queen's Own Hussars

We were on foot patrol in one of the Catholic estates, and as always when patrolling in these areas we were extra cautious. Anyway the brick comes to a street corner which is on my side of the street; I knelt down to take a look around the corner and just as I'm about to peek, I look over to my buddy across the road (Chris Bales). There was a look of terror on his face and he was pointing to the rear of my position, mouthing something. I mouthed in return: 'What? What?' and it was at this point that I could feel hot breath on the back of my neck and I slowly looked behind me from my kneeling position. There standing proud and steadfast is an Irish Wolfhound the size of a small horse! I just thought: 'Shit!' and I thought that my days were numbered; eaten to death by a dog the size of a horse! Fortunately for me, the dog was docile and thank God it didn't do a thing.

I'm sure all the squaddies who served remember the dogs that would chase us around the streets and there were those, trained by their owners just to attack soldiers. Well, there was one particular Alsatian which would chase us whilst we were on mobile patrol in one of the estates. Although it looked vicious and it would be barking like mad, no noise would come from its mouth! Apparently a Para from an earlier tour was being attacked by this dog, and stuck his SLR barrel down its throat, which took away its voice, hence the silent bark.

Light Infantry soldiers prepare to detonate IRA explosives (Brian Sheridan)

The remains of Royal Hotel bomb in quarry. Sergeant Graham
Lightfoot, ATO and Cpl Brian Sheridan, 1LI (Brian Sheridan)

Safe explosion. The remains of Royal Hotel bomb (Brian Sheridan)

Three days after the outrage at the 'Bloody Tower,' a punishment squad from an unnamed wing of the IRA, dragged Daniel Harkin (47) out of his bed at his home in Strabane in the very early hours of the morning. The hooded men forced a family member into the bathroom, barricaded her in and took Mr Harkin outside. He was killed, it would seem, by being dropped onto his head; whether this was an intentional death or not, may never be known.

Brian Shaw (21) was loosely known to the author; he was a former member of the Royal Green Jackets who had, following three tours, opted to purchase his discharge. He had met and fallen in love with a Belfast woman and returned from his native Nottinghamshire to live in Belfast. The pair had married and were living on Carncaver Road, close the arterial A55 Knockbreda Road in the east of the city. Brian Shaw possibly thought that the love of a local Catholic girl, and his departure from the Army would ensure that the IRA would leave him in peace. The Provisional IRA could be tarred with many epithets; being reasonable and forgiving are not amongst them. The former Jacket was last seen in a bar close to the Markets area and was lured to a house in Divis Street. At some stage, he was beaten and tortured, before being shot in an empty house in the Lower Falls area. His lifeless body was found by soldiers who were patrolling around Arundel Street after an explosion.

The IRA later claimed that, not only had Shaw never left the Army, but that he was a member of the SAS and had been sent to Belfast as an agent provocateur. Their statement that he had "confessed under interrogation" was obscenely outrageous, even by their perverted standards.

Londonderry had been quiet for a few weeks, as the Army was controlling the main source of trouble in the city; the Creggan, Bogside and the Gobnascale estates. With a

The end result of the IRA's car scrappage scheme in Kilkeel (Brian Sheridan)

An injured soldier receives treatment after a bomb blast (Brian Sheridan)

constant and flexible VCP policy, they had very much put a stranglehold on the movement of arms and explosives. However, outside of the city it was a far different matter. Twenty-five miles east of the city is a small Londonderry town called Garvagh. Very late on the night of Tuesday, 23 July, an alert group of local vigilantes in Garvagh had warned the Army, that they suspected that a bomb had been planted. A mobile patrol of UDR soldiers was sent in, in order to clear residents living in the town centre. Corporal John Conley (23), father of three and a part-time soldier was standing very close to the suspect car when it exploded, killing him instantly. He was the tenth member or former member of the Regiment to die so far this year.

On 24 July, a member of Omagh District Council, Mr Patrick Kelly (33) and father of three, vanished from the village of Trillick, Co Fermanagh as he walked home from his part-time job. Some mystery and not a little controversy surrounds the disappearance and the subsequent discovery of his body, over a year later. Mr Kelly's body was found, weighted down in Lough Erne, just a few miles west of where he was last seen; it was found on 10 August the following year. It was claimed that he had been stopped, either by UDR soldiers and taken away to be murdered, or by men in stolen UDR uniforms. This author feels that the latter explanation is far more plausible, given the UFF's antipathy towards Nationalist politicians and the fact that they had already carried out a machine gun attack on the bar in Trillick where he worked. The abduction and eventual murder of Mr Kelly can be confidently laid at the door of this branch of the Loyalist paramilitaries. There was further tragedy to come for his family, as less than two weeks later, his brother in law, Patrick 'Paddy' McElhone was shot and killed by soldiers.[2]

Romper Room was a children's television series which ran in the United States from 1953 to 1994 as well as at various times in Australia, Canada, Japan, Puerto Rico, New Zealand and the United Kingdom. The programme was aimed at children five years of age or younger. Australians, with their proclivity to copy anything remotely American, often keep a room in which their children can play, and name it a 'romper room.' In Northern Ireland during the Troubles, the Loyalist paramilitaries gave a whole new meaning, a whole new connotation to that innocent term. On the very same day as the disappearance of Patrick Kelly, the Ulster Defence Association (UDA) abducted Ann Ogilby (31) from a bus in Belfast, and together with her six-year-old daughter, took her to one of their clubs in Sandy Row. A gang of 11 women and a man informed club members that Miss Ogilby was going to be 'rompered' and took her into the 'romper room' where they proceeded to savagely beat her with a house brick until she died from her appalling injuries. All the while, her young daughter was held captive in another room whilst her mother was slowly and systematically beaten to death. Her body was later dumped near the M1 motorway in Belfast.

These 'romper rooms' were a feature of Loyalist paramilitary torture and many, especially in the Shankill and Crumlin Road area were used to torture and eventually murder Catholics. They were also used to 'interrogate' suspected informers and also to settle internal feuds. The mad dog Lenny Murphy, sadistic leader of the Loyalist 'Shankill Butchers' was also a proponent of the use of 'romper rooms.' Eight months after they had battered Ann Ogilby to death, all 11 women, one of who was the Commander of the Women's section of the UDA, were found guilty and received prison sentences.

2   See Chapter 20, August 1974.

Corporal Brian Sheridan took this photograph just seconds before the device
exploded and he and the others were blown off their feet (Brian Sheridan)

On the same day of Ann Ogilby's vicious death and Patrick Kelly's abduction and
likely death, Thomas Croarkin (35) who was injured in the Monaghan attack on 17 May,
died of his injuries. He was from Tyholland in Co Monaghan and was the last of the
Dublin/Monaghan bombing victims to die.

On 27 July, two soldiers from separate Regiments died and about whom, little
has been made public. Lance Corporal Michael Francis Norris (24) of the Royal Irish
Rangers died in 'unknown circumstances.' UDR soldier Private Robert Joseph William
Rainey (30) was killed, possibly in an RTA in the Newtownhamilton area. The author
regrets that he has no further information on these two soldiers.

In the very early hours of Monday 29 July, John Morgan (44) a Protestant from
Mount Vernon Park, Belfast, was returning home after a night out. He was walking
along Shore Road, where today, the M2 Motorway sweeps past, when a gunman stepped
out of the shadows as he passed, and shot him in the back. Mr Morgan was walking
northwards after socialising in a Loyalist Club in Ivan Street, which is about a 15 minute
walk to where he was living with his pregnant wife. A murder squad from the Provisional
IRA, though not actively targeting Mr Morgan, would have easily surmised that he was
a Protestant and that was enough for the gunman to shoot and kill the lone walker.

The following evening, the New Lodge area of North Belfast witnessed the death
of another soldier, and the third from the Royal Artillery in just over three years. The
Army had sited a permanent OP on the Antrim Road above a funeral parlour, close
to where Gunner Kim MaCunn was shot and killed on 22 June.[3] The OP had been

---

3   See Chapter 18, June 1974.

'Wheelbarrow' about to enter Royal Hotel, Kilkeel to check suspect device (Brian Sheridan)

Made safe! IRA explosives from a defused device (Brian Sheridan)

there for some considerable time and was constantly manned. A soldier from the Royal Artillery had earlier reported suspicious activity from a nearby betting shop but the incident was not investigated. Shortly afterwards, a foot patrol from the regiment had just passed the junction between Edlingham Street and Hillman Street (where Gunner Robert 'Geordie' Curtis was shot and killed in February 1971), when an IRA gunman opened fire from Spamount Street.

Just seconds earlier, a member of the patrol had been alerted by the way all civilians seemed to have "… just vanished from the street …" Sergeant Bernard 'Bernie' Fearns (34), father of three, had either just taken cover or was in the process of doing so, when he was hit twice, and collapsed. The gunmen were hiding in an alleyway close to Spamount Street and Stratheden Street, having gained entry through 'friendly' houses. After the shooting, they escaped in a stolen car, abandoning it about a mile away. Sergeant Fearns was from North Yorkshire and was described as a 'popular soldier' by other former squaddies with whom I have spoken.

The author recalls the moment, back in 2008, when he spoke with a soldier who was there at the time. He remembers well that the man he was interviewing was in tears and unashamedly so; the author too was in tears and attempting to write down the other man's words, through his own veil of tears. I am honoured that the same soldier has again written about the incident and, later, about the capture of the IRA gunman, allegedly responsible for the shooting of Sergeant Fearns.

THE SHOOTING OF 'BERNIE' FEARNS
Steven Corbett, 13 Troop, Royal Artillery

It was whilst training for the 1974 tour that I got to know Bernie. He took us under his wing a bit for the various aspects of our training before deployment to New Lodge in June 1974. After we reached Belfast, I hardly ever saw him again, as we went to Girdwood Barracks with 97 Battery; we operated very much as a separate unit; at least that's how it appeared to me at the time.

On Monday 29 July, our section took over the Parlour OP for a two day period of duty. The OP was situated just to the left of the Presbyterian Church at the junction of Antrim Road and New Lodge Road, and it got its name from its previous use as a funeral parlour. It used to stink of embalming fluid and when you sat upstairs, in the dark at the observation slit, you could hear the rats scurrying about under the floorboards. In the very early hours of the following morning, at about 1 am, a single shot was fired a few hundred yards away from the OP; but we were unsure if it was actually directed at our post. Later in the day around 4 pm I started my two-hour stint at the viewing point. Fifteen minutes later, I made a report to call sign G3 (Battery HQ) that six to eight men had run out of a betting shop over the road and scattered in various directions. A mobile was sent to investigate, but nothing suspicious was found. At around 4:45pm, I heard what can only be described as several 'popping' sounds but I really thought nothing of it. Two minutes later, the OP in Artillery House flats came on the air, and reported hearing two shots in the area of Stratheden Street. I then saw a man running away from the area and into the Sheridan Bar. I again contacted G3 and reported what I had seen.

Everything remained quiet for a minute or so, and then the radio crackled into life. A sobbing voice came on the air pleading for help. It was only then that

I realised that the man I had seen running away must have been a gunman. That poor lad was trying his best to explain that their patrol (G11) had been ambushed and his Sergeant had just been shot. It was awful to listen to his obvious distress on the air. The poor bastard had to go over to Bernie's body to retrieve the radio from his breast pocket, before he could make the call. I can't begin to imagine what it must have been like for him to have to do that. Eventually, the MO went out with the armoured ambulance to recover Bernie's body.

After a while the radio again crackled into life and the MO came on the air describing Bernie's injuries. He explained how the first bullet had hit him just below the heart and had come out of his back, the second caught him in the abdomen as he was falling and went through his leg. I couldn't understand why he would come on the air and explain in such a matter of fact way how Bernie had died. To hear the distress of the lad on the radio who had witnessed the shooting, and then to hear from the MO a description of the wounds to Bernie's body made it even worst. It wasn't so many weeks ago that Kim MacCunn had been shot dead either.

I discovered later that Bernie had actually seen the gunman in the alley, between Spamount Street and Stratheden Street. He went down on his knee to fire, but the gunman shot first. The patrol was at the junction of Hillman Street and Edlingham Street when the shooting happened. Edlingham Street had a terrible reputation for ambushes. It ran as straight as an arrow from a building on the New Lodge Road (which we referred to as 'The Butts') to Tiger's Bay in the Protestant area. We would paint the wall of this building green, and then the locals would go over it in white so that we stood out when crossing Edlingham Street. You really did feel like a target when you crossed at any point along its length.

The gunman who shot Bernie had used an American supplied Garand rifle. In fact at that time, most weapons used against us seemed to be of American origin.

The July of 1974 had ended, and the death tally for the month was 17. Of these seven were soldiers or former soldiers, (five of whom were killed by the IRA), and nine civilians. The Loyalists lost one member, killed by the IRA. Of the civilians, the Loyalists killed five; of the nine civilians killed, at least five were purely sectarian. In total, the Provisional IRA was responsible for the loss of nine lives and the Loyalists for five during the course of the month.

Chapter 20

August

Augustwould witness the death of the 50th British soldier in 1974; it would also witness the cold-blooded killing of a civilian by the Provisional IRA as he was collecting information for the 1974 census; it would also witness the fatal consequences of the IRA's penchant for turning residential areas into battlefields.

On the third day of August, an explosive booby trap was placed under the lorry of a Protestant haulage firm, driven by a protestant driver and employed by a firm whose workforce was predominantly Protestant. Charles McKnight (25) was killed by an explosion which tore his cab apart as he started the vehicle which had been parked outside a house in the Newtownabbey area. There is some question about the intended target and which of the paramilitaries planted the device; it bore all the hallmarks of a sectarian attack by the Provisional IRA.

On the same day, in one of the interminable, internecine feuds carried out between the Official and Provisional wings of the IRA, the British Army, somewhat improbably and certainly ironically, lent a hand. Volunteer Martin Skillen (21), listed in the NORAID IRA 'Roll of Honor' (sic) as a member of the Second Battalion, Belfast Brigade, was killed by the Army. Skillen was planning an attack on the Official IRA at Sevastopol Street, close to the Falls Road. The street, which still exists, was known in Army intelligence briefings as the 'Clonards' and at one stage was the location for the Clonard Cinema. The cinema, one of what we British describe as a local 'flea pit,' opened in the heyday of the silent movie in 1913, before finally closing in March, 1966. A Falls resident described it thus: "It had beautiful Italian ornate masonry. Italian craftsmen did the fancy plaster work on the Clonard Cinema." By 1974, it had been eight years derelict and it was used by the Army as a covert OP.

Martin Skillen, a former internee, was observed by a soldier in the cinema holding a rifle and pointing it in his general direction; in accordance with ROE (rules of engagement) he opened fire and hit the IRA man. As was common with the IRA, a dicker or sympathiser, in this case a female, ran over to his body and grabbed the rifle and ran off. She was a very lucky lady, because under ROE, the soldier was entitled to shoot her as had happened in 1972, when a soldier from the Royal Green Jackets shot and killed a female helper who was carrying an Armalite after a shooting.

In removing the weapon, the IRA were able to save a very valuable Armalite, and prevent it from being forensically examined and being linked to other murders, but also to convey the impression to journalists and Irish-American supporters, that the Army was shooting unarmed members of the IRA. The author further understands that Skillen, from the Turf Lodge, was the man who invented the 'letterbox shoot.' This involved the risky tactic of one man holding open the letterbox of a house facing into the street where soldiers were likely to pass, whilst the gunmen fired through the slot as a soldier walked into view. Because the gunman would be sitting well back from the

Aftermath of IRA bomb attack in Newtownhamilton (Brian Sheridan)

Seconds after Newtownhamilton bomb explosion, fire-fighters
tend to badly injured colleague (Brian Sheridan)

An injured fire-fighter is moved to a safer area for treatment (Brian Sheridan)

One hour after Newtownhamilton bomb, fire-fighters
struggle to contain the blaze (Brian Sheridan)

Fire-fighters continue their battle in Newtownhamilton (Brian Sheridan)

door, the mizzle flash would not be observed and the letterbox would quickly close, thus adding more confusion to the unfortunate soldier's comrades.

That day was not yet over and Reserve Constable Ronald Alexander Winder (45) was called to an incident whilst he was out on a mobile patrol. As he reached the scene, he collapsed and tragically died. He too, was a victim of the Troubles.

CO LONDONDERRY
Richard L Shelton, King's Regiment

Our Londonderry tour was split into two sections; Ops north and Ops south. Ops north were mainly in the Waterside district of Derry and mainly dealt with the Protestant population; not a great deal happened up there. HQ was based in Ebrington Barracks, which I believe was an old Navy base. Ops South was a different kettle of fish entirely; we had just about everything there!

Sion Mills was the Recce Platoon base and that was like Fort Apache! The only thing missing were the Indians riding around it shooting arrows. My best mate Colour Sergeant Tony Hollingsworth (now Lt Col MBE – retired) was the two i/c. They patrolled the border around Clady and a Republican estate called the Ballycolman. They had numerous sorties and I remember them being ambushed there with grenades and automatic weapons. How the hell they didn't have any fatalities and wounded was incredible.

The resident company manned the sangars in the town; the cross border bridge known as the 'hump VCP' (Strabane – Lifford crossing) carried out foot patrols in the town and another area known as the 'head of the town.' They also had to have a QRF (quick reaction force) on immediate standby. The Kingos enjoyed going to Strabane as there was always something going on. I was the IC INT in Strabane and known as a LINCO (Liaison Intelligence NCO) and we had a FINCO (Field Intelligence NCO) with us who was supposed to work with the RUC Special Branch, but after a month they ditched him and everything went through me.

People were often mistaken when they thought that the Official IRA and the Provisional IRA had no link; untrue. We had 14 knee-cappings in Strabane in the first 12 months and 21 before I left. This was the Official IRA's punishment to anyone who committed robbery without their consent.

Proxy car bombs were most frightening. The Provisionals would enter a family house, hold them at gunpoint and then take the car, and load it with a bomb. They would then instruct a family member to drive it to a specific location or they would shoot everyone. They also told the driver that he would be watched all the way. The driver had to drive into Strabane over numerous 'sleeping policemen' and his heart must have been in his mouth. He also risked getting shot when he delivered the bomb.

One of the most enjoyable tasks the soldiers did was Helicopter VCPs. They would just set the Helicopter down on a main road and set up the VCP. Radio controlled IEDs were not established fully then, so most bombs were placed under culverts. They had command wires attached to the device and were set off by observing us and just contacting the wires to the battery.

Strabane had the highest unemployment of any town in UK. Why? They all drew dole there and worked over the border! Salmon Poaching was also a thriving business (it also supplemented mess dinners when we caught them).

Throughout the Troubles the Provisional IRA, as well as the Officials, showed no compunction or hesitation in turning the residential streets of the Republican areas into battlefields. Soldiers in the British Army had the constraints of the yellow card directives for when they could, and could not open fire, upon an armed terrorist; they also had the rules of chivalry and fair play enshrined within the accepted ROE; rules of engagement. Once they came under fire, once they saw an armed man – or woman – and once they felt that they were in mortal danger, they could both initiate as well as return fire. One such incident occurred on 5 August; in the Ardoyne area of Belfast.

Mrs Martha Lavery (66), an old age pensioner, living in Jamaica Street spent the last evening of her life, watching TV with family members. Whether or not she supported the IRA and wanted the troops off her streets is not known; what can be safely assumed is that she didn't wish to live in the middle of a battlefield. An Army land rover came under attack from gunmen from the Official IRA close to her home and two soldiers were wounded in the initial volley. The soldiers, as they were entitled to do, returned fire and may have hit and wounded a gunman as a small firefight – more an exchange of rounds – took place. Sadly for Mrs Lavery two of the rounds came through her front door and hit and killed her. Both the coroner and forensic testing were later unable to determine the origin of the bullets which killed her. What was certain, however, was that the IRA had again turned a residential area into a shooting gallery through its own arrogant irresponsibility.

On 7 August there was a most regrettable incident at a farm in Limehall, Co Tyrone when a patrol from the Royal Regiment of Wales (RRW) had cause to affect a search. Their motto is *Gwell angau na Chywilydd* (Death rather than Dishonour) but the following incident is one which will not be easily forgotten. Back in 2008, this author interviewed an officer who had been present that day and he spoke honestly and frankly. The MoD decided that it must not be reported in the first person, so one will discuss it, without the use of 'reported speech.'

Patrick McElhone (22) cultivated a medium-size farm close to Pomeroy and had been questioned earlier that day, and sent on his way. Later in the day, a further patrol of RRW soldiers, under the command of a junior officer returned to the farm and spoke to Mr McElhone. He was allegedly truculent and un-cooperative, was dismissed by the officer and walked away. A minute or two later, the same soldier instructed one of the Privates to bring the farmer back, as he wished to ask him another question. The soldier duly obeyed and left to find him; a minute or two later, there was the unmistakable sound of an SLR being discharged and the officer ran around the corner of the farm building and found Mr McElhone's body on the ground. He immediately questioned the soldier who stated that the farmer had tried to run away and that he had had no recourse other than to shoot him. The NCO was later charged with manslaughter, and appeared in court. At first he said that the man was running away and that he feared that he might be a terrorist and fired at him from 20 yards; later he stated that the discharge was accidental. The soldier was later acquitted, but it left a rather nasty taste in the mouth, and was more mill for the grist of IRA propaganda.

Sad end for suspect Morris Minor close to Irish border; pity that
the IRA chose to use such a nice motor (Brian Sheridan)

Not many spare parts left on this vehicle (Brian Sheridan)

Felix fires SSG shot at another suspect vehicle near Irish border (Brian Sheridan)

Sergeant Graham Lightfoot (AT) and ADU soldier and his friend
pictured close to the Irish border (Brian Sheridan)

The following day, there was a falling out amongst Loyalist paramilitaries and UFF member, Terence Miskimmon (24) who had only recently been released from prison was shot and killed in Belfast. He had been accused of being over friendly with Republicans, possibly whilst he had been behind bars, and had been earmarked for execution. Such were the psychopaths who both ran and manned the Loyalist organisations that the man's own friends terrified for their own safety, actively conspired to lead him to his death. He was shot in a car somewhere in North Belfast and his body was dumped near Shore Road, close to a recent sectarian murder scene.

On 12 August, Charles Apcar, a member of the British security services was killed, probably by the IRA at a location in Northern Ireland. The author is not permitted to say more, and his age and service details, including the background to the mission he was engaged upon are withheld by the MoD. Of course, the causes of his death may be more prosaic than one might imagine. One believes that his death must be mentioned, and it is fitting that his name appears on the Roll of Honour of British deaths, during the Troubles.

The following day, in what was an unbelievable lapse in security; two Royal Marine Commandos were killed by a massive bomb blast in Drumuckaval, Co Armagh. Their deaths brought into question the total lack of professionalism of their senior officers. An observation post, some two miles outside of Crossmaglen had been left unattended for the best part of a week; in the very heart of 'bandit country'. The Provisional IRA was a heartless, ruthless killing machine; they were also professional, vigilant and always willing to watch and learn. Their South Armagh Brigade would have been aware of the location of the OP, not only through their own observations, but also through the eyes of their legion of 'dickers'. Ever vigilant, ever desperate to kill British soldiers they were unable to resist this opportunity, and booby-trapped the post with at least 200 lbs of explosives. Marine Michael John (20) from St Albans, and Corporal Dennis Leach (24) from Leeds were killed when the IRA detonated the device which they had clandestinely planted during the period between occupations of the OP.

Shortly before the explosion a Royal Marine patrol had actually searched the OP before settling in to watch the border with the Irish Republic, several hundred yards away. An IRA unit observing the men then triggered the device by a command wire which had been located inside the post and which led several hundred feet away to the actual border. Both Marines were killed instantly and two of their comrades were seriously injured. The Royal Marines (motto: *Per Mare, Per Terram* which means By Sea, By Land) were very badly let down by the officers who felt that it was safe to return to a position which had been unmanned for a week and in an area where the IRA were dominant.

Castlewellan, Co Down is approximately 30 miles due south of Belfast, and just three miles from the coast at Dundrum Bay; it is a picturesque part of South Down. In the north of the town is the St Malachy's Estate and though nowhere near as nasty as its Republican sisters to the north, such as Turf Lodge, Andersonstown, Ballymurphy and Creggan, it is nonetheless, a hard line Nationalist area. On 14 August, whilst on a routine foot patrol on the estate, soldiers spotted a known player, Paul Magorrian (21) in possession of a rifle. Under ROE, they opened fire and killed the man, described as an Adjutant in the IRA's South Down Brigade. Although locals, including the town priest claimed that the man had not been armed, the soldiers recovered a rifle and sniper scope.

The terrorists knew the rules of law and the rules of engagement, and if they were seen to be armed, they were aware that the Army could, and would shoot. The IRA was playing big boys' games and thus, big boys' rules applied.

The senseless sectarian slaughter continued, but this time, a 13-year-old boy, barely into his teens was cut down by a UFF sniper; this truly *advanced* the Loyalist cause.[1] Joseph McGuinness (13) lived in the New Lodge area and was walking with friends in North Queen Street, en-route to buy fish and chips. There was an altercation with some Protestant youths (*'blue noses'* as they were called by Catholics) from the Loyalist Duncairn Gardens, which was clearly a ruse to lure the Catholic boys into the gunman's sights. Young Joseph walked across towards the youth when a single shot rang out, and he fell mortally wounded to the ground. He staggered back towards his home, some instinct taking over as he sought the sanctuary of his family; he collapsed in Hillman Street; close to where Robert Curtis became the 22nd British soldier to die in the Troubles. Some three hours later, he died in the RVH, another victim of the sectarian killers.

'Sneaky beakies' was the name generally given to undercover soldiers engaged on covert operations in Northern Ireland. Several secretive military units were allegedly engaged throughout the Troubles, however the MoD have consistently maintained a NCND stance in relation to the existence of such units. It would appear that term 'sneaky beakies' was also applied by some regiments to their covert patrols.

'SNEAKY BEAKIES'
Gerry Chandler 3 RGJ

'Sneaky Beakies' was the name given to undercover soldiers who went on foot patrols, usually at night and wearing soft shoes or slippers; these were designed to gather intelligence. After one such SB we were watching a Republican drinking club on the Falls Road. We later raided the pub to search for suspected 'players'. I remember the place was packed with drinkers and the customary way of dealing with that, was for us all to race in and form a line across the bar linking arms. Then one by one we would check each person and throw them to the other side of the line assuming they were 'clear'. The thing which sticks with me was the pure hatred in the eyes of some of those men and women. I remember thinking 'where does that hatred come from?' and later seeing paintings of William of Orange celebrating the Battle of The Boyne in 1699, notably the large one in The Rodney area. I realised that if hatred goes back that far, this conflict would go on and on because there was no way politicians in Westminster could ever comprehend it. I also found myself thinking how I myself would feel if Irish troops were fulfilling a similar function in mainland Britain. Whilst I hoped I could see their point of view there was one thing I was absolutely certain about; there was no way I would ever kill or maim anyone, least of all innocent women and children.

On 18 August, a total of 19 IRA members escaped from Portlaoise Jail after overpowering guards and using gelignite to blast through gates. The prison itself is in is the county town of County Laois in the midlands of Ireland. This escape was a major

---

1   Author's own italics.

propaganda coup for the Provisionals and an even more major embarrassment for the Republic's Government, which faced many calls to resign. Harold Wilson, the British Prime Minister was reportedly unhappy.

There then followed an uneasy lull in the violence and, other than the seemingly daily rioting by Catholic youths, there were no fatalities for a period of eight days. On or around, 18 August, an IRA punishment squad, acting on an unsubstantiated rumour, seized a 56-year-old dockworker, Arthur Rafferty and dragged him to Newington Street, in the New Lodge area. Despite the fact that no crime had been reported and despite the fact that this was just unfounded gossip, they found him guilty of sexual assault against a child. He was shot and left in a terrible state, with a cardboard sign nearby, accusing him of sexual assault. It is likely, however that it was placed around his neck and became dislodged. The sheer hypocrisy of the Provisional IRA simply knows no bounds; their thought processes in anti-social crimes (e.g. excluding those which they perpetrated) were uncluttered by thoughts of right or wrong or by evidence! He died in hospital on 8 September.

Then, on 23 August, an RUC Special Branch officer, Inspector Peter Flanagan (47) was shot dead in the 'Diamond Bar' in Omagh as he drank whilst off-duty. He had been dicked by a female IRA member and his routines were 'sussed' out by the IRA who had stalked him to his 'local'. The man who shot him was IRA man Sean O'Callaghan who was also responsible for the death of the UDR 'Greenfinch' Eva Martin. O'Callaghan, who became an informer for the Garda Síochána and who allegedly informed for the UK's MI5 in the Netherlands, wrote his autobiography *The Informer* following his release from jail.

In 1976, aged 21, O'Callaghan resigned from the IRA, and moved to England, where he later decided to become an informer. He returned to Tralee, where he had a meeting with a local Garda, who had previously arrested him, and disclosed that he wanted to inform on the IRA. O'Callaghan stated that he was the head of the IRA Southern Command, and a substitute delegate on the IRA Army Council, both in print and before a Dublin jury under oath. However, these claims have been denied. He was elected a local councillor for Sinn Féin, and was in regular contact with its leaders, Gerry Adams (now MP for Belfast West) and Martin McGuinness (now MP for Mid Ulster). In 1984, he helped to foil a bomb attack on a theatre in London where Prince Charles and Princess Diana were to attend a benefit concert which featured Duran Duran and Dire Straits, among other performers. He escaped to Ireland as he was wanted by the British police.

The Provisional IRA, from its birth arising from the split with the Official wing, had immediately declared that all members of the occupation forces would be killed routinely. These 'occupation forces' naturally included soldiers and policemen, Judges, prison officers, civilian security searchers and, apparently, census-takers. They had also marked for execution those former members of the UDR who had resigned and severed their links with part-time soldiering. William Hutchinson (30) fell into two of those categories; he was a former member of the UDR and was also employed by the Department of the Environment (DOE) as a traffic census taker. On 24 August, he was sitting in a van with a colleague in Calbragh, Co Tyrone, close to Dungannon. A stolen car drove alongside the DOE van and sprayed it with automatic gunfire.

Mr Hutchinson was killed instantly and his colleague was very badly injured. Whatever prompted the Provisionals to then claim that he was an undercover soldier on spying duties is simply beyond comprehension. One wonders if, in all honesty, their spokespeople actually believed the ludicrous comments they made publically. Whether or not the Sinn Féin puppet who uttered those words, managed to say them with a straight face is not recorded. The vast bulk of statements made by this organisation varied between piousness and the outrageous.

On the 25th, another UDR soldier was killed in a seemingly ubiquitous road traffic accident, when Private Samuel Gilmore Workman (21) was killed in an RTA, just a few short weeks after his 21st birthday. A former serving soldier put the whole RTA thing into some kind of stark perspective:

Mike Sangster, Royal Artillery

Take a 9 till 5 day job; add an 8 till 4 night job. No weekends off. Put the whole mix into a land rover on a narrow country road at night, together with live weapons and add a terrorist threat. Does anybody wonder why the death rate from RTA, ND and what is euphemistically called violent and unnatural causes was so high amongst those lads? I should probably think that the divorce rate amongst the married lads was pretty high as well which could account for some of those 'violent and unnatural' causes.

I don't know how some of them did it, bearing in mind that a high proportion of them were over 30 years old; some in their 50's. We were in our late teens or early 20's and pre training made sure we were pretty fit, yet after four months, I was physically and mentally knackered. Those lads did this for years!

The Royal Pioneer Corps, whose origins go back to Calais in 1346, are known as 'grave diggers' and 'chunkies' among other regiments of the British Army. Often saddled with the more mundane tasks, they have given stout and resolute service to the Crown and Commonwealth War Grave Commission cemeteries throughout the world are dotted with the fallen of that Corps who died alongside the more 'glamorous' of units. Their motto is *Labor omnia vincit* (Latin: Hard work conquers all) and they lost soldiers in Northern Ireland during the Troubles; ten in all died between 1972 and 1988.

On 26 August, a land rover containing members of 3 Brigade, members of the Royal Signals and one Royal Pioneer Corps sharpshooter, Private Philip Drake (18), came under fire at Craigavon, Co Tyrone. The vehicle had just entered a roundabout near Drumbeg, and it was there that IRA gunmen sprung their ambush. Over a dozen rounds were fired at the soldiers and Private Drake from Kettering, Northamptonshire was hit in the head and died shortly afterwards. Of those involved in the periphery of then shooting, including a woman who moved the weapons through Army checkpoints in a baby's pram and others who assisted, the courts handed down only suspended sentences. It would appear that a soldier's life was not worth tuppenth!

The day after the murder of Private Drake, an IRA member succeeded in blowing himself up with his own device. Patrick McKeown (29) was a member of an IRA bombing-making team and was assembling a bomb in an IRA 'safe house' in Newry, Co Down. Together with at least two other members, he worked on the device when it suddenly prematurely detonated. He was killed instantly and the two others were badly wounded but were whisked over the border into the Republic, where they would have received medical treatment from sympathisers. The border crossing close to Kelly's Road is a mere four miles away and from there, another mile to the Provo sanctuary of Dundalk where medical treatment was given, no questions asked. Once over, there was a further six-mile dash to Louth County Hospital and treatment for the injured bombers.

The IRA team had been working on the device in the kitchen of the safe house, in order to pack it into a hijacked vehicle, presumably to leave in the centre of Newry. He had intended to kill security forces; he succeeded only in killing himself.

August 1974 had ended, and the death tally for the month was 15. Of these six were soldiers or former soldiers, (four of whom were killed by the IRA) two Policemen died and four civilians. The IRA lost three members, two of whom were killed by the Army. Of the civilians, the Loyalists killed two; of the four civilians killed, at least two were purely sectarian. In total, the Provisional IRA was responsible for the loss of six lives and the Loyalists for three during the course of the month.

Chapter 21

September

The month of September saw a further fall in troubles-related deaths, and *only* one British soldier died during the month; even then, from 'circumstances unknown.' There was a turning point, however in that the Provisional IRA focused their attention on legal figures and assassinated two judges on the same day and then killed a former prison officer. The Loyalist murder gangs stepped up their sectarian murder campaign and both sides of the paramilitary fence vied with each other to see which one could inflict the largest amount of human suffering.

THE CAPTURE OF AN IRA GUNMAN
Steve Corbett, 13 Troop, Royal Artillery

On Monday, 2 September there was a fair bit of shooting in and around the 'Lodge'. At 6:10pm three shots were fired by a gunman armed with a Garand rifle at a foot patrol. They gave chase, and one member of the patrol actually managed to get close enough to snatch the rifle off the gunman, but he still managed to get away. At 9:20pm the gunman – Patrick Campbell – was caught by a foot patrol from 97 Battery; this man was widely considered to be the killer of Bernie Fearns. The idiots in the patrol somehow managed to let him escape, and even managed to miss him when they opened fire on him at close range. Over the next half hour, there were three more contacts with Provos in the 'Lodge. On Saturday, 7 September, Patrick Campbell was again captured, and this time he didn't get away. I was on mobile patrol at the time, and I just happened to be at North Queen Street RUC Station, when he was brought in for questioning. He was hauled into a small yard and put, spread-eagled against a wall. Feelings were understandably running very high amongst members of 97 Battery. I took a picture of him against the wall just before we left to continue our patrol. Campbell later admitted to many shootings he was involved in.

I can't forget that poor lad's voice who came on the radio pleading for help, and I can't forget how the MO came on the air describing Bernie's injuries. It all seemed so heartless to me to do such a thing. I knew that Bernie was dead, but was there any need for everyone to be told the extent of his injuries? Every year I place a cross on the Cenotaph bearing Bernie's and also Kim MacCunn's names. I have never forgotten them, and I never will.

On Thursday, 5 September, a lone RUC officer attempted to foil an Official IRA bank raid in North Belfast. He was fatally wounded as he challenged armed raiders at a bank in Rathcoole, Newtownabbey. Alerted by his radio, Inspector William Elliott (48) raced to the bank and confronted the robbers as they fled; for his pains, he was shot and mortally wounded, dying very shortly afterwards. He was the 55th policeman to die in the Troubles, and was posthumously awarded the Queen's Police Medal. A soldier from the Royal Artillery was present in the aftermath and recounts below his brief but frightening experience.

CATCHING IRA BOMBERS
John 'Wooly' Woolgrove, Royal Artillery

In September 1974, we were attached to 4th Field Regiment. There was a bank robbery at the Ulster Bank in the Diamond shopping centre in Rathcoole and two of the robbers were reported as being still in the area. As it happened, we were on mobile patrol and were called to the incident. I was 2IC of the patrol and we were tasked to go along Shore Road to Greenisland, which I recall was a small estate which seemed to be comprised of just blocks of flats. This particular entrance overlooked the Rathcoole estate, and as we drove in at the back of the estate, there was a small path. After getting out of the land rover, we started walking up a path with small bushes on either side. As we did so, a man came running around the corner and stopped suddenly as he saw us. Instantly, I pointed my weapon at him as he was holding a pistol; I screamed at him: "Put that fucking weapon down!" and he did so, but my heart was going 'ten to the dozen!'

However, after searching him, he turned out to be a plain clothed policeman! He told us that two men had run through the estate just minutes before; we radioed through to HQ and were told to join back up with the rest of the patrol in the Diamond Centre. It was about a week later that we were sent to Flax Street mill in the Ardoyne area of Belfast; the patrols were a lot different in the Ardoyne as most were foot patrols. We got used to the area, going from Flax Street mill up to the bus station where some of our other lads were based.

About a week or so before leaving Belfast, we were on an OP at Alliance Avenue, looking down Jamaica Street. We were in an upstairs room of a house overlooking some waste ground and spent five boring, tedious days just checking out vehicles; every vehicle, whether it was coming or going!. Eventually we were relieved and a Makralon land rover picked us up; we drove off and then we had a burst of activity on the radio. The call alerted us to look out for a stolen two tone, brown Austin Cambridge. Minutes later, as we headed in the direction of Flax Street mill, one of the lads – 'Taff' – shouted out that it was parked along the side of the road in Oldpark Road.

I looked over and could see that there were two men sitting in it and I immediately told the Staff Sergeant and he ordered the vehicle to stop. The rest of the lads were getting shitty with me because they wanted to get back to the Mill for some food and rest. He told Lenny, the driver to drive past and then turn around, further down the road. I was ordered to jump out and get the driver out of the car and grab the car keys. I ran straight to the Austin and yanked the door open whilst Taff ran around to the passenger side. As I did so, I pointed my rifle at the driver's face; he turned white immediately! I screamed at him to get out and Taff did the same at the other side. The poor driver was terrified and he was shaking like a leaf! Staff Sgt Smith got the other lads into all round defence and they took up firing positions pointing in all directions. I ordered the driver to open the boot and I was shitting myself in case it was a car bomb.

The driver didn't want to open the boot so I pushed my gun barrel into his face and made him open it. As he did, there was a very strong smell of marzipan and I could see lots of plastic bags all filled with a yellow-coloured material. I pushed him away and began searching him; I found some detonators in his pocket and a couple of bits of wire. I handcuffed him and in the meantime, we had called for backup on the radio; he was properly arrested and put in the back of the land rover. We then searched the passenger and found some bits of paper with names and vehicle numbers, which we later discovered were policemen's private details. Obviously they had intended to use the bomb-making material in booby traps under the individual officers' cars, probably at their homes. I often wondered how the IRA obtained all this info and I suppose that they must have had a 'mole' inside the RUC Records Office.

We drove the car back to North Queen Street RUC station, although we had to smash the windscreens to let that sickening marzipan smell out. Later on that day, the homes of the two IRA men were searched and the search team found detonators, timing devices, reels of wire and a whole load of paper work. This IRA intelligence contained personal info on the police, Army tactics etc; even down to numbers of soldiers in a land rover and stuff like that. That same week, the 4th Regiment had three other separate finds of bomb-making equipment in the same area!

After the tour was over, we returned to Germany but were later called back in order to give evidence against the two IRA men. To this day, I have no idea what sentence they were given, because as soon as we had said our pieces, we were whisked out of the courtroom and back to Germany.

In terms of IRA intelligence, it is clear that they were well informed and it is highly probable that they had sympathisers, even active members, working inside RUC HQ, probably even inside HQNI. As the old wartime adage goes, 'loose lips sink ships' and 'walls have ears.' Even innocent remarks, overheard by the wrong people could mean so much more to terrorist organisations such as the IRA and the Loyalist paramilitaries. Individual soldiers recall how, even after one or two foot patrols, locals calling out 'What about ye, Dave?' or 'Morning, Billy' as they walked through a Republican area. In these cases, it is however, more likely that the residents had overheard individual soldiers calling out each other's names. Furthermore, the number of RUC officers and UDR men who were targeted at their homes and places of work do show that the IRA's intelligence gathering was vastly superior than the SF originally thought. The late IRA man, Eamon Collins' autobiography *Killing Rage* details his work as an IRA 'mole' inside HM Customs. It is a fine example of the organisation's intelligence work and in the instance of Collins, demonstrates how he was able to facilitate the targeting of a UDR man who worked for Customs, as well as other part-time soldiers and policemen.

Eamon Collins was a PIRA activist during the late 1970s and 1980s periods. He turned his back on the organisation in the late 1980s and later wrote 'Killing Rage' telling of his experiences in the IRA. He was killed in 1999, it is presumed by his former PIRA colleagues, for testifying against IRA volunteer Thomas 'Slab' Murphy in a civil trial in Dublin. After leaving the organisation, he became increasingly critical of the leadership and was an intended 'supergrass' during the 1980s. He had intended to give evidence against the IRA at trials against its members but rescinded his statements at the last moment.

Collins wrote in his book that he never felt able to kill anyone himself, but instead became the South Down Brigade's intelligence officer. He also publically admitted to being a member of the IRA's notorious 'nutting squad.' Eamon Collins was killed on 27 January 1999 whilst walking his dogs near his home in Newry. He was stabbed and beaten so badly that police initially thought he had been hit by a car. Sinn Féin President and former Belfast Brigade commander for the IRA, Gerry Adams wrote that Collins' death was "regrettable" but added that Collins had "many enemies in many, many, many places."

The Saturday following the Rathcoole raid, an IRA unit took over the grounds of a Care Home in Dungannon, with the intention of attacking an Army patrol as it passed by. Several gunmen opened fire with automatic weapons and hit the foot patrol, wounding one soldier, but they either ignored a passing civilian vehicle or fired anyway. They hit a civilian car, fatally wounding a passenger; cynically uncaring, just as long as they achieved their primary goal of killing soldiers. Mrs Mary Bingham (59) died after her daughter had rushed her to a nearby hospital. The 'brave urban guerrillas' had injured a soldier, so what did it matter if they had also ended the life of an innocent civilian?

The day after – a Sunday – Arthur Rafferty (56), who had been badly wounded by an IRA punishment squad on 18 August, died of his wounds. It was yet another triumph for Republican 'justice.' It was clearly a case of execute first, and then listen to the evidence. The author wishes to point out to the family of Mr Rafferty, that there is no evidence whatsoever of the crimes for which the Provisional IRA murdered him; the killing was without the slightest cause or provocation.

The Provisional IRA, however, had bigger fish to fry and eight days after the death of the falsely accused dockworker; they shot and killed two senior symbols of the 'British occupation forces'. On the morning of Monday 16 September, they almost simultaneously attacked two separate judges in Belfast. Both of the Judges were killed and it is thought that a third attack was thwarted.

Martin McBirney QC, (52) was targeted at his home in Belmont Road, to the east of Sydenham as the IRA struck in the Belfast suburbs. The Magistrate was sitting down at a table, when an IRA gunman burst into the house, and shot him several times, leaving him fatally wounded; he died shortly afterwards. Another IRA gang then struck at Malone Road in the south of the city, close to the Ormeau Road. Judge Rory Conaghan (54) was eating breakfast with his young daughter, when an armed gang burst in and shot him dead in front of the horrified little girl. Despite neither Judge having an anti-Republican stance, nor showing anything other than blind impartiality in court cases dealing with the IRA, both were assassinated. A later Sinn Féin/IRA statement stated that the men had been killed for "collaborating with the British war machine." Magistrate McBirney's sister, who lived in the Republican Andersonstown, was so shocked at the news of her brother's death that she had a massive heart attack and died immediately.

VICIOUS DOG MEETS ITS END IN THE RODNEY
Gerry Chandler, 3 Royal Green Jackets

On foot patrols I was always 'tail end Charlie,' probably by virtue of the fact that I arrived a few days later in Belfast than the rest of the battalion. It involved an awful lot of walking backwards up and down the streets of Belfast. These were largely uneventful, except for the regular tests carried out by the section commander who was not averse to diving over a hedge and screaming 'Contact, wait out' into his Pye radio; or pretending to do so, just to keep everyone on their toes. It resulted in quite a few broken fences and rifle barrels full of mud where leaping over the fence meant they got impaled in the gardens.

During one of these amusing interludes there was another shout of 'Contact!' I one of the Riflemen – I think his name was 'Scouse' McGarry – dropped a tobacco tin full of cigarette cards that he was collecting as he began to run across the road. Unbelievably, he stopped and bent over and started to pick them up. I encouraged him to desist with a stream of choice obscenities from my cover, deep in someone's garden hedge. 'Scouse' McGarry, was later, to die in West Berlin, around 1976, whilst messing about with a diver's knife at the Sergeant's mess. Actually it was more than messing about as someone was later charged with his murder. What was unbelievable, was that had there been an IRA gunman, 'Scouse' would almost certainly been shot as he risked his life for his collection of cards. The gunman would have thought that it was his birthday, Christmas and Easter all rolled into one!

I remember one particular patrol in the Rodney, where the natives were doing the usual dustbin-lid banging to alert the local IRA sharpshooters that a foot patrol was about.[1] We'd had a number of nasty receptions in the area and one in particular from a rather feral dog which had obviously been trained to go for any soldiers they happened to meet. He'd inflicted quite a few injuries during the course of the tour. After a few run ins with the brute, I remember someone from the section, whose name I know well but who shall remain anonymous, asking if he could replace me as tail end Charlie on that patrol, and I was happy to agree. When we came to the street with the rabid dog, it went for the lad, and he caught hold of it, took a Bowie knife from his belt, promptly slit its throat and laid it on the doorstep of the house in question. It sounds a terrible thing to do now but at the time I think a lot of people were glad that he had done it. Another day, another patrol and one less threat to us all.

The UVF were busy over the next three days; busy that is, spreading the gospel of violent and senseless death. Michael McCourt (31) ran an engineering plant at Pomeroy, Co Tyrone and he came to the attention of the Loyalists because he was a Catholic and employed Catholics. One or more members of a UVF bombing team left two devices inside the factory at closing time and when Mr McCourt handled one it exploded and killed him instantly. Three days later, close to midnight, a UVF murder gang was driving along Clifton Street, on the sectarian interface between the Crumlin Road and the New Lodge. They spotted several youths in and outside a small café and simply opened fire

---

1   This was sometimes referred to as 'hen patrols' on account of the fact that it was usually the women banging the lids.

indiscriminately. Patrick McGreevy (16) was hit and fatally wounded; he died in the early hours of the following morning. McGreevy was a member of the Official wing of the IRA and Republican death notices lauded him as a member of *Fianna Éireann*.

The organisation describes itself thus:

> Fianna Éireann is a [sic] independent Republican youth movement, dedicated to upholding the true principles of republicanism amongst Irish youth both male and female. We are committed to the establishment of a united Ireland free of all foreign oppression and the establishment of a 32 county socialist Irish republic proclaimed on Easter week 1916 and ratified by Dáil Éireann 1919. Although we are not aligned to any other political organisation we show solidarity to the various organisations that make up the vanguard of Irish republicanism, we promote the use of the Irish language by our members and Irish classes will be made available for members how want to learn there [sic] native language. As a republican youth movement we do not feel obliged to accept a half-way house solution or puppet parliament in Ireland it is all or nothing, Fianna upholds the right of the Irish working class to the ownership of Ireland and all her natural resources and to this end we will campaign against all forms of capitalism and foreign exploitation.

On the 20th, Corporal Geoffrey Hall (21) of the Royal Army Ordnance Corps (RAOC) died in circumstances unknown, whilst on duty, and somewhere in Northern Ireland. The author has no further information on this young soldier; he was the only soldier to die during the month of September.

The IRA then turned its attentions towards another arm of the 'occupation forces' the Prison Service. During the course of the Troubles, they murdered a total of 29 members of the Prison Officers Association (POA) in Northern Ireland. On 22 September, they targeted William McCully (58) who was himself, a former officer, although such distinctions rarely mattered to the psychopaths who seemingly killed for pleasure. Mr McCully had retired from the prison service some three years before, and was now employed as a school caretaker. He must have inadvertently mentioned the fact in the company of preying ears, and he was marked for execution. Late in the evening, he answered a knock at the door of his house at Hillmount Gardens in the south of Belfast and was immediately shot and died shortly afterwards; his wife was wounded in the attack.

As stated previously a total of 29 prison officers, including two females, were murdered by Republicans between 1974 and 1993. In the appendix to another volume is a full list of those killed for the crime of doing their jobs. The murdered officers included Agnes Wallace, mother of six, who was killed in Armagh on 19 April 1979, and Elizabeth Chambers, killed by INLA in Armagh on 7 October, 1982. William McCully was the first to be killed.

The Provisional IRA, and the Republican movement as a whole, have often accused the Army of colluding with the Loyalist paramilitaries, in order to destroy them, the Republicans. It is a fanciful thought, and one which must have certainly crossed the minds of HQNI and the British Government. It would have been certainly, a most attractive proposition for the beleaguered soldiers to let the two sides – Loyalist and Republican – wipe each other out, and thus save bloodshed amongst the troops. How

IRA explosives after successful defuse (Brian Sheridan)

Army roadblock to safeguard civilians whilst IRA bomb is examined (Brian Sheridan)

easy might it have been, for an Army patrol to delay going into an area for 15 minutes or so whilst a Loyalist assassination squad took out a top Sinn Féin member or a top IRA member?

This author believes that it may well have happened, from time to time but, in the main, the British Army played with a 'straight bat' and conducted their affairs within the rule of law and within the guidelines of ROE. On 25 September, the Army played with an exceptionally 'straight bat,' and their reaction and decisive timing saw a young man's murderers caught and put behind bars. Two members of the UVF, on a stolen motorcycle, pulled up to an electrical store on Limestone Road, North Belfast, knowing that a young Catholic boy, Kieran McIlroy (18), worked there. Waiting until closing time, they watched him come out of work, and calmly shot him dead, before driving off. A passing Army mobile patrol was hailed down by eyewitnesses and the soldiers raced off, catching up with the murderers stuck in traffic on the Antrim Road. Both men were convicted and jailed for life. One wonders if the bearded one, in West Belfast, actually in private praised the soldiers for their prompt action. One rather suspects not.

THE NIGHT WE ARRESTED GERRY ADAMS
Gerry Chandler, 3 Royal Green Jackets

This would be the August or September; over the course of the years, memories fade and sometimes the dates became blurred as one day passes into another. On a foot patrol, one night, we were walking along the Lower Falls Road right outside the Whiterock Cemetery on the corner where it meets the road that which leads to McCrory Park. We had received intelligence to suggest that an IRA player would shortly be passing by on the top deck of a bus. INT told us that this man was wanted for at least one killing and that he was on his way to see his girlfriend who was a nurse at the RVH (Royal Victoria Hospital). There was a bit of a wait and the usual sight of children with jeans with tartan flashes, Bay City Rollers style, halfway up their legs. They generally were on roller skates, clinging to the back of the Belfast black taxis as they made their way home for free. Although VCPs were a common sight, to stop a bus was unheard of at the time.

Eventually the bus came into sight and we stopped it. Two of the guys went to the top deck and hauled off none other than Gerry Adams. I was given the task of ensuring that he stood against the wall with his hands and legs splayed, as was standard practice at the time. This meant that the whole body weight rested on the man's fingers, which was extremely uncomfortable for those who were detained. Also as it was about the right height it also gave a great opportunity of resting a rifle barrel against his 'crown jewels'.[2] He was there for some time, as we first P-checked (personnel checked) him, before the section commander spoke to INT about him. We needed to understand what we should do with him once we had sure who he really was. I'm pretty sure that in the end he was released, as there was no tangible evidence to detain him. This was odd I thought, as at the time he was known to be the Battalion Commander of PIRA's West Belfast battalion.

---

2   For non-British readers, this refers to the testicles!

Ever vigilant. Private Musset (LI) in South Armagh (Brian Sheridan)

Private Joe Gribben (1LI) on sangar duty in South Armagh (Brian Sheridan)

Over the years, Gerry Adams has undergone a startling political metamorphosis, and is now a leading and 'respectable' Sinn Féin politician and *Teachta Dála* (TD) for the constituency of Louth. His title is currently President of Sinn Féin. Adams has stated repeatedly that he has never been a member of the Provisional IRA. However, authors such as Ed Moloney, Peter Taylor, Mark Urban and historian Richard English have all named Adams as part of the IRA leadership since the 1970s. Adams has denied Moloney's claims, calling them 'libellous.' Ed Moloney's recent works *Voices From The Grave* contains allegations from IRA man and former colleague, the late Brendan Hughes that Adams was the architect of the bombing campaign in Belfast in the early 1970s. Hughes alleges that Adams was behind the Abercorn bombing in March 1972 and the 'Bloody Friday' bombings in Belfast in July of the same year.[3] The author invites the reader to draw his or her own conclusions as to the culpability of Adams as a terrorist and IRA commander.

There was no let-up in the sectarian murders, and a gang of UDA/UFF thugs chanced upon a lone Catholic boy walking in the direction of Andersonstown after a night out. Gerard McWilliams (25) was a Belfast boy who had lived the previous six years on the British mainland, and was possibly not street-wise enough to appreciate the dangers of walking home alone, at night, with so many sectarian murderers stalking the streets. He was caught and half-beaten to death and then finally stabbed, and his body dumped like so much rubbish, at Lecale Street, between Windsor Park and Milltown cemetery. Mr McWilliams was a victim of both his own naivety, and of Loyalist thugs.

The inherent dangers of being a Catholic, employed in a Protestant company and in a Protestant area were many and very real. For many, unable to find work in a predominantly Catholic-owned company and in a Catholic area, there was of course, no alternative. The Loyalist murder gangs knew this also and constantly targeted people who had to travel from a 'safe' area into an 'unsafe' one in which to work, and earn money in order to feed their families.

One such employer was Sunblest Bakeries, for whom the author in his student days worked, in Bradford, West Yorkshire. They employed a small number of Catholics. Ralph Laverty (55) was a Catholic from Andersonstown, he had a large family – four children – who needed feeding and clothing, and so worked at the Bakery. He was described as an innocent man, doing his best for his family, even if it meant travelling to the Loyalist Castereagh area. The UVF spy network had already reported him to the leadership; in all probability through a sympathiser in the Personnel Department, who could easily access personal details, or simply because a workmate had informed on him. Whatever the reason, he was killed just outside by a man who shot him five times in the back. Some years later, a former colleague of Mr Laverty was jailed for life for the murder. The intimacy of the killer to his victim sums up the sheer evil and lack of a defined goal that the paramilitaries had, in that the killer had, in all probability, shared a tea break, cracked a joke or even swapped photos with his victim.

A Loyalist gang was involved on the same day in another killing; this time in the Catholic Cliftonville area, but this time it was a case of mistaken identity. John Cameron (57) and father of three was, ironically enough, a Protestant who lived in a Catholic area and was regarded as a good friend by his Catholic neighbours. Cliftonville is on

---

3   For more details see Wharton, Ken, *The Bloodiest Year: Northern Ireland 1972*, (Stroud: History Press, 2011).

the tip of the hard line Ardbone area – known locally as the 'Bone – and close to the sectarian interface with Protestants. A gunman from either the UVF or the UFF fired several shots through the window of the Cameron's house; the shots hit Mr Cameron, but it would appear that the gunman was shooting blind and thankfully, the bulk of the family were out at the time. He died at the scene, collapsing amongst the paint and wallpaper with which he was decorating the front room.

The excellent *Lost Lives* notes the following quote from his widow: "He was a man who had no enemies and was not capable of doing anybody any harm. He was not a member of any organisation and had no interest in politics."[4]

September 1974 had ended and the death tally for the month was 14. Of these one was a soldier, one was a Policeman and 11 were civilians. The IRA lost one member, killed by the Loyalists. Of the civilians, the Loyalists killed five and the IRA also killed five; of the 11 civilians killed, at least five were purely sectarian. In total, the Provisional IRA was responsible for the loss of six lives and the Loyalists for six also during the course of the month.

4   McKitterick, David et al, *op cit*. pp. 477-478.

Chapter 22

October

In October the Loyalists stepped up their pointless and insane sectarian murders; the IRA killed a member of a soldier's family; an IRA 'mule' died transporting a bomb and the England Team struck again.

On 3 October a foot patrol from the Staffordshire Regiment was in the vicinity of Racecourse Road in the northern suburbs of Londonderry. The border with the Republic is less than a mile away, and even though Lenamore Road, which leads from Racecourse Road to Ireland would be heavily controlled by VCPs, there were enough other crossing places for IRA members to bolt over. Lieutenant Michael Simpson (21) from Sunbury-on-Thames in London was leading the patrol when a single shot rang out; he slumped to the ground, fatally wounded. He died later on 23 October in hospital. One of the gun team was a 17-year-old girl who was sentenced to life in prison in 1977. She was released after just four years when her weight fell dramatically and several British Labour MPs somewhat incredulously obtained her freedom!

RVH GUARD
Gerry Chandler, 3 Royal Green Jackets

From time to time we were required to provide guards for the RVH, for wounded soldiers. In some cases, for patients also, who had been shot by the IRA just in case they came back in to finish the job. In fact a year or so earlier, two IRA gunmen wearing doctors' coats had done just that. I remember sitting by the bedside of a young officer who had been shot in the back by an IRA sniper. The bullet hole had made a small hole in his back but it had taken a huge amount of his chest away as it exited and the screams that he made when they changed his dressing night and morning were terrible. It was heartbreaking and I felt so sorry for him; I sat by his bed with a 9mm pistol but there was very little I or anyone could do for him. I remember his parents arriving to visit one day and I think the next day he died. I'm pretty sure this was Lieutenant Michael Simpson of the 1st Battalion The Staffordshire Regiment, and from Sunbury-on-Thames, Middlesex, who died on 23 October 1974 aged 21, three weeks after being shot by an IRA sniper whilst on foot patrol racecourse Road, Shantallow, Londonderry.

Whilst looking at the Operation Banner website recently I came across the following post from a former colleague in 1 Staffordshire Regiment, written on 8 July 2007 and now living in Birmingham. I hope they don't mind me reproducing it here, it seems a fitting tribute to the ultimate sacrifice which Mike Simpson gave all those years ago whilst fulfilling his peacekeeping duties on the streets of Londonderry.

Mike, your death, which saddened us all at the time, has not been in vain.
A few of us visited the Shantallow, Rosemount, Creggan estates in July 2006

and then we made a memorial visit to where you were shot and subsequently died. It was pleasing to see that no troops were patrolling and no aggressive or life-threatening situations seemed to be around the corner as it was in our days in 1974 with the regiment. Young children were playing happily and without fear on the streets, whereas in our day they would have been stoning or petrol bombing us. Here we were 32 years after 1 Staffords had first patrolled the Londonderry province and it was so uncanny to see the exacting change. We and all other serving soldiers have had a part to play in the peace process. Your sacrifice was far greater than those soldiers that were lucky to survive and we will never forget you or our other colleagues who have lost their lives on the road to peace. Long may it last.

The Royal Victoria Hospital, which is situated at the junction of the Falls Road and Grosvenor Road in Belfast, was, at one stage, the world's premier hospital for the treatment of gunshot wounds. The medical staff there, by the mid-70s had experienced more shooting injuries and fatalities than any other hospital, definitely in Europe and almost certainly in the world.

On the morning of 4 October two Catholic friends, who worked for an engineering company, were walking the short distance from their bus to Boucher Road, in South Belfast. They walked along Moonstone Street which runs parallel to the main Lisburn Road, intending to cross a footbridge over the main Dublin-Belfast railway line, from there Boucher Road is a few hundred yards away. With the consummate ease with which they discovered employee's confidential information, the UVF had set a trap for the two Catholics. Before they reached the footbridge, a gunman opened fire, fatally wounding Mr Robert Willis (33) and badly wounding his colleague. Both men were barely able to stagger back to the main road, where they both collapsed; Mr Willis died on the way to the nearby Musgrave Park Hospital.

The day after, an IRA 'mule', Eugene McQuaid (35), father of five and an unemployed Catholic, was tasked by the IRA to transport parts of a mortar tube and explosives. It is stretching it somewhat, to accept that Mr McQuaid was unaware of the contents of the 'package' which he was instructed to carry. However, the evidence suggests, somewhat incredulously that the IRA gave him the 'package' without informing him of the danger in which he had placed himself. There was also a grave danger to the general public as he drove through residential areas. As he was about to cross the Irish border and into Northern Ireland, the device exploded, injuring him terribly and he died shortly afterwards.

The Provisional IRA said nothing at the time, but then in April 2006, almost 32 years later, they made one of their staggeringly pious and 'sincere' apologies; 32 years too late. A spokesman said:

On October 5 1974 Eugene McQuaid was killed as the result of an explosion, near the border at Newry. The leadership of Óglaigh na hÉireann was asked by the McQuaid family to investigate the circumstances surrounding the death of Eugene McQuaid. Our investigation has found that:

An IRA operation was in place on that day aimed at a British Army patrol that was known to travel that particular stretch of the road regularly. Eugene McQuaid was killed when an explosive device, intended for that patrol, was detonated prematurely. Eugene McQuaid was not a member of the IRA. He was not involved in the IRA operation. At the time the IRA did not acknowledge its involvement in the incident. The IRA leadership offers its sincere apologies to the McQuaid family for the death of Eugene and for the heartache and trauma that our actions have caused.

Signed P O'Neill, Irish Republican Publicity Bureau, Dublin.

Later, on the same day as Mr McQuaid's demise, the IRA set up a hoax bomb call knowing that both the RUC and the Army would attend; it was a clear IRA 'come on' designed to lure the security forces into a vulnerable position where a well concealed gunman could open fire. They had called in the warning on the Shantallow Estate, Londonderry and they took aim at a policewoman who was shepherding motorists away from the 'bomb.' As they fired, the officer was hit in her upper arm, but the high velocity round continued and struck a pregnant woman, Asha Chopra (25) and a mother of two very young children. Her car crashed and she died seconds afterwards, as her killer slunk back to his hovel on the Creggan or in the Bogside. Her unborn child died and her young children were left motherless, as the Provisionals showed not a jot of compassion or regret about turning the Shantallow into a battlefield. The author will be anxiously scouring the press for an apology from the IRA, for the death of Mrs Chopra around about 2020.

Guildford in Surrey is a typical English county town; long used by the British Army in order to garrison its troops. In the last 40 years, it has been a main administrative centre for the Royal Military Police and the now defunct, Women's Royal Army Corps (WRAC). In early October, 1974, part of the Provisional IRA's England Team, later to become infamous as the 'Balcombe Street gang' attacked several pubs in the Guildford area. They chose two in particular, which were popular with off-duty military personnel. Their bombing team manufactured two 6 lb gelignite bombs in London, one of which was placed in the Horse and Groom in North Street. A second device was planted in the Seven Stars.

IRA members, including at least two girls had walked into the pub, buying drinks in order to blend in. They had observed the drinkers, mostly young men and women, some soldiers, some civilians, with an average age of around 19; knowing of the carnage that they would be about to cause. Acutely aware of what was to unfold, they left their 'packages' or bags, placing them surreptitiously underneath tables, chairs or, in the case of the Horse and Groom, underneath a bench. After that, they would have walked calmly out of the pub, possibly without a backwards glance and left the drinkers to their fate.

A device, containing 6 lbs of nitro-glycerine and manufactured, according to the later trial of the bombers, at a bomb-making factory in Fulham, London, was left under a bench. Moments after the bomb was placed, an off-duty female soldier sat down there. Her name was Caroline Slater, there for an evening's drinking with her friend Ann Hamilton. At 10:30pm on Saturday 5 October 1974, without warning, the device exploded.

A bomb blast in a confined space is devastating. First the shock wave spreads out, faster than the speed of sound. Some heavy objects deflect the waves, but other solid material is changed instantly into gas, creating an enormous increase in volume and pressure. People in the way can have their limbs torn off, and in the millisecond which follows, the energy waves go into their mouths and upwards, taking off the tops of their skulls and other parts of the body so that sometimes all is left is the spine, held together by the vertebrae. The shock wave, travelling at 13,000 miles per hour pulverises the floor immediately below the explosion. It slows down quickly, but more damage is done by the blast wave which follows at half the speed. This has the pressure of pent-up gas behind it and it can also tear off limbs, perforate eardrums and smash up furniture, the pieces of which in turn become deadly weapons. For a few seconds a fireball goes with it, singeing hair and removing eyebrows and eyelashes.[1]

Five people – four soldiers and a civilian – were killed instantly and a further 65 were wounded; some dreadfully. Those killed were WRAC Private Jean Slater (18), from Staffordshire, who was still in Basic Training; WRAC Private Ann Hamilton (19) from Crewe, who had only been in the Army for four weeks; Guardsman William Forsyth (18), Scots Guards, from Renfrewshire, and still in basic training; Guardsman John Hunter (17), also in the Scots Guards, and also from Renfrewshire, and Paul Craig (22), a Plasterer from Borehamwood, Herts. Mr Craig would have celebrated his 23rd birthday the following day and was in the pub to celebrate a friend's birthday.

Eyewitness survivors told afterwards that one of the dead soldiers had just returned to his seat after selecting 'Long Tall Glasses' by Leo Sayer on the pub's jukebox when there was: "a flash and a bang". A soldier from the Scots Guards, Jimmy Cooper, told newspaper reporters from the *Guildford Times* and the *Daily Express*:

I had just leaned forward to get up and buy my round when there was a bang. I must have gone straight through the window because I was lying outside with my hair and clothes on fire. Some people tore off my jacket and shirt to save me from serious burns. My two mates were killed outright and another was critically injured.'
The blast caused the entire floor to disintegrate, forcing people downwards, thus saving lives; a photograph taken at the time shows the entire front wall collapsed. The journalist from the *Guildford Times* further reported: 'People were running, shouting and screaming. Many of them were young girls and they were clutching bleeding heads. There was blood everywhere....there was rubble everywhere, glass, bricks, timber. People were scrabbling among the debris, trying to pull people out of the mess. It was panic and chaos.

There was another pub in Guildford which was also popular with soldiers, the nearby Seven Stars and, alerted by the blast at the Horse and Groom just a few hundred yards away, the landlord, Mr O'Brien cleared his pub of drinkers. Together with his staff, he began searching for suspicious looking packages. One was found and as they left the pub, it exploded, injuring the pub landlord, five members of his staff and a teenage customer

1   Hamill, Desmond, *Pig In The Middle: the army in Northern Ireland, 1969-1984*, (London: Methuen Books, 1985) pp. 100-101.

who had strayed back into the pub. However, the landlord's prompt and brave action prevented further carnage; the death toll could have been horrendous.

The Monday morning (7 October) edition of the *Daily Express* printed photographs of the four dead soldiers but not of the civilian Paul Craig, under the sub-headline: "Dead: Four young victims of IRA terror" and showed grainy black and white images of the two girls and less than recent ones of the two boys, both resplendent with rock-star long haircuts. Under another headline: "Girl Bombers on the Run" it read:

> Two girl terrorists were being hunted last night as police swooped on homes in the wake of Saturday's horrific pub-bomb blast which claimed the lives of five people. Sixty-eight people were hurt in the bloody Guildford explosion – last night, 30 of them, including ten girls from the Women's Royal Army Corps were still in hospital, some of them critically ill. The girls, believed to be members of an IRA revenge squad, were seen scuttling down an alley leading away from the two pubs, the Horse and Groom and the Seven Stars after the second bomb blast. Seven teenage Scots who only joined the Army three weeks ago, and a group of young WRAC girls they were chatting up…caught the full horror of the explosion.

The Express also went on to report the words of an Irish barmaid, Maureen Sullivan who was from Co Kerry in the Irish Republic. She had been in England only four months and was pulling pints in the Horse and Groom when the bomb exploded: "I feel ashamed to call myself Irish after what I saw last night." Other newspapers wrote of dazed and bloodied survivors, walking around in the ruins, screaming: "Bastards! Bastards!" as they searched desperately for friends in the smoking rubble of what had been the most popular soldiers' pub in Guildford.

The 'Balcombe Street gang' were not finished however, and the IRA's England Team would strike a month later at another pub, this time in Woolwich in South London; again with devastating results.

The RUC, surely the most beleaguered police force in the western world, lost two more officers in the space of three days; one to terrorist activity and the other to a dreadful RTA whilst going about his lawful duty. On the 8th, two RUCR officers were alerted to a suspicious looking vehicle which had been abandoned in the town centre. Instead of waiting for EOD team from the Army, Reserve Constable Arthur Henderson (31) tried the door of the car; it exploded, killing him instantly, injuring a comrade and dreadfully injuring a passing civilian.

On 8 October, a UFF gang had lain in wait outside Belfast's City Hospital, in the south of the city. They were expecting a group of five Catholic workmates to arrive for their shift at the busy hospital. As the five men arrived, they opened fire on the men with at least one sub machine gun, hitting two of them. One of the men fell, mortally wounded, and the gang escaped in a stolen vehicle. Anthony Morgan was rushed into hospital for emergency treatment, but he was to die of those wounds on Christmas Eve.

The Provisional IRA, despite its 'holier than thou' attitude to random and senseless sectarian killings, was not averse to shooting Protestants from time to time, in order to keep up the 'sectarian scores.' On October 9, they attacked a workman's' hut on a building site in the Loyalist Woodvale, badly wounding two Protestant workmen; fortunately neither died. The day after, RUC officer Constable John Campbell Harris

(42) was involved in a terrible RTA, just as his shift was about to finish, and fatally injured. Hours later, REME soldier, Lance Corporal Alister David McCallum Stewart (21) from North Berwick in Scotland, was also killed in an RTA.

On that same day, Loyalists launched a sectarian murder blitz, killing four innocent Catholics in the space of just 72 hours. Albert Greer (30), living on the Ardoyne in Belfast, was visiting friends in the Ballyduff Estate, in Newtownabbey, north of Belfast for the day. The Ballyduff is a Loyalist heartland and it came to the attention of the media in 2009 when Democratic Unionist politician Alderman Nigel Hamilton spoke to the *Newtownabbey Today* newspaper in vivid language. The newspaper reported how the Loyalists:

> ... launched a stinging attack on the untidiness of Ballyduff, calling the area a 'pigsty'. Alderman Nigel Hamilton, who does not represent the area, made his claims after a recent walkabout in the estate. He claimed he has since registered a full complaint to the Housing Executive and the council. 'The upper parts of Ballyduff are like a forgotten wilderness of laneways which are strewn with debris, cans, papers, condoms and broken bottles,' he claimed. 'I do not think I have seen such a dilapidated mess and regard this as total neglect. It is unacceptable that people are not being listened to. I spoke to one man who complained that his son, an occupant of a property close to the quarry side of the estate, had complained that rats were frequently seen scuttling around bin bags dumped by opportunists.

By what means the UVF were alerted to the presence of a Catholic on the Ballyduff is unrecorded. However, they burst into the house where Mr Greer was visiting and shot him three times, killing him instantly. The men who covered their faces, made good their escape in a stolen car. The killing was claimed in the name of the Protestant Action Force, which was a red herring as it merely sought to disguise the involvement of the UVF.

The same organisation – irrespective of its *nom de plume*, it was the same UVF murderers – struck again on the 11th, this time in Cambridge Street, Belfast. James Hasty (40) lived in the Catholic New Lodge and was walking to work in the morning along Brougham Street, which is on the sectarian interface with the Loyalist Tiger Bay area. Masked gunmen from the UVF sprang out of a side street and shot dead Mr Hasty who had lost an arm as a result of an industrial accident some years earlier; he died at the scene.

Exactly two and a half hours later, on the British mainland in London, the IRA's England Team struck again. They carried out two bomb attacks on clubs in the centre of London, when a hand-thrown bomb with a short fuse was thrown through a basement window of the 'Victory', an ex-servicemen's club in Seymour Street near Marble Arch. A short time later an identical bomb was thrown into the ground floor bar at the Army and Navy Club in St. James's Square; thankfully, only one person was injured in these two attacks.

The day after the murder of Mr Hasty, and whilst their Republican counterparts were causing mayhem in London, the UVF, in their terrorist coat-of-many-colours (and many names) ambushed two workmen in Carrickfergus, Co Antrim. Carrickfergus is a small seaside town which sits on the shores of Belfast Lough. Michael McKenzie (21)

Sergeant Graham Lightfoot, ATO, defuses an IRA bomb at the
Royal Hotel, Kilkeel. Brave man (Brian Sheridan)

was a Catholic who had friends on both sides of the sectarian divide and refused to discriminate on the basis of which temple a man worshipped at. On the morning of his death, he was walking home with a Protestant workmate, at the end of a night out. UVF gunmen lay in wait at Hawthorne Avenue in the town, and opened fire from very close range. Both young men were hit in the head, with the Protestant boy being badly wounded, but young Michael died at the scene. This author and other like-minded historians may rail and rage at the sectarian murderers and their illogical, counterproductive violence, but in this instance, one defers to the words of the Judge at the killer's later trial.

The Judge spoke to the convicted man in his summing up:

> You have pleaded guilty to the cold-blooded murder of a young man whom you knew and with whom you were reasonably friendly. But his religion happened to be different to yours and the sole motive for this murder was a sectarian one. You then turned around and attempted to murder his friend who was also your friend, because he had seen too much.[2]

The fourth Sectarian killing in 72 hours took place on the 13th, when Kieran Murphy (17) and a relative of the IRA's Belfast Brigade Commander at the time, according to Brendan Hughes, Gerry Adams. Adams was interned at the time in the Long Kesh prison when his nephew was abducted in the Antrim Road, Belfast by the

---

2   McKitterick, David et al, *op cit.* pp. 483-484.

UVF. He was beaten and then eventually murdered and his body was dumped close to Hightown Road on the northern outskirts of the city. The young man was walking back from a Chinese restaurant when he was abducted by his eventual killers. Four innocent Catholics now lay dead and the day of the Shankill Butchers still lay ahead.

On the 15th, mass disturbances broke out at HM Prison the Maze, and a number of huts were destroyed by fires which had been started by Republican prisoners. British troops were called into the prison to re-establish control.

Merlyn Rees, then Secretary of State for Northern Ireland, announced that nine Republican prisoners from the Maze Prison had been hospitalised following disturbances the previous day. Fifteen prison officers and 16 soldiers were also hurt during the disturbances. The unrest spread to Magilligan Prison where a number of huts were destroyed. In Armagh Women's Prison the governor and three women prison officers were held captive before being released following mediation by clergymen.

Following a spate of hijackings on the Derrybeg Estate in Newry, the Army had set up a covert OP in one of the estate's derelict houses. This was extremely dangerous, and though the soldiers were well-armed, a life-or-death situation would arise if they were discovered. What was considered unique about the Derrybeg estate was that, for the first time in Northern Irish history, young families were up-rooted from closely-knit communities, and transplanted to a green field site and housed among complete strangers. This move was seen as a bold and imaginative initiative by Newry Urban Council, to provide badly-needed homes for the growing population of newly-weds, forced to live with parents or in-laws. The new tenants found themselves crammed into 360 houses, devoid of social or recreational facilities, far from shops, pubs or cinemas. A bus service was non-existent, few owned cars, and there was a dearth of taxis. It was a symbol of the downtrodden Catholic in the South Down area, and as such, it was a rabid breeding ground for Irish Republicanism and for the Provisional IRA.

STA, STA, STAYING ALIVE
Erich Modrowics, Queen's Own Hussars

It was around internment anniversary time of year where you get the intense riots and shootings. I was driving the company's covert car; a Brown Hillman Hunter. When I look back, I realise that it was probably known to all the Fianna boys. I was wearing civilian clothes and had a 9mm Browning for 'protection.' It was madness to be on duty and unarmed, just as it was equally insane to be in unsafe areas whilst unarmed even when off duty.[3] I had been to Lisburn, in order to drop someone off and then return later to pick him up; very probably the Colonel. I was driving back along the Andersontown Road in West Belfast, in order to get back to Fort Monagh, and as we got near to the roundabout, I saw an odd sight! There was a Military Police (RMP) land rover driving quickly towards me. It was on its own which I thought was strange as we were instructed to always drive in pairs.

Suddenly, I could see bricks and other debris in the road between our two vehicles, and as they neared me, a load of youths appeared from nowhere and began picking up the bricks in the road to throw at the RMP land rover. The guys saw this and proceeded to do an immediate 'U' turn which wasn't particularly

---

3   The author has, *passim*, identified at least a dozen regular soldiers who were killed whilst off-duty over the course of the Troubles.

good for me as I was coming towards the brick-carrying youths from the rear and I thought if they see the car they will know it's an Army vehicle. I had my 9mm cocked with one up the spout and ready to use, and I would have used it, mark my words. I wanted to keep Mrs Modrowics' little boy to stay alive and I also wished my mates to stay in one piece. I dropped the car into third and gunned it, and I actually closed my eyes as I came upon the youths as I thought I was bound to hit one or more. To this day I don't know if I did or not but I made it through and got back to the camp safely. I was scared shitless by the whole incident!

On the evening of 17 October, a young Yorkshire soldier was fatally injured in a dreadful RTA in the centre of Belfast. The soldiers involved, from the Royal Artillery have often spoken about their disquiet over the accident, which they felt was not only never apportioned to the right quarters, but was also 'swept under the carpet' at HQNI. Gunner Keith Bates was only 20 when he was killed in Belfast's Market's area. He was from Shipley, in West Yorkshire and, although his name appears on the Wall at the AFM in Staffordshire, he does not appear in the 'official' roll of honour, a fact rectified in this author's detailed ROH. Young Bates lingered for 18 days, before, on the evening of 4 November, he succumbed to his injuries in the RVH.

'BASHER' BATES
Ian 'Scouse' Mitchell, Royal Artillery

My main story begins towards the back end of our first tour of 1974, when, in the early hours of the 17th October, we were on a mobile patrol in the city centre in the pursuit of a suspected terrorist vehicle. As we approached a main set of lights which were on 'green', an RMP Makralon Police vehicle jumped a set of red lights. In doing so it caught the back end of our land rover, and, in the process, catapulted all of us out of the vehicle. As the four of us were thrown out, Keith 'Basher' Bates was impaled onto nearby wrought iron railings. As the Land rover spun around and crushed him against them, I hit a metal traffic sign. The other two occupants shot along the road and pavement, sustaining minor injuries. Basher had fatal wounds, and died a number of weeks later; I had serious injuries, broken back in five places, closed head injury, multiply fractures to my pelvis and was casevaced to England.

I have to say that I received first class medical treatment for the length of time I convalesced, but it took a very long time, and I now suffer with a compressed fracture of my D6 vertebra. The RMPs were investigated over the incident but were acquitted and there were no charges. The incident resulted in one dead Gunner and another one was given the last rites by a Catholic priest, at the request of his Mother. Funny, I don't remember this incident making the national news.

On 18 October, as a bus driver drove onto the Derrybeg, he was immediately surrounded by youths with blunt instruments and bricks and forced out of his cab. Undercover soldiers then broke cover and charged towards the mob, one of whom, according to a soldier, was armed. Ignoring the challenge, the young man Michael Hughes, who was also a member of the Provisional IRA, pointed a pistol at the troops who shot him dead. In the confusion, the pistol went missing and it is not beyond the realms of probability that it was snatched and spirited away by the IRA man's comrades. In instances such as those, the Army then have not the evidence to defend themselves of shooting an unarmed man. The IRA were well practiced when it came to propaganda, and seized with alacrity an obvious opportunity to coin in more dollars from the gullible and naïve Irish-Americans; the Provisionals definitely had no peers.

The blood-letting sparked a frenzy of deaths, and over the next four days, a total of ten people throughout the province would lose their lives. It would affect civilian and military and the deaths were as a result of several different causes. First to die, and one of four to die that day, October 21, was UDR Private, William James Bell (41) whose death was recorded as 'unknown circumstances' by the MoD, but his former comrades and commanders must know the true facts behind the passing of this, still young soldier.

Minutes afterwards, two young Catholic brothers were on their way to work when a car containing Loyalist gunmen pulled up alongside them, and opened fire. Edward Morgan (27) and his half-brother Michael Loughran (18) were walking down the Falls Road/Divis Street to commence work for the day, instead of catching a bus due to the public transport strike. As they passed the turn off for Northumberland Street, which leads north to the Shankill, the car which had been stolen earlier, paused for a second or two and shots rang out. As it sped off, both brothers slumped to the ground dead. The UVF had sent out a further message of hatred to the Catholics and it would bring swift retribution from their sectarian counterparts. The Loyalist murder gangs were cold-blooded men who simply toured Belfast, looking for victims, purely at random.

The day was not over and, before it ended, the Provisionals would have continued the tit-for-tat murders. Samuel Gibson (28) was a Protestant van driver who did laundry delivery and collection in Belfast. He was also a Ranger in the Territorial Army. On the same day on which three people had already been killed, he was abducted by an armed gang of Republicans – in all probability the Provisional IRA – in the Ardoyne as he did his final deliveries. He was taken to a derelict house at Velsheda Park, where he was beaten, before being shot eight times. It was a purely sectarian murder, designed to extract some sort of retribution for the activities of the UVF and lost the Republicans what they laughingly claimed as the 'moral high ground'. What was unknown was if the IRA were aware that they were also killing a British soldier.

On the following day, the UFF got in on the act, when one of their men walked into a betting shop in Marquis Street in Belfast's city centre. On the pretext of studying the odds and runners for the day, he left a transistor radio, packed with as much explosive as could be fitted in, and walked out. Later in the day, Dominic Donnelly (48) found the apparently lost radio and decided that he would sell it. As he walked out of the shop with his 'find,' he spoke to a young boy in a van parked outside the betting shop. As the two spoke, the booby-trapped radio exploded, killing Donnelly instantly and badly wounding the younger man at the same time. The younger man was blinded and lost an arm by the blast, thought to contain 5lbs of explosives. The intention of the UFF was that a punter might turn on the radio inside the shop in order to listen to a race, thus killing many in the building.

On that same day – the 22nd – the IRA's England Team carried out a bomb attack on the Brooks club, in St James's Square in London. Although the bomb was thrown into an empty dining room, two members of the kitchen staff were severely injured in the blast. One of the first on the scene was Conservative Party leader, and recently deposed Prime Minister, Edward Heath who was dining nearby. "I don't think it was meant for me. I didn't decide to have dinner out until a quarter of an hour before," he said when being interviewed. He continued: "There is a lot of damage, the ceiling is down in one room and it is a shambles." The two injured waiters had been relaxing in the restaurant area after all the diners had left when the bomb went off. One of them said later that they had heard a noise and as they went to investigate the bomb exploded.

Commander Robert Hardy of Scotland Yard stated afterwards that there was a possibility that the device could have been thrown. The bombing was the latest in a series of attacks on clubs with military connections, and although Brooks Club had no serving officers as members it did attract retired officers.

On 23 October, Lieutenant Michael Simpson from the Staffordshires who had been wounded in Londonderry, earlier in the month died of his injuries. The man convicted of killing the young officer, was also found guilty of the murder of Asha Chopra, the pregnant woman shot dead in an IRA 'come on' on 5 October.

The day after, the IRA's England Team continued their bombing campaign, and, fresh from Guildford and the Brooks club incidents, carried out a bomb attack on a cottage in the grounds of Harrow School in north-west London. No one was injured in the explosion. The time bomb, estimated to have contained 5lbs of explosives, exploded shortly before midnight just outside the cottage which had, until just before this date, been occupied by the head of the school's Combined Cadet Force. At 11.30pm a telephone warning about the bomb had been given to the Press Association.

On 25 October the UDR lost another soldier, again under that ubiquitous catch-all banner: 'unknown circumstances'. Private Robert George Allen (39) died, in Ulster; that is all that is known, publically about this soldier.

Two days after the death of Private Allen, two young Catholic men were hitchhiking on the Sunday afternoon to Portadown from Loughall, when they unknowingly accepted a lift from men from the UVF. At some stage on the journey, the driver stopped at a remote farmhouse and attacked the two Catholics. One of the pair managed to break free and ran off into the rural area and managed to hide. His friend, however, was not so lucky and was severely beaten before being bundled back into the car and driven to a house in Portadown. He was further tortured, before being shot dead and his body dumped. There was evidence which showed that Anthony Duffy (18) had also been strangled before being shot.

The sand-dunes and beaches to the east of the inner bay at Dundrum, Co Down, had seen occasional use as a military training area since the mid-1700s, but its formal existence as an army barracks began during the Boer War with c.1600 men 'housed' in bell tents adjacent to the hamlet of Ballykinler. The first permanent accommodation, a 'Tin Camp' of corrugated iron-faced huts with their coal-burning stoves, was erected in late 1914 for the newly-formed 36th 'Ulster' Division. However, in 1902 a Sandes Soldiers' Home, one of the series founded in 1877 by a Tralee lady, Miss Elisabeth Anne Sandes, had been built at what became Ballykinler's entrance gates and it was a familiar off-duty refuge for generations of soldiers through both World Wars and into the Op Banner troubles era; (Alex B fondly remembers the superb bacon butties from his UDR annual camp and range-day visits).

Its weakness was its location, just beyond the camp perimeter; a fatal flaw noted and exploited by the Provos on Monday 28th October when, in a typically cowardly, but cunning, attack, they parked a 300 lbs van bomb on the road outside the barracks, opposite the timber-framed, corrugated-iron clad building. At 10:30am, the explosives detonated.

A huge explosion rocked the camp; in the main barracks, windows blew out, and the walls shuddered with the shock wave. Outside the main gates a thick greasy cloud of grey and black smoke pillared skywards from what had been the Sandes Home building. The leisure area became a shell of torn corrugated iron and burning timber; rapidly reducing to a pile of ashes as an inferno of flame raged at its centre. In the explosion, 1st Battalion Duke of Edinburgh's Royal Regiment soldiers, Lance Corporal Alan 'Taffy' Coughlan (22) from Newport in South Wales and Private Michael Swanick (20) from Merseyside, were killed instantly in the blast. Thirty-one soldiers and two civilians were injured in the attack. In the circumstances, it was a miracle that 'only' those two 'Farmersboys' soldiers died – though that's of no comfort to their families and friends. However, the extent of the Provos callous disregard for even children's lives was amply demonstrated by the fact that they'd abandoned their bomb close to a school. The *Belfast Telegraph* report noted that, "Windows in Ballykinler Primary School, about a hundred yards away, were shattered and glass showered into the classrooms. A number of people were treated for shock, but none of them were injured." It was a miraculous escape there too. Do PIRA's 'veterans' really consider it another courageous blow struck for 'Irish Freedom?'

The Sandes Home was rebuilt on the original site and during a subsequent 1 Battalion tour in 1986 the DERR's CO, RSM and a party of soldiers from the battalion unveiled

An injured fireman is taken away to hospital for emergency
treatment, Newtownhamilton (Brian Sheridan)

Job done! Graham Lightfoot walks away from Royal Hotel, Kilkeel (Brian Sheridan)

a memorial stone dedicated to the memory of Lance Corporal Coughlan and Private Swanick. The plinth stands just outside the new home. As for Ballykinler's Abercorn Barracks, one of the most modern facilities in the UK, rumours persist that, as part of the 'demilitarisation' process, it will close when the present resident battalion, 2nd Rifles, leaves the Province in 2016.

On the same day as the Ballykinler blast, the wife and young son of Sports Minister Denis Howell survived a bomb attack on their car. The attack was known to be the work of the Provisional IRA's England Team and was the first on a serving minister during their 1970s campaign. The car, a white Ford Cortina, exploded as Mrs Howell reversed out of the driveway of their house in Birmingham. Experts believe they survived as a result of the device falling from the exhaust onto the road. Mrs Howell and her son, both of whom were in the car at the time, escaped unhurt. Her older sons also escaped unhurt despite the windows of the house being blown in by the force of the explosion. Mr Howell, a Labour MP in Birmingham, was in London at the time of the attack and heard about it in a newsflash. "I have no idea how the bomb could have been planted or how bad the damage is, but I gather from my wife on the phone that all the windows and neighbours' windows were smashed. I haven't the faintest idea why I was picked on. One just uses one's imagination. I'm like a lot of other victims in all of this nonsense."

There was worse to come for the MP's hometown of Birmingham and that day was coming increasingly closer. It would be the worst terrorist outrage in mainland Britain of the Troubles and the IRA's England Team was already drawing up plans for the forthcoming carnage.

As the month of October drew to a close, the IRA targeted a UDR family living on the outskirts of Belfast. The Catherwood family lived at Upper Hightown Road, just

north of the main A52 Ballyuroag Road, shortly before it takes the more famous title, the Crumlin Road. Two of the family, the wife and her son were part-time soldiers in the UDR, but Gordon Catherwood (44) had not joined. At around teatime on the 30th, an IRA sniper, firing from the cover of bushes, shot Mr Catherwood, in the head, killing him instantly. Although another UDR friend in the house returned fire, the gunman escaped.

The ranks of the Provisional IRA were thinned by the death of Michael Meehan (16) who was killed in a classic 'own goal' explosion outside a petrol station in Londonderry on the same day as the Catherwood murder. The Provisionals were clearly entrusting their dirty work to babies, and the young boy was sitting in a car, at Strand Road when it exploded, killing him instantly. A petrol pump attendant, standing next to the car, was blown off his feet and the driver of the car also had a miraculous escape. The dazed driver ran off, leaving behind a loaded revolver, but was later caught and received a long jail sentence.

October 1974 had ended and the death tally for the month was 28; twice the previous month. Of these there were ten soldiers; two were Policemen and 14 civilians. The IRA lost two members. Of the civilians, the Loyalists killed nine and the IRA also killed six; of the 15 civilians killed, at least ten were purely sectarian. In total, the Provisional IRA was responsible for the loss of 15 lives and the Loyalists for nine during the course of the month.

Chapter 23

November

N ovember was a month to remember in many ways. The IRA's England Team bombed with an ease which contradicted how difficult the British security services were making it for them. In many instances they were thwarted, but they only had to get lucky every once or twice. One of those instances occurred in Birmingham towards the end of the month. It produced the largest terrorist outrage of the Troubles on the mainland, the third worst of the entire period. Both sets of paramilitaries indulged in the blood lust of sectarian killings, with 22 civilians shot dead purely on the basis of their religion. The IRA actually killed a young Protestant teenager, just to provide a 'come on' to lure the Army into an ambush. This sickening depravity did not slow for an instant, the financial contributions of the unbelievably naive Irish-Americans. The 'come on' was also used in England for the first time and the target was the police and ambulance services.

Lorenzo Sinclair (44) had, unfortunately for him, made his contempt for the Republican bombers very public. He had approached the manager of the Park Bar in Lawther Street, in North Belfast, to offer his services as a security manager with a 'guarantee' that he could protect its patrons from the IRA. The bar, which was close to the Limestone Road, and not far from the Republican Oldpark, was within a few minutes journey of the sectarian divide. A car, later abandoned, drove past the bar and gunmen shot Mr Sinclair as he stood on guard; he died within the hour.

As sure as day follows night, there was a retaliatory strike from the UFF on 4 November, and two armed men walked calmly up to the entrance of the Club Bar on University Road, Belfast where doorman Ivan Clayton (48) was on duty. The father of four had no time at all to react, and the gunmen shot him dead, before running off in the direction of the Loyalist Sandy Row. The club was located to the south of the city centre and close to Queen's University.

On the same evening Gunner Keith Bates (20) who was fatally injured in a contentious RTA the previous month, died of those injuries in Belfast's RVH. There are many within the solid ranks of former Royal Artillerymen who feel that both the Royal Military Police and the RUC knew more than was admitted; it is a source of bitter contention to the Gunners who felt much was not revealed about the circumstances of the accident.

On Wednesday 6 November 1974, 33 Republican Prisoners escaped from the Maze Prison (Long Kesh) through an elaborately constructed tunnel. The break-out assumed all the trappings of the Steve McQueen film *The Great Escape* and was a tribute to the IRA's own 'tunnel rats.' IRA member Hugh Coney (24) from Coalisland was shot dead by a soldier during the escape. The IRA had armed men outside the wire and the soldier concerned stated that he saw what he thought was the glint of a weapon, and opened fire; Coney died at the scene. Thirty-two of the prisoners were captured by the end of the day, and the remaining three were back in custody within 24 hours.

The escape was the prelude to two days of violence, in which four soldiers were killed. In the early afternoon of that same day, an armed IRA gang held a Crossmaglen family hostage – one wonders just how much coercion was actually needed – and set up a firing point in an upstairs window. Whilst the family was held 'captive,' an IRA gunman opened fire with a Second World War Bren gun, no doubt stolen from a raid on the UDR or the Cadet Force, some years previously.

As a six-man foot patrol from the Duke of Edinburgh's Royal Regiment (DERR) walked through the town square, the gunman opened fire and hit three of the soldiers in a series of short bursts, firing 20 rounds in all. Private Brian Allen (20) was hit and fatally wounded and died in the casevac helicopter; he was from Ilkeston in Derbyshire. Corporal Steven Windsor (26) from Devon was also fatally wounded, and he died a few hours after the same helicopter reached hospital. Corporal Windsor was from the Devon & Dorsets Regiment and was on attachment to the DERR. Private Allen was the third member of the Regiment to die in less than two weeks, following the bomb blast at the Sandes Home in Ballykinler.

Stewartstown, Co Tyrone is set in sweeping, rural countryside a few miles west of Lough Neagh. The electricity generating company thought it an ideal place to site a substation; it was remote and a tempting target for the IRA. Sometime before the morning of the 7 November, they planted and detonated a device, fully cognisant that the Army would be called out to investigate. They knew that amongst the soldiers sent, there would be specialists from EOD and a secondary device was planted, specifically aimed at them. After an initial inspection, no further devices were found and several workmen were allowed onto the site to begin clearing up.

Staff Sergeant Vernon Rose (30), from Hampshire, of the Royal Army Ordnance Corps and Staff Sergeant Charles Simpson (35), of the Royal Hussars were at the forefront of the search party. Aided by an RUC constable, they were carrying out a final search, when they accidentally disturbed some plastic bags. The bags exploded, killing both soldiers instantly, maiming another and blinding the policeman. A further six soldiers and three of the workmen were also injured in the blast, which left a 10' wide crater. Staff Sergeant Simpson was on attachment to EOD, and came from Aberdeenshire; he left four young children.

That Thursday, 7 November 1974, was still not over, and events were taking place south of the Thames in London, as the IRA continued their mainland blitz. But before the bloody events of that Thursday evening unfolded there, it was 'business as usual' in the Province. There was an on-going internal feud in North Belfast and Billy Hull, a former leader of the Loyalist Association of Workers (LAW), and Jim Anderson, a former Ulster Defence Association (UDA) leader, were shot and wounded in attacks by fellow Loyalist paramilitaries.

Woolwich is described thus by the fascinating, but unreliable, Wikipedia:

> ... a district in south London, England, located in the London Borough of Greenwich. The area is identified in the London Plan as one of 35 major centres in Greater London. Woolwich formed part of Kent until 1889 when the County of London was created. It is notable as a river crossing point, having the Woolwich Ferry (and the lesser-known Woolwich foot tunnel) to North Woolwich, and as the

one-time home of the Woolwich Building Society (now relocated in Bexleyheath and owned by Barclays.

Even as CVOs (Casualty Visiting Officers) were imparting news of the tragedy in Stewartstown to the Rose and Simpson families, the IRA's England Team were in the process of executing yet another mainland pub blast. 'The King's Arms' which still stands today, in Frances Street, Woolwich was a pub, popular with not only civilians, but also with soldiers from nearby barracks. There was also a military hospital nearby, and many of the 'walking wounded' would often arrange 'escape parties' to have a pint or two. The Provisional IRA knew this and would have carried out reconnaissance trips in order to plan routes of attack and more importantly, escape routes. They would have been well aware of the military clientele and would have considered the death of an 'English' civilian nothing more than collateral damage.

Just after 10:15pm on that Thursday evening, an IRA gang walked up to the window of the pub, ignited a 6 lb blast bomb and hurled it with force, into the pub; they quickly ran off. As it landed, with its fuse burning down to detonation, a very brave and quick-thinking member of the bar staff, Alan Horsley (20) dived on top of the bomb. It detonated, dreadfully and fatally injuring him and killing off-duty soldier, Gunner Richard Dunne (42); dozens were injured and several lost limbs. The device was packed with nuts and bolts, a nasty IRA invention, designed to cause maximum shrapnel wounds.

The *Daily Express'* headlines on the morning after, raged:

Bombers Blast London Pub.
It happened at 10:17am as business in the King's Arms in Frances Street, Woolwich – just 50 yards from Woolwich Barracks – mounted to its evening peak. Some of the injured were WRACs. No warning was given. Casualties were rushed to the Brook Hospital at Shooters Hill and one man [sic] – thought to be a soldier – died from his injuries there. Two soldiers arrived early today to identify the body. All four operating theatres at the hospital were in use, and eight off-duty surgeons living nearby were called in.

The *Express* continued:

The injuries they were treating including damage to the chest and stomach as well as broken bodies. At first the police said a package containing the bomb had been left in the bar. But a soldier who was inside the pub said a car drove past and the bomb was lobbed through the window in a satchel. Still dazed and deafened from the blast, he said: 'I was sitting inside when the window smashed and the bag exploded almost immediately. A pal of mine was thrown off his feet. At that point everything went black and I came round as I was being helped out of the pub by friends …

… Inside the pub the purple and pink wallpaper hung over twisted and broken chairs and tables. Drinks and glasses were smashed over the floor. A man's torn jacket hung out of one of the gaping holes where the pub's front windows used to be. And pools of blood were evident as police and forensic experts sifted through the debris. Ironically, the only thing which remained intact was a dartboard which laughing Army girls had been using only minutes before the blast.

A cordon of uniformed soldiers in battle dress [sic] threw a ring round Army personnel flats in Artillery Place which runs into Frances Street. People were stopped and asked for identification as they approached the area, and at least two of the soldiers patrolling the flats across the main road from the barracks, carried heavy wooden staves. Meanwhile hundreds of relatives and friends crowded outside the King's Arms in a desperate search to see if any of their families were involved. At the barrack gates, a captain stood checking names of soldiers returning from a night out. A soldier who was inside the pub at the time of the blast, escaped uninjured. He wandered the nearby streets in total shock before returning to the scene. There he refused offers of medical aid but just stood sipping a cup of tea, and smoking a cigarette with shaking hand. He could not say anything – but gazed at the shattered bar.

Underneath a grainy black and white photograph of the shattered pub, the reporters quoted a neighbour of the pub, Mr Bill Edwards, as saying: "The whole area was strewn with debris," He said. "I saw about a dozen people lying on stretchers on the pavement outside. There were still some injured people inside the pub. Soldiers, policemen, firemen were tearing the rubble with their fingers to try and reach them." At the very bottom of the report, separated by a small black dot, were five short lines about the earlier tragedy at Stewartstown; they read: "An Army bomb expert and another soldier were killed yesterday when a booby-trap landmine exploded near Stewartstown, Co Tyrone."

The death toll of the Woolwich blast stood at two; but for the incredible bravery of Alan Horsley, a 20-year-old sales clerk, it would have stood much higher. After Guildford and now Woolwich, one wondered what else the IRA's England Team could throw at us. The answer was 100 miles further north and just 14 days away.

Over the course of the last 70-odd years, the magnificent city of London has withstood the evil might of Adolf Hitler's Luftwaffe, the bombs of the psychopathic IRA and the Moslem terrorist bombs of July 7 2005. The greatest city in the World has withstood all that could be thrown at it. The IRA tried to destroy the heart of London; it failed!

Somewhat ironically, and unknowingly insensitive, the Ministry of Defence in London had chosen that very day to state that the names of British soldiers killed during the conflict in Northern Ireland, would not be added to war memorials. The reason given was that the conflict in Northern Ireland was not classified as a war. Tell that now, to the families of the 1,300 killed and the 7,000 injured during the bloody course of the Troubles!

On 8 November, an Army foot patrol on the Twinbrook Estate in South West Belfast, below Andersonstown chanced upon an attempted van hijacking. They spotted Gerard Fennell (28) a 'Lieutenant' in the IRA, armed with a pistol and they shot him, fatally wounding him; he died later in hospital. The death of this IRA man was the first of a staggering 18 deaths in just 13 days, leading up to the carnage of Birmingham.

On the very same day, Paul Armstrong (18) a merchant seaman home on leave in Belfast, was abducted by a UVF gang as he walked towards the family home in the

Corporal Brian Sheridan climbing aboard bomb-damaged
train at Meigh Crossing (Brian Sheridan)

Catholic New Lodge. He was severely beaten, before being shot four times and his body was dumped in a derelict house in the Oldpark area. Taking a leaf out of the same book of pathetic and convenient excuses, used by the Provisional IRA, the UVF claimed that the sectarian murder was revenge for the Stewartstown and Guildford bombings. One does rather form a mental image of the paramilitary murderers, sitting around in 'discussion groups' mentally grappling with the complexities of the English language, expatiating on which excuse to use for their latest sordid actions.

On the 9 November, a UVF gang burst into a Catholic-owned and run garage at Clady Corner, Muckamore close to what is now the site of George Best International Airport in Belfast. The masked gang screamed at Patrick Courtney (29) and his mechanic, William Tierney (31) to kneel on the ground as this was a robbery. The two did as ordered, and Mr Courtney, a haulage contractor threw some money to the men; as he did so, one of the UVF murder gang shot him in the head, killing him instantly. Mr Tierney tried to make a run, but he was hit almost a dozen times in a burst of automatic gunfire. Mr Courtney's young child was sitting in a car outside and, miraculously escaped unhurt despite the amount of lead which was flying around. Over the course of the next five years, two of the murder gang were tried and sentenced for the garage murders. One of the men was convicted of five other murders and another UVF member was convicted of a further two.

Private Dixon's Saracen moments after a landmine explosion at Crossmaglen.
His actions saved several lives that day (Brian Sheridan)

There was a third murder that day, again involving Loyalist paramilitaries, this time the UFF. In what would appear to have been a drunken act of bravado, John McQuitty (40) was singled out by a UDA/UFF member for no apparent reason. He was shot and fatally wounded, dying en-route to hospital by a UFF member who seems to have taken part in the murder for no reason other than he was led astray by another.

On Remembrance Day, 1988, the Provisional IRA showed their utter contempt for that most sacred of British traditions; the act of remembering the nation's fallen not only in both World Wars but in many other conflicts at home and abroad. The attack at Enniskillen which left 11 dead and will forever be known as the 'Poppy Day Massacre' was one of the most despicable and sordid atrocities carried out by the staggeringly evil Irish Republican Army. One is still waiting, 23 years on for an apology for this crime, for it was not a political act; it wasn't striking a blow against the 'occupation forces'; it was a cold-blooded and calculated act of evil.

On Remembrance Day in 1974, they killed two of the Army's civvie workers and then had the gall to accuse the two men of being in the pay of the UDR and also of working undercover for British Intelligence. Hugh Slater (29), a labourer, and Leonard Cross (18), a painter, were employed by the Army at Ebrington Barracks, Londonderry. The two men had crossed the nearby border with the Republic for a drink, and were probably abducted shortly after leaving the pub that evening. They were taken to a safe house on the Creggan Estate where they were interrogated – the Provisionals denied torture – before being taken to a remote country road near Sheriff's Mountain, and shot. The road chosen was close to Croarty Road and very close to the border. Their hands were tied and then both were shot at very close range, several times in the head. Leonard

Cross was not a member of British Intelligence, no more than his older friend was; young Cross was a member of the Army Cadet Force and had intended to join the Army.

It is worth quoting elements of the statement by Sinn Féin/IRA, as it aptly sums up their sublime ignorance and thoroughly destroys what little credibility this organisation ever possessed. The statement described how they had "interrogated" the men' and had discovered that one was working directly for British Intelligence' and had done undercover work in the Bogside. Further, it stated that the man had been "directly involved" in the arrest of IRA men and had divulged information on informants in the area. The statement continued: "The men were not abused in any way during the interrogation but received superficial cuts during the struggle to overcome them. Last night both men were executed." The words are chilling, and one can only speculate the terror which young Cross and his older friend felt, being questioned by these ruthless men; those last moments before death must have been absolutely indescribable. One does wonder, however, just who actually believed the insane rhetoric spouted by these people; that is, other than their sycophantic and obsessed supporters on the Republican estates and of course, their Brit-hating adoring audience in 'Irish-America.'

If one thought that the IRA had plumbed the depths of depravity, their next efforts 'to advance the cause of Irish freedom' proved all observers wrong. The Provisionals possessed an unerring ability to sordidly outdo each staggering outrage. This was illustrated by an attack on a petrol station on the West Circular Road in Belfast. The road takes traffic north-west from the city and begins as the Springfield Road sweeps towards the Whiterock Road and the Ballymurphy Estate. Joseph Taylor (17) started work at the petrol station on the morning of Tuesday, 12 November; almost exactly one hour later, he was dead. The young boy lived in the nearby Ballygomartin area and was a victim of the Provisional IRA's tactic of sickening the British and the Loyalists into contemplating vacating the North. Four gunmen pulled up in a stolen car and forced Taylor and a workmate into the cash office where they cold bloodedly shot him dead, before planting a bomb and rushing outside, ignoring the other employee. Just before the gang raced off, the 'heroes' of the IRA opened fire on a group of Boy Scouts outside a clubhouse; directly opposite the petrol station. The young boys dived for cover as the gang sprayed them with machine gun bullets; by a miracle, none of them were hit.

Within minutes, the RUC and Army had arrived, and were inspecting the premises when the device exploded. No-one was hurt, but it was clear that the death of this young man served merely as a 'come on' to the security forces. The senseless killing was simply an act of depravity, designed to lure soldiers and police into an ambush.

The day was not yet over when a car containing a UFF murder gang cruising through Londonderry's Waterside area spotted two Catholic men and fired at them. William Elliott (21) was hit in the chest and fell to the ground, mortally wounded; his friend was unhurt. A passing police patrol found the pair, but were sadly unable to save the young Catholic. The Bishop of Londonderry publically condemned the three murders, two by the IRA (of Slater and Cross) and this latest one, in retaliation for the first. He was quoted as saying: "Over the past three years almost 140 people have died in this area through violence. Surely it must be obvious now that the way of violence is the road to misery and suffering and grief."

Earlier, Michael Brennan (26) a teacher was helping out in a Youth Club at Carolan Road, near to the Ormeau Road, when a UVF gunman fired indiscriminately into the building. St Mary's Youth Club was attended by Catholic children from the Ormeau Road area, and it was full at the time of the shooting. Through sheer good fortune, none of the children were hit, but Mr Brennan was fatally wounded; he died the following day. On that day – the 13th – a soldier from the Royal Anglians collapsed and died whilst on duty. Private Parry Lloyd Hollis (20) from Southend-on-Sea was rushed to hospital, but he was dead on arrival; exhaustive enquiries from the author have failed to elicit any further details on the death of this young Essex boy.

A LOT OF WASTED BOTTLES.
Erich Modrowics, Queen's Own Hussars
The colonel decided that we would go out on a mobile patrol in the late evening around the time of the internment anniversary riots. I was his driver and was in the lead rover with the RSM behind; naturally we took helmets but wore berets. For some reason it seemed darker that usual that night as we left the relative safety of the camp at Fort Monagh. We drove down to the first roundabout and then turned onto the Andersontown Road. It was eerily quiet, the streets were deserted but there was the smell of burning in the air. We drove past a burning car – and the usual detritus of the urban battleground which was Belfast – and approached a pedestrian crossing which changed to Red as we neared it. There was no one there, so we drove through it and then a little further the Colonel told me to turn left. I did so and started to turn left down a side street, the name of which I don't know but as we turned there was a telegraph pole burning across the road.

We stopped and were getting out of the rover, and I recall I was one of the last to get out and as my foot touched the road a glass bottle landed a foot or two away and smashed. The calm had become the storm and more bottles started raining down around us; the Colonel told us to get back in and turn around which we did with haste! The journey back along the Andersontown Road was alive with bottles raining down from both sides of the street yet there was no one to be seen. I assume they were hiding behind the hedges of the houses but it was a surreal experience, and it seemed like everyone had donned their helmets by this time. However, as I couldn't get to mine as I was driving, I was forced to use my gloved hand to protect my head. We were almost back at the camp and about to turn up to the driveway to the back gate when a frantic voice sounded on the radio. We were urgently informed that there was an impending ambush close to the back gate! I did a quick turn over the grass and we went to the front gate where we were able to get in without incident; just another mobile patrol in West Belfast!

The contributor writes about a waste of bottles and whilst not strictly germane, this puts the author in mind of one of his boyhood heroes, one Freddie Trueman, the Yorkshire cricketer. Whilst this may be somewhat apocryphal the following took place on the cricket tour of the West Indies in 1953/4. At Georgetown, volatile sections of the crowd began hurling bottles on to the pitch, putting players and umpires at risk and quite naturally, the players left the pitch. All, that is, with the exception of one Freddie Trueman, who was seen collecting bottles with a nonchalant alacrity. When questioned as to his sanity by the riot police, Trueman is rumoured to have stated: "Eh, lad, where ah come from, there's three-pence each back on these bottles!"

On 14 November, a member of the IRA's England Team, James McDaid (26) from Belfast's Ardoyne, was engaged in planting a device at a GPO office in Coventry's Greyfriars district. This act had grim echoes of 35 years earlier when, some nine days before the declaration of War, an IRA team had packed a bicycle frame with explosives and left it outside Astley's shop in Coventry's Broadgate. On that morning of 25 August 1939, no warning was given and when the device exploded, five people were killed and 70 injured; some dreadfully. The dead were listed as Elsie Ansell, John Corbett Arnott, Rex Gentle, Gwilym Rowlands and James Clay; their number would be added to in the Luftwaffe raid on the city the following year.

In the 1974 re-enactment McDaid was killed instantly as his bomb exploded prematurely; his accomplices escaped unscathed. The Irish community announced plans to give the dead terrorist a Republican military funeral in Birmingham, but Roy Jenkins, the Labour Home Secretary, refused this and the IRA promised revenge. That revenge was not long in coming; in fact, it would take only a week.

On November 15, an IRA gun team secreted itself in a bombed out building in Strabane's Fountain Street, awaiting the approach of a patrol from the Royal Regiment of Fusiliers. As a four man brick approached, the men were suddenly lit up by the headlights of a passing car. This author believes that this was the deliberate act of an IRA 'dicker' in order to illuminate the soldiers and make them a better target. Fusilier Anthony Simmons (19) from North Manchester was hit and mortally wounded; he was rushed to hospital but died en-route.

On the same day that Fusilier Simmons was killed, a UVF gang attacked Maguire's Bar in Larne, Co Antrim. Larne itself is a sea and ferry port on the north-eastern coast of Northern Ireland. It is a mixed town, but there are some very obviously Catholic areas and Maguire's was situated in Lower Cross Street, in such an area. The bar was thankfully not busy and there was more luck in store for the drinkers when one of the gunmen had a stoppage. However, Kevin Regan (26) was hit and fatally wounded; he died a few days later, on 20 November.

On the 16th, an Army mobile patrol, including UDR men, was ambushed by IRA gunmen in High Street, Newry, just a few miles from the Irish border. As the soldiers took cover, they came under non-automatic, but sustained fire and at least six rounds impacted on or near the vehicles. One soldier was hit, and the other rounds wounded a pregnant woman and her sister; the wounded soldier was Private Thomas McCready (34). He was rushed to hospital but the Kilcoo, Co Down man died shortly after admission. It clearly mattered little to the gunmen that there had been 'collateral damage,' as they turned Newry into a battleground.

The killings continued and the clock counted down to the Birmingham attacks. On the 17th, a stolen car, containing an IRA gang stopped on the Crumlin Road and fired several shots at two Protestant teenagers as they walked along. The father of one of the boys was actually walking towards them. John Bailey (17) who was only 100 yards from his home in Silverstream Road, in the North Western suburbs of Belfast, fell mortally wounded. His distraught father was forced to watch the murder of his son and had to be comforted at the scene by friends and neighbours. The younger teenager was hit in the chest but survived. As the stolen car raced back towards Republican territory, the occupants also opened fire at a group of people outside a Protestant church, further down the road.

Two more soldiers died the following day; one from an RTA and the other as death due to 'circumstances unknown', officially at least. Private Samuel John Martin (20) of the UDR was killed in an RTA whilst on duty; a victim of exhaustion no doubt. The Royal Scots Dragoon Guards lost Trooper Donald Roy Davies (24); all that the author has been able to ascertain with any certainty, is that his funeral took place at Clochaenog Parish Church, near Ruthin in North Wales.

Constable Robert Forde (29) had joined the RUC after service in the Royal Navy; he was, by all accounts, a dedicated policeman who served his country to the utmost. Married with two young children, he was on duty on the night of 20 November, in Craigavon, Co Armagh. The Provisional IRA had telephoned the newspapers in order to warn the residents of the Rathmore Estate to evacuate their houses, as some unstable explosives had been left there. This 'humanitarian' face of the Provisionals was simply too good to be true. The entire operation was a sick 'come on' in order to lure the Army and police into a trap. Constable Forde unwittingly walked on a paving stone, underneath which a bomb had been placed. It was triggered by a watching IRA member via remote control, and the policeman was killed instantly.

On the same day that Forde was murdered and Regan died of his wounds, the UVF carried out another machine gun attack on a Catholic bar, this time at Aughamullan, Co Tyrone. The gang burst into the bar and opened fire with machine guns, hitting one customer in the chest, somehow missing his heart, but Patrick Falls (45) from Coalisland was fatally wounded and died at the scene. The gang escaped in a stolen car, later found abandoned in a Loyalist area of Belfast.

Even though Catholics suffered the most from sectarian slaughter, the author is left with the impression that they condemned the senseless killings, more so than the Protestant community. The Provisional IRA had therefore the most to lose from their own supporters in prolonging the sectarian killings, and risked alienating their core support. That the IRA did indulge in the killing on the basis of religion is axiomatic, but that they indulged less so than the Loyalists must not detract from their sectarian image. One instance took place at 18:30 on the evening of November 21, one hour and 47 minutes before the carnage in Birmingham began. William Burns (39), father of five, was a baker in Eliza Street, Belfast; in the Markets area. As a Protestant, he had been warned by the IRA to leave the bakery but had refused to obey their demands. On the same night as the Birmingham outrages, he paid for that refusal with his life. He was picked up by the IRA, killed and his body dumped close to the Ormeau Road.

The 21st day of November, 1974, fell on a Thursday; for many people in Britain, Thursday was 'pay day' and for many people in Birmingham, especially amongst the young, it was a reason worth celebrating – in the pub. For twenty one people in Birmingham, it was their last day on Earth, as the IRA moved north and targeted Britain's 'second city.'

Several teams of IRA bombers had based themselves in the area and as quietly as they came, they left in the same way, leaving behind a devastated and shocked city and almost 200 families completely distressed; 21 people were killed and 160 were injured, some critically and many were maimed for life. Two of the city centre's favourite 'watering holes' – today the young would refer to them as nightclubs – were the Mulberry

Bush and the Tavern in The Town. At 8:11pm, a caller with an Irish accent telephoned the local newspaper, the *Birmingham Post and Mail* and gave the correct password and warned of two bombs in the city centre. The caller mentioned the Rotunda, a circular office block in the city centre, and the Inland Revenue Office in New Street, nearby. There was no mention of specific locations in either place; the Mulberry Bush was on two floors of the Rotunda and the Tavern in the Town was in New Street. At 8:17pm, a scant six minutes after the warning was telephoned in, a device left by an IRA member or members underneath a table in the Mulberry exploded.

A policeman told the later inquest:

"We were just 300 yards away, just cresting the hill, when there was the largest thunderclap and rumbling and ground shock. Debris was coming down all over the road. It was like a volcano had erupted, people running and screaming. The Mulberry Bush had sort of exploded out onto the pavement; rubble, half a staircase, glass, carpets, bar tops and furniture blown to bits, and injured people staggering out."

The Tavern in the Town was only a few hundred yards away, and was packed as the first bomb went off over in the Rotunda building. The sound of the blast would have been clearly heard and whether or not some of the drinkers left to investigate and thus saved their lives, is open to conjecture. At 8:20pm, just three minutes after the first bomb, another device exploded in the second pub in which around 100 people were drinking. Just minutes later, a third device went off inside a nearby Yate's Wine Lodge, but it had already been evacuated and there were no deaths.

On the Friday morning, the *Daily Express* which earlier that year had relegated the M62 coach bomb to page 5, screamed: "It's Slaughter By IRA Bombs" from its banner headlines. Beneath the headline is a photograph of dead men, lying sprawled midst the wreckage of one of the shattered pubs and alongside is a photograph of a man, clinging desperately to the roof of a car, being driven frantically away from the bomb scene. Four of their journalists co-wrote: "The thugs of the IRA declared war on Birmingham with a sickening vengeance last night, leaving at least 17 [sic] people dead and 120 injured – many of them terribly maimed – in the worst toll of any bomb incident in Britain or Ulster in the recent troubles. Three explosions rocked the city – two of them in pubs packed with young people – in bloody revenge for the ban on IRA men marching in honour of dead Provisional bomber James McDaid.[1]

It came within two days of Provo Chief of Staff David Connell promising all-out war on British civilians unless the Army was withdrawn from Ulster." The journalist went on to describe the carnage and mayhem inside the pubs. "One man who was about to go inside the pub said: 'I was hit by a tremendous rush of air. You couldn't see. There was pandemonium. People were falling over one another to get out." Survivor Anthony Bailey said:

> We were sitting by the toilets. Suddenly there was one howl of an explosion. It went off by the jukebox. The ceiling fell down on top of us and water began pouring everywhere. His fiancée, Susan Edkin added: 'There was a tremendous rush to get out. People were shouting and screaming....I remember there was a man lying on the floor who couldn't see because his eyes had gone. It was terrible.' Sheet metal

---

1   McDaid was killed in an own goal explosion on 14 November planting a bomb in Coventry.

worker, Eddie Gallacher said: I had just gone for a pint and played the jukebox. I was just turning away to pick up my drink when the blast – from the jukebox corner – lifted me off my feet and threw me the length of the bar as the lights went on. The ceiling crashed and I fell on top of the bodies of a number of women customers. I tried to get up, but people were running and trampling on us. It was horrible. Some of us tried to get back in to rescue people, but it was impossible.

The scene can only be imagined; smoke, broken glass, people screaming, sobbing as they searched for friends, shocked and dazed, their eyes too glazed yet to see the shattered bodies and torn limbs which adorn a blast scene. Moving on to the second blast, this time at the Talk of The Town, the *Express* reporters continued: "Factory worker Mitch Wheeler said: 'There was this terrific blast and I was hurled off my feet. Everything went black and there was choking fumes. People were screaming and moaning. There were bodies everywhere. It was horrible, but as I struggled to get out, I knew I was trampling over bodies. About five minutes earlier we had heard a dull thud and someone when someone said it's probably a bomb. Some people went up to investigate. They were the lucky ones and escaped." The *Express* interviewed the manager of the second pub, Mr Dick Lawn; he said: "It was bloody murder. My place was full. When I got back there, they were carrying out the bodies. People were running around crying and screaming."

By an incredible coincidence, his counterpart at the Mulberry was also on a night off and he too escaped the carnage. He was seen walking around in the ruins of his demolished pub, no doubt reflecting upon his incredibly lucky escape. Another survivor was also interviewed, saying:

I saw bodies and blood everywhere. There were at least 30 brought out injured from the pub. I brought some out myself." The reporter continued: "His wife Moira who was serving behind the bar has been taken to hospital. She is badly injured. Hardly anyone inside escaped unscathed. A wounded man in a bloodstained shirt being helped away by two policemen said: "The swines – the bastards. Everyone was talking quite happily and laughing and joking when suddenly we were all hit by this fantastic blast. There were women and young girls screaming, blood pouring everywhere. I saw one young man who seemed to have half his body blown off. It was horrible.

There were over 200 casualties on the night, as we shall see in a moment, but had the Provisionals had their way, the toll would have been much higher. In addition to the third explosion at Yates' Wine Lodge, bombs were also either defused or failed to detonate at the Ivy pub in Hagley Road, where a device was placed on top of a 2,000 gallon oil tank; another was placed outside the British Airways office in the city and yet another device was defused at New Street Railway Station.

The recently re-elected Prime Minister, Harold Wilson said: "My colleagues in the Government and I are profoundly shocked to learn of the outrages which have been committed in Birmingham this evening." The former Prime Minister and leader of HM Opposition, Edward Heath spoke of his shock and anger and added: "…the whole country will be shocked and angered by the appalling loss of life and injury to innocent people by tonight's senseless bombing." Finally, the Lord Mayor of Birmingham said that: " ... the appalling outrage would build up hate and prejudice against the settled Irish community... I suspect (that) is what this outrage was intended to do."

A doctor, desperately trying to save lives and limbs at the City's main hospital said: "You went to put drips on an arm and there isn't one. You look for a leg and there isn't one."

The 'Mulberry Bush' and 'Tavern on The Town' dead were: Michael Beasley (30); Lynn Bennett (18); Stanley Bodman (51); James Caddick (40); Paul Davies (20); Charles Gray (44); Maxine Hambleton (18); Ann Hayes (19); Neil Marsh (17); Marilyn Nash (22); John Jones (51); Pamela Palmer (19) who was there with her boyfriend who lost a leg; Maureen Roberts (20); John Rowlands (46);Jane Davies (17); Desmond Reilly (21) and his brother Eugene (23);Trevor Thrupp (33) and Stephen Whalley (24). Additionally the following two people were fatally injured: Thomas Chayter (28) a barman at one of the pubs, who died in hospital on 28 November, and James Craig (34) who died on December 10. Twenty-one people, including the two fatally wounded, were killed in the first blasts and 182 were wounded; some dreadfully.

In May, the UVF had slaughtered 33 in Dublin and Monaghan, and the Provisional IRA had killed 28 in Guildford, Woolwich and now Birmingham. The troubles were far from over and this phase had still a further 23 years left to run.

Later that same evening of the twin blasts, Birmingham, still in shock and grieving for the dead and injured, had a further blow to its already battered senses. The family of dead IRA member James McDade, had by an unfortunate coincidence, chosen that evening to fly the terrorist's body back to Northern Ireland from Birmingham Airport. This was done, either through a total lack of sensitivity on their part or a deliberate attempt to provoke more of anti-Irish backlash. It is staggering also, that the West Midlands police did not try and have the coffin diverted to another airport with links to Belfast. Whatever the reason, bomb warnings from callers with English accents were phoned through to the airport and staff walked out. The families of some of those injured as well as other supporters grappled with police and McDade's family and IRA sympathisers at the Coventry hospital where his body was being stored. The two sides fought each other and there were several arrests. IRA supporters had hoped to march with the coffin, displaying the tricolour but this had been banned by Coventry and West Midlands police.

The scuffle intensified and insults were exchanged by the two sets of people, with objects including a bag of flour and a bottle were aimed at the hearse, before police managed to get the McDade family and coffin onto the waiting plane.

There was naturally, widespread outrage amongst the general public and the British government came under pressure to be seen to be acting against the threat of further bombs. On 29 November 1974 the Prevention of Terrorism Act was passed. Additionally, six Irish men, thereafter known as the 'Birmingham Six', were arrested and convicted of causing the explosions and served 16 years in prison before being freed on appeal on 14 March 1991. This author would have been delighted that the Birmingham six been the main perpetrators and served their time; the fact that they were, in all probability innocent and rightly released, however pours shame on the police. The West Midland Serious Crimes Squad was shown to have lied, falsified evidence and 'probably' beaten confessions out of the six innocent men. The disbanding of the squad is a testimony to their corruption; it was a shameful performance by people to whom we all looked for better things.

The killings were not over for the month; far from it. In the remaining nine days, 13 people would lose their lives; nine of who would be murdered in sectarian tit-for-tats, as both sides stepped up the senseless slaughter.

Around the time that the emergency services were pulling out the dead and dying from the two Birmingham pubs, just across the Irish Sea, a UFF gang had attacked a petrol station in a Catholic area, during which they had shot a customer in the face; thankfully he lived. On the 22nd, the same Loyalist gang then attacked the 'Peoples' filling station in Springfield Road, by this time, predominantly if not totally, Catholic. They had cold-bloodedly shot Geraldine Macklin (20), one of the station employees and left her dying and also wounded one of her male colleagues in the process. The murder gang raced off and the RUC quickly arrived on the scene; Miss Macklin was rushed to the RVH which was only several hundred yards away. She sadly died that afternoon.

That evening, with the entire city alert with tension and Army and RUC patrols stepped up, the UFF targeted the Catholic-owned 'Hole in the Wall' pub in Ballycarry Street. The club was located in the Ardoyne and Oldpark area and was frequented by Catholics only; it had a secure system of entry which was designed to prevent Loyalist attacks. However, on this occasion, a UFF gang waited until a customer had knocked for entry and then burst past him, opening fire as they did so. The manager of the bar, Michael Hanratty (44) pushed a customer out of the way, thus saving his life, but he himself was shot in the head. He died shortly afterwards in the RVH. Another customer was also wounded, as the gang made good their escape into a Loyalist area.

This was now proving to be the worst month of the Troubles so far, for sectarian murders. There were still more to come in this month of November, and the RUC simply didn't have the resources to investigate in depth, any of them. It didn't help that they were unable to 'flood' an area with men, or examine the forensics; they were unable to even spend any great length of time there without an Army escort. The sectarian killers knew that they were unlikely to be caught without the RUC having the benefit of a paid informer. Given the number of actual convictions made, it is a major tribute to the RUC's efforts, especially when taking into consideration the constraints and restrictions under which they had to operate.

In the early hours of the morning of 23 November, Thomas Gunn (34) was at a dance at a hotel in Holywood, a little over a mile from what is now George Best International Airport, Belfast, and around the same distance from Palace Barracks. He left the party of friends with whom he was drinking, and went to the toilets. He had already been earmarked by members of a UVF murder gang and he was grabbed, dragged through a rear entrance and bundled into a waiting car. His abductors drove Mr Gunn through Belfast and into the northern outskirts in a 'borrowed' taxi, where they beat him before shooting him dead in a field. The taxi, traced to a UVF member who was later convicted of murder (in 1977) became bogged down in the field where they had killed him, and had to be abandoned.

The day after Mr Gunn's murder, there were a further four sectarian murders, two by Loyalists and two by the Provisional IRA; all in Belfast. The blood spilled on purely sectarian grounds in this period, was amongst the worst of the entire troubles. Again, petrol filling stations were targeted, and it was an 'independent' operation by three members of the IRA who attacked the Edenderry filling station on the Crumlin Road. Three Provisionals, having stolen a car, pulled up to the petrol pumps and jumped out, brandishing handguns. They forced Heather Thompson (17) and John McClean (24) who was the manager into the back office, and forced both to kneel. As the pair did so, one gunman emptied his pistol into the young girl and Mr McClean was shot nine times at very close range. The trio of cowards then sped away, leaving the two employees lying dead; shot in cold blood. The killings formed part of what the *Irish News* later called "the bloodiest weekend since the start of the sectarian assassination campaign". One of the killers of the Edenderry pair, claimed later in court: "Do you know that I have prayed for that wee girl since I went inside?" Such a pity that he too, didn't 'find' God before the murder of the two innocents.

Before the day had finished, two more innocent people had been killed; this time Catholics, murdered by the UFF. Mrs Mary Sheppard (41), mother of four and William Hutton (50) were shot dead by UFF gunmen at a taxi office in Clifton Street, Belfast. The offices were just north of the city centre and Clifton Street itself is a continuation of the Loyalist Crumlin Road. Mrs Sheppard was the wife of the owner of the taxi firm, and was working late on the Saturday night, despatching drivers; Mr Hutton was a passenger, waiting in the office to be picked up and was watching the television. The murder gang had called at the office, ostensibly to hire a taxi, but on entering, they turned up the volume of the TV and then shot Mr Hutton, before shooting Mrs Sheppard in the face. The weekend had witnessed a staggering five sectarian killings and seven in total in the three days since the Birmingham attacks.

On the first day of the week, following the bloody weekend, Roy Jenkins, Home Secretary, announced to the House of Commons, that the Irish Republican Army (IRA) was to be proscribed. In other words, declared illegal in the United Kingdom with further emergency powers to be introduced through legislation. As though in response, the 'England Team' carried out three bomb attacks in the centre of London. In each case a small bomb with a timer was placed inside a post office pillar-box. The first bomb exploded at 5:50pm in King's Cross and injured two people. The second bomb exploded at 6:00pm in a pillar-box in Piccadilly Circus injuring 16 people. The final bomb exploded at 6:50pm outside Victoria Station and two people were injured.

Earlier on the day of Mr Jenkin's announcement, the IRA carried out another sectarian attack, this time in the Loyalist suburb of Woodvale, west of the Shankill and north of the Ballymurphy Estate. James Murdoch (55) and two workmates were walking through the Protestant area on their way to work, when a masked IRA gunman who had had been hiding behind parked cars, stepped out and shot at the men with a sub machine gun. The indiscriminate spraying left Mr Murdoch dead, one workmate seriously injured and the third man fell to the ground but was unhurt.

At 11:00PM hours on that fateful Monday, the UFF targeted a lone Catholic, Patrick Cherry (36) as he sat in his car in Newtownards, waiting for friends. He worked in the Rolls Royce factory – an equal rights employer with no discernible sectarian prejudices – at nearby Dundonald. As he waited, a masked gunman walked up to the car and shot him several times; he died at the scene. Mr Cherry left behind two young daughters.

Throughout my works, it has been constantly stressed that the overwhelming bulk of sectarian murder victims were at random, by happenchance; generally on the unscientific method of through which area one was walking through, into or out of. On the 26th, John Ramsey (44) a Protestant from the Crumlin Road area, was murdered by the Loyalist and Protestant UFF. He had the misfortune to be walking past the Holy Cross Monastery in the Catholic Ardoyne when the murder gang spotted him; that was enough for them and he was shot dead, because he was 'thought' to be a Catholic.

The final sectarian murder of 'mad November' occurred on the 26th, when the Provisional IRA targeted a Protestant shop-owner in Duncairn Gardens. Duncairn Gardens is situated very close to the sectarian interface with the Catholic New Lodge. Mr Thomas Hamilton (34) was tending his shop and his eight-year-old daughter was assisting. IRA gunmen burst in and opened fire with little consideration for the child. The young girl threw herself to the ground and her father was hit and died almost immediately. The cowardly gunmen ran out of the shop, and raced away in a waiting stolen car, towards the New Lodge.

PERSONAL THOUGHTS ABOUT THE NEW LODGE
Stephen Corbett, Royal Artillery

After the time I had in Andersonstown back in 71/72, I went to the Lodge with a fair bit of anger in me towards the Irish Catholics. I had also witnessed hatred when I went home on leave in Manchester from some of my long-standing Irish neighbours as well; and all because I chose to join the British Army.

I remember the looks we used to get when out on patrol in the Lodge, and on one occasion, outside the Starry Plough pub, a man in his 70's tried to goad me into punching him. In the whole of the four months tour, I was only once shown any true kindness; that was when an elderly lady slipped me an apple one night while I was on foot patrol. I often used to see a well-known scumbag by the name of Marie Docherty when I was in the Parlour OP. She was one of the hard-line Republicans that lived in the Lodge. She seemed to have a permanent scowl on her face whenever I saw her.

Then there was Winnie 'S.' Her husband had been 'murdered, by the Brits, or possibly by a Loyalist gang. It really depended very much on whose version you wanted to believe, but she hated us anyway. I remember a young girl who was known as (censored)[2]. I can't recall why she got that name, but she used to give us the odd bits of information about possible planned attacks and stuff like that. Whenever we met up with her she always had her back against an alley-wall, fag in hand and her boyfriend stuck between her legs.

There was a woman down near Harding Street who had a very fierce Alsatian; she used to give us drinks of tea occasionally. But I always had my doubts about her. After all, would the Provos really allow a Catholic woman living alone to give a squaddie a cup of tea on their patch? I think not! I always got the impression she herself, was probably after bits of information.

We had another tea stop at a lady called Lizzie. She and her family were Protestants, living amongst utter desolation near the Docks. You were always sure of a brew whatever time of night or day you went. I am sure the family must be remembered with reverence by those soldiers who went to the New Lodge. It was such a homely feeling when you rolled up outside the house.

---

2   For obvious reasons of personal security, the author has decided to remove the woman's name.

I know it couldn't have been pleasant for the locals when we were doing head-checks at their homes, and I really did hate doing that. But if they had any feelings towards us at all, that would have been their chance to show it, behind closed doors when we were in their house. And that is something that hardly ever happened.

When we were in hot pursuit of gunmen we would hammer on doors to gain entry, but most of the time the occupants wouldn't respond quick enough for our liking, and we would end up kicking the door in. I recall going down the full length of a street doing this once, after a gunman had opened fire on a patrol. It's no wonder we were hated so much really. Towards the end of the tour I started thinking; 'How would I like it if some soldier did that to my house?' I'm sure there must have been many good people there, but you hardly ever met them.

I detested the Republicans with a vengeance, and I still do. There has always been tension simmering just below the surface, despite the so-called Peace Process. The former Provos, who are now MP's, must know who the present terrorists are in the Province. And even the so-called 'good' Catholics must know who the Republican sympathisers are living amongst them. But they choose to ignore what is going on, either through fear, or because they don't really care. I never believed the Provos put all their weapons 'beyond use' either. The Provisional IRA has never gone away; they just changed their name.

Two days after the initial announcement, Roy Jenkins, introduced the Prevention of Terrorism (Temporary Provisions) Bill into the House of Commons. One of the provisions of the Bill provided the police with powers to arrest and detain suspected terrorists for up to 48 hours, in the first instance and for up to seven days if the police applied to the Home Secretary for additional time. The provision also allowed for exclusion orders to be made against people suspected of involvement in terrorism. Jenkins described the provisions in the Bill as "draconian measures unprecedented in peacetime." The Bill became law on 29 November.

The day after these 'Draconian measures,' Thomas Chayter (20) a barman in Birmingham's 'Tavern in the Town' who had been dreadfully injured in the earlier bomb blast, died of his wounds; he was the 20th fatality of the atrocity. On that day, the Labour government rushed through the Prevention of Terrorism (Temporary Provisions) Bill. The new Act gave the police powers to detain people for up to seven days without any charge being brought against them. The Act also allowed the authorities to 'exclude' people from entering Britain. Although it was initially viewed as a temporary measure, the Prevention of Terrorism Act was to be renewed each year, and was eventually made permanent by a Conservative government in 1988. Many critics of the Act claimed that it was mainly being used as a means of monitoring the movements of innocent Irish people. Indeed many thousands of, mainly Catholic, Irish people were screened under provisions in the act, although never charged with any offences.

On the 29th and 30th respectively, two more soldiers died; one was killed in a tragic on-duty RTA and the other died from what the MoD euphemistically term "death by violent or unnatural causes." Trooper John Major (22) 15/19 Hussars, died under such circumstances, and regrettably the author is not permitted to comment further. Private John Taylor (37) of the UDR was killed in an RTA.

The Provisional IRA's England Team in spite, or possibly even because of, the carnage that they had caused, carried out two bomb attacks near the National Army Museum in Tite Street, Chelsea, London. Initially a small bomb exploded in a post office pillar-box at 8:30pm, and approximately 20 minutes later a second, larger bomb, exploded behind a hedge just a short distance away from the first explosion. Twenty people were injured in the second explosion including an explosives officer, six policemen and two ambulance men. This was intended as a 'come on' and this tactic of the 'come-on' bomb was one which the IRA used, on many occasions in Northern Ireland.

In Belfast, the UVF had launched a gun and bomb attack at a Catholic-owned bar in Church Street, Newry. The bar in the town centre was frequented, in the main, by Catholics; it was an obvious target for the Loyalists. Although given that Newry was in the IRA's own heartland, it was a risky attack. On the evening of the 29th, at least two members of the UVF placed an explosive device in a hallway, lit the fuse and walked out. The resultant explosion injured a score or more, but John Mallon was mortally injured; he died the following month.

Then, on the final Saturday of that bloody month – the 30th -, the IRA carried out a bomb attack on the Talbot Arms public house in Little Chester Street, Belgravia, London. Two small bombs, each with a short fuse, were thrown at the window of the pub. One bomb went through the window but failed to explode; the second rebounded off the window frame and landed in the street, but the explosion still injured five customers inside the pub.

November had finally ground to a halt; together with May, it was the worst month since the carnage of July 1972. In all, 63 people had died. 12 were soldiers, one policeman and 47 civilians. The IRA lost three members. Of the civilians killed, the Provisional IRA killed 31 and the Loyalists 16. A shameful 22 of the civilian deaths were overtly sectarian; it was the second worst month of the Troubles for these senseless and random killings based on religion alone. In the month, the Provisional IRA was responsible for 37 deaths and the Loyalists for 16.

Chapter 24

December

After the insanity of the previous month December was less violent and the number of fatalities, although painfully high for the families concerned, was mercifully low in comparison. In all 13 people were to die, although *Lost Lives* list 15 people killed. This author does not attribute two of the deaths to the Troubles and will explain the rationale behind this thinking within this chapter. However, a high proportion of the deaths were sectarian killings.

Gortmullen in Co Fermanagh is a remote place; situated close to the border with the Republic and opposite Co Monaghan. Sometime around the 28 November, the Provisional IRA booby trapped an empty milk churn with explosives and left it close to one of the houses in the hamlet, near to Derrylin. A civilian had moved the churn away from a relative's house and the Army bomb disposal team (EOD) were called to defuse it. On 2 December, Sergeant Major John Maddocks (32), a father of three from the RAOC, was tasked to examine the device. As he reached into the churn for a better look, it exploded, killing him instantly and obliterating his body. His stunned comrades also came close to death, as the Provisionals had planted a secondary device in a nearby field. This was later defused by the EOD team.

On 4 December, a UFF gang had carried out an armed raid on a shop belonging to James Davidson (64) in Upper Glenfarne Street, Belfast. The shop was situated midway between the Shankill Road and Crumlin Road; right in the heart of Loyalist territory. Mr Davidson was shot in the neck and died from his injuries two days later. Loyalist sources stated that the raid was a 'homer', a term which described a robbery for personal gain rather than one to swell party funds.

On Thursday, 5 December, the Prevention of Terrorism Act, which had been introduced in Britain on 29 November was extended to Northern Ireland. In essence, the Act, or a reasonable facsimile thereof, had been in use previously. The powers of arrest and detention and the use of the Diplock Courts had already extended similar powers to the security forces.

The Diplock courts were established by the Government in Northern Ireland on 8 August 1973. This was in an attempt to overcome widespread jury intimidation by the paramilitaries of both sides. The right to trial by jury was suspended for certain scheduled offences and the court consisted of a single judge. The Diplock courts, which were abolished in 2007, were established in response to a report submitted to parliament in December 1972 by Lord Diplock. This report addressed the problem of dealing with paramilitary violence through means other than internment. The report marked the beginnings of a policy known as criminalisation, in which the state removed any legal distinction between political violence and normal crime, with political prisoners treated as common criminals.

On 7 December, there was a double IRA 'own goal' and two of their bomb-makers died in premature explosions, in separate incidents less than a mile apart. Ethel Lynch

(22) from the Creggan Estate in Londonderry was constructing a device in an IRA bomb-making factory in the east of the city, close to the University. She was killed instantly and other members of the team were slightly injured, but made good their escape. John McDaid (16) one of the youngest IRA bomb-makers to be killed, was constructing a device in a side street off the Strand Road. He had already prepared one and was working on a second, destined for attacks on Protestant bars in the city. He was killed instantly when it too, prematurely detonated and a companion was also injured; as his wounded fellow-terrorist limped away, he was arrested by an RUC patrol.

On 8 December, the Irish Republican Socialist Party (IRSP) was formed following a split within Official Sinn Féin; among its leading members were Séamus Costello, leader of the IRSP, and Bernadette McAliskey, a former Member of Parliament. The Irish National Liberation Army (INLA) was formed in 1975, many people viewed it as the military wing of the IRSP. The INLA was an organisation more ruthless and more violent, if that were possible than the Provisional IRA or the Officials who had spawned them. Constantly in bitter, deathly feuds with other Republicans and constantly in a state of internal turmoil, the INLA was always likely to implode.

They did, however, claim many notable 'scalps', none more so than Margaret Thatcher's right hand man, Airey Neave MP. Neave was loathed by the Republicans and was likely to play a major role in their suppression if, or when, the Conservatives were returned to power. On 30 March, 1979, his car was targeted in the underground car park of the House of Commons, in an alarming lapse in security, and a UVBT (under vehicle booby trap) was placed underneath fitted with a mercury tilt device. Once his car drove up the car park's incline, it detonated, killing him almost instantly. The INLA had arrived on the scene, and would add its bloody contribution to the Troubles over the next 20 or more years.

On 10 December, the final victim of the previous month's Birmingham pub attacks passed away in hospital. James Craig (34), a car worker, became the 21st and final victim of the IRA's slaughter of innocent civilians in Britain's second city.

On 11 December, a debate on the reintroduction of capital punishment for acts of terrorism was held in the House of Commons. The specific motion came in the form of an amendment which was proposed by a Conservative MP. Following a five-hour debate the amendment was defeated by a free vote of 369 to 217. Whilst the debate was taking place, the England Team carried out a bomb attack on the Long Bar of the Naval and Military Club in Piccadilly, London. At 6.30pm, IRA members threw a small bomb through the window of the bar; no one was injured. As two IRA members were leaving the scene they were followed by a taxi cab and they fired two shots at the driver; the driver was not injured. Almost at the same time a second group of IRA members carried out a gun attack on the Cavalry Club; again there were no injuries.

Forkhill (Irish: *Foirceal*) is a small village in south Co Armagh and, during the course of the Troubles, at least 13 people died violently there. It is a rural community, close to Newry and with quick, easy links to the border with the Republic. The border is approximately 1,300 yards away and the area was of crucial importance to both the Provisional IRA and the security forces. On the night of 14 December, the RUC were called in to what appeared to be a 'routine' burglary on a house at Killeavy. Nothing could ever be described thus, and the police attended in a joint patrol with the Royal

Green Jackets. The 'burglary' was an IRA 'come on' and, as such, a carefully laid ambush had been set.

At least four gunmen in well placed firing points opened up on the border side of the house, using automatic weapon as the RUC/Army car drove towards the site. At least 40 rounds were fired and Constable David McNiece (19) was hit several times and killed immediately. Rifleman Michael Gibson (20), 1RGJ a London boy was mortally wounded, and died in hospital four days after Christmas with his family at his bedside. The deaths of the two young security force members were premeditated and cowardly and served to illustrate just how dangerous the jobs of soldiers and policemen really were.

On 14 December John Mallon (21), who had been injured in the UVF attack in Newry the previous month, died of his injuries. Though terribly injured, he had clung to life for 16 days.

In the week between Saturday 14 December and Saturday 21st, the IRA's England Team carried out four further attacks in London. They carried out a gun attack on the Churchill Hotel in Portman Square, London on the 14th; three people were slightly injured by flying glass. On the 17th, an IRA unit placed three time bombs at telephone exchanges in London. In one of the explosions George Arthur (34), a post office telephonist, was killed.

Mr Arthur was also a part-time student, studying nights for a Law degree; he had been due to fly out of the country that evening on a holiday, his wife was in the middle of packing when police turned up at the family home. A member of the England Team had walked into the sorting offices at Tottenham Court Road, close to London's West End, and placed a device inside a duffle bag in a corridor. The building was immediately evacuated but, in the confusion, George Arthur was overlooked and he died instantly in the blast.

On the 19th, they carried out a bomb attack on Selfridge's department store in Oxford Street, London. A time bomb had been placed in a car which was then parked outside the store. Three telephone warnings were given and the area was evacuated. Finally they left a bomb in Harrods department store in Knightsbridge, London. The bomb was discovered, prior to a telephone warning, and later defused by explosives officers.

AFTERWARDS
Stephen Corbett, Royal Artillery

The Postman always used to make sure that my wife, Pam, got my mail before she left for work. That way, she would sit there reading my letters with a cup of tea while the radio was on. I had always told her that if anything happened to me, she would hear it from the Army and nobody else. But on one particular morning, whilst gardening and listening to the radio, she thought that she heard that '"a Gunner Stephen … from Wythenshawe, Manchester had been shot dead in Northern Ireland." She didn't catch the surname, but managed to convince herself it was me. I was told later that she was absolutely distraught and that no-one could console her. It was only when the next bulletin came on, an hour later that she started to calm down. I came home a few weeks later on R&R leave, but when it was time for me to go back, she was truly heartbroken. She was convinced that something was going to happen to me. When the taxi drew up outside the house to take me to the airport, she wouldn't let go of me. I wanted to stay, but I really had no choice other than to go back. It was one of the hardest things I have ever had to do when I left her again that day.

I recall that several months after I left the Army, a letter arrived for me from Northern Ireland. I opened it and a typewritten note warned me never to go back to Belfast. I was rather worried about it at the time, so I went to the local police with it; but they didn't want to know. I could never figure out how they got my address. But I remember an advert being in 'Visor' offering to deliver flowers to your loved ones in England for £10. I placed the order and told Pam to be in on such and such a date, but the flowers never arrived. And I wondered if that was how they did it. I kept the letter for years, but I don't know where it is now. I know much of this sounds far-fetched, but it's perfectly true.

Incidents such as these were not isolated and the Provisional IRA was known to have obtained the addresses of soldiers who had been killed in the conflict. Several families then received letters which both taunted them and gloated over their loss. One family contacted the author to describe a very emotional incident involving such a taunt. The mother of a soldier killed in the early 1970s, who specifically asked not to be identified, wrote:

About a week after he was killed and a few days after the funeral, we received two letters both with Belfast postmarks. Inside the first envelope was a blank piece of paper but in the second, there were three or four lines of neat handwriting. It started off by saying that we were responsible for the loss of our son and we had only ourselves to blame. We had signed for our boy to join as a boy soldier as he was under 18, and this person said that as we had done that, the responsibility for his death was ours. To lose your child at such a young age was terrible enough, but to receive such a hateful letter so soon afterwards left us feeling even more devastated.

Mrs Felicity Townsend, wife of Peter Townsend, a soldier of the Green Howards, was similarly taunted after the wounding of her husband in the Ardoyne in 1971. An intruder had gotten into the common area of her flat in Middlesbrough whilst Peter was recovering in hospital and she was severely alarmed; whether or not this was the Provisional IRA playing mind games is a moot point. They were quite clearly prepared and ruthless enough to take the war to their 'own' civilians, so why not to the vulnerable and freshly grieving loved ones of soldiers?

MY SOLDIER HUSBAND
Pam Corbett

I hated Stephen being in the army, but he promised me that after the tour in Ireland he would be out for good. I suppose that may be why I worried so much about him. We hadn't been married all that long before he went over, and I convinced myself I wasn't going to see him ever again. After I heard on the news one day about a soldier being shot dead – and I thought they said it was Stephen – I just went to pieces. I could never relax after that; I don't think that I ever got over the shock properly.

Stephen never understood what it was like for me at home. It was alright for him; he knew where he was and what he was doing, but I didn't know anything. I was never able to speak to him on a phone or anything like that; all I had were the letters he sent almost every day. If I didn't get one I would start to worry. I listened to the news all the time and I couldn't sleep of a night. I used to sit there in the dark and wonder if he was out on patrol and if everything was alright.

I worked at Marshal-Wards in Manchester at that time; sometimes, when I walked into the office of a morning, my friends would be gathered around talking. When they saw me they would go silent, so I knew they were talking about me and probably wondering if anything had happened to Stephen. My friend Sandra had left Belfast to escape all the trouble over there and she was always apologising to me about what was going on. I think she thought I would blame her if anything happened to Stephen. The happiest day of my life was when he finally came home for good on Saturday 12 October 1974.

As Christmas approached the continued depravity of the sectarian killers left even the most optimistic observer of the Troubles beginning to question if an end to the conflict would ever come. The Loyalist UFF was responsible for one of the most sickening acts of betrayal witnessed to date in the present conflict. Joseph McDermott (37) was a roofing contractor who was a Catholic and worked with, and was befriended by, two workmates who were Protestant. The two workmates were also members of the UDA/UFF and talked their Catholic colleague into staying behind in a UDA club where the three of them had enjoyed pre-Christmas drinks. The three left the club during the early hours of the 21 December, the two Protestants told Mr McDermott that they were going for more drink. As they led him across waste ground at Ballycoan Road in North Belfast, he became suspicious and tried to leave. As he did so, they shot him several times at close range and, in order to finish him off, strangled him with a tie. This act of betrayal demonstrated clearly that they would stoop to any level in the sectarian war. Indeed, such a comment is superfluous as there were clearly no depths to which they would stoop.

Some hours later, another member of the Provisional IRA's England Team died in a self-inflicted 'own goal', albeit not with an explosive device. Brian Fox (27) had been fooling around with a revolver in a safe house in the Staffordshire town of Newcastle-under-Lyme. Apparently unaware of the trigger action, he put the gun against his forehead, squeezed the trigger and succeeded in removing himself from the gene pool. Fox was mourned by no-one other than his family, and of course his fellow terrorists.

NEWLY ARRIVED
Erich Modrowics, Queen's Own Hussars
We arrived at Aldergrove airport on a Hercules transporter and got into the trucks that were to take us to the camp in Armagh. I remember thinking, "we have no ammunition and are a sitting target"; all of the way to the camp I sat and looked at a hole in the floor of the truck and imagined a bomb going off and blowing us to pieces. That was probably the scariest time I had, after I had gone out on patrol the first time. I believe my personality changed and I enjoyed the rush of adrenaline that came with fear. It was like a drug and I craved it, and consequently I volunteered to do all the crazy things that most sane squaddies

ATO at work (Brian Sheridan)

ATO and Light Infantry escort prepare to examine Newtownhamilton bomb (Brian Sheridan)

ATO and Light Infantry escort prepare to examine Newtownhamilton bomb (Brian Sheridan)

ATO team after successful defusing of an IRA bomb at Newtownhamilton (Brian Sheridan)

wouldn't have done. I kicked doors in that could have been booby trapped, went into buildings through windows that could have pressure pads waiting for unsuspecting squaddies; I did that and always got a buzz from that adrenaline rush. Northern Ireland changed my personality; I became more aggressive and to this day being an old fart still am that way inclined.

There are numerous incidents that I recall from my 2 tours but one that stands out was in Armagh City. It was summertime and the Irish girls all seemed to be beautiful; we spent many hours yearning for female company but the nearest we got was looking at the wank mags that were passed around. I did have a crush on a girl at one of our tea stops and we met now and again when it was safe to do so, the highlight of which was a kiss (I still remember you Dorothy). Anyway, I digress. Our brick was on foot patrol in the city, and we went down an alley to the back of a building where they were doing some renovation work inside. There was a pile of rubble and right on top of it was an Army trip flare minus the poles; just the flare itself. One of the guys (Stew Goldstone) went right over picked it up and said: 'Look at this!' The rest of us stared at him, our faces contorted in horror as we knew through our training about the way that the IRA left booby traps. Stew realised immediately what he had done by the look of pure horror on our faces! The entire incident probably lasted a minute but seemed like hours; we told him to place it back where he found it, which he did very, very carefully. We then radioed ATO (Bomb disposal) and they came down and cordoned off the area. I can't remember what happened after that but that was one of the closest I ever came to being blown up!

The year's bombing campaign ended with three further attacks by the England Team, both in towns with a large military garrison. On the same day – the 21st – a bomb left by the IRA on a platform of the railway station in Aldershot, England, was defused by explosives officers. Later that day, another unexploded bomb was discovered and defused at the King's Arms public house, known to be popular with soldiers in Warminster, Wiltshire.

On 22 December, the London home of the Conservative leader, and former, Prime Minister Edward Heath was bombed; he had not been home at the time of the attack but arrived ten minutes later. The 2 lb device caused some exterior damage and also caused further damage inside the house in Victoria. Witnesses described seeing a man emerging from a Cortina car and throwing the bomb on to the first floor balcony of the house. Two policemen and a patrol car chased the vehicle as it drove off, and it crashed a few minutes later in Chelsea and several men fled from the vehicle. Mr Heath, who had been conducting a carol service at his home town of Broadstairs, Kent, was driven off by police to an undisclosed location after his arrival at home.

BATTALION CHANGEOVERS
Gerry Chandler, 3 Royal Green Jackets
It always amazed me that when battalions switched over at the end of their tour, they weren't targeted by the IRA. Basically a huge convoy of four tonners would roll down to the docks, accompanied by support vehicles. As far as I am aware these convoys were never targeted.

On Christmas Eve, Anthony Morgan (34) died in hospital after a long fight for life following a UFF gun attack outside a Belfast hospital the previous October.[1] On the 29th, Rifleman Michael Gibson (20) of the Royal Green Jackets died of the wounds he had received in the IRA 'come on' at Killeavy, near Forkhill, Co Armagh. Rifleman Gibson from Deptford in London was the last person killed as a consequence of the Troubles in 1974. He was the 188th soldier killed during the two years covered by this book and the 16th Royal Green Jacket to die in the Troubles to date.

Twelve people had died in December; two were soldiers, one policeman and six civilians. The IRA lost three members, all to 'own goals'. Of the civilians killed, the Provisional IRA killed two and the Loyalists four. At least three of the civilian deaths were overtly sectarian. During the month, the Provisional IRA had caused the deaths of eight people, including three of their own.

So 1974 was over; the Troubles had now run for 64 months. The death toll of British soldiers over the five years had reached a staggering 448; approximately half of those suffered during Britain's involvement in the Korean War. Although the mandarins inside the MoD building in Whitehall would contend that they had not all died as a 'direct' result of terrorist action, there were still 448 grieving families throughout the United Kingdom. Amongst these fatalities would be men who had died from negligent discharges, accidental shootings, road traffic accidents and from that MoD euphemism, 'death by violent or unnatural causes.' All 448 had died in or as a consequence of the Troubles; another great euphemism which only the English language, and the British, can produce.

I will leave the last words to the poetry of Hathcock

'A WEE DANDER'
It's a short walk from North Howard Street mill,
or if you're a local "a wee dander".
Past the republican news office to Leeson Street,
and then McCann's the butcher.
McCann's son Dan was shot on the rock,
stopped in the process of his daddy's profession,
made a mistake in taking us on …
and now he's learnt his lesson.
Next on the left Bell Star Taxis, dickers leaning on the wall,
pretending to read their papers.
Their eyes flit up from the pages, greasy haired and unshaven,
Fall Road, West Belfast, a town far far from heaven.
The damp autumn morning, still dark grey,
with the eggy sulphurous stench of a 1000 coal fires.
I'm dodging the dog shit and piles of windblown litter,
and see hate dripping faces all twisted and bitter.
Scanning their faces, looking for players,
scanning and scanning and scanning.

---

1   See Chapter 22, October 1974

My eyes
are everywhere, rooftops and windows, parked cars and alleys, hyper, hyper alert.
Wanting to live another day, than a six foot hole in the dirt.
We hang a right as we pass Dunville Park,
me and my muckers: Jim, PJ and Mark.
And there in the distance sits our mesh wrapped redoubt,
so we run the remaining metres and yards.
Hard targeting with a zig and a zag, and our hearts beating hard,
running as fast as a horse on the canter.
The patrols at an end and we start to unload,
Have a brew and a fag while we swop banter,
at our home in Springfield Road.

1974: The Final Tolls

Over the year, beginning with the sectarian murder of John Whyte and ending with the death from wounds of Rifleman Michael Gibson, a total of 322 people had lost their lives in, or as a direct consequence of the Troubles.

The tolls were as follows:

British Army	79
RUC	14
Civilians	200
IRA	25
Loyalists	4

Further, it is worth noting, that of the 200 civilian deaths in 1974, at least 101, or c. 50% were killed in sectarian murders.

Over the course of the two years under study in this book, the totals were as follows:

British Army	189
RUC	26
Civilians	328
IRA	61
Loyalists	19

Postscript

1972

In a previous works by this author (*The Bloodiest Year*) reference was made to the accidental death of Private Dennis Porter of the Royal Army Medical Corps on 24 April, 1972. This author was finally able to speak to someone who, although not present at the incident was, nevertheless, involved through an accident of fate, and his words are printed below.

DEATH FROM AN ND
John, Royal Army Pay Corps

Dennis was attached to 2 Field Regt RA for the period of the tour; he was already there when I arrived. We had a portakabin 'barracks' within the Musgrave Park Hospital Grounds. The room with his bed-space in the portakabin had, I think, eight from the attached Field Ambulance, and four bunks.

One of the soldiers in his room was due to go on R&R and started to take the rounds out of his SLR magazine, doing it properly. Dennis was on the other side of the room leaning against his bunk with his back to them whilst reading. An RCT Private saw the magazine being unloaded and said to the other soldier: 'I'll show you a quicker way.' He took the SLR and put the mag on and started to eject the rounds. When he got to what he thought was the end, he took the mag off and as he went to pass the SLR back, accidentally pulled the trigger. Tragically, there was one up the spout and it hit Dennis in the back. The round went through him, exiting via his heart; it went through the wall, across the path into the next cabin, in to the first room and through the wall on the other side ending in a second room.

I can't remember the name of the RCT Private but he was charged with manslaughter and found not guilty!

Roll of Honour: 1973-4

14/20 King's Hussars and 15/19 King's Royal Hussars

TROOPER JOHN TYSON	28/02/74:	RTA
CPL MICHAEL COTTON	20/03/74:	Killed in friendly fire Co Armagh
CPL MICHAEL HERBERT	20/03/74:	Killed in same incident

15/19 Hussars

TPR JOHN MAJOR	29/11/74:	Death by violent or unnatural causes

17/ 21st Lancers

CPL TERENCE WILLIAMS	05/05/73:	Booby Trap bomb Crossmaglen
TROOPER JOHN GIBBONS	05/05/73:	Killed in same incident
TROOPER KENEALY	14/09/73:	Killed in training accident Gosford Castle

16/5th Lancers

2/LT ANDREW SOMERVILLE	27/03/73:	IRA landmine near Omagh

05 Regiment Army Air Corps

C/SGT ARTHUR PLACE	18/05/73:	Booby trap bomb, Knock-na-Moe Hotel, Omagh
C.O.FH. BR COX	18/05/73:	Killed in the same incident
SGT DB READ	18/05/73:	Killed in the same incident
WO. D C ROWAT	12/04/74:	Killed in helicopter crash, Co Armagh

5th Royal Inniskilling Dragoon Guards

SGT FREDERICK WILLIAM DRAKE	03/06/73:	Died of wounds: bomb, Knock-na-Moe Hotel Omagh

Air Cadet Force

CDT Leonard Cross	11/11/74:	Murdered by the IRA nr Creggan, Estate,

Cheshire Regiment

CPL DAVID SMITH	04/07/74:	DoW after being shot, Ballymurphy Estate, Belfast

Coldstream Guards

GUARDSMAN ROBERT PEARSON	20/02/73:	Killed by IRA snipers, Lower Falls, Belfast
GUARDSMAN MICHAEL SHAW	20/02/73:	Killed in same incident
GUARDSMAN MICHAEL DOYLE	21/02/73:	Killed by sniper, Fort Whiterock, Belfast
GUARDSMAN ANTON BROWN	06/03/73:	Killed by sniper, Ballymurphy Estate, Belfast
CAPTAIN ANTHONY POLLEN	14/04/74:	Shot on undercover mission, Bogside, Londonderry

Devon & Dorset Regiment

CPL STEVEN WINDSOR	06/11/74:	Killed by sniper, Crossmaglen

Duke of Edinburgh's Royal Regiment

CPL JOSEPH LEAHY	08/03/73:	DoW, booby trap, Forkhill, Co Armagh
S/SGT BARRINGTON FOSTER	23/03/73:	Murdered off-duty by the IRA
CAPTAIN NIGEL SUTTON	14/08/73:	Died in vehicle accident, Ballykinler

PTE MICHAEL SWANICK   28/10/74:   IRA van bomb attack, Ballykinler
PTE BRIAN ALLEN   06/11/74:   Killed by sniper, Crossmaglen

Duke Of Wellington's Regiment
PTE BRIAN ORAM   07/04/73:   RTA
CPL DAVID TIMSON   07/04/73:   Killed in same incident
PTE JOSEPH MCGREGOR   24/05/73:   RTA
WOII PETER LINDSAY   28/08/73:   Unknown
2ND LT HOWARD FAWLEY   25/01/74:   Landmine attack, Ballyronan Co Londonderry
CPL MICHAEL RYAN   17/03/74:   IRA sniper at Brandywell, Londonderry
PTE LOUIS CARROLL   07/04/74:   Cause of death unknown

Gloucestershire Regiment
PTE GEOFFREY BREAKWELL   17/07/73:   IRA booby trap, Divis St Flats, Belfast
PTE CHRISTOPHER BRADY   17/07/73:   Killed in same incident

Gordon Highlanders
PTE MICHAEL GEORGE MARR   29/03/73:   Shot by sniper, Andersonstown, Belfast

Green Howards
PTE RAYMOND HALL   05/03/73:   DoW: Sniper attack, Belfast
PTE FREDERICK DICKS   05/06/74:   IRA sniper, Dungannon

King's Own Royal Border Regiment
C/SERGEANT WILLIAM BOARDLEY   1/02/73:   Shot in Strabane by IRA gunman

Life Guards
CPL of HORSE LEONARD DURBER 21/02/73:   DoW after riot in Belfast

Light Infantry
LCPL. A KENNINGTON   28/02/73:   IRA sniper, Ardoyne area of Belfast
CPL. T P TAYLOR   13/05/73:   Killed in bomb attack, Donegall Road
PTE. J GASKELL   14/05/73:   DoW from same incident
PTE. R B ROBERTS   1/07/73:   Shot by sniper in Ballymurphy Estate, Belfast
LCPL. C R MILLER   18/09/73:   Shot in West Belfast
PTE. STEPHEN HALL   28/10/73:   Shot in Crossmaglen

Parachute Regiment
CPL. S N HARRISON   07/04/73:   IRA landmine, Tullyogallaghan
L/CPL. T D BROWN   07/04/73:   Killed in same incident
L/CPL. D A FORMAN   16/04/73:   Accidentally shot, Flax Street Mill, Ardoyne
WOII. W R VINES   05/05/73:   IRA landmine, Crossmaglen
A/SGT. J WALLACE   24/05/73:   IRA booby trap, Crossmaglen
PTE. R BEDFORD   16/03/74:   Shot in IRA ambush, Crossmaglen
PTE. P JAMES   16/03/74:   Killed in same incident

Prince Of Wales' Own Regiment of Yorkshire
PTE JAMES LEADBEATER   11/02/73:   Unknown Cause of death
PTE MICHAEL MURTAGH   06/02/73:   Killed in rocket attack Lower Falls area,
PTE EDWIN WESTON   14/02/73:   IRA sniper Divis Street area, Belfast
PTE GARY BARLOW   04/03/73:   Disarmed and murdered by IRA, Belfast
PTE JOHN GREEN   08/03/73:   Shot whilst guarding school in Lower Falls

Queen's Own Highlanders
PTE JAMES HESKETH   10/12/73:   Shot dead on Lower Falls, Belfast

Royal Anglian Regiment

PTE ANTHONY GOODFELLOW	27/04/73:	Shot at VCP Creggan Estate, Londonderry
PTE N MARWICK	12/09/73:	Cause of death unknown
L/CPL ROY GRANT	2/11/73:	Death by violent or unnatural causes
PTE PARRY HOLLIS	13/11/74:	Died of natural causes during his tour

Royal Army Dental Corps

SGT RICHARD MULDOON	23/03/73:	Murdered by the IRA whilst off duty.

Royal Army Medical Corps

PTE DENNIS 'TAFFY' PORTER	24/04/72:	Violent or unnatural causes
CAPTAIN HARRY MURPHY	15/03/73:	Violent or unnatural causes

Royal Army Ordnance Corps

CAPTAIN B S GRITTEN	21/06/73:	Killed explosives, Lecky Road, Londonderry
SSGT. R F BECKETT	30/08/73:	Killed by bomb in post office Tullyhommon
CAPTAIN RONALD WILKINSON	23/09/73:	IRA bomb, Edgbaston, Birmingham
2ND LT L. HAMILTON DOBBIE	03/10/73:	IRA bomb, Bligh's Lane post, Londonderry
SSGT. A N BRAMMAH	18/02/74:	Examining IRA bomb Crossmaglen
CPL GEOFFREY HALL	20/09/74:	Cause of death unknown
SSGT. V I ROSE	07/11/74:	IRA landmine, Stewartstown, Tyrone
WOII. J A MADDOCKS	2/12/74:	Examining milk churn bomb Gortmullen

Royal Army Veterinary Corps

CPL BRIAN CRIDDLE, BEM	22/07/73:	DoW; wounded defusing IRA bomb

Royal Artillery

GUNNER IVOR SWAIN	23/03/73:	RTA: North Belfast (ATT: Royal Marines)
GNR IDWAL EVANS	11/04/73:	IRA sniper Bogside area of Londonderry
GNR KERRY VENN	28/04/73:	IRA sniper Shantallow Estate, Londonderry
SGT THOMAS CRUMP	03/05/73:	DoW after being shot in Londonderry
GNR JOSEPH BROOKES	25/11/73:	Shot in IRA ambush in Bogside area of Londonderry
BOMBARDIER HEINZ PISAREK	25/11/73:	Killed in same incident
SGT JOHN HAUGHEY	21/01/74:	Remote-controlled bomb, Bogside, Londonderry
GNR LEONARD GODDEN	04/02/74:	Killed by IRA bomb on M62 in Yorkshire
BDR TERRENCE GRIFFIN	04/02.74:	Killed in same incident
LT/COL JOHN STEVENSON	08/04/74:	Murdered by IRA gunmen at his home in Northumberland
GNR KIM MACCUNN	22/06/74:	IRA sniper New Lodge, Belfast
SGT BERNARD FEARNS	30/07/74:	IRA sniper New Lodge area of Belfast
GNR KEITH BATES	04/11/74:	RTA: Central Belfast
GNR RICHARD DUNNE	08/11/74:	IRA bomb in Woolwich, London pub bombings

Royal Horse Artillery

GNR DAVID FARRINGTON	13/03/74:	Shot by IRA gunmen in Chapel Lane, Belfast
GUNNER TIMOTHY UTTERIDGE	19/10/84:	Shot by IRA, Turf Lodge, Belfast

Royal Corps of Signals

Sgt DAVID MCELVIE	13/03/73:	Unknown
CPL JOHN AIKMAN	06/11/73:	Shot by IRA gunmen Newtownhamilton
Signalman MICHAEL E. WAUGH	04/02/74:	Killed by IRA bomb, M62, Yorkshire
Signalman LESLIE DAVID WALSH	04/02/74:	Killed in same incident
Signalman PAUL ANTHONY REID	04/02/74:	Killed in same incident

Royal Corps of Transport

DRIVER MICHAEL GAY	17/03/73:	IRA landmine, Dungannon
SGT THOMAS PENROSE	24/03/73:	Murdered off-duty with two others, Antrim road, Belfast
CPL ANDREW GILMOUR	29/08/73:	RTA
L/CPL EDMOND CROSBIE	23/11/73:	RTA
DRIVER NORMAN MCKENZIE	11/04/74:	IRA landmine, Lisnaskea, Co Fermanagh

Royal Electrical & Mechanical Engineers

CPL DAVID BROWN	14/03/73:	Unknown
SGT MALCOLM SELDON	30/06/74:	Violent or unnatural causes
L/CPL ALISTER STEWART	09/10/74:	RTA

Royal Engineers

WOII IAN DONALD	24/05/73:	IRA bomb, Cullaville, Co Armagh
MAJOR RICHARD JARMAN	20/07/73:	IRA booby trap Middletown, Co Armagh
SAPPER MALCOLM ORTON	17/09/73:	Cause of death unknown
S/SGT JAMES LUND	19/01/74:	Cause of death unknown
L/CPL IAN NICHOLL	15/05/74:	RTA
SAPPER JOHN WALTON	02/07/74:	IRA booby trap Newtownhamilton

Royal Green Jackets

RFN NICOLAS ALLEN	26/11/73:	Death by violent or unnatural causes
RFN MICHAEL GIBSON	29/12/74:	Shot along with RUC constable at Forkhill on joint patrol

Royal Hampshire Regiment

PTE JOHN KING	13/03/73:	IRA booby trap, Crossmaglen

Royal Hussars

S/SGT CHARLES SIMPSON	07/11/74:	IRA booby trap, Stewartstown, Co Tyrone

Royal Irish Rangers

L/CPL MICHAEL NORRIS	27/07/74:	Cause of death Unknown
RANGER H THOMPSON	06/12/77:	RTA

Royal Marine Commandos

MARINE JOHN SHAW	26/07/73:	RTA in highly controversial circumstances[1]
MARINE GRAHAM COX	29/04/73:	IRA sniper, New Lodge, Belfast
MARINE JOHN MACKLIN	28/03/74:	DoW after being shot in the Antrim Rd, Belfast
CPL DENNIS LEACH	13/08/74:	IRA bomb, Crossmaglen
MARINE MICHAEL JOHN	13/08/74:	Killed in same incident

Royal Military Police

CPL ALAN HOLMAN	11/02/73:	Cause of death unknown
CPL RODERICK LANE	20/05/73:	RTA
SGT SHERIDAN YOUNG	18/05/73:	Killed in IRA atrocity at Knock-na-Moe Hotel
CPL RICHARD ROBERTS	30/05/73:	RTA
CPL STUART MILNE	20/02/74:	RTA
L/CPL PAUL MUNDY	20/02/74:	Killed in same incident

---

1   Marine John Shaw's death is recorded by the Royal Marines as 'killed in action'

Royal Pioneer Corps

SGT JAMES ROBINSON	08/02/73:	Died of natural causes whilst on duty
PTE PHILIP DRAKE	26/08/74:	IRA sniper, Craigavon, Co Armagh

Royal Regiment of Fusiliers

CPL. D NAPIER	09/03/73:	RTA
FUSILIER. CHARLES J MARCHANT	09/04/73:	DoW after being shot in ambush at Lurgan
L/CPL JAMES J MCSHANE	04/02/74:	Killed in IRA bomb outrage, M62, Yorkshire
FUSILIER JACK HYNES	04/02.74:	Killed in same outrage
CPL CLIFFORD HAUGHTON	04/02/74:	Killed in same outrage
FUSILIER STEPHEN WHALLEY	07/02/74:	DoW: from same outrage
FUSILIER. ANTHONY SIMMONS	15/11/74:	Shot by IRA at Strabane

Royal Scots Dragoon Guards

TROOPER DONALD ROY DAVIES	18/11/74:	Cause of Death unknown

Royal Welch Fusiliers

CPL DAVID SMITH	21/06/73:	IRA booby trap, Strabane
CPL ALAN COUGHLAN	28/10/74:	Van bomb attack at Ballykinler Army camp

Scots Dragoon Guards

TROOPER DONALD DAVIES	17/11/74:	Cause of death unknown

Scots Guards

GUARDSMAN ALAN DAUGHTERY	31/12/73:	IRA sniper, Falls Road, Belfast
GUARDSMAN WILLIAM FORSYTH	05/10/74:	Killed in IRA bomb outrage, Guildford
GUARDSMAN JOHN HUNTER	05/10/74:	Killed in same outrage

Staffordshire Regiment

2ND LT MICHAEL SIMPSON	23/10/74:	DoW after being shot by IRA sniper, Londonderry

Ulster Defence Regiment

CAPTAIN JAMES HOOD	04/01/73:	Murdered by the IRA at home
CPL DAVID W. BINGHAM	16/01/73:	Abducted and killed by the IRA
PTE THOMAS J FORSYTHE	16/10/73:	Killed in a shooting accident
PTE JOHNSTONE BRADLEY	23/01/73:	Unknown
SGT DAVID C.DEACON	03/03/73:	Abducted and murdered by the IRA
PTE WILLIAM L. KENNY	16/03/73:	Abducted and murdered on way to UDR barracks
CPL PATRICK DAVIDSON	17/03/73:	Unknown
PTE ALEXANDER MCCONAGHY	10/04/73:	Unknown
PTE SAMUEL BEATTIE	14/04/73:	Unknown
CPL FRANK CADDOO	10/05/73:	Shot by IRA at his farm in Rehagey
L/CPL HUGH WATTON	24/05/73:	Unknown
PTE SIDNEY W. WATT	20/07/73:	Ambushed by the IRA at a friend's
PTE KENNETH HILL	28/08/73:	Shot in Armagh City on duty
PTE MATT LILLY	07/09/73:	Shot by the IRA on his milk round
PTE COLIN MCKEOWN	17/10/73:	RTA
PTE WILLIAM MAGILL	19/10/73:	Unknown
L/CPL THOMAS BEATTY	04/11/73:	Unknown
CPL WILLIAM MARTIN	20/11/73:	RTA
PTE DAVID SPENCE	20/11/73:	RTA
PTE ROBERT N. JAMESON	17/01/74:	Shot by IRA as he got off a bus at Trillick
CAPTAIN CORMAC MCCABE	19/01/74:	Abducted and murdered by IRA in Irish Republic
CPL ROY T. MOFFETT	03/03/74:	IRA landmine on Cookstown to Omagh road
WOII DAVID SINNAMON	11/04/74:	IRA bomb in house in Dungannon

PTE EVA MARTIN	03/05/74:	Killed by IRA in rocket and gun attack at Clogher
PTE EDWARD GIBSON	30/05/74:	Unknown
PTE NOEL SEELEY	26/06/74:	Unknown
CPL JOHN CONLEY	23/07/74:	IRA car bomb in Bridge Street, Garvagh
PTE ROBERT RAINEY	27/07/74:	RTA
PTE SAMUEL WORKMAN	25/08/74:	RTA
PTE WILLIAM BELL	21/10/74:	Unknown
PTE ROBERT ALLEN	25/10/74:	Unknown
PTE THOMAS MCCREADY	17/11/74:	Shot by the IRA IN Newry
PTE JOHN S. MARTIN	18/11/74:	RTA
PTE JOHN TAYLOR	30/11/74:	RTA

Former Ulster Defence Regiment Soldiers Killed in Northern Ireland

MR ISAAC SCOTT	10/07/73:	Shot by IRA in Belleek, Co Armagh
MR IVAN VENNARD	03/10/73:	Shot dead by IRA on his postal round, Lurgan
MR GEORGE SAUNDERSON	10/04/74:	Shot by IRA at his school in Co Fermanagh
MR WILLIAM HUTCHINSON	24/08/74:	Shot by IRA at work

Welsh Guards

GUARDSMAN DAVID ROBERTS	24/11/73	Killed by IRA bomb, South Armagh

Security Services (Date and cause of death withheld by MoD)

CHARLES APCAR	12/08/74:	Death by violent or unnatural causes

The following Army Women and Children were also killed as a result of terrorism.

MRS LINDA HAUGHTON	04/02/74:	M62 Coach Bomb outrage
MASTER LEE HAUGHTON	04/02/74:	Killed in same outrage
MASTER ROBERT HAUGHTON	04/02/74:	Killed in same outrage
MR GORDON CATHERWOOD	30/10/74:	Killed by IRA sniper aiming at his UDR son and wife.

Temporary British Army Bases

Belfast

Agnes Street.
Albert Street Mill
Andersonstown Bus Station
Ardoyne Bus Depot
Broadway Hotel, Falls
Brown's Square, Shankill
Carnmoney, Glengormley
Casement Park, Andersonstown
Donegall Pass RUC
Flax Street Mill
Fort Monagh
Fort Whiterock (AKA Fort Jericho)
Girdwood Barracks, Nr Antrim Road
Glassmullan, Andersonstown
Grand Central Hotel
Hastings Road RUC
Henry Taggart Memorial Hall, Ballymurphy Estate
Lenadoon Avenue
Leopold Street RUC, Crumlin
McCrory Park RUC station
Mission Hall, Markets Area
Mulhouse Street. Rear annexe of the RVH, Grosvenor Road.
Musgrave Park Hospital (Echelon)
North Howard Street Mill
North Queen's Street RUC
Paisley Park
Silver City
Snugville Street off Springfield Road
Springfield Road RUC
St Teresa's, Turf Lodge
Sunnyside Street TA Centre.
Telephone Exchange, Markets
Vere Foster School, Ballymurphy Estate
Woodburne RUC Station

Londonderry

Bligh's Lane
Bridge Camp

Clooney Park West
Diamond Masonic Hall
Fort George
Gasworks, Bogside
Gorton Coal Hill
Hawkin Street, Fountains area.
HMS *Upton* (Minesweeper)
Knicker Factory, Creggan
Magilligan HMP
Masonic Hall, Bishops Street Within.
Piggery Ridge, Creggan
Rosemount RUC
Short Strand Bus Depot
Slieve Gallion
Strand Road RUC

Army Civilian Workers
Killed by The IRA

Noor Baz Khan	26/06/73	Murdered by the IRA, Londonderry
John Dunn	11/01/74	Murdered by the IRA, Londonderry
Cecilia Byrne	11/01/74	Murdered in the same incident
Donald Farrell	23/03/74	Army Careers Officer, shot by IRA
Mohammed Abdul Khalid	22/04/74	Murdered by the IRA, Crossmaglen
Hugh Slater	11/11/74	Murdered by the IRA, Londonderry
Leonard Cross	11/11/74	Murdered in same incident[1]
Patsie Gillespie	24/10/91	Killed by IRA , Coshquin in 'Proxy' Bomb

---

1   Leonard Cross was a member of the Army Cadet Force and is commemorated as such.

Select Bibliography

Barzilay, David, *The British Army in Ulster* Volume 1 (Belfast: Century Books, 1973)

Bradley, Gerry and Feeny, Brian, *Insider: Gerry Bradley's Life in the IRA* (Dublin: O'Brian Press, 2009)

Clarke, A.F.N., *Contact* (London: Secker & Warburg, 1983)

Clarke, George, *Border Crossing: true stories of the RUC Special Branch, the Garda Special Branch and IRA moles* (Dublin: Gill & Macmillan, 2009)

Cusack, Jim & McDonald, Henry, *UVF*, (Dublin: Poolberg Press, 1997)

Dillon, Martin, *The Shankill Butchers: a case study of mass murder* (London: Hutchinson, 1989)

Gilmour, Raymond, *Dead Ground: Infiltrating the IRA* (London: Little, Brown & Co, 1998)

Hamill, Desmond, *Pig In The Middle: the Army in Northern Ireland, 1969-1984* (London: Methuen Books, 1985)

Harnden, Toby, *Bandit Country: the IRA and South Armagh* (London: Hodder & Stoughton 1999)

Latham, Richard, *Deadly Beat: Inside the Royal Ulster* Constabulary (Edinburgh: Mainstream, 2001)

Maloney, Ed, *Voices From The Grave: two men's war in Ireland* (London: Faber & Faber, 2010)

McGartland, Martin, *Fifty Dead Men Walking* (London: John Blake, 2009)

McKitterick, David et al, *Lost Lives: The stories of the men, women and children who died as a result of the Northern Ireland Troubles* (Edinburgh: Mainstream, 2000)

Myers, Kevin, *Watching the Door: Cheating Death in 1970s Belfast* (London: Atlantic Books, 2008)

O'Callaghan, Sean, *The Informer* (London: Bantam, 1999)

Potter, John, *A Testimony To Courage: the Regimental History of the Ulster Defence Regiment* (London: Leo Cooper: 2001)

Urban, Mark, *Big Boys' Rules: the secret struggle against the IRA* (London: Faber & Faber, 1992)

Van der Bilj, Nicholas, *Operation Banner: the British Army in Northern Ireland, 1969-2007* (Barnsley: Pen & Sword, 2009)

Ware, Darren, *A Rendezvous with the Enemy: My Brother's Life and Death with the Coldstream Guards in Northern Ireland* (Solihull: Helion, 2010)

Wharton, Ken, *A Long Long War; Voices From the British Army in Northern Ireland, 1969-98* (Solihull: Helion, 2008)

Wharton, Ken, *Bloody Belfast; An Oral History of the British Army's War against the IRA* (Stroud: Spellmount, 2010)

Wharton, Ken, *Bullets, Bombs and Cups of Tea; Further Voices of the British Army in Northern Ireland* (Solihull: Helion, 2009)

Wharton, Ken, *The Bloodiest Year: Northern Ireland 1972* (Stroud: History Press, 2011)

Internet Sources:

http://www.flintshirechronicle.co.uk/flintshire-news/local-flintshire-news/2010/04/01/
    holywell-cadet-centre-dedicated-to-fallen-guardsman-david-roberts-
    reopens-51352-26148949/
http://www.noraid.org/roll_of_honor.html
http://www.ukpressonline.co.uk/

Index

Note: Neither the IRA or RUC are indexed as both are mentioned on virtually every page of the book.

Related titles published by Helion & Company

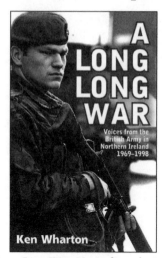

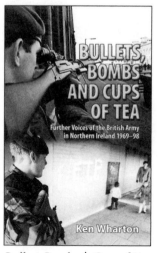

A Long Long War: Voices from the British
Army in Northern Ireland 1969-98
Ken Wharton
544pp Paperback ISBN 978-1-906033-79-8
eBook ISBN 978-1-907677-60-1

Bullets, Bombs & Cups of Tea:
Further Voices from the British Army
in Northern Ireland 1969-98
Ken Wharton
536pp Paperback ISBN 978-1-907677-06-9
eBook ISBN 978-1-907677-89-2

A selection of forthcoming titles

Four Ball, One Tracer. Commanding Executive Outcomes in Angola and Sierra Leone
Roelf van Heerden as told to Andrew Hudson
ISBN 978-1-907677-76-2

'Young Citizen Old Soldier'. From Boyhood in Antrim to Hell on the Somme. The Journal
of Rifleman James McRoberts, 14th Battalion Royal Irish Rifles, January 1915-April 1917
Edited by David Truesdale
ISBN 978-1-908916-48-8

LZ Hot! Flying South Africa's Border War
Nick Lithgow
ISBN 978-1-908916-59-4

HELION & COMPANY
26 Willow Road, Solihull, West Midlands B91 1UE, England
Telephone 0121 705 3393   Fax 0121 711 4075
Website: http://www.helion.co.uk